LARA

THE ENGLAND CHRONICLES

LARA

THE ENGLAND CHRONICLES

Brian Lara

with

Phil Walker

fairfield books

I know you didn't miss any of it Dad,
375 was for you

First published by Fairfield Books in June 2024
Reprinted in September 2024 with minor revisions

fairfield books

Fairfield Books
Bedser Stand
Kia Oval
London
SE11 5SS

Typeset in Garamond and Ridley Grotesk
Typesetting by Rob Whitehouse

This book is printed on paper certified
by the Forest Stewardship Council

Every effort has been made to trace copyright and any oversight
will be rectified in future editions at the earliest opportunity

The views and opinions expressed in this book are those of the author
and do not necessarily reflect the views of the publishers

© 2024 Fairfield Books & Brian Lara
ISBN 978-1-915237-40-8
Ebook ISBN 978-1-915237-46-0

A CIP catalogue record for this title is available from the British Library

Printed by CPI Group (UK) Ltd

I shall be telling this with a sigh
Somewhere ages and ages hence:
Two roads diverged in a wood, and I—
I took the one less traveled by,
And that has made all the difference.

ROBERT FROST, *THE ROAD NOT TAKEN*

CONTENTS

CO-WRITER'S NOTE

Phil Walker

"SO, WHAT'S HE LIKE THEN?" I've had that one a lot recently. I might answer with something about the singular focus, and the wild mercury flashes that always keep you guessing; or maybe the vampiric approach to sleep, or the off-the-cuff gift for narrative structure – the last of which often humbled the best writing/editing team we could assemble – or how it all seemed to spool out from a mind as restless as it is instinctively creative. Somewhere along the line I've gained a little sense of what it might have been like to sit on your bat at the non-striker's when he was having one of *those* days. It's been an interesting few months.

This is Brian's 'England' book. He wanted us to start there. The rivalry is so rich and deep and his magics so intricately woven into its tapestry that it was the natural place to start.

And that's the point here: this is just the start. It may not surprise you to learn that Brian Charles Lara (everyone refers to him like that) has more to say.

London, June 2024

FOREWORD

Jimmy Adams

THE THING WITH BRIAN, it all happened so fast. He produces this masterpiece at Sydney in January 1993, his first Test hundred, and then barely a year-and-a-half later, he's the owner of two world records and this icon of West Indies cricket. An immortal at 25.

All of which coincided with this unprecedented media explosion, and Brian was that generation. No one in the West Indies, not even Viv Richards, had ever had to deal with where the media was heading in the mid-Nineties and I don't think anybody had a formula for dealing with it. Brian and his management team were feeling their way around it too.

I wasn't in Brian's bubble, but I was watching it happen. It was an interesting phenomenon. The only other person in the game who would have known about this kind of stuff would have been Tendulkar. Brian was living with a level of scrutiny and pressure that no other cricketer bar Sachin could relate to.

He was the first truly global West Indian superstar, bringing our cricket into that space for the first time, and with everybody becoming more aware of the commercialisation that was starting to underpin the game, Brian's power forced the West Indies authorities to look at players differently. And I don't think that was a bad thing at all.

Was there some degree of resentment from the previous generation towards him? Look, while I have enormous respect for all our past players, I strongly believe some resented the way he proactively asserted his worth inside the global cricket 'marketplace'.

Brian has always been conscious of his own value, and for some former players, that was an aspect of him that they struggled to accept. It's almost as if they wanted to say, "Well, we sucked it up for all those years, you should do the same thing." To which Brian would basically say: "OK, sure, but I'm not going to do what you all did, I'm going to get what I'm worth, and if you boys don't like it, that's fine by me."

This kind of stuff dogged him for a while. I can't speak my reality as fact, but the perception of Brian's behaviour before he got the captaincy in 1998 was that he was manipulating the situation to get the job, and so when the board appointed him in place of Courtney Walsh, it left a few of that generation wondering, "Hey what's happening here?"

I don't know if that was fair or not. What I do know is that I started with Brian when we were kids. I grew up playing with him and he captained me at under 19s level. Outside of cricket we were good friends. We wouldn't hang out together, we never did, but we were, and are, good friends. I was part of a group who played a few Test matches and we were very comfortable playing under Brian. We believed in his leadership and like any captain, he liked having people around him who believed in him. No doubt, he cared deeply for the West Indian cause.

On the 2000 tour of England that I captained, Brian seemed detached. He'd been captain for a couple of years, taken some time away from the game, and this was his return. He scored his runs, went about his business, there was never any controversy per se. But this was a quieter version of the Brian I'd seen around. Not in a negative sense, but it was almost as if he'd gone into himself. I wondered if he thought that the best way to get through coming back into cricket was to focus on his batting, to stay within his shell; you see, I'd known Brian long enough to know that he is never short of an opinion.

I'll tell you something about Brian, about how Brian's brain works. If I look at a situation and he looks at the same situation, it will take me 10 hours of planning to get somewhere close to a solution. Brian will look at the same situation and grab a pen and paper and say "Jimmy, listen, look at this." And he'd have a solution. His mind, I find it amazing.

We'd be on tour, and we'd have all these discussions, about anything and everything. Questions with him are a dime a dozen because he works things out so quickly and always gives you food for thought. On the 2000 tour we hardly had those conversations, not because he said to me that he didn't want to speak. It was just that he seemed to be in a very calm bubble. For me, it was too calm for Brian. It was like it was self-induced.

I remember thinking to myself, we're just happy to have him back, and to give him as much space as he needed. He was never disruptive, so best just let him score his runs, and work through his own stuff in his own way. Even when he was quiet he still fascinated me.

Everybody is unique. But I think we're always particularly interested in what the geniuses do and how they see the world. And without doubt, Brian was one of a couple of geniuses around the game at the time. Shane Warne was the other. And look, they're interesting kids.

Brian proved himself 10 times over on the field, that's not in doubt. I've heard it said a million times over: kids and people around the Caribbean saying that he's the reason why they play, why they watch, why they support. But still I wonder, if I were to relay those stories back to him, would he hear me, really?

There have been times over the years when I've wondered whether he is content. Something I've wondered about a few of our great players in the past. I watch and listen to them and think, "For all that you've achieved in the game, are you truly content?" For a mortal like me, if I had achieved what Brian did, I wouldn't have a care in the world. I could be driving down the motorway butt naked and be like, "So what, I've scored 30 Test hundreds!". Yet when I look at Brian, I see someone who's still searching. Perhaps this is the price of genius.

He has matured over the years, becoming more reflective over time. In that spirit, I hope this book gives him some peace and closure. If nothing else, it will bring all those memories flooding back, transporting us to those beautiful days when Brian's strokeplay took the game to another plane. That'll be enough for me. The greatest batting genius I ever shared a field with.

Jimmy Adams
Jamaica, June 2024

FOREWORD

Dwight Yorke

GROWING UP in little Tobago, getting to play my football against the boys from the big island of Trinidad involved a tricky journey. If I wanted to compete against the best of their guys, I had to take a 20-minute propeller flight across the water and then make my way to the ground, but it was always worth it, even as the youngest boy in our team.

It was on one of my trips over to play against Trinidad's national schoolboys under 12s that I first encountered this small, skilful dribbler called Brian Charles Lara. We hit it off straight away. Along with Russell Latapy, we formed a little group of good footballers, pushing each other on, the three of us joined together right from the beginning. I was the youngest of the three, I was only about 9 at the time and they were near enough 12, but it didn't matter. We clicked over football. It was the start of a lifelong friendship.

A few years later, when we were teenagers, it dawned on us that Brian's future would not involve a ball at his feet, but a bat in his hands. Myself and Russell were doing well in football while Brian was excelling in cricket at a rate beyond what any of us could imagine. He was probably about 16 years old when I realised that our boy was already well on his way to becoming a national treasure, and he's lived with that pressure ever since.

Brian was a good lad, just a nice, pleasant kid, and although we lived on separate islands we could feel our friendship getting stronger every time we saw each other. We had a lot in common. We both came from a very big family. Our mothers were both religious and they tried to keep us on the straight and narrow. Back then our parents didn't have too much to worry about. We came from very disciplined families, so breaking curfew was walking a fine line. We only really got up to mischief when we were adults...

* * *

We were making inroads. We'd passed the phase of being little teenagers. At 18 I made my way to England on a contract with Aston Villa, experiencing something completely different outside of our country, while Brian was already pushing up into the West Indies team. We were moving onto the international stage at such a rate. It was quite something, and the elevation, certainly from Brian's perspective, was dizzying. He was hitting numbers and breaking records like you'd never seen before.

And that was quite frightening. I was still there trying to make my way at Villa, and I fed off what Brian was doing. He was a true inspiration. Watching him gave me a bit more juice. Here was my best friend doing what he was doing, and it made me think that maybe I could achieve something similar in my sport. And so, I thank Brian. I've told him this before, but it doesn't hurt to say it again.

When Brian joined Warwickshire in 1994 we became inseparable. We took every opportunity to spend time with each other. We had our jobs to do, training every day, but we always found the time to link up when we could. The reason he came to Warwickshire was because I was based in Birmingham, it became an easy sell for the club. We lived together, shared cars, we were living a boyhood dream. Two young boys from the Caribbean who'd taken different paths to end up in the same country, doing what we were doing. Brian was a phenomenon at the top of his game, and I was now becoming Aston Villa's best player. The combination was lethal. We were living a dream life, everyone in Birmingham knew that we were untouchable. Wherever we turned up it was chaos, in the best possible way... It was fun of the highest level, yet we were still doing the business on the pitch. Certain people lost sight of the fact that all the fun we were having off the pitch, and all that surrounded us, was only possible because of our achievements on the field of play.

We've racked up 40-plus years of friendship. We're godfathers to each other's kids. We might have had disputes down the line, but I can't think I've ever had a full-on argument with Brian. Then again, I think I'm probably a bit more laid-back than he is. In Tobago the pace of life is so slow compared to Trinidad, and so I would take that trophy for sure.

I hope this book helps you see who Brian really is. Me? I see a person who I would give my last penny to, just as he would to me. My brother for always.

Dwight Yorke
Dubai, June 2024

EVERYWHERE IS UPROAR

'Signal everybody, signal
Signal everybody, signal
Start the carnival
Start the carnival
Lara! Lara!
We ain't goin' home,
Jump up
We ain't goin' home,
Jump up'

'SIGNAL TO LARA', SUPER BLUE

I DON'T SWITCH OFF. That's not how this thing works. I never feel tired. I never will feel tired. Switch on and switch off? Between deliveries? *That's* tiring. That's not me.

Out there is my ring. You think I'm switching on or off when backed into a corner? I'm gonna dance and sway and throw another hit. It's a fight between them and me. Win it and the innings belongs to me.

I don't put myself under undue pressure. There's more than enough of that kicking around. Pressure is a thick winter coat I never take off. Wasting time on what this guy's gonna bowl, worrying about technique, those things don't factor.

It's never a strain. They talk about fatigue, exhaustion, the mind playing tricks. This means nothing to me. Batting and concentrating is second nature. I *never* get out because I'm tired.

The affair deepened after Sydney. Gave me a taste and now I'm obsessed. Infatuated. Big runs. Huge scores. Going bigger than anyone went before. It's all I can think about. I got close at Sydney. This time I'm thinking the longer I bat, the closer I get, the stronger I become. Think about it, who's going to be more exhausted? I'm the one plundering. I am the spectacle, and they are there to provide for that spectacle.

* * *

As a kid, when there was no one to play with, I'd use plant pots for fielders. I'd throw a ball against the wall in the back yard at home and use my wrists to hit the spaces between them. In my scorebook my batting order's always Greenidge-Haynes-Richards-Lara-Gomes-Lloyd and it's always a Test match against England. Playing against a golf ball, an orange, a tennis ball on the street, it's always about excitement. I'm learning the thrill of scoring runs, right out of the garage.

When it comes to the big stuff, and those pots become people, I have a mental picture of the field in my head. I know where every guy is. I can calculate when that ball is delivered, what I need to do with it. I don't need to be technically correct; I just need to find a gap.

I see countless beautiful batters hit a perfect cover drive straight at a fielder. Good for them. I'm never happy with that. The slight angle of the bat, the delay in the shot, sweeping it fine to make sure I get two, shifting the pieces around. It's a game of chess, and I want value for my moves.

They're tired. They don't want to do it. All the while I'm ready to go. Lunchtime on the second day, teatime on the second day, I'm ready to go.

Evening session, day two, the numbers start to fall. Sydney comes and goes. Next is Viv's 291. I don't need to be told. I felt terrible at Sydney, getting so close. This one matters. To go past the Master Blaster. Now that's something.

Just before the close Angus Fraser beats my bat. I try to play a straight drive to one that leaves me. At least, he says, he can say he beat my bat after I had 300.

I go in 320 not out. Forty-six to get. There's no talk of a declaration. Curtly makes that clear. He's not bowling on *that*. Let the boy go for it, he says.

* * *

I can't be stuck in my room. I need to feel the scene outside. We're in a hotel in Five Islands, up where Richie Richardson's from. I go into town to lap up the atmosphere and think about what's to come. I burn some energy in the city, eat some food with friends and go back to the hotel. I don't break the curfew. Not this time.

Still no sleep. Everything's pumping, racing. My roommate Junior Murray has these videos. I watch one. Still wired. At 5am I call a friend and we go out to play nine holes. It doesn't matter where I hit the ball, I just need to do something different. I'm back in time for breakfast, but I don't want a hotel one. This one's special. I go find my man in Antigua, Shipwreck, who brings me my favourite saltfish from downtown.

Down at the Rec it's teeming. People been getting busy overnight. Paraphernalia everywhere, T-shirts, caps, keyrings, all produced in anticipation of what's to come, what *has* to come. This be Antigua, the place shaking to Chickie's tunes, Gravy and Mayfield up on the rafters, the English sweating it out in the shade. You can feel the vibrations, this small ground smack in the heart of the city, and today the centre of the world.

I hear The Greatest is in town. That he's actually *here*.

This game, man. It's not just about playing and doing your best. It's entertainment. To entertain is the thing. It's always been with me. Make them dance. Make it a spectacle.

My mind is fresh. Adrenaline takes over. No sleep. If I sleep, I might miss something. I'm not wasted or tired. I have a quick knock up, then Clive Lloyd asks me, do I mind if the TV people hand me my bat on the way out. I'm cool with that, it's all part of the show, I say. By day three my shirt is pretty stained, but I pull it on anyway. I'm not superstitious. It just feels right. Bell rings. The crowd lose their minds. Gower and Botham wait on the outfield with their microphones. One of them hands me my bat. Showtime.

* * *

They bowl well. Fields set deep, not many boundaries. Tight bowling, questions asked. You can see they're into it. Everyone's connected. I play one loose shot, the ball lobs over the covers for two. Settle down. No rush. More singles.

I know he's in the building. I can feel it.

My confidence doesn't go backwards. That false shot locks me back in the right frame of mind. Man, you've had these guys in the sun for two days. They'll throw something at you now, but it'll get easier. They've had a night's sleep so wake up and pay attention. I'm into my groove and cruise to the landmarks. Gooch, Bradman, Hanif. They come up loud on the PA system, but I don't need to be told. Hutton next.

And then the one. He's here, I know he is.

People always talked about my size. How small I was next to Desmond, Gordon, Richie, Viv. Boy got the power to be a world-class player? And he always say, 'This young man is going to be one of the best.'

I was puzzled, many times, by that. The only one who truly believed in me. And now he's here. On 361 Caddick bowls a full one. I feel my body flow into the shot. And in that moment, we are inseparable. For a second, it feels enough just to be up there next to him.

I pass Shiv mid-pitch, he nods. Next over, he takes a single off Chris Lewis to get me back on strike.

* * *

Michael Atherton takes an age to set his field. Our eyes meet. He smiles. I smile back. We both know the game. It's a play by the English to have me wait. Fans are up on the fences waiting to invade.

My mindset never changes. Ever. Attack first, and if the ball is good enough, go into a defensive shot.

Lewis runs in with an aggression I haven't seen before. Deep backward square leg is in the circle. The field suggests it'll be a good length ball on off stump, but I can see the bluff coming. It's there in his run-up. I know this guy will try to bowl the fastest short ball he ever bowled. I'm in position quickly. Waiting to slap it through midwicket.

Before the ball is through the infield, I see hordes of men eluding the police on to the field. I wheel away in the shot, almost swaying off my feet. There's Shiv, just a kid in his first series, the two of us tied in now forever. We share some words, whatever they are, a moment of stillness in the chaos.

The crowd and the police run for each other. Men lying on the turf, crying, shouting. Hundreds of them, all trying to get a touch. Everywhere is uproar. It's turned into a ceremony in the middle of a Test match. The England boys don't mind.

The crowd disperses a little, and now I see him striding out, leading a delegation onto the field. Sir Garfield. And for a few seconds it's just him and me. No one loves their record to be broken. I would learn that myself. But for Sobers, being here to pass the mantle? I can feel he wants it too. It's us two now, locked together.

* * *

At Sydney I'd thought a lot about my dad, felt his absence sharply. This night brings it all back again. Everyone's a part of it and happy and claiming to be there, but the one man who would have truly made the innings worth it, is not there to see it. Everything that happened came after he passed.

I understand a lot about expectation, and a little about adulation. Coaches, teachers, parents of other kids, I grow up with people looking at me. Some people fear it. They shrink in the face of it. I don't. From the very first time I saw Viv walk through customs at Heathrow into that mad mass of photographers, I knew that nothing would stop me getting to where I have to be.

And I have this idea, you see, that love and beauty will always win out. But I'm naïve. So very, very naïve.

CHAPTER 1

STEPPING OUT

'As a kid, you're just kind of floating around; sport was our way of coming together'

DWIGHT YORKE

MAYBE IT'S PLANNED. Marlon Samuels on strike, pushes to mid-on, "Yes" is the call. I respond, take off, and hear the shout that says Marlon's changed his mind. It's late, late in the day, too late to turn around and start again. I'm stood there, mid-pitch, alone. All I can hope for is one final reprieve, one last shot for old time's sake, but Kevin Pietersen's throw is arrowing into the stumps and I can see already even before the ball breaks the bails that it's deadeye and yes, this really is it.

My international career comes to an end on Saturday, April 21, 2007. RUN OUT in the 31st over for 18 at 11.53am at the Kensington Oval, Barbados, playing against England in a nothing match between two teams already out of the World Cup. I walk off. Remove my helmet. Look up to the bleachers, then the skies. Wow. *Wow.* So *this* is how it's meant to be.

I believe that if something is destined to happen then no outside power can change its course. Everything happens for a reason. It wasn't bad luck that day. It was all of a piece with everything that went before it. Don't get me wrong, I don't feel comfortable with it. I'm *definitely* not happy about it. But what can you do? It's all part of my story.

Cricket is the cruellest of all games. When you're out, there's no second chances. You're done. There's only one place you can retreat to, and that's the sanctuary of the pavilion, where at least a man can be alone with his thoughts.

I also believe that we get what we deserve. I guess we have to call this karma.

What I do know is that I've had enough. I can't wait to get out of it all. It's been on my mind a lot throughout my career, this feeling – the lure of walking away, the deep appeal of breathing a cleaner air – but never has it been so strong, so near the surface, as these past few weeks. I *have* to walk away. I have to surrender my energy to something else that might make me happy. There is nothing more I can do as a cricketer representing the West Indies.

I exist in the grey when it comes to some persons of power in the Caribbean. And I'm talking about power in the Caribbean at large, not just the corridors of West Indies cricket. Everyone has an opinion about me, and no one's in the business of keeping it to themselves. Island prime ministers, politicians, pastors, judges, lawyers, doctors, street influencers, everyone has a view. I've lived in their gaze for the best part of two decades.

A man should never think he is invincible. We are all dispensable. I know I'm high on the hit list of some people in authority, and this is not a new thing. I've played every day of my career like I've had to prove something. Thankfully, I learnt very quickly what motivated me. Team was everything. When I was at Fatima College it was playing for the whole school. Playing for Trinidad & Tobago, it was that red, white and black; and then as a West Indies player, to see a Jamaican, Bajan or Trinidadian jumping for joy, it had to be that. Point my energies at a greater cause, and I could do great things.

I can say now that I love every single one of my teammates, even if some of them couldn't care less if I fell down dead in front of them. They were still my major motivating force. Together, we represented something so much bigger than ourselves. I've had the greatest career I could ever have dreamed of, and I wouldn't swap it for anything. No other sport, no other period in West Indies cricket. This was my calling, my destiny. This was my fate.

* * *

To understand me, we have to go back to where I came from, what I was fed, what I loved, how I slept at night and woke in the morning, what I was taught, what I read, and what I saw with my own eyes.

OK, here goes.

I have a sporadically addictive personality. I don't know if you googled it whether you would find a medical term for it. But it seems self-explanatory to me. I can throw my mind, body and soul into something or someone until I get my desired result, or I fail. Down the road I can see the same challenge, the same person appears in front of me and even then, I give it no importance. I can forgive but no one forgets. I move on very quickly to the next thing that catches my attention and conjures up my emotions. I have started countless books but only finished a few. I like history, geography and I was good at accounting.

West Indies cricket meant a lot to a household that had male testosterone peeling off the walls. My father, Bunty Lara, and six older brothers meant that me and my four sisters had no choice but to learn the game of cricket and its history. Transistor radios were our connection to sport in the Seventies and Dad loved cricket immensely. There were other sports, but none captivated him like cricket and cricketers. Was I named Brian Charles after the Trinidadian brothers Bryan and Charlie Davis, West Indian cricketers around the time of my birth? I don't think so. But you can't be sure.

I came from a once sleepy little village called Cantaro in the Santa Cruz valley. Misty mornings, cold and beautiful, the sun took its time to get to us. We were locked between two very high mountains that were part of the northern range. Windows and doors were open throughout the day and night, the sound of village life whistling through from house to house. We were a tight village, with aunts and uncles and their siblings living in close proximity.

We weren't too far from the sea, the northern beaches were a half-hour drive away or, as we did on many occasions, a two-hour hike up and down the mountains. I loved that hike, but only the *going* part; after a day in the salt playing cricket and football on the beach, and then a big meat-pelau meal, those mountains started to look colossal and impossible. Being the youngest boy, I was allowed to travel back with the girls in my dad's white Kingswood. The boys didn't mind because they knew I'd only hold them back, ending up on one of their backs for part of the journey back.

So, 11 of us kids. There was Junior and Marlene from my mother Pearl's previous relationship, and nine of us from Bunty Lara. The first nine kids carried my mother's last name, Eustache; and only the last two, myself and Karen, took the surname of Lara, as we were born after our parents were finally married. Was it tough living in a three-bedroom house? No, it was a joy. Though on some occasions one toilet made things difficult.

Village people were very good at building onto the structure of their house. Junior and Marlene migrated to Canada and New York when I was still a baby, and Winston and Robert moved into part of the garage, which created a fourth bedroom. Our parents had the front room, and Agnes, the eldest of the nine of us still at the house, took me under her wing – or perhaps I was placed in her care – and slept in the middle room, while the rest piled into the back room.

As a young man, Dad worked at an agricultural station, starting off as a labourer and worked his way up to manager. Maybe that's how I learnt my survival skills. Certainly, I came to understand from him that there's always something better to come if you hang in there.

Vegetables and some fruits, then, were never a problem. In fact, food itself was never an issue. My brothers were great divers and they spent hours in the open ocean bringing back all types of fish, lobsters and other shell creatures from the sea. My parents made sure that there was always enough to share with neighbours and friends.

We were fed what I would call heavy food. There might have been a coleslaw or a green salad but I wasn't interested. My favourite, and I had to have it weekly, was boiled dumplings, green fig and salt fish. Put that meal in front of me with a few tomatoes and a large slice of avocado – my dad brought home loads of that – and I was in heaven. I was addicted to that, and to green, not-yet-ripe fruits eaten with salt, black pepper and chilli sauce, or even just the raw chilli. A habit I haven't yet been able to kick.

Preparation for Sunday lunch would start on Saturday at the San Juan market. My parents would leave home at 5am and be back by 8am with all the ingredients that weren't available at Dad's workplace. My mother would make breakfast, lunch and dinner every day of the week, but Saturdays, while she did this, she'd also start prepping for the big Sunday lunch. It'd be stewed chicken, baked chicken, and barbecue chicken, white rice, Spanish rice, rice and peas, callaloo, beans – red or lentils for me – some salad or a coleslaw, and don't dare put food in front of me without avocado. That butter-like taste was a must, especially if my mother was trying to force things down my throat that I didn't like. A small bit of that and a big piece of avocado was the only way I could stomach all that beetroot.

* * *

Some memories never fade, only deepen. The sun was blaring that day in 1975 when the West Indies won the first men's World Cup. I'd just turned six, old enough to have some feeling for what it meant, and like every kid I wanted to play cricket. And I was lucky, though I didn't feel it at the time, having to contest with kids twice, three times my age, and my six bigger brothers. It was actually the perfect sporting education.

It wasn't just cricket. I played table tennis to a high level in my early years, competing with some great names, Nigel and Ian Christopher, Seamus Clarke and others, who went on to play for our national team. I was playing all the sports I was allowed to, but Dad's love of cricket was such that I was always pushed in that direction.

Cricket and football, the two main sports in Trinidad & Tobago, were seasonal. Dry season, January to June: cricket was the game. Then, come the rainy season, end of June to December, we'd all go out on the streets, the open savannahs or any other space to play football. Football season was always an exciting time in the village of Cantaro in the Santa Cruz valley.

It was the No.1 sport in the village and it wasn't long before we formed our own team. We called ourselves Santa Cruz Hotspurs after my favourite team as a kid, Tottenham Hotspur. We chose Hotspurs because of their back-to-back victories in the FA Cup in the early Eighties. I was only 11 years old, but I already knew something about *style* – I didn't want us to be called United or City, or in our case, a village team. Santa Cruz Hotspurs just had a special ring to it.

Glenn Hoddle was my favourite footballer. He kept the ball at his feet so beautifully. His skills were magical to watch. A playmaker, a wonderful dribbler. He could pick out the head of his teammate in the opposition's box with precision from either foot.

My football dreams were short-lived but they did hold some significance. In 1980, when I was 11, I saw an advert in the newspaper calling on kids who were interested in football to trial at various centres across the country, firstly to represent their county, and ultimately for the chance to represent Trinidad and Tobago under-12s.

The coaches set up a centre at St Augustine College for the North East Zone kids, and when I turned up there were 300 kids standing in the torrential rain. It was impossible to play outdoors, and so under cover, the coaches got rid of 200 kids just by letting us pass and trap the ball.

With 100 of us left, one of the coaches threw the ball to this kid who caught it on his thigh, flipped it up onto the back of his neck, rolled it down his back and trapped it dead. My eyes opened up *huge*. That kid was Russell Latapy. I got into the North East Zone team, and then into the Trinidad final 20. We also had a lad called Shaka Hislop with us. He came in on the North East Zone team trying to play as a forward until they stuck him in goal.

Latapy was our captain, our magician, when we played against Tobago's equivalent of our team. We beat them 4-3, but they had this eight-year-old, who scored all three goals with his toes poking out of his boots. I later learned that this was Dwight Yorke. Soon enough we were inseparable.

Dwight says I could have gone all the way but I was much too worried about being tackled to play rough and tough top-level football. I wanted to be a winger, collecting the ball with a defender coming towards me and I was skilful enough to beat them. But when you play in the middle, going up for headers and sticking your foot into dangerous places? That wasn't for me. I didn't have the physique of Dwight or the skill of Russell Latapy. Those guys were on a different level.

And so it was that three of my closest friends went on to play at a very high level. Dwight was with Aston Villa from the age of 18, later playing for Manchester United when they famously won the treble, and having stints at Blackburn Rovers, Birmingham City, Sunderland and Sydney FC.

Russell played for Academica de Coimbra and Porto in Portugal, and Hibs, Glasgow Rangers, Dundee United and Falkirk in Scotland, while our goalkeeper, Shaka, played for Reading, Portsmouth, West Ham and Newcastle. These friendships, forged on the pitch in the rain, are unbreakable.

The highlight of my football career came long after my youthful dalliance with the game. The UNICEF Soccer Aid match at Old Trafford in 2010 was packed with true legends of the sport, from Henrik Larsson and Luis Figo to the untouchable Zinedine Zidane. There were other football stars there that day – plus a few celebrities, like Mike Myers and Woody Harrelson – but I will stop at Zizou.

The football skills of the non-football celebs weren't great and there were constant turnovers every time the ball found their feet. Inevitably, the greats started to play a little more amongst themselves.

I was brought on in the second half along with Figo and a few others. Anxious to get into the game I stood in an open position to receive the ball shouting "Figo!" "Zizou!" but to no avail. Maybe they didn't trust my skills. Eventually on one forward move it went like this: Zidane to Figo, back to Zidane, but Zidane was stuck, so he looked up, saw me, and passed the ball. I saw Larsson making a run and gave a through pass to him, he ran on to it and narrowly slapped it wide.

Instantly I started getting more of the ball. I couldn't believe I was on a field with such greats in front of over 65,000 fans. Some Trinidadians love football more than cricket, and one of them, my very good friend Christian Mouttet, travelled up for the match with his family, renting a box just to be there. I still smile today just thinking about it.

* * *

Sport dominated my life. I hardly had time for homework and sometimes even my academics during school hours. I represented the school six days a week at sport. I would get home exhausted but happy, living my best life, hit my bed and lie there reminiscing about my day and how well we'd played. If I had to continue the next day I would be strategising how to keep ahead of the opposition. I struggled to sleep with the buzz and level of excitement ahead of me.

When I did fall asleep I dreamt a lot, sometimes wildly. I felt that my brain was so hot and wired. I didn't just dream about the good things. I sometimes dreamt about stuff that made me jump up and out of my bed, sweating, screaming and running until someone caught hold of me. My mother would have to bathe me in Limacol, a scented refreshing ointment, pouring a generous amount in her hand to pat my head and face. It took some time, I was later told, for me to calm down and I would only fall asleep in my mother's arms next to her, in bed with my dad.

In the morning I would have little recollection of the previous night's fiasco. My thoughts would only be on the day ahead, on the limitless games we could play.

CHAPTER 2

FATHERS AND SONS

*'I never seen a prouder man
when you scored runs'*

AGNES EUSTACHE CYRUS

BUNTY LARA was a no-nonsense man. My brothers always said I got the tamer side of him. He was older and wiser by the time I came along, not so much of a disciplinarian as back in his heyday, when my siblings were moving from being kids to teenage life.

He didn't laugh with us much. He provided for us, ensured we didn't stray, and pulled us back in line if he saw reason to, or if any complaints came from elders in the village. Neighbours and other elders were allowed to scold you if they found you doing something you weren't supposed to do, and you weren't a smart kid if you took that scolding back to your parents. "You must have done something wrong for Mr Martin to put his hands on you."

My dad was disciplined, hard-working and an inspiration to his children. He was held in high esteem by his peers. He made the Lara name a respected and proud one in the village.

He was never big on football, but cricket was his obsession. He wanted to dissuade me from football so I could concentrate my energies on cricket. Years later, Colin Murray, my college first XI football coach, told me that Dad would recommend I spend more time on the bench watching the game rather than playing. I was small and skinny, and breaking a leg would have seriously dented his ambitions for me.

Cricket, he never missed a match. I remember once being upset about something or other. I had a match the next day and very early the next morning, still angry with him, I snuck out with my cricket gear. I walked a half-mile, passing through the orange and grapefruit estate – which is now the Brian Lara Recreation Ground – till I got to the main road that led to the hills and down into Maraval and then Port of Spain.

I stuck my hand out at every passing car begging for a lift to the capital where my game was taking place. It was the norm back then for a car to pick up strangers on the side of the road. Eventually, I picked up a lift and made my way to the ground. When I arrived, he had already set himself up under his favourite shaded tree. He truly never missed a match.

I passed my Common Entrance exams and was sent to San Juan Secondary School for a year. The school was big on football but they didn't have a cricket team, so as a boy I played my cricket on weekends either in the village or on Sunday mornings at the Harvard Cricket Club.

If my dad harboured dreams and ambitions for me, then Harvard was the club to bring them out. My sister Agnes had read a newspaper advert from Harvard which was looking to recruit kids for their cricket coaching clinic. It was November, 1975. I was six, and the clinic was starting in January, start of the dry season. Agnes told Dad that they should get me there. He agreed. I was learning a lot playing in the streets and on bad dirt pitches in the village, but it was time to move up.

Registration for Harvard took place on the first Sunday of the new year and Agnes got me up early. We thought there'd be loads of parents with their kids coming to register and the later ones might get turned away. It was still dark, around 5.30am when we left home, my dad, me and my nephew Marvin, who was also six years old. Yes, I was his uncle: my big sister Marlene – at no time did I ever think she was my half-sister – was living in New York, married and trying to make ends meet working day and night, and Marvin and his brother Ronnie were sent down to live with us and get an education in Trinidad. But to me Marvin was more like my kid brother, and the one I was closest to.

We were inseparable. We did everything together. We would leave home and wander through the village just being kids. We would head either to the cocoa estate or the orange and grapefruit field, ignoring the NO TRESPASSING signs to fill our jerseys, or any plastic bags we'd smuggled out of the house. If you left home with plastic bags in your hand and you weren't going to fetch something for your parents, they knew you were up to no good.

When we drove out of the village that morning to Harvard, we could hear in almost every yard we passed the sound of the roosters, cock-a-doodle-doo-ing. Driving out onto the Saddle Road, the beauty of the valley revealed itself. I liked the back seat, left side window, where I could stick my hand out and feel the breeze pushing against my hand as I tried to defeat the wind. I leant my head out of the window, to catch the nice, cool air that would continue to whisper through the valley all day.

The greenery was spectacular. Bamboo and mango trees lining the great Saddle Road. Poon Tip's horse farm touched the side of the road and there was no greater beauty than to see these majestic animals chewing the grass and breaking into a sudden gallop. That five minutes before we got to the top of the mountain and the road split was magical. Take a right, our normal route, and you'd head to Maracas Bay. That day, for the first time in my life, we went left.

We cruised into Maraval, a much bigger village with much bigger cars. The place even had a *gas station*. I pulled my head right in, rested my chin on the top of the front seat and fixed my eyes on the windscreen. This was my first trip into Port of Spain. We arrived outside the locked gates of the Harvard Cricket Club at 6.30am but not before we caught sight of the vast, stunning houses of St Clair. There was this one property, it was so big, I imagined that all the houses on Mitchell St where we lived could fit inside it.

The Harvard gates opened at 8am. We were close to the top of the line but some parents had come earlier. I don't know why I was dressed in whites because it was only registration day but Roy Fredericks was my hero and I wanted to bat and look like him, so I had the long-sleeve white shirt, buttons down the middle, sleeves down and buttoned, white slacks with the fasteners at the side and a pair of Bata white shoes. Registration took some time, so I was left to wander around with the other kids.

A couple of kids had brought bats and balls with them. I didn't have a fancy bat at the time; my coconut branch shaped into a bat wouldn't have gone down well with the big city kids.

A couple of games started up. The owner of the bat would have a hit first. At the end, I got my chance, and just like on the streets, I was determined not to get out. After a few shots a crowd of parents had gathered to watch, as their kids were getting restless. Before I knew it, I was a spectacle.

I was just batting and batting. Some of the kids dropped out and joined the other game. Eventually a parent came up to bowl, dropped me a short fast one and I pulled it out of the nets. In street games, it's out when you hit it into the neighbour's yard. At Harvard, it's the tennis courts.

After registration Dad didn't take us the same way home. He pointed out King George V Park just across from Harvard. He asked me if I knew about the place on the right, just opposite the park. It was my first time, so he knew I didn't.

"This is the Queen's Park Oval," he said. It was still alien to me. All I could see was a high red-brick wall that curved round the corner till I could see no more. "This is where the West Indies team plays." He paused to let me take it in.

Later, he stopped for coconut water, and he let us have a crushed-ice snow cone, with an extremely sweet syrup poured over the top.

Some days you remember every last detail.

* * *

I didn't see the absence of cricket at San Juan Secondary as a problem. I figured that come January, I'd be playing on the weekends at Harvard anyway. But Dad didn't see it that way, so he secured an interview through one of the coaches at Harvard at a place called Fatima College in Port of Spain.

I can tell you now, I was not happy about it. San Juan Secondary was a co-ed, and I was thinking I'm not the brightest boy, so I was happy where I was. But Dad insisted we do this interview. I remember during the summer holidays, the principal of Fatima, the late Clive Pantin, was interviewing my dad as I was sitting there, this little boy, and Dad was saying how good a cricketer I was, and how great it would be for his son to be at Fatima playing cricket. And Mr Pantin said, "Well, Mr Lara, I don't really want a cricketer." To which my father said: "My sentiments *exactly*."

Academics were important to my father. Unfortunately, his boy didn't feel the same way.

* * *

A little reluctantly, I accepted my move to Fatima, and what I found when I got there was *privilege*. For a village boy it was an eye-opener. I was surrounded by predominantly white college students, high-society types, and it was here where I met the former West Indies player and Trinidad captain Joey Carew via my new friends at Fatima, Joey's boys, Michael and David.

Some of the proudest moments of my life were seeing Dad, an agricultural labourer who'd pulled himself up over countless years to make manager of his station, sitting there sharing stories with former West Indian players. Joey Carew, Charlie Davis, Bryan Davis, Willie Rodriguez, all these great names. They all had sons there. Fatima was the place. And there he was, Dad, the village man, carrying on the conversation.

Those names had the pedigree. So whenever I did well, you could see the joy on Dad's face. First of all, he was just in awe of the company he was keeping. Then to see his son matching the feats of those kids on the field, the joy flowed out of him.

David Carew once asked me if I could stay over at his place because we had a first XI game that started on Friday evening and continued all of Saturday. They lived about half a mile from the school so it made sense. My dad asked me if I was sure about it. I said, "Yeah, why not?" And so from that first Friday night ahead of games for the college on a Saturday, it just became a regular thing, and it certainly wasn't something Dad was going to stop. This was Joey Carew's house, after all, where the elites of Trinidad & Tobago cricket came round for dinner.

Many times I would sit down with Joey and his sons and talk cricket. It was a major influence in my life. I was sitting with knowledgeable people who really knew the game. We would watch the West Indies, getting up in the middle of the night to see them play abroad. Joey was a very well-respected figure within the game, a selector for the West Indies team, and sometime chairman of selectors. He was a big boy.

I remember many times when the West Indies were in town, all these greats stopping by Joey's house. Jackie Hendriks, Allan Rae, Wes Hall. I got to meet all these great former cricketers. They'd come over to the Carew house and we'd talk cricket over dinner. Just to be in their presence was enough. One evening, Clive Lloyd – the *actual* West Indies captain – came over for dinner.

It was a cricket family, all the way through, and I became virtually part of the household. Marion and Joey treated me like a son and

I love Michael and David, who treated me like a brother, dearly. I treaded carefully with granny Burke, but Hurricane, the maid, was a woman and a half. She controlled the house, barked at Michael, David and me as if we were no different to Arthur, her son. She cooked great food, proper creole food that everyone loved.

I grew closer and closer to the Carew family. I'd go home after my college game on Saturday and prepare for Harvard the next morning, and after that session, Dad would drive me over to the Queen's Park Oval where Michael and David would be practising. One of the security men would have to find one of the boys before they would open the gates for us.

I walked into the Queen's Park Oval for the first time in 1977. The West Indies were playing Pakistan and I was eight years old. I came a few times after that but never through the Members' Gate. I may have had more college teammates at Queen's Park than I did at Harvard, but not kids who looked like me. If they weren't white, they were a very light brown.

At that point in time I wanted to remain loyal to the Harvard Coaching Clinic, but through playing for Fatima College and spending time with the Carews, the opportunity came to join Queen's Park Oval, the most elite club in Trinidad.

I was torn. I didn't want to turn my back on Harvard after all they had done for me. Yet, when I told Harvard about the offer from Queen's Park they literally pushed me out of the door.

They must have felt they'd done their job. They knew where I was heading.

* * *

It came to a point where I was literally living at the Carew residence. There were always cricket books lying around the house.

I picked them all up at one time or another, reading random bits based on their chapter headings, returning to books I'd discarded the previous week, re-reading sections I'd found interesting. I wasn't one to read an entire book in order; my brain didn't work like that, but what I did read I soaked up. Stories about the black Bradman, Sir George Headley. Tales of the great allrounder Sir Learie Constantine and his exploits as an overseas star in faraway England.

Headley and Constantine, and all the other black cricketers of their era, their struggles between the wars were *real* struggles. They were standout players but they had to toe the line set by their white teammates and administrators. Captaincy was never something they could aspire to, such positions were exclusively open to those who did not look like them.

From there, I read about our first victory at Lord's in 1950, and this explosion of music, dance and jubilation as our Caribbean brothers and sisters spilled onto the streets of London. I learnt about the three Ws – about the awesome power of Sir Clyde Walcott and the technical brilliance of Sir Everton Weekes, who controlled his ferocity, I read, by keeping the ball on the ground. And, of course, I read about the class and elegance of Sir Frank Worrell, who was always referred to in a slightly different tone. As our first black captain, he is perhaps our most respected figure for the era in which he played and the cause he championed. He died painfully young, just 42. How I wish I could have shaken his hand.

Then into the Sixties I'd go, reading up on Sir Garfield Sobers and Rohan Kanhai, these wonderfully stylish cricketers playing the game like they were performing on Shaftesbury Avenue, competing amongst themselves for the right to be called the best and embedding the idea in my mind that these guys were the true forefathers of West Indian flair.

They may not have had the same burdens as the founding fathers but they still had mountains to climb in their quest to become fully-fledged professional cricketers, foregoing further education to put food on the table for their families. Sobers' allround ability and star quality, not to mention having a world record in his back pocket, made him the most marketable cricketer in the West Indies at that time. His story and style captivated me.

Sir Clive Lloyd became the main man in the Seventies and this is where I began to inch my way in. I could vividly recall the first World Cup, and I got a handle on Kerry Packer's World Series Cricket and, more darkly, the rebel tours to South Africa. These were all watershed moments in world cricket, and with each new shift, so my understanding of the social complexities of cricket would deepen again. It was so much more than a game.

Clive's genius was to keep the West Indies team at the forefront of the hearts and minds of all cricket lovers. We were double world champions, in 1975 and 1979 – only losing in the final to India in 1983 going for the treble – and were indisputably the greatest Test team on the planet.

The only thing I could compare to those World Cup wins, the only sporting event that carried the same significance at home, was when the 100-metre runner Hasely Crawford of Trinidad and Tobago ran past the rest of the world to bring the first Olympic gold medal to our shores in 1976. Thousands of people turned up at Piarco Airport for his return. My dad packed the boys into his car to join the crowds. I remember sitting on the airport's second floor with my feet dangling through the railings and my dad stood over me to protect me, fixed on Hasely and dreaming it was me.

Sir Clive and then Sir Viv Richards led us through a period where we became one of the most dominant teams in world sport. If the period between the wars was about black West Indians fighting for a spot in the West Indies team, and the Fifties and Sixties about showing our colonial masters that we can govern ourselves politically and socially, then the Seventies and Eighties were about showing the world that when we're strong and united, we're *untouchable*.

I barrelled through all this stuff with tireless enthusiasm, all the while wondering how all this history, all these stories, would infuse what was still to come. How, I dared wonder, would the *Nineties* be remembered? We were arriving at my own time.

ENGLAND v WEST INDIES

Venue: Lord's Cricket Ground, St John's Wood
Toss: West Indies won the toss and decided to bat
Umpires: D Davies, FS Lee

Date: 24th, 26th, 27th, 28th, 29th June 1950
Result: West Indies won by 326 runs
Scorers: WH Ferguson (West Indies), W Mavins (England)

WEST INDIES	1ST INNINGS	R	B	2ND INNINGS	R	B
AF Rae	c and b Jenkins	106		b Jenkins	24	
JB Stollmeyer	lbw b Wardle	20		b Jenkins	30	
FMM Worrell	b Bedser	52		c Doggart b Jenkins	45	
ED Weekes	b Bedser	63		run out	63	
+CL Walcott	st Evans b Jenkins	14		(6) not out	168	
GE Gomez	st Evans b Jenkins	1		(7) c Edrich b Bedser	70	
RJ Christiani	b Bedser	33		(8) not out	5	
*JDC Goddard	b Wardle	14		(5) c Evans b Jenkins	11	
PEW Jones	c Evans b Jenkins	0				
S Ramadhin	not out	1				
AL Valentine	c Hutton b Jenkins	5				
Extras	(10 b, 5 lb, 1 nb, 1 w)	17		(8 lb, 1 nb)	9	
Total	(all out, 131.2 overs)	326		(6 wickets, dec, 178 overs)	425	

Fall of wickets: 1-37 (Stollmeyer), 2-128 (Worrell), 3-233 (Weekes), 4-262 (Walcott), 5-273 (Rae), 6-274 (Gomez), 7-320 (Goddard), 8-320 (Christiani), 9-320 (Jones), 10-326 (Valentine, 131.2 ov)
Fall of wickets: 1-48 (Stollmeyer), 2-75 (Rae), 3-108 (Worrell), 4-146 (Goddard), 5-199 (Weekes), 6-410 (Gomez)

ENGLAND	O	M	R	W	Wd	Nb		O	M	R	W	Wd	Nb
Bedser	40	14	60	3	-	-	Bedser	44	16	80	1	-	1
Edrich	16	4	30	0	-	-	Edrich	13	2	37	0	-	-
Jenkins	35.2	6	116	5	1	-	Jenkins	59	13	174	4	-	-
Wardle	17	6	46	2	-	-	Wardle	30	10	58	0	-	-
Berry	19	7	45	0	-	1	Berry	32	15	67	0	-	-
Yardley	4	1	12	0	-	-							

ENGLAND	1ST INNINGS	R	B	2ND INNINGS	R	B
L Hutton	st Walcott b Valentine	35		b Valentine	10	
C Washbrook	st Walcott b Ramadhin	36		b Ramadhin	114	
WJ Edrich	c Walcott b Ramadhin	8		c Jones b Ramadhin	8	
GHG Doggart	lbw b Ramadhin	0		b Ramadhin	25	
WGA Parkhouse	b Valentine	0		c Goddard b Valentine	48	
*NWD Yardley	b Valentine	16		c Weekes b Valentine	19	
+TG Evans	b Ramadhin	8		c Rae b Ramadhin	2	
RO Jenkins	c Walcott b Valentine	4		b Ramadhin	4	
JH Wardle	not out	33		lbw b Worrell	21	
AV Bedser	b Ramadhin	5		b Ramadhin	0	
R Berry	c Goddard b Jones	2		not out	0	
Extras	(2 b, 1 lb, 1 w)	4		(16 b, 7 lb)	23	
Total	(all out, 106.4 overs)	151		(all out, 191.3 overs)	274	

Fall of wickets: 1-62 (Hutton), 2-74 (Washbrook), 3-74 (Doggart), 4-75 (Parkhouse), 5-86 (Edrich), 6-102 (Evans), 7-110 (Yardley), 8-113 (Jenkins), 9-122 (Bedser), 10-151 (Berry, 106.4 ov)
Fall of wickets: 1-28 (Hutton), 2-57 (Edrich), 3-140 (Doggart), 4-218 (Parkhouse), 5-228 (Washbrook), 6-238 (Evans), 7-245 (Yardley), 8-248 (Jenkins), 9-258 (Bedser), 10-274 (Wardle, 191.3 ov)

WEST INDIES	O	M	R	W	Wd	Nb		O	M	R	W	Wd	Nb
Jones	8.4	2	13	1	-	-	Jones	7	1	22	0	-	-
Worrell	10	4	20	0	-	-	Worrell	22.3	9	39	1	-	-
Valentine	45	28	48	4	-	-	Valentine	71	47	79	3	-	-
Ramadhin	43	27	66	5	-	-	Ramadhin	72	43	86	6	-	-
							Gomez	13	1	25	0	-	-
							Goddard	6	6	0	0	-	-

CHAPTER 3

1990
THE WRITING'S ON THE WALL

'Yuh calling our boy a thief?'

WEST INDIES FAN, BARBADOS

I FIRST GOT SELECTED in a West Indies squad against India in 1989. I was 19 years old, impatient and massively ambitious. After two good first-class seasons and the Youth World Cup in Australia, I could almost touch it.

The previous season, my first in senior cricket, I'd come up against Joel Garner, Malcolm Marshall and Curtly Ambrose and lived to tell the tale. In 1989 you could add Michael Holding, Courtney Walsh and Patrick Patterson to that list.

I didn't debut against India that year, I was 12th man in the series, but I'd already got a taste of playing the big boys in India's tour match at St Kitts against West Indies Under 23s. The 182 I hit that day sealed the deal for me. After two years of first-class cricket I'd played enough to make an assessment and answer the question which had burned me up since I was a kid: Did I have what it took? Well, did I?

Going into 1990, our top six was formidable. Gordon Greenidge and Desmond Haynes were an all-time opening pair, while Richie Richardson, Keith Arthurton, Viv Richards and Gus Logie, with our keeper Jeffrey Dujon at No.7, offered a powerful mix of greatness and promise.

I was only a teenager, but I deserved my place among the support cast. With the incredibly talented Carl Hooper heading up a list also featuring Carlisle Best, Phil Simmons and myself, that was a serious top 10 of batters.

It wasn't always a smooth ride. A poor run of form in early 1990 threatened to derail me but luckily I'd already left my mark on our first-class game, and when the English tourists got to the Caribbean I was given an early chance against them for the West Indies Board President's XI in a pre-series warm-up. My knock of 134 against Devon Malcolm and the rest put me back in the reckoning and into the squad for the Test series. I was close, so very close.

In the event, that series would come too soon for me. But I had a front row seat, carrying the drinks, soaking it up, and I'll never forget what I saw.

* * *

Fourth Test, Kensington Oval, it's late on the fourth evening, the sun's dropping behind the stands, Ambrose is bowling fast and the place is off the hook.

Barbados is the most popular tourist destination in the English-speaking Caribbean. When England tour, the tourism industry goes into overdrive, and with Barbados and Antigua attracting the lion's share of English folks, those venues tended to get the final Tests of a series. In 1990 we needed to win both to keep our winning record.

The mood's turned wild. Someone in the bleachers throws a coconut into a mass of bodies, striking a spectator in the head as a war of words turns physical, forcing play to be stopped while the police stepped in. No one takes the blame.

Meanwhile out in the middle, England's No.3, Rob Bailey, in his third Test match, is just about hanging in there. After a pair in the third Test and 17 in the first innings, Bailey's on 6 from 15 balls. He's playing for his country and his career.

Three slips, gully, short leg. Ambrose comes pumping in. Any second, this stage will catch fire.

I'm watching from the players' pavilion. We're one-down in the series. Out of nowhere, that famous decade-long winning streak is under threat, and not from Australia or even Pakistan, but from *England*.

* * *

For a while, no one had believed that we'd get to this point. Even when they won the opening Test at Jamaica, a first win on Caribbean soil in 16 years, the idea that they might win the series just isn't taken seriously. We're so accustomed to dominating that it feels impossible to think we won't be back on top.

But Jamaica was no fluke. Allan Lamb was brilliant with the bat, Robin Smith and Graham Gooch backed him up, and an unlikely pace attack led by the Jamaica-born Malcolm and the Barbados-born Gladstone Small turned us over twice to seal a famous victory.

For the second Test, not a ball was bowled in Guyana for three days and by the time the rain stopped and the canals were cleared for the water to run off, that match was dead.

So we had to pay proper attention to the third Test. An England victory at Port of Spain would mean a minimum drawn series, and a drawn series against the English, let alone a winning one, is not allowed to happen.

Well, we get lucky. Defeat could and should have come at Trinidad.

It's a strange match. We bat first on an uneven surface with a generous amount of grass on it, losing five wickets for 29 before a brilliant 98 by our local boy Logie saves us some major embarrassment. We're bowled out for 199 having been 103-8 but England respond well, taking a lead of 89 with Gooch, an amazing player of the quicks, holding things together.

Chasing 151 to win, the game's in England's grasp on the final day before a thunderstorm takes out most of the afternoon. When it clears, the ground's soggy in some areas but the umpires feel it's good for play. With 78 needed, nine wickets in hand and a scheduled 30 overs to get them, the equation's still in their favour, even without Gooch, whose hand had been smashed up from a nasty lifter from Ezra Moseley. Sitting on the players balcony I'm biting my nails alongside our manager Clive Lloyd. England's players and staff are also visibly uneasy. This is history in the offing.

Suddenly Clive taps me on the shoulder. Our stand-in skipper Desmond Haynes is coming off so I run on to replace him. An over later he's back out there, and I'm given instructions to have water and a towel ready. I'm thinking maybe the bowlers are gonna turn it up and I need to be there to refuel them, but it's the exact opposite. Instead I'm summoned onto the field at the end of every over. Drinks, towels, anything. At one point I'm sent on with a new set of bowling shoes with supposedly longer spikes. Bowlers start losing their run-ups blaming it on the sawdust-filled outfield. Anything to drag the game out.

It works. Only 17 of those overs are bowled before the light becomes too dangerous. England finish up five wickets down, still 31 runs shy. To see the mighty West Indies reduce the game to a snail's pace with time-wasting tactics doesn't exactly resonate with this idealistic 20-year-old.

After getting away with one at Trinidad, I can see the pressure on the faces of our players. There's an uneasy atmosphere that night. This is uncharted waters.

After a decade of chaos, England have landed on a formula. Discipline with bat and ball, led by a brilliant opening batter in Gooch, who pays more attention to preparation and fitness than any other England captain before him, and a bowling attack that revolves around limiting the bad balls and not going looking for gold, knowing that if they do they'll get spanked.

So, *this* is why Bridgetown is so hot that evening. England have turned up for once.

* * *

Set 356 to win, with an hour on the fourth day plus a full fifth day to negotiate, England are under pressure for the first time in the series. Our boys sense blood. A win is a must.

Ambrose's delivery is fast but heading down the leg-side. It jags off the pitch past Bailey's attempted leg glance, flicking his thigh pad on the way through as Dujon, with no foot movement as usual, dives to gather the ball up. It's not close to the bat but the cordon goes up, with Viv Richards the most animated; only Ambrose shows any doubts.

The umpire Lloyd Barker stands unmoved as the prolonged appeal gets more airtime now with Viv totally convinced that there's some bat on ball. The whipped-up crowd is screaming for the catch, pressure really buss pipe, and up goes Barker's finger. Bailey has to go. I'm jolted by the scene and it's a tough thing to see him walking off, the fall guy in our desperation not to lose a series. I had great sympathy for him. He'll play just one more game for his country.

The crowd is still wired when time's called for the day. "Barker, that's unfair, you're killing the game..." the English supporters shout, as the umpires and players leave the field.

"Yuh calling our boy a thief?" the locals hit back.

I watch it all, this scene that *Wisden* would write up as 'at best undignified and unsightly and at worst calculated gamesmanship'.

It stays with me long after that match is done. Long after Curtly takes eight wickets to win the game in the final hour on day five, and long after the finale at Antigua, which falls to us thanks to a record-breaking opening stand from Greenidge and Haynes, a total dismantlement of an attack which had lost its belief, plundering 298 to ensure that the West Indies took the series 2-1. Antigua was becoming a doomsday venue for England. Four years earlier, Viv had butchered them for the fastest Test hundred ever recorded, from just 56 balls, and now this, the all-time record opening stand for the West Indies. There was a scheduled tour for 1994 and my plan was to be a permanent fixture by then.

I couldn't shake what I saw in Trinidad and Barbados, but I had to accept it. I guess it was all part of my education. I had my ideas about how things should be done, I believed in the values of the game. I'd sat at Joey's table and listened hard to big men talk softly about what cricket stood for, why it was important, what it meant. But the curtain had been peeled back. I was no longer such a wide-eyed innocent.

As the dust settled on the series, what had become clear to me above all else was that teams were closing in on us. We may have been the undisputed champions of Test cricket, but the gap was narrowing. We had to take heed of it before it was too late and we suffered more than just a surface scratch.

WEST INDIES UNDER-23s v INDIANS

Venue: Warner Park, Basseterre
Toss: Indians won the toss and decided to bat
Umpires: AE Weekes, PC Whyte

Date: 14th, 15th, 16th March 1989
Result: Match drawn

INDIANS	1ST INNINGS	R	B	2ND INNINGS	R	B
*K Srikkanth	c and b Allen	28				
J Arun Lal	c Morgan b Perry	40		(1) not out	21	
NS Sidhu	lbw b LA Joseph	114				
SV Manjrekar	c Perry b Dhanraj	109				
AK Sharma	c Adams b LA Joseph	18				
RR Singh	not out	37				
+SS Karim	c Dhaniram b Benjamin	16		(2) not out	13	
Arshad Ayub	not out	20				
SK Sharma						
M Venkataramana						
ND Hirwani						
Extras	(12 b, 7 lb, 10 nb)	29		(5 nb)	5	
Total	(6 wickets, dec, 119 overs)	411		(no wicket, 9 overs)	39	

Fall of wickets: 1-38 (Srikkanth), 2-86 (Arun Lal), 3-257 (Sidhu), 4-300 (AK Sharma), 5-335 (Manjrekar), 6-368 (Karim)

WEST INDIES UNDER-23S	O	M	R	W	Wd	Nb		O	M	R	W	Wd	Nb
Benjamin	23	4	71	1	-	4	LA Joseph	5	1	19	0	-	3
Allen	19	2	57	1	-	3	Benjamin	2	0	16	0	-	2
LA Joseph	20	1	57	2	-	3	Perry	2	1	4	0	-	-
Perry	26	7	79	1	-	-							
Dhanraj	31	4	128	1	-	-							

WEST INDIES U23S	1ST INNINGS	R	B	2ND INNINGS	R	B
DS Morgan	b SK Sharma	39				
S Dhaniram	c Karim b SK Sharma	61				
DA Joseph	b Arshad Ayub	31				
*BC Lara	c Manjrekar b Hirwani	182				
JC Adams	lbw b Arshad Ayub	1				
+JR Murray	lbw b Hirwani	14				
NO Perry	c Arshad Ayub b Venkataramana	22				
IBA Allen	lbw b Hirwani	25				
KCG Benjamin	lbw b Hirwani	9				
R Dhanraj	lbw b Hirwani	1				
LA Joseph	not out	9				
Extras	(9 lb, 2 nb)	11				
Total	(all out, 127.3 overs)	405				

Fall of wickets: 1-44 (Morgan), 2-100 (DA Joseph), 3-195 (Dhaniram), 4-197 (Adams), 5-232 (Murray), 6-293 (Perry), 7-362 (Allen), 8-388 (Benjamin), 9-395 (Lara), 10-405 (Dhanraj, 127.3 ov)

INDIANS	O	M	R	W	Wd	Nb		O	M	R	W	Wd	Nb
SK Sharma	17	0	61	2	-	2							
Singh	6	0	25	0	-	-							
Arshad Ayub	35	6	69	2	-	-							
Hirwani	36.3	6	150	5	-	-							
Venkataramana	26	6	72	1	-	-							
Srikkanth	7	4	19	0	-	-							

WEST INDIES BOARD PRESIDENT'S XI v ENGLAND XI

Venue: Guaracara Park, Pointe-a-Pierre
Toss: WIPB XI won the toss and decided to field
Result: England XI won by 113 runs

Date: 17th, 18th, 19th, 20th March 1990
Umpires: F Ali, M Hosein

ENGLAND XI	1ST INNINGS	R	B	2ND INNINGS	R	B
*GA Gooch	c Harris b Haynes	66		c and b Haynes	61	
W Larkins	c Harris b Patterson	1		lbw b Haynes	13	
AJ Stewart	c Adams b Benjamin	6		b Benjamin	15	
RA Smith	c Morgan b Haynes	29		not out	99	
RJ Bailey	lbw b Baptiste	52		b Haynes	7	
DJ Capel	c Harris b Arthurton	1		(7) lbw b Benjamin	0	
+RC Russell	c Harris b Baptiste	25		(8) c Lambert b Haynes	16	
PAJ DeFreitas	not out	10		(9) lbw b Haynes	15	
CC Lewis	lbw b Patterson	21		(10) lbw b Haynes	6	
EE Hemmings	b Baptiste	3		(6) lbw b Benjamin	1	
DE Malcolm	b Baptiste	8		b Patterson	4	
Extras	(5 lb, 20 nb, 5 w)	30		(10 b, 7 lb, 21 nb, 3 w)	41	
Total	(all out, 95.1 overs)	252		(all out, 112.5 overs)	278	

Fall of wickets: 1-12 (Larkins), 2-36 (Stewart), 3-107 (Smith), 4-136 (Gooch), 5-150 (Capel), 6-201 (Bailey), 7-206 (Russell), 8-239 (Lewis), 9-243 (Hemmings), 10-252 (Malcolm, 95.1 ov)
Fall of wickets: 1-38 (Larkins), 2-98 (Stewart), 3-104 (Gooch), 4-131 (Bailey), 5-132 (Hemmings), 6-132 (Capel), 7-166 (Russell), 8-209 (DeFreitas), 9-249 (Lewis), 10-278 (Malcolm, 112.5 ov)

WEST INDIES BOARD PRESIDENT'S XI	O	M	R	W	Wd	Nb		O	M	R	W	Wd	Nb
Patterson	9	1	45	2	-	9	Patterson	23.5	7	59	1	-	11
Benjamin	15	2	34	1	2	2	Benjamin	27	7	70	3	3	2
Baptiste	33.1	5	91	4	3	9	Haynes	40	11	90	6	-	-
Haynes	32	12	57	2	-	-	Baptiste	22	6	42	0	1	9
Arthurton	5	0	18	1	-	-							
Morgan	1	0	2	0	-	-							

WIBP XI	1ST INNINGS	R	B	2ND INNINGS	R	B
CB Lambert	b Malcolm	12		c Capel b Malcolm	0	
DS Morgan	run out	0		c Bailey b Malcolm	12	
KLT Arthurton	c Russell b Capel	37		b DeFreitas	2	
BC Lara	b DeFreitas	134		lbw b DeFreitas	1	
*AL Logie	c Russell b Hemmings	40		(6) c and b Hemmings	26	
JC Adams	lbw b DeFreitas	8		(5) c Russell b DeFreitas	8	
+LL Harris	run out	8		lbw b Malcolm	0	
RC Haynes	c Russell b Malcolm	20		b DeFreitas	30	
EAE Baptiste	c and b Malcolm	9		lbw b Capel	19	
KCG Benjamin	c Russell b DeFreitas	2		not out	6	
BP Patterson	not out	0		lbw b Hemmings	11	
Extras	(3 b, 5 lb, 15 nb, 1 w)	24		(8 nb)	8	
Total	(all out, 83.5 overs)	294		(all out, 36.4 overs)	123	

Fall of wickets: 1-17 (Morgan), 2-21 (Lambert), 3-98 (Arthurton), 4-229 (Logie), 5-245 (Lara), 6-260 (Adams), 7-271 (Harris), 8-286 (Haynes), 9-292 (Baptiste), 10-294 (Benjamin, 83.5 ov)
Fall of wickets: 1-0 (Lambert), 2-3 (Arthurton), 3-6 (Lara), 4-26 (Morgan), 5-26 (Adams), 6-26 (Harris), 7-58 (Haynes), 8-106 (Logie), 9-110 (Baptiste), 10-123 (Patterson, 36.4 ov)

ENGLAND XI	O	M	R	W	Wd	Nb		O	M	R	W	Wd	Nb
Malcolm	19	4	60	3	-	3	Malcolm	11	3	29	3	-	2
DeFreitas	26.5	1	89	3	1	7	DeFreitas	13	2	54	4	-	5
Lewis	11	2	47	0	-	3	Hemmings	7.4	2	31	2	-	-
Capel	9	0	42	1	-	-	Capel	5	3	9	1	-	1
Hemmings	18	5	48	1	-	2							

WEST INDIES v ENGLAND, FIRST TEST

Venue: Sabina Park, Kingston
Toss: West Indies won the toss and decided to bat
Umpires: LH Barker, SA Bucknor

Date: 24th, 25th, 26th, 28th February, 1st March 1990
Result: England won by 9 wickets

WEST INDIES	1ST INNINGS	R	B	2ND INNINGS	R	B
CG Greenidge	run out	32	65	c Hussain b Malcolm	36	87
DL Haynes	c and b Small	36	115	b Malcolm	14	22
RB Richardson	c Small b Capel	10	23	lbw b Fraser	25	45
CA Best	c Russell b Capel	4	16	c Gooch b Small	64	136
CL Hooper	c Capel b Fraser	20	60	c Larkins b Small	8	19
*IVA Richards	lbw b Malcolm	21	31	b Malcolm	37	52
+PJL Dujon	not out	19	40	b Malcolm	15	30
MD Marshall	b Fraser	0	5	not out	8	17
IR Bishop	c Larkins b Fraser	0	1	c Larkins b Small	3	5
CA Walsh	b Fraser	6	29	b Small	2	11
BP Patterson	b Fraser	0	4	run out	2	5
Extras	(9 b, 3 lb, 4 nb)	16		(14 b, 10 lb, 1 nb, 1 w)	26	
Total	(all out, 64 overs)	164		(all out, 72.3 overs)	240	

Fall of wickets: 1-62 (Greenidge), 2-81 (Richardson), 3-92 (Best), 4-92 (Haynes), 5-124 (Richards), 6-144 (Hooper), 7-144 (Marshall), 8-150 (Bishop), 9-164 (Walsh), 10-164 (Patterson)
Fall of wickets: 1-26 (Haynes), 2-69 (Richardson), 3-87 (Greenidge), 4-112 (Hooper), 5-192 (Richards), 6-222 (Best), 7-222 (Dujon), 8-227 (Bishop), 9-237 (Walsh), 10-240 (Patterson)

ENGLAND	O	M	R	W	Wd	Nb		O	M	R	W	Wd	Nb
Small	15	6	44	1	-	-	Small	22	6	58	4	-	-
Malcolm	16	4	49	1	-	2	Malcolm	21.3	2	77	4	-	-
Fraser	20	8	28	5	-	-	Capel	15	1	50	0	-	-
Capel	13	4	31	2	-	2	Fraser	14	5	31	1	-	1

ENGLAND	1ST INNINGS	R	B	2ND INNINGS	R	B
*GA Gooch	c Dujon b Patterson	18	30	c Greenidge b Bishop	8	37
W Larkins	lbw b Walsh	46	120	not out	29	60
AJ Stewart	c Best b Bishop	13	12	not out	0	6
AJ Lamb	c Hooper b Walsh	132	205			
RA Smith	c Best b Bishop	57	161			
N Hussain	c Dujon b Bishop	13	12			
DJ Capel	c Richardson b Walsh	5	21			
+RC Russell	c Patterson b Walsh	26	72			
GC Small	lbw b Marshall	4	14			
ARC Fraser	not out	2	21			
DE Malcolm	lbw b Walsh	0	1			
Extras	(23 b, 12 lb, 12 nb, 1 w)	48		(1 lb, 3 nb)	4	
Total	(all out, 109.2 overs)	364		(1 wicket, 16.3 overs)	41	

Fall of wickets: 1-40 (Gooch), 2-60 (Stewart), 3-116 (Larkins), 4-288 (Smith), 5-315 (Hussain), 6-315 (Lamb), 7-325 (Capel), 8-339 (Small), 9-364 (Russell), 10-364 (Malcolm)
Fall of wickets: 1-35 (Gooch)

WEST INDIES	O	M	R	W	Wd	Nb		O	M	R	W	Wd	Nb
Patterson	18	2	74	1	-	3	Patterson	3	1	11	0	-	1
Bishop	27	5	72	3	1	-	Bishop	7.3	2	17	1	-	-
Marshall	18	3	46	1	-	2	Walsh	6	0	12	0	-	-
Walsh	27.2	4	68	5	-	7							
Hooper	6	0	28	0	-	-							
Richards	9	1	22	0	-	-							
Best	4	0	19	0	-	-							

WEST INDIES v ENGLAND, THIRD TEST

Venue: Queen's Park Oval, Port of Spain
Toss: England won the toss and decided to field
Umpires: LH Barker, CE Cumberbatch

Date: 23rd, 24th, 25th, 27th, 28th March 1990
Result: Match drawn

WEST INDIES	1ST INNINGS	R	B	2ND INNINGS	R	B
CG Greenidge	c Stewart b Malcolm	5	11	lbw b Fraser	42	124
*DL Haynes	c Lamb b Small	0	8	c Lamb b Malcolm	45	89
RB Richardson	c Russell b Fraser	8	34	c Gooch b Small	34	86
CA Best	c Lamb b Fraser	10	36	lbw b Malcolm	0	2
+PJL Dujon	lbw b Small	4	10	b Malcolm	0	1
AL Logie	c Lamb b Fraser	98	139	c Larkins b Malcolm	20	52
CL Hooper	c Russell b Capel	32	67	run out	10	47
EA Moseley	c Russell b Malcolm	0	2	c Lamb b Malcolm	26	31
CEL Ambrose	c Russell b Malcolm	7	11	c Russell b Fraser	18	42
IR Bishop	b Malcolm	16	65	not out	15	34
CA Walsh	not out	8	16	lbw b Malcolm	1	10
Extras	(4 lb, 7 nb)	11		(2 b, 13 lb, 12 nb, 1 w)	28	
Total	(all out, 65.1 overs)	199		(all out, 84.2 overs)	239	

Fall of wickets: 1-5 (Greenidge), 2-5 (Haynes), 3-22 (Richardson), 4-27 (Best), 5-29 (Dujon), 6-92 (Hooper), 7-93 (Moseley), 8-103 (Ambrose), 9-177 (Bishop), 10-199 (Logie)
Fall of wickets: 1-96 (Greenidge), 2-100 (Haynes), 3-100 (Best), 4-100 (Dujon), 5-142 (Logie), 6-167 (Richardson), 7-200 (Moseley), 8-200 (Hooper), 9-234 (Ambrose), 10-239 (Walsh)

ENGLAND	O	M	R	W	Wd	Nb		O	M	R	W	Wd	Nb
Small	17	4	41	2	-	-	Malcolm	26.2	4	77	6	1	6
Malcolm	20	2	60	4	-	4	Small	21	8	56	1	-	-
Fraser	13.1	2	41	3	-	2	Capel	13	3	30	0	-	1
Capel	15	2	53	1	-	1	Fraser	24	4	61	2	-	5

ENGLAND	1ST INNINGS	R	B	2ND INNINGS	R	B
*GA Gooch	c Dujon b Bishop	84	264	retired hurt	18	28
W Larkins	c Dujon b Ambrose	54	156	c Dujon b Moseley	7	24
AJ Stewart	c Dujon b Ambrose	9	56	c Bishop b Walsh	31	32
AJ Lamb	b Bishop	32	81	lbw b Bishop	25	48
RA Smith	c Dujon b Moseley	5	27	lbw b Walsh	2	7
RJ Bailey	c Logie b Moseley	0	1	b Walsh	0	13
DJ Capel	c Moseley b Ambrose	40	122	not out	17	44
+RC Russell	c Best b Walsh	15	67	not out	5	8
GC Small	lbw b Bishop	0	4			
ARC Fraser	c Hooper b Ambrose	11	56			
DE Malcolm	not out	0	6			
Extras	(6 b, 13 lb, 16 nb, 3 w)	38		(2 b, 7 lb, 6 nb)	15	
Total	(all out, 137.2 overs)	288		(5 wickets, 33 overs)	120	

Fall of wickets: 1-112 (Larkins), 2-152 (Stewart), 3-195 (Gooch), 4-214 (Smith), 5-214 (Bailey), 6-214 (Lamb), 7-243 (Russell), 8-244 (Small), 9-284 (Fraser), 10-288 (Capel)
Fall of wickets: 1-27 (Larkins), 2-74 (Stewart), 3-79 (Smith), 4-85 (Bailey), 5-106 (Lamb)

WEST INDIES	O	M	R	W	Wd	Nb		O	M	R	W	Wd	Nb
Ambrose	36.2	8	59	4	-	4	Bishop	10	1	31	1	-	-
Bishop	31	6	69	3	-	-	Ambrose	6	0	20	0	-	1
Walsh	22	5	45	1	-	6	Moseley	10	2	33	1	-	3
Hooper	18	5	26	0	-	-	Walsh	7	0	27	3	-	2
Moseley	30	5	70	2	2	6							

WEST INDIES v ENGLAND, FOURTH TEST

Venue: Kensington Oval, Bridgetown
Toss: England won the toss and decided to field
Umpires: DM Archer, LH Barker

Date: 5th, 6th, 7th, 8th, 10th April 1990
Result: West Indies won by 164 runs

WEST INDIES	1ST INNINGS	R	B	2ND INNINGS	R	B
CG Greenidge	c Russell b DeFreitas	41	77	lbw b Small	3	17
DL Haynes	c Stewart b Small	0	4	c Malcolm b Small	109	177
RB Richardson	c Russell b Small	45	89	lbw b DeFreitas	39	49
CA Best	c Russell b Small	164	245			
*IVA Richards	c Russell b Capel	70	110	(4) c Small b Capel	12	23
AL Logie	c Russell b Capel	31	51	(5) lbw b DeFreitas	48	80
+PJL Dujon	b Capel	31	74	(8) not out	15	30
MD Marshall	c Lamb b Small	4	5	(7) c Smith b Small	7	12
CEL Ambrose	not out	20	44	c Capel b DeFreitas	1	5
IR Bishop	run out	10	31	not out	11	16
EA Moseley	b DeFreitas	4	19	(6) b Small	5	8
Extras	(8 lb, 18 nb)	26		(12 lb, 4 nb, 1 w)	17	
Total	(all out, 121.5 overs)	446		(8 wickets, dec, 68 overs)	267	

Fall of wickets: 1-6 (Haynes), 2-69 (Greenidge), 3-108 (Richardson), 4-227 (Richards), 5-291 (Logie), 6-395 (Dujon), 7-406 (Marshall), 8-411 (Best), 9-431 (Bishop), 10-446 (Moseley)
Fall of wickets: 1-13 (Greenidge), 2-80 (Richardson), 3-109 (Richards), 4-223 (Haynes), 5-228 (Logie), 6-238 (Marshall), 7-238 (Moseley), 8-239 (Ambrose)

ENGLAND	O	M	R	W	Wd	Nb		O	M	R	W	Wd	Nb
Malcolm	33	6	142	0	-	2	Malcolm	10	0	46	0	1	3
Small	35	5	109	4	-	-	Small	20	1	74	4	-	-
DeFreitas	29.5	5	99	2	-	14	DeFreitas	22	2	69	3	-	4
Capel	24	5	88	3	-	2	Capel	16	1	66	1	-	2

ENGLAND	1ST INNINGS	R	B	2ND INNINGS	R	B
AJ Stewart	c Richards b Moseley	45	61	c Richards b Ambrose	37	80
W Larkins	c Richardson b Bishop	0	1	c Dujon b Bishop	0	2
RJ Bailey	b Bishop	17	19	c Dujon b Ambrose	6	16
*AJ Lamb	lbw b Ambrose	119	224	(6) c Dujon b Moseley	10	35
RA Smith	b Moseley	62	246	(7) not out	40	150
N Hussain	lbw b Marshall	18	49	(8) lbw b Ambrose	0	11
DJ Capel	c Greenidge b Marshall	2	6	(9) lbw b Ambrose	6	14
+RC Russell	lbw b Bishop	7	31	(5) b Ambrose	55	238
PAJ DeFreitas	c and b Ambrose	24	30	(10) lbw b Ambrose	0	1
GC Small	not out	1	6	(4) lbw b Ambrose	0	2
DE Malcolm	b Bishop	12	15	lbw b Ambrose	4	18
Extras	(14 b, 9 lb, 25 nb, 3 w)	51		(8 b, 9 lb, 15 nb, 1 w)	33	
Total	(all out, 109.3 overs)	358		(all out, 91.4 overs)	191	

Fall of wickets: 1-1 (Larkins), 2-46 (Bailey), 3-75 (Stewart), 4-268 (Lamb), 5-297 (Smith), 6-301 (Capel), 7-308 (Hussain), 8-340 (Russell), 9-340 (DeFreitas), 10-358 (Malcolm)
Fall of wickets: 1-1 (Larkins), 2-10 (Bailey), 3-10 (Small), 4-71 (Stewart), 5-97 (Lamb), 6-166 (Russell), 7-173 (Hussain), 8-181 (Capel), 9-181 (DeFreitas), 10-191 (Malcolm)

WEST INDIES	O	M	R	W	Wd	Nb		O	M	R	W	Wd	Nb
Bishop	24.3	8	70	4	-	-	Bishop	20	7	40	1	-	-
Ambrose	25	2	82	2	-	10	Ambrose	22.4	10	45	8	-	7
Moseley	28	3	114	2	3	12	Marshall	18	8	31	0	-	7
Marshall	23	6	55	2	-	-	Moseley	19	3	44	1	1	3
Richards	9	4	14	0	-	-	Richards	10	5	11	0	-	-
							Richardson	2	1	3	0	-	-

WEST INDIES v ENGLAND, FIFTH TEST

Venue: Antigua Recreation Ground, St John's
Toss: England won the toss and decided to bat
Umpires: DM Archer, AE Weekes

Date: 12th, 14th, 15th, 16th April 1990
Result: West Indies won by an innings and 32 runs

ENGLAND	1ST INNINGS	R	B	2ND INNINGS	R	B
AJ Stewart	c Richards b Walsh	27	49	c Richardson b Bishop	8	29
W Larkins	c Hooper b Ambrose	30	103	b Ambrose	10	17
RJ Bailey	c Dujon b Bishop	42	101	(4) c Dujon b Bishop	8	14
*AJ Lamb	c Richards b Ambrose	37	70	(5) b Baptiste	35	59
RA Smith	lbw b Walsh	12	43	(6) retired hurt	8	31
N Hussain	c Dujon b Bishop	35	87	(7) c Dujon b Bishop	34	70
DJ Capel	c Haynes b Bishop	10	31	(8) run out	1	10
+RC Russell	c Dujon b Bishop	7	34	(9) c Richardson b Ambrose	24	30
PAJ DeFreitas	lbw b Bishop	21	22	(10) c Greenidge b Ambrose	0	3
GC Small	lbw b Walsh	8	20	(3) b Ambrose	4	23
DE Malcolm	not out	0	5	not out	1	11
Extras	(5 b, 11 lb, 15 nb)	31		(1 b, 8 lb, 11 nb, 1 w)	21	
Total	(all out, 91.1 overs)	260		(all out, 47 overs)	154	

Fall of wickets: 1-42 (Stewart), 2-101 (Larkins), 3-143 (Bailey), 4-167 (Smith), 5-167 (Lamb), 6-195 (Capel), 7-212 (Russell), 8-242 (DeFreitas), 9-259 (Small), 10-260 (Hussain)
Fall of wickets: 1-16 (Larkins), 2-20 (Stewart), 3-33 (Bailey), 4-37 (Small), 5-86 (Lamb), 6-94 (Capel), 7-148 (Russell), 8-148 (DeFreitas), 9-154 (Hussain)

WEST INDIES	O	M	R	W	Wd	Nb		O	M	R	W	Wd	Nb
Bishop	28.1	6	84	5	-	-	Bishop	14	2	36	3	-	-
Ambrose	29	5	79	2	-	4	Ambrose	13	7	22	4	-	1
Walsh	21	4	51	3	-	7	Walsh	10	1	40	0	-	6
Baptiste	13	4	30	0	-	4	Baptiste	10	1	47	1	-	4

WEST INDIES	1ST INNINGS	R	B	2ND INNINGS	R	B
CG Greenidge	run out	149	207			
DL Haynes	c Russell b Small	167	317			
RB Richardson	c Russell b Malcolm	34	52			
CL Hooper	b Capel	1	6			
*IVA Richards	c Smith b Malcolm	1	2			
AL Logie	c Lamb b DeFreitas	15	31			
+PJL Dujon	run out	25	38			
EAE Baptiste	c Russell b Malcolm	9	23			
CEL Ambrose	c DeFreitas b Capel	5	13			
IR Bishop	not out	14	36			
CA Walsh	b Malcolm	8	15			
Extras	(5 lb, 13 nb)	18				
Total	(all out, 120.5 overs)	446				

Fall of wickets: 1-298 (Greenidge), 2-357 (Richardson), 3-358 (Hooper), 4-359 (Richards), 5-382 (Logie), 6-384 (Haynes), 7-415 (Dujon), 8-417 (Baptiste), 9-433 (Ambrose), 10-446 (Walsh)

ENGLAND	O	M	R	W	Wd	Nb		O	M	R	W	Wd	Nb
Small	31	3	123	1	-	-							
Malcolm	34.5	3	126	4	-	3							
Capel	28	1	118	2	-	5							
DeFreitas	27	4	74	1	-	5							

CHAPTER 4

1991

THE KING, THE KID AND THE CALIBRA

'You wanna drive it? Let's go'

SIR VIVIAN RICHARDS

HERE'S THE THING about the '91 tour: Viv was right. Even though I might have been anxious to play, I was not ready. I may have been impatient, of course I was. As a young player, you're not thinking about whether or not you're ready. You're not being rational. You're watching the form of some of the guys and wondering why you can't get in.

Looking back now, I can understand why he held me back. It was one of those things. You want to play so badly, but then you look back and realise it was probably a good thing. I might have been scraping myself off the floor by the end of it.

I was beyond elated to be selected. My dreams were being realised at a quick pace. I was being pulled into this whole other world and even before the squad was announced I caught a glimpse of the tensions lurking under the surface. We were in Barbados playing a Test match against Australia. I was 12th man, it was late evening after play. I was sitting alone by the pool at the Rockley Resort when our captain came by mumbling to himself. I'd dreamt of moments like this, Viv and me alone, but most of them had us in the middle, beating the bowling. This would have to do for now. I was inquisitive to find out what was wrong.

"What's wrong, Skip?" It was the first thing that came out of my mouth. He didn't even look at me. I felt like he wasn't even talking to me, yet he got louder.

"These selectors, man, they want to get rid of me."

"What?" I said.

"You shut up... You know you're going, you're Joey's son, your father is a selector, two weeks before the tour starts and no captain yet."

I didn't say another word. He ranted a little longer and then disappeared.

* * *

This tour would leave its mark. This was *England*, with everything that went with it. The biggest tour out there. I knew about the battles between us, when it started, how it started, the significance of every tour, every match. The history between England and the people of the Caribbean stretches to corners of the world far beyond the limits of our borders. It's been written about by some of the most illustrious names you could imagine. This would be my little piece, my understanding of it, coming from books I read but also from the heart.

When I got up from my seat to deplane, stretching for my oversized West Indies blazer above, slipping it on and looking at all the passengers thrilled by our presence, I knew I was joining something special. This was further emphasised when we cleared immigration and customs and proceeded to push our trolleys towards the exit doors. As they opened up for us, there it was. The first thing I saw. Scores of media men falling over themselves to get shots of the great man, Sir Isaac Vivian Alexander Richards, on his last tour of England. I remember photographers pushing some of us players out of the way to catch a shot of the man behind the shades, the swagger and the felt hat.

Some people see superstardom in, you know, an *envious* way. That wasn't it for me. I saw him as an example. I said to myself at that very moment: *that* is how I want to be treated one day.

I knew there were going to be limited opportunities to play, I knew that I had to really impress if I wanted to push myself into the side. To break into this West Indies team, I had to do more than the norm. At 22, I'd already broken records for the most runs in first-class cricket and still found myself sitting on the bench watching. If a player made those runs in today's cricket they'd be elevated very close to the captaincy.

But for all that, what I saw that year were the first signs that we weren't as invincible as we used to be. We were still successful as a team, and we'd go unbeaten in the Test series that summer, but we weren't dominating as we did in the past.

Cracks were starting to appear in the great West Indies cricket team. Just as I was trying to push through.

* * *

Still, those *names*. Not so long ago they were fantasy figures, legends that I'd impersonate to play Test matches in the yard at home, batting against a tennis ball. Suddenly there they were. It was thrilling to be around them. But for a young kid making his way, it was a tough school.

Early on we were staying at the Westbury Hotel in Mayfair, in the heart of London. One morning I walked outside and Viv was taking some pictures for his latest sponsorship deal. It was a Vauxhall Calibra, a two-door affair, just a lovely car. We were travelling to Birmingham that day ahead of the first ODI – the first international match of the tour.

"What a beautiful car," I say to Viv.

"You like it?"

"Of course I like it! I mean, it's nice…"

"You wanna drive it?"

I say, of course, I'd love to. What else could I say? It's Sir Viv, the main man. And so he gives me the keys, jumps in the passenger seat, settles in and tells me to drive us to Birmingham.

Now, I could drive fine, but coming from Trinidad & Tobago, you don't know about two-hour drives, and you *really* don't know about motorways. No matter. Viv just sits in the passenger seat and lets me get on with it.

I was surprised, for one, that he gave me the keys. But I'm feeling happy to be in the same car with the captain. I drive all the way to Birmingham behind a bus. I didn't know the way. We play the game, and a few days later I'm heading to the team bus to find my seat and all I hear is that famously deep, strong voice calling out for Pups. Now, that was my nickname in the team – there were big dogs and there were pups.

I don't look up. Instead, I bury myself in my seat. I hear it again. Then again. Eventually I look up.

"Let's go."

And I realise. I'll be driving this man around for the entire summer. He buys the big book, the A-Z of England, and away we go.

You'd think I'd learn a lot, right? Asking questions, picking his brains, my own audience with the King? All I'll say is it's hard to get much insight out of a man who's asleep. Viv, he slept a *lot*. We didn't spend much time talking. Or at least I thought he was sleeping. Every so often my foot would get a bit heavy on the gas, and every time I pressed that pedal and pushed it up around 75-80mph he would grunt, a real deep grunt through his nose, and say to me, "Pups, listen to me, this is England, they would *love* to put me in jail round here. Slow down, man."

Whatever deal he had with Vauxhall, Viv was *not* gonna drive. And why would he? He's playing all the cricket, I'm playing the practice games, and he needs a driver. I guess he didn't want to hire one when he already had one in the team.

And so it went, Viv and me in the Calibra, all through that summer. I never set foot on the bus again.

* * *

We played a couple of first-class games against the counties, then into the one-dayers, and after a few more county games we'd get into the Test series. I knew no one was gonna do me any favours. I needed to have a strong first-class season and keep pounding on the door to break it down.

It was my first experience of English conditions and starting off in Worcestershire, it was ironic that at the other end of the scale, Ian Botham was also trying to play his way back into the Test team. He came out to play that week, and I'd also heard a lot about Graeme Hick, the Zimbabwean who was scoring tons of runs and about England wanting to pick him for the Tests now he was qualified.

That game was a very important one for me because, even though I knew I don't start the series, I was determined to be the leading batsman in the first-class game when the first Test was announced. My goals were well-planned. Get runs in the warm-up games and let the selectors and captain do whatever they had to do.

What I didn't factor in was just how different the conditions are in England to the Caribbean. Sure, I'd played against Marshall and Patterson. Faced up to Garner, Walsh, Mikey Holding. But I'd never faced bowlers in *England*. Even though they didn't have any bowlers of the pace of these guys – Devon Malcolm excepted – the conditions made them difficult. I didn't pay enough attention to adapt my game.

First game, Worcester, I got 26, bowled by Phil Newport, driving at one and feeling sure I'd middle it and missing it altogether. Welcome to England. I would have to learn quick.

Sir Viv scored a hundred in that game and with this being his last tour it was great to see him in form. And then there was Botham, who hit a big hundred. I remember that Viv was not too unhappy about that.

* * *

The one-dayers came before the Tests and unfortunately Gordon Greenidge got injured in the second one-day international which gave me the opportunity to play at Lord's for just my second ever one-dayer.

Losing two early wickets, I was in. It was an amazing feeling because I slotted in before Viv Richards to bat at No. 4. Looking back on it, that top seven was all right-handers so maybe I shouldn't feel too privileged about it, perhaps I was just in there to break it up a bit. No matter. What an honour. Walking through the Long Room, onto the field, the crowd rising up, that feeling will never leave me. When I got out there, 'Big Syd' Lawrence was bowling. I played an on-drive for four and I remember getting into the groove, building a partnership with Richie Richardson, before he was out.

Now listen, every young man's dream is to be waiting in the middle, watching The Greatest walk through the gate and onto the field where I'm standing. Immediately the mood was different. A different feeling in the air. Everyone knew this was Sir Vivian's last series, he was 39 at the time, and they all just stood up, everyone, as one. It was amazing. I'm watching this in *awe*.

What happened next, I don't even know *what* it was. I think I must have felt under observation, or like I was sitting an exam. All these thoughts. You can't hog the strike, you can't be pinned down, you have to look classy. All these emotions and feelings are running through me, now I'm batting with Viv. We put on a small partnership, just 20 runs, when I skipped down the wicket to hit the left-arm spin of Richard Illingworth to deep mid-off and it took the inside half of the bat. You're talking elementary stuff. *Elementary stuff*. I allowed it to bounce and turn and I spooned an easy catch back to him.

I was distraught. It was the first time I'd ever batted with Sir Vivian Richards in an international match and I didn't want it to stop because I didn't know when I would next get to do it. The answer to that was never. That was it. My one time ever. Think of all the runs we scored for the West Indies, and we combined for just 20 of them, one cold morning at Lord's.

Back in those days a one-day international match was broken up by lunch and tea and our dressing room at tea was a steaming place as Viv and Curtly Ambrose got into each other.

We were in the field, and Carl Hooper was bowling to Neil Fairbrother when Fairbrother late-cut the ball past Ambrose at short third man and picked up two runs. Ambrose gathered and threw the ball back to the keeper but before he could get back into the circle, Hooper bowled another ball. So the umpire called no-ball due to there being three men in the circle, not four. I was stood at backward point and saw Viv, who was at extra cover, raise his hand in anger. Ambrose brushed him off, and I kept turning to my left to see Viv Richards and back to my right to see Curtly Ambrose, two fellow Antiguans, gesturing to each other.

At tea, Viv goes up the stairs first and we all file in, all the greats one after the other, and he slams the door behind us.

"Something happened on my field today and if that ever happens again that person will not represent the West Indies as long as I'm in charge."

The room is dead quiet. Curtly gets up.

"I know where you're from, we're from the same island, I came here with nothing, and I will *leave* with nothing."

It was a direct threat to quit the tour. Viv was slumped in his chair. He said to Lance Gibbs, the manager, "You take care of this meeting."

I'd been around Sir Viv for a couple of years by then, and while I thought Curtly was disrespectful to the captain for laying down a threat like that, this was the first time I'd seen anyone answer back to him in anger.

* * *

From Lord's we jumped back in the Calibra and headed to Taunton, Viv's old stomping ground. I hadn't crossed fifty yet on tour. I needed runs. As a young player and part of that batting unit, I knew I'd get the opportunity to play these practice games as the senior guys would be taking a break. So, *this* was my Test match.

I was as zoned in as possible and again was so disappointed not to make a hundred. I made 93, and while it was a good feeling to retrace the steps of Sir Viv to make some runs at that ground, I was hugely disappointed that I didn't carry on. I knew it was gonna be tough to make the team. Phil Simmons was an automatic pick to open after the injury to Greenidge, and then when you looked at the line-up, Richie and Viv and one of the best talents that the West Indies ever produced in Carl Hooper, I knew it would be tough. As Viv had said to me a couple of years before, I would have to wait my turn.

Leicestershire was next on the road, and I knew I had at best only an outside chance of getting picked for the first Test. Simmons' hundred at Worcester had cemented him as opener, and Carl's runs at Somerset had done the same for him. I wouldn't say it licked the fight out of me, but something was missing for me at Leicester.

I remember it was cold. Overcast. Freezing. We were in the field and I was standing at second slip, Viv was at first and Richie Richardson was at third. Damien Martyn edged one off one of our fast bowlers and we both, Richie and me, shouted "Catch it!". It flew between us for four, and I didn't dare look in his direction.

All I heard was Viv's cough, you know? He does that cough a lot.

"If there's one thing I don't want in my team it's any coward boys. When the ball come to you, catch it."

I didn't say anything because I knew it split between myself and Richie, but at that stage, let's be honest, you're freezing and you don't want anything to come near you. A few overs later, I think it might have been Ambrose bowling, and Martyn nicked again and it went straight into the lap of Viv Richards, and out again. And he starts to wring his hands, "Jeez, this place is *cold*, man."

Something's about to come out my mouth and I look at Dujon and he just puts his finger to his lips. After that, I shut my mouth. I may not have scored any runs, but I guess I was still learning.

* * *

I was fascinated by players who could play pace, and I'm talking real, serious pace. I knew how difficult it was to face our guys. I'd faced them in the nets and against them in the Caribbean, so I knew what batters were up against. I would always look out for the best players of pace and study their movements, because any batter who defied the West Indies was worthy of fascination.

What Graham Gooch did at Headingley in that first Test match was a lesson in batsmanship. It was incredible. My mind was so young, so inexperienced in my learnings about the game. I'd played a lot of first-class cricket but this was different, this was levels up.

I was struck that Gooch was dominating in his late thirties more than in the early part of his career. What had he learned? That innings at Leeds, 154 not out to carry his bat, was the result of all the experience he had gained over the years, and I'd yet to find myself. I remember thinking: *this* is the level. I wanted to spend some time with him, to pick his brains. I wasn't upset that he scored those runs. Disappointed that we lost, sure. But in awe of what I'd seen. No one else scored a hundred or got close to it, only Viv really stood up for us with the bat with 70-odd in the first innings.

Something else from that Test match. There was a lot of talk in our dressing room about Devon Malcolm and Phil DeFreitas, these two West Indians opening the bowling for England. Back then I felt there was this need to show West Indian fast bowlers coming up against us that the only team they could make was the one they were in.

It wasn't disrespect, but it wasn't far off. It didn't work in that match. DeFreitas picked up eight wickets and Malcolm bowled fast. For us, it was our first loss in England since the Seventies.

So this is where I was. After that first Test defeat, I went into the zone of thinking that there is an opportunity here. Brian, man, you've gotta score runs. It doesn't matter what happens in the match, whether we win or draw, they're practice games, and there's maybe three, four innings before the Lord's Test and I'll be on trial in every one of them. I got myself into that way of thinking.

And what happened? I couldn't score a run. Back-to-back failures. I couldn't understand it. I was focused, sure, but I was nervous, too uptight. My feet wouldn't move properly and I couldn't time the ball. That was me done. Three low scores and that was me out of Lord's. Don't even think about it.

Yet still I couldn't shake it, I was so confused. I wasn't doing the business to even be *considered*, and it hurt. My brain was working overtime, over-thinking, tying myself up with all these ideas. My tour was hanging by a thread.

* * *

When I think back to that Lord's match I see the class of Carl Hooper. Man, what a player. The ease in which he batted brought out a kind of awe in us, and in *all* of us, even the senior players. You felt that when Carl went out to bat, they enjoyed it – Haynes, Richards, Greenidge, all these guys would stop what they were doing just to watch him.

He was so talented, yet he didn't understand just how good he was. People would ask why he didn't do full justice to his brilliance, and you know what, there is no clear reason for it. Carl was easily one of the best players I've ever seen. I would say that not even Tendulkar and myself would come close to that talent. Separate Carl's career from playing to captaining, and his numbers are very different. As a captain he averaged near to 50, so he enjoyed the responsibility. It's sad that only as a captain did he fulfil his true potential.

That week at Lord's, there was a lot going on. After Carl's hundred, we were in the field and at the end of play Viv called a team meeting. He sat us all down and went round to the bowlers.

"Curtly, big man, good effort, keep working hard."

"Maco, *soldier.*"

"Young Allen. Good effort, young man. First Test match. Impressed."

Then he pauses. "But some of us don't wanna bowl the ball."

So Courtney Walsh starts getting emotional and he's stood up and shouted, "Manager, give me my ticket."

Lance says to him, "Why, what happened?"

And Courtney says, "What you mean, what happened? The man calls everybody else and I ain't called and now he says some of us don't wanna bowl the ball. He must be talking to me!"

Lance has to try and talk Courtney down, but Viv won't shift. Eventually our reserve keeper David Williams, who's very religious, got us all to put our hands on each other's shoulders and he said a prayer. That seemed to do the trick, but it was that kind of mood.

Viv's tone of voice is intimidating and if you're not strong enough, you can take that personally and be affected by it. Me, I was never really affected by it. In a way I welcomed it, because I was so much under his arm that I knew abuse was coming and I was a strong personality.

I don't think Viv wilfully intimidated you. It was just his make-up. He's not a bully. Viv Richards is not a bully. But Viv has a very strong personality. He's a very aggressive person who dealt with most things that way. If we had a team meeting, he would inspire. He would back his players forever. He would talk in such a way that it left a mark on you. Even now, he's not a soft person. Maybe he has a soft *side*, but a soft person?

Put it this way. Viv was Viv, with everything that went with it, at *all* times. I was on his tail all the time so I might have received more tongue lashings than most, but it never affected me badly because I knew that what he was talking about was what West Indies cricket needed to hear. If you sift out all the toughness and the so-called arrogance and listen to what he's really saying, he means well for West Indies cricket. Sure we had a couple of run-ins, especially later when I was captain and he was selector, but I think I stood up to him most of the time.

A lot of players wouldn't dare admit they didn't like Viv Richards, or that they felt intimidated by him. I would say that I love Viv Richards and he did try to intimidate me but never succeeded. I have seen with my own eyes big men brought to tears, including me, under the wrath of the King.

Now listen, it needs to be said that Viv Richards never cried down on a person because he didn't want them to be great like him. His sternness was who he was, but he never wanted you not to do well. It was just how he was.

With Viv, he doesn't understand if he's hurting someone or not. The Lord's match was a wet one and I remember at one point the players came off the field for rain. I was making sure that as the guy on the bench, everybody's comfortable. You help the fast bowlers with their boots, knocking the turf off the soles, and you go to the captain and vice-captain with any requests. They're your focus. I did that job as professionally as I could. I remember taking Ambrose and Marshall's boots and cleaning them up as best I could, and taking their wet tops to the dryer.

Lunch was called, and after doing all that and preparing the lunches for the senior men to have downstairs, I went back upstairs to see the legendary Nancy, who dished up the Lord's lunches, for my own plate. So I'm up there in the line, waiting for my lunch, and Viv looks at me and says, "What are you doing?" I say to him that I'm queuing for my lunch, and that his lunch and the other lunches are all prepared downstairs, where he likes to eat.

"Put that plate down," he says. "I want you to go for a run."

So I have to go out and run around the Lord's outfield for 15 minutes, until the umpires are heading out again, at which point I have to run back in and change into my whites to prepare for any eventualities as 12th man! Man, I was hungry that day.

Same Test match, I broke the curfew.

* * *

So a couple of touring Trini's, Colin Borde and Ricky Farfan, heard about this soca party happening in Brixton. I understood how to play it. Even if you go out through the front door at 8pm, you've got to know where the fire exit is on the way back. I overstayed past the midnight curfew because the party was going so great and, you know, I come back in about 2am via the back door and crawl into the room I'm sharing with Malcolm Marshall and quietly into my bed.

The next day or two, things aren't going great. The tour manager is talking about guys disturbing their roommates and stuff like that, but I didn't remember Malcolm stirring or getting up so I didn't think too much more of it. And look, trust me, I'm not the only person in that team breaking the curfew.

Rain was falling at Lord's, and I'd done all my duties. I'm slumped in my chair, dozing a little. And suddenly I'm feeling like I'm in an MRI machine, and I open my eyes and he's right there, his face up against mine.

"Did you have a late night?"

"No Skip, the rain is falling so, you know, and I thought the guys were OK, and, you know, it's raining…"

"OK, if the rain is falling, get yourself up and go and watch it."

I go to sit on the little balcony and watch the drizzle.

A little time later, I hear Lance, the manager, who likes horse racing as

I did, come running in and I can hear him saying "Where's Brian?" So he finds me alone on the balcony and says, "Come, come, I've got a horse!" But as I get back up to re-enter the room, I see Viv standing there with his towel around his waist, staring me down. I make an immediate U-turn and sit back on the bench. You see with Viv, he knew *everything*.

The following that the West Indies had on that tour was just amazing. Unlimited amounts of Caribbean food delivered to our hotel, London teeming with West Indians wanting to be with you. So yes, I enjoyed myself and yes, I broke the curfew that one time.

OK, it might have been twice.

But I wasn't a reckless person who smoked or drank a lot. My eyes were open to London. You'd go down to Piccadilly Circus and you're alive to it all. I spent a lot of time looking around London and cutting it close to the curfew and I don't mind that. I knew that the West Indian presence in London was very heavy so there was always a phone call, always an offer of something. I was 22, just turned. You felt like you were right in the heart of it. The Caribbean melting pot. And then you had your travellers who would follow the team around. There was Keith the Pipe Guy, and all these characters. It was beautiful.

Not so beautiful: I got fined. Twenty percent of my tour money. That late night caught up with me. I only found out after the tour was done. I had to travel to Barbados to meet with the board and I had my lawyer with me, because I was a little surprised. He said to me, "What did you do to lose money on that tour?" Turns out it was for breaking that curfew.

Man, so much went on during that tour, I had to ask who else lost 20 percent? There should have been a few, I can say that much. I couldn't deny that I broke that curfew, and if 20 percent was the norm and the same for everyone then fine, I deserved it. But it left a sour taste. I was a first-timer and I guess I got what was coming to me. I took it on the chin but it was hard not to feel a little more cynical by the end of it.

* * *

After Lord's we drove down, Viv and me, to Hampshire, where I decided I got to be a little more aggressive. I'd been poking around and I felt I needed to free myself up and be more attacking. I walked out to bat at Hampshire and let it all go – square cuts, drives, pulls, flicks, every shot in the book, and I was on 30-odd in no time. I look up and see David Williams running onto the field with a pair of my gloves in his hand. I haven't asked for any gloves but there he is anyway.

"What's wrong, what you out here for?"

"I have a message from Viv, he says to stop batting like a millionaire."

"Tell him where to go."

Now, David is from my country. We know each other pretty well. He's already turned to head back to the pavilion and now I'm shouting back at him.

"David, David! Where you going?!"

"Well, Brian, you've got a message for Viv, I'd better go tell him."

"Come on, man, were you really gonna tell him that?!"

"Of course not, Brian. But I was sent out to send this stupid message, what choice did I have?"

"OK, cool," I say. "Just *please* don't tell Viv I told him where to go, alright?"

Viv wasn't wrong. I *was* playing a shot a ball. I'd had no runs on the tour, I felt anxious, all I could think about was, 'What's next?' So I went out blazing away, perhaps out of desperation. I think, again, it's Viv's way. He was watching me closely, could see what I was doing, and was concerned. I think it was his way of saying, 'Slow down, man, it'll happen, it'll happen'. I most likely wasn't gonna get anything out of that sort of approach. A shot a ball, you might score a hundred one day, but that's not the way to play in England. You need to grind. And it was his way of telling me that, and showing me love.

* * *

One down with three to play, our senior men stepped up. Ambrose was so dominant at that time, the best fast bowler in the world, and he was our most penetrative bowler that summer. He took eight wickets at Trent Bridge to lead us to a big win, our first international victory of the tour, while Viv made a brilliant 80, his third score of fifty of the series.

Ambrose took 28 Test wickets that summer and had the wood over Hick, nicking him off twice at Nottingham. Hick, in his first full series, ended up in pieces after it. The attitude towards him was that he was coming up against the wrong opposition. I remember the conversations vividly, the talk was all about how he had no chance of scoring runs. We were going to show him. It was similar to the attitude we had to the Caribbean-born England fast bowlers, trying to prove a point. Hick came up against the wrong guys to be making his debut. That West Indies team was not gonna allow him anything. They build you up? We're gonna break you down. Pride plays a defining role in West Indies cricket. They take a personal attitude to these things. It stemmed from *grovel*. That word. That word that no West Indian cricketer is unaware of. Nothing personal against him, but Hick, a white African, that meant something to us. That was the attitude.

After Nottingham we rocked up in Darlington for a two-day affair against the Minor Counties. Man, what a schedule. By this stage of the tour the senior guys, quite rightly, were resting up, so Viv was looking for bowlers. On day two, this game is just meandering along, it's pretty boring for all of us. All I'm doing is running from one side to the other at the end of each over, so I start to flex my shoulder, getting loose. Viv keeps ignoring me, until eventually after a few overs of this nonsense he stops me and says, "What, you wanna bowl?"

I say, "It's a fun game, nice crowd, of course I wanna bowl."

So he chucks the ball to me. Now, listen, I'm not very good *at all*. A very below average legspinner. But this game is a fun game, so I start rolling a few out. After about five overs my shoulder starts getting tired, but no matter, Viv chucks the ball to me for another one. And another one. And another after that. The lengths start getting bad, the full tosses start happening, and after eight overs I'm done. Ten overs in, I'm really done. "Hey, young man, what you stopping for?"

In all I bowl 22.3 overs, none for 104. After it, my shoulder is knackered, my fingers are raw, I can barely lift my hand up. That night I ask him why.

"You wanted to bowl. Since you wanna bowl, you better bowl."

From Darlington we drove to Wales to play Glamorgan, and then down to Kent. The routine was well in place by then. Viv would sleep, I'd drive, I'd put my foot down, take the car up past 70mph, and then he'd snort and grunt out of his sleep and tell me to keep my foot off the pedal because the English would love to throw him in jail. This one time on the way south I woke him up and took my chance. "Skip, why won't you give me a chance?"

He looked at me, paused, and finally said, "Go away and score some runs. Go on. Go get me a hundred."

At Kent I go out to bat, and for the first time in my life I'm thinking about Brian Lara and not the team position. That was new to me. From school to first-class, to any game I played, even a cricket game in the village, it was always about the team position and what the team required. That was what inspired me, what drove me to play. It was never about blanking out what the team requires and going out there as an individual to score runs for myself, but that game against Kent was the first time I'd ever felt like that. And what happened? I couldn't hit the ball off the square. Timing, footwork, everything was lacking. I could not do *anything*.

The way my mind was working was not how I was accustomed to. I was so focused on myself scoring runs that I took myself away from what really motivated me as a cricketer. I failed, and that was that. I resumed my place on the bench.

* * *

I did a *lot* of bowling in the nets that summer. Spin, pace, whatever was required. I wasn't any good, but I enjoyed it. This one particular morning we were practising in the nets at Edgbaston in preparation for the Fourth Test. One thing: back in those days you could tell if you were being considered for selection by the time you batted at net practice. If as a batter you're ignored till almost the end of the session then you know it's going to be towel and water responsibilities for you for the next five days. So that was me by then, having the odd hit and doing a lot of bowling.

The batter's Sir Viv. I grab a new ball and decide to bowl some pace. I normally run and angle my body and arm to swing the ball into the right-hander. My first three balls are wide down the legside and each time Viv bends down, looking at me, to chuck the ball back. The last one comes with a menacing stare. I decide to try and bowl it straight with a little more side-on action and this time it swings away very wide. I don't look up because I know what I'll see, a face to terrify the best bowlers in the world.

I contemplate putting down the ball but that will bring a different kind of problem with the King. Next ball, I run in, trying my in-swinger again from a wider off-stump line and out comes the front foot, bat away from the pad, big drive, but through the gate and the ball crashes into leg stump. I'm about to jump in joy, when I see him looking like he could kill me.

Next ball, with more confidence after finally getting my line and length, I run in and let go but before I can finish my post-delivery shenanigans, I see this red thing coming back at me head high. Sir Viv strikes it with so much power that I literally have no time to react. In the split-second I have to avoid being decapitated I end up falling and twisting my ankle. I'm on the floor in agony and the first thing I hear is Desmond Haynes who's batting in the next net. "Good, you look for that."

I limp away from the nets in the direction of the dressing rooms. By now tears are flowing and this isn't from just the incident, but from two months of frustration on that England tour – maybe even two years of frustration, being a part of the West Indies team and really not getting a chance.

I'll say it again. I'm not saying that I should have been in the side, I'm just saying it was a tough period. It honestly turned out to be the best thing that ever happened to me. It made me appreciate the value of getting in and staying in.

At this stage I've played one Test and a few one-day games and I tell myself the next opportunity I get, there is no way they are getting me out of this team. I'm taken to the hospital and put in a cast. I have torn ligaments. My tour is over.

Patched up in a cast, it's a miserable way to finish my first full England tour with the West Indies team. But I wasn't unhappy that I was heading home in a few days. I thought I would surprise my family and my girlfriend, sneaking back into the country without telling them. Well, I got the surprise of my life when I found out that my girlfriend replaced me and returned to her ex-boyfriend.

Back home, newly single and on crutches, all I could do was watch the rest of the series from a distance. It was clear that as our big guys warmed up, the series would swing to us and sure enough, victory at Edgbaston thanks to a brilliant hundred by Richie Richardson, who showed his class on that tour, ensured that Viv would never lose a Test series as captain. I just wish I'd been there for it. Viv's last stand at the Oval, the whole of the cricket world rising as one to see him off.

The Master Blaster was done. He left the scene still undefeated, removing his cap one last time and saluting every corner of the ground. I remember wondering if Viv would be going to the World Cup that winter. I don't know the facts, but I think he wanted to go and just wasn't selected. For me that would have been an amazing thing, to share one last experience with him. But it wasn't to be. I was learning. This is big-man business, the real deal, and you've got to be able to live with it. No friends, no favours.

Those two years with Viv Richards were the most important period of my career. Our paths on the field crossed all too rarely, just those 20 runs in some one-day game before a Test series. And now, just like that, he was done.

With Viv going, so went a little of the power and beauty of West Indian cricket.

WORCESTERSHIRE v WEST INDIANS

Venue: County Ground, New Road, Worcester
Toss: West Indians won the toss and decided to bat
Umpires: JH Hampshire, KE Palmer

Date: 15th, 16th, 17th May 1991
Result: Match drawn

WEST INDIANS	1ST INNINGS	R	B	2ND INNINGS	R	B
CG Greenidge	c Lampitt b Botham	26		not out	12	
PV Simmons	b Illingworth	134		not out	24	
RB Richardson	c Moody b Botham	6				
BC Lara	b Newport	26				
*IVA Richards	c Illingworth b Newport	131				
CL Hooper	c Illingworth b Dilley	42				
+PJL Dujon	c Bevins b Dilley	0				
HAG Anthony	not out	33				
IBA Allen	did not bat					
CA Walsh	did not bat					
BP Patterson	did not bat					
Extras	(1 b, 4 lb, 6 nb)	11			0	
Total	(7 wickets, dec, 114.2 overs)	409		(no wicket, 16 overs)	36	

Fall of wickets: 1-54, 2-75, 3-139, 4-278, 5-341, 6-346, 7-409 (114.2 ov)

WORCESTERSHIRE	O	M	R	W	Wd	Nb		O	M	R	W	Wd	Nb
Dilley	21.2	4	68	2	-	-	Dilley	3	2	3	0	-	-
Botham	29	5	83	2	-	-	Newport	8	2	20	0	-	-
Newport	29	6	110	2	-	-	Lampitt	5	3	13	0	-	-
Lampitt	17	2	81	0	-	-							
Illingworth	18	4	62	1	-	-							

WORCESTERSHIRE	1ST INNINGS	R	B	2ND INNINGS	R	B
TS Curtis	c Lara b Patterson	30				
GJ Lord	c Hooper b Patterson	1				
GA Hick	b Allen	11				
TM Moody	run out	11				
*PA Neale	run out	34				
IT Botham	c Allen b Anthony	161				
PJ Newport	c Greenidge b Patterson	0				
SR Lampitt	c Allen b Walsh	3				
RK Illingworth	b Walsh	4				
+SR Bevins	c Allen b Walsh	6				
GR Dilley	not out	0				
Extras	(2 b, 11 lb, 13 nb, 1 w)	27				
Total	(all out, 69.1 overs)	288				

Fall of wickets: 1-15, 2-40, 3-50, 4-60, 5-196, 6-222, 7-245, 8-272, 9-288, 10-288 (69.1 ov)

WEST INDIANS	O	M	R	W	Wd	Nb		O	M	R	W	Wd	Nb
Patterson	20	5	49	3	-	-							
Allen	18	5	64	1	-	-							
Anthony	13	1	63	1	-	-							
Walsh	13.1	1	64	3	-	-							
Simmons	5	1	35	0	-	-							

ENGLAND v WEST INDIES, THIRD ODI

Venue: Lord's Cricket Ground, St John's Wood
Toss: England won the toss and decided to field
Umpires: MJ Kitchen, DR Shepherd

Date: 27th May 1991
Result: England won by 7 wickets

WEST INDIES		R	B	ENGLAND		R	B
PV Simmons	c Russell b DeFreitas	5	16	*GA Gooch	run out	11	29
+PJL Dujon	b Lawrence	0	1	MA Atherton	c Dujon b Marshall	25	46
RB Richardson	c DeFreitas b Illingworth	41	56	GA Hick	not out	86	102
BC Lara	c and b Illingworth	23	40	NH Fairbrother	c Richards b Patterson	113	109
*IVA Richards	c Illingworth b DeFreitas	37	57	MR Ramprakash	not out	0	0
AL Logie	c and b Gooch	82	99	DA Reeve			
CL Hooper	c Fairbrother b Lawrence	26	29	DR Pringle			
MD Marshall	c DeFreitas b Lawrence	13	16	+RC Russell			
CEL Ambrose	not out	6	12	PAJ DeFreitas			
CA Walsh	lbw b Lawrence	0	2	RK Illingworth			
BP Patterson	not out	2	10	DV Lawrence			
Extras	(1 b, 9 lb, 5 nb, 14 w)	29		Extras	(4 b, 12 lb, 4 nb, 10 w)	30	
Total	(9 wickets, 55 overs)	264		Total	(3 wickets, 46.1 overs)	265	

Fall of wickets: 1-8 (Dujon), 2-8 (Simmons), 3-71 (Richardson), 4-91 (Lara), 5-164 (Richards), 6-227 (Hooper), 7-241 (Logie), 8-258 (Marshall), 9-258 (Walsh)
Fall of wickets: 1-28 (Gooch), 2-48 (Atherton), 3-261 (Fairbrother)

ENGLAND	O	M	R	W	Wd	Nb	WEST INDIES	O	M	R	W	Wd	Nb
Lawrence	11	1	67	4	-	-	Ambrose	8	0	31	0	-	-
DeFreitas	11	1	26	2	-	-	Patterson	10	0	62	1	-	-
Reeve	11	1	43	0	-	-	Marshall	11	1	49	1	-	-
Illingworth	11	1	53	2	-	-	Walsh	11	1	50	0	-	-
Pringle	9	0	56	0	-	-	Hooper	4.1	0	36	0	-	-
Gooch	2	0	9	1	-	-	Simmons	2	0	21	0	-	-

SOMERSET v WEST INDIANS

Venue: County Ground, Taunton
Toss: West Indians won the toss and decided to bat
Umpires: SB Hassan, KE Palmer

Date: 29th, 30th, 31st May 1991
Result: Match drawn

WEST INDIANS	1ST INNINGS	R	B	2ND INNINGS	R	B
PV Simmons	b Graveney	10		(2) lbw b Caddick	51	
*DL Haynes	c Roebuck b Caddick	1		(1) retired hurt	16	
RB Richardson	c Cook b Caddick	7		not out	91	
BC Lara	c and b Trump	93		c Cook b Graveney	50	
CL Hooper	lbw b Hayhurst	123		not out	48	
AL Logie	c Harden b Trump	48				
MD Marshall	c Harden b Hayhurst	14				
+D Williams	not out	14				
CEL Ambrose	not out	16				
HAG Anthony						
IBA Allen						
Extras	(13 lb, 3 nb)	16		(2 lb, 3 nb, 2 w)	7	
Total	(7 wickets, dec, 96 overs)	342		(2 wickets, dec, 51 overs)	263	

Fall of wickets: 1-7, 2-21, 3-71, 4-158, 5-265, 6-298, 7-313
Fall of wickets: 1-95, 2-178

SOMERSET	O	M	R	W	Wd	Nb		O	M	R	W	Wd	Nb
Caddick	20	2	85	2	-	-	Caddick	12	0	68	1	-	-
Lefebvre	12	3	27	0	-	-	Hayhurst	4	0	23	0	-	-
Hayhurst	10	2	42	2	-	-	MacLeay	7	0	33	0	-	-
MacLeay	11	3	32	0	-	-	Graveney	14	2	51	1	-	-
Graveney	21	3	68	1	-	-	Trump	14	0	86	0	-	-
Trump	20	2	69	2	-	-							
Roebuck	2	1	6	0	-	-							

SOMERSET	1ST INNINGS	R	B	2ND INNINGS	R	B
SJ Cook	not out	162		c Williams b Ambrose	14	
PM Roebuck	c Lara b Ambrose	10		b Allen	3	
AN Hayhurst	lbw b Marshall	22		b Ambrose	5	
*CJ Tavaré	lbw b Ambrose	10		not out	109	
RJ Harden	c Williams b Marshall	7		c Williams b Marshall	6	
+ND Burns	c Hooper b Anthony	0		b Hooper	14	
KH MacLeay	b Simmons	15		c Richardson b Allen	14	
RP Lefebvre	b Hooper	5		(11) not out	0	
HRJ Trump	not out	20		(8) c Allen b Hooper	9	
AR Caddick				(9) lbw b Hooper	0	
DA Graveney				(10) lbw b Anthony	8	
Extras	(2 b, 1 lb, 16 nb)	19		(5 b, 1 lb, 10 nb)	16	
Total	(7 wickets, dec, 87.4 overs)	270		(9 wickets, 66 overs)	198	

Fall of wickets: 1-45, 2-94, 3-141, 4-159, 5-160, 6-199, 7-214
Fall of wickets: 1-16, 2-20, 3-26, 4-46, 5-109, 6-131, 7-140, 8-156, 9-192

WEST INDIANS	O	M	R	W	Wd	Nb		O	M	R	W	Wd	Nb
Ambrose	18	7	35	2	-	-	Ambrose	18	7	35	2	-	-
Allen	15.4	1	71	0	-	-	Allen	12	1	61	2	-	-
Marshall	15	4	35	2	-	-	Marshall	8	0	35	1	-	-
Anthony	16	0	72	1	-	-	Anthony	9	5	34	1	-	-
Hooper	16	1	38	1	-	-	Hooper	19	7	27	3	-	-
Simmons	7	1	16	1	-	-							

LEICESTERSHIRE v WEST INDIANS

Venue: Grace Road, Leicester
Toss: Leicestershire won the toss and decided to bat
Umpires: BJ Meyer, AGT Whitehead

Date: 1st, 2nd, 3rd June 1991
Result: West Indians won by 6 wickets

LEICESTERSHIRE	1ST INNINGS	R	B	2ND INNINGS	R	B
TJ Boon	c Dujon b Patterson	15		lbw b Anthony	5	
*NE Briers	c Allen b Anthony	68		c Anthony b Allen	9	
PN Hepworth	c Logie b Simmons	68		c Dujon b Anthony	21	
DR Martyn	c Richardson b Allen	35		not out	60	
L Potter	c Anthony b Richards	53		lbw b Anthony	2	
BF Smith	c Simmons b Walsh	13		not out	29	
CC Lewis	c Lara b Anthony	72				
+PA Nixon	not out	9				
MI Gidley	not out	0				
DJ Millns						
JN Maguire						
Extras	(1 b, 8 lb, 6 nb, 7 w)	22		(9 lb, 1 w)	10	
Total	(7 wickets, dec, 86 overs)	355		(4 wickets, dec, 42 overs)	136	

Fall of wickets: 1-27, 2-105, 3-158, 4-253, 5-253, 6-317, 7-352
Fall of wickets: 1-14, 2-27, 3-46, 4-48

WEST INDIANS	O	M	R	W	Wd	Nb		O	M	R	W	Wd	Nb
Patterson	20	4	75	1	-	-	Patterson	11	7	15	0	-	-
Allen	16	3	65	1	-	-	Allen	11	3	46	1	-	-
Anthony	13	1	69	2	-	-	Anthony	8	3	28	3	-	-
Walsh	19	5	60	1	-	-	Walsh	8	5	18	0	-	-
Simmons	9	3	45	1	-	-	Simmons	2	0	6	0	-	-
Richards	9	3	32	1	-	-	Lara	2	0	14	0	-	-

WEST INDIANS	1ST INNINGS	R	B	2ND INNINGS	R	B
PV Simmons	c Nixon b Maguire	42		c Boon b Lewis	0	
CB Lambert	b Maguire	4		c Hepworth b Maguire	51	
RB Richardson	lbw b Maguire	63		not out	135	
BC Lara	c Nixon b Maguire	3		c Gidley b Maguire	26	
AL Logie	c and b Lewis	32		b Lewis	10	
*IVA Richards	b Maguire	45		not out	39	
+PJL Dujon	not out	9				
HAG Anthony	c Potter b Millns	9				
IBA Allen	not out	0				
CA Walsh						
BP Patterson						
Extras	(1 lb, 8 nb)	9		(12 lb, 4 nb)	16	
Total	(7 wickets, dec, 60.3 overs)	216		(4 wickets, 48.1 overs)	277	

Fall of wickets: 1-7, 2-100, 3-117, 4-122, 5-179, 6-207, 7-216
Fall of wickets: 1-0, 2-121, 3-166, 4-183

LEICESTERSHIRE	O	M	R	W	Wd	Nb		O	M	R	W	Wd	Nb
Lewis	19	5	60	1	-	-	Lewis	15	0	63	2	-	-
Maguire	17	3	44	5	-	-	Maguire	14.1	0	86	2	-	-
Millns	13.3	1	64	1	-	-	Millns	14	1	78	0	-	-
Potter	11	2	47	0	-	-	Gidley	5	0	38	0	-	-

ENGLAND v WEST INDIES, FIRST TEST

Venue: Headingley, Leeds
Toss: West Indies won the toss and decided to field
Umpires: HD Bird, DR Shepherd

Date: 6th, 7th, 8th, 9th, 10th June 1991
Result: England won by 115 runs

ENGLAND	1ST INNINGS	R	B	2ND INNINGS	R	B
*GA Gooch	c Dujon b Marshall	34	49	not out	154	331
MA Atherton	b Patterson	2	16	c Dujon b Ambrose	6	33
GA Hick	c Dujon b Walsh	6	31	b Ambrose	6	20
AJ Lamb	c Hooper b Marshall	11	37	c Hooper b Ambrose	0	1
MR Ramprakash	c Hooper b Marshall	27	103	c Dujon b Ambrose	27	109
RA Smith	run out (Ambrose->Dujon)	54	88	lbw b Ambrose	0	1
+RC Russell	lbw b Patterson	5	29	c Dujon b Ambrose	4	12
DR Pringle	c Logie b Patterson	16	73	c Dujon b Marshall	27	94
PAJ DeFreitas	c Simmons b Ambrose	15	34	lbw b Walsh	3	27
SL Watkin	b Ambrose	2	9	c Hooper b Marshall	0	5
DE Malcolm	not out	5	31	b Marshall	4	11
Extras	(5 lb, 14 nb, 2 w)	21		(4 b, 9 lb, 7 nb, 1 w)	21	
Total	(all out, 79.2 overs)	198		(all out, 106 overs)	252	

Fall of wickets: 1-13 (Atherton), 2-45 (Gooch), 3-45 (Hick), 4-64 (Lamb), 5-129 (Ramprakash), 6-149 (Smith), 7-154 (Russell), 8-177 (DeFreitas), 9-181 (Watkin), 10-198 (Pringle, 79.2 ov)
Fall of wickets: 1-22 (Atherton), 2-38 (Hick), 3-38 (Lamb), 4-116 (Ramprakash), 5-116 (Smith), 6-124 (Russell), 7-222 (Pringle), 8-236 (DeFreitas), 9-238 (Watkin), 10-252 (Malcolm, 106 ov)

WEST INDIES	O	M	R	W	Wd	Nb		O	M	R	W	Wd	Nb
Ambrose	26	8	49	2	-	-	Ambrose	28	6	52	6	-	-
Patterson	26.2	8	67	3	-	-	Patterson	15	1	52	0	-	-
Walsh	14	7	31	1	-	-	Marshall	25	4	58	3	-	-
Marshall	13	4	46	3	-	-	Walsh	30	5	61	1	-	-
							Hooper	4	1	11	0	-	-
							Richards	4	1	5	0	-	-

WEST INDIES	1ST INNINGS	R	B	2ND INNINGS	R	B
PV Simmons	c Ramprakash b DeFreitas	38	62	b DeFreitas	0	1
DL Haynes	c Russell b Watkin	7	38	c Smith b Pringle	19	51
RB Richardson	run out (Gooch->Malcolm->Russell)	29	62	c Lamb b DeFreitas	68	141
CL Hooper	run out (Ramprakash)	0		c Lamb b Watkin	5	25
*IVA Richards	c Lamb b Pringle	73	98	c Gooch b Watkin	3	8
AL Logie	c Lamb b DeFreitas	6	15	c Gooch b Watkin	3	7
+PJL Dujon	c Ramprakash b Watkin	6	13	lbw b DeFreitas	33	62
MD Marshall	c Hick b Pringle	0		lbw b Pringle	1	7
CEL Ambrose	c Hick b DeFreitas	0	3	c Pringle b DeFreitas	14	26
CA Walsh	c Gooch b DeFreitas	3	16	c Atherton b Malcolm	9	23
BP Patterson	not out	5	14	not out	0	0
Extras	(1 lb, 5 nb)	6		(1 lb, 6 nb)	7	
Total	(all out, 54.1 overs)	173		(all out, 56.4 overs)	162	

Fall of wickets: 1-36 (Haynes), 2-54 (Simmons), 3-58 (Hooper), 4-102 (Richardson), 5-139 (Logie), 6-156 (Dujon), 7-160 (Marshall), 8-165 (Ambrose), 9-167 (Richards), 10-162 (Walsh, 54.1 ov)
Fall of wickets: 1-0 (Simmons), 2-61 (Haynes), 3-77 (Hooper), 4-85 (Richards), 5-88 (Logie), 6-136 (Richardson), 7-137 (Marshall), 8-139 (Dujon), 9-162 (Ambrose), 10-162 (Walsh, 56.4 ov)

ENGLAND	O	M	R	W	Wd	Nb		O	M	R	W	Wd	Nb
Malcolm	14	0	69	0	-	-	DeFreitas	21	4	59	4	-	-
DeFreitas	17.1	5	34	4	-	-	Malcolm	6.4	0	26	1	-	-
Watkin	14	2	55	2	-	-	Pringle	22	6	38	2	-	-
Pringle	9	3	14	2	-	-	Watkin	7	0	38	3	-	-

DERBYSHIRE v WEST INDIANS

Venue: County Ground, Derby
Toss: West Indians won the toss and decided to bat
Umpires: BJ Meyer, RA White

Date: 12th, 13th, 14th June 1991
Result: Match drawn

WEST INDIANS	1ST INNINGS	R	B	2ND INNINGS	R	B
CB Lambert	lbw b Base	5		lbw b Cork	4	
*DL Haynes	lbw b Base	31		b Warner	0	
RB Richardson	c Warner b Folley	114		(6) not out	48	
BC Lara	lbw b Base	1		(3) lbw b Cork	20	
CL Hooper	c Cork b Base	82		not out	95	
AL Logie	not out	3		(4) b Warner	9	
MD Marshall						
+D Williams						
HAG Anthony						
CEL Ambrose						
IBA Allen						
Extras	(10 lb, 12 nb, 3 w)	25		(1 b, 10 lb, 12 nb)	23	
Total	(5 wickets, dec, 76.4 overs)	261		(4 wickets, dec, 50 overs)	199	

Fall of wickets: 1-23, 2-82, 3-84, 4-248, 5-261 (76.4 ov)
Fall of wickets: 1-0, 2-14, 3-33, 4-48

DERBYSHIRE	O	M	R	W	Wd	Nb		O	M	R	W	Wd	Nb
Base	22.4	7	44	4	-	-	Base	9	1	19	0	-	-
Warner	17	3	52	0	-	-	Warner	10	2	26	2	-	-
Folley	11	2	67	1	-	-	Folley	10	0	52	0	-	-
Griffith	10	3	39	0	-	-	Griffith	6	1	28	0	-	-
Cork	16	3	49	0	-	-	Cork	10	2	27	2	-	-
							Bowler	5	0	36	0	-	-

DERBYSHIRE	1ST INNINGS	R	B	2ND INNINGS	R	B
*KJ Barnett	b Allen	1		not out	12	
PD Bowler	c Lambert b Marshall	13		c Lambert b Allen	63	
TJG O'Gorman	b Ambrose	4		c Haynes b Hooper	23	
M Azharuddin	c Ambrose b Hooper	72		b Anthony	35	
CJ Adams	b Anthony	55		run out	3	
FA Griffith	b Anthony	6		(7) st Williams b Hooper	4	
+KM Krikken	c Richardson b Hooper	6		(8) run out	3	
DG Cork	not out	11		(9) c Williams b Hooper	4	
AE Warner	b Hooper	7		(6) st Williams b Hooper	9	
I Folley				b Marshall	0	
SJ Base				not out	9	
Extras	(5 b, 16 lb, 8 nb)	29		(15 lb, 5 nb)	20	
Total	(8 wickets, dec, 65.2 overs)	204		(9 wickets, 50 overs)	185	

Fall of wickets: 1-5, 2-10, 3-51, 4-135, 5-171, 6-181, 7-182, 8-204 (65.2 ov)
Fall of wickets: 1-70, 2-139, 3-153, 4-156, 5-161, 6-165, 7-172, 8-173, 9-185

WEST INDIANS	O	M	R	W	Wd	Nb		O	M	R	W	Wd	Nb
Ambrose	11	3	26	1	-	-	Ambrose	7	2	18	0	-	-
Allen	11	3	35	1	-	-	Allen	8	0	37	1	-	-
Anthony	13	0	45	2	-	-	Anthony	9	0	42	1	-	-
Marshall	8	1	27	1	-	-	Marshall	9	2	22	1	-	-
Hooper	22.2	7	50	3	-	-	Hooper	16	4	49	4	-	-
							Lara	1	0	2	0	-	-

NORTHAMPTONSHIRE v WEST INDIANS

Venue: County Ground, Northampton
Toss: West Indians won the toss and decided to bat
Umpires: JC Balderstone, B Dudleston
Date: 15th, 16th, 17th June 1991
Result: Match drawn

WEST INDIANS	1ST INNINGS	R	B	2ND INNINGS	R	B
PV Simmons	c Cook b Curran	29				
DL Haynes	c Ripley b Curran	60				
BC Lara	c Cook b Baptiste	4				
AL Logie	lbw b Curran	19				
+PJL Dujon	c Cook b Thomas	82				
*IVA Richards	c Lamb b Thomas	47				
CL Hooper	not out	49				
HAG Anthony	b Cook	6				
IBA Allen	lbw b Cook	8				
CA Walsh						
BP Patterson						
Extras	(1 b, 4 lb, 1 nb)	6				
Total	(8 wickets, dec, 75.2 overs)	310				

Fall of wickets: 1-74, 2-95, 3-95, 4-136, 5-232, 6-269, 7-284, 8-310 (75.2 ov)

NORTHAMPTONSHIRE	O	M	R	W	Wd	Nb		O	M	R	W	Wd	Nb
Thomas	15	1	87	2	-	-							
Taylor	10	2	36	0	-	-							
Cook	16.2	1	74	2	-	-							
Baptiste	12	5	25	1	-	-							
Curran	16	4	60	3	-	-							
Capel	6	0	23	0	-	-							

NORTHAMPTONSHIRE	1ST INNINGS	R	B	2ND INNINGS	R	B
A Fordham	not out	34				
NA Felton	b Anthony	20				
RJ Bailey	not out	1				
*AJ Lamb						
DJ Capel						
KM Curran						
EAE Baptiste						
JG Thomas						
+D Ripley						
JP Taylor						
NGB Cook						
Extras	(2 b, 4 lb, 6 nb, 1 w)	13				
Total	(1 wicket, dec, 20 overs)	68				

Fall of wickets: 1-66 (Felton)

WEST INDIANS	O	M	R	W	Wd	Nb		O	M	R	W	Wd	Nb
Patterson	0.3	0	2	0	-	-							
Walsh	7.3	1	13	0	-	-							
Allen	7	0	27	0	-	-							
Lara	3	1	9	0	-	-							
Anthony	2	1	11	1	-	-							

ENGLAND v WEST INDIES, SECOND TEST

Venue: Lord's Cricket Ground, St John's Wood
Toss: West Indies won the toss and decided to bat
Umpires: BJ Meyer, KE Palmer

Date: 20th, 21st, 22nd, 23rd, 24th June 1991
Result: Match drawn

WEST INDIES	1ST INNINGS	R	B	2ND INNINGS	R	B
PV Simmons	c Lamb b Hick	33	88	lbw b DeFreitas	2	11
DL Haynes	c Russell b Pringle	60	106	not out	4	18
RB Richardson	c DeFreitas b Hick	57	124	c Hick b Malcolm	1	3
CL Hooper	c Lamb b Pringle	111	202	not out	1	5
*IVA Richards	lbw b DeFreitas	63	89			
AL Logie	b DeFreitas	5	10			
+PJL Dujon	c Lamb b Pringle	20	43			
MD Marshall	lbw b Pringle	25	40			
CEL Ambrose	c and b Malcolm	5	17			
CA Walsh	c Atherton b Pringle	10	14			
IBA Allen	not out	1	11			
Extras	(3 b, 7 lb, 19 nb)	29		(2 lb, 2 nb)	4	
Total	(all out, 120.1 overs)	419		(2 wickets, 5.5 overs)	12	

Fall of wickets: 1-90 (Simmons), 2-102 (Haynes), 3-198 (Richardson), 4-322 (Richards), 5-332 (Logie), 6-366 (Hooper), 7-382 (Dujon), 8-402 (Ambrose), 9-410 (Marshall), 10-419 (Walsh, 120.1 ov)
Fall of wickets: 1-9 (Simmons), 2-10 (Richardson)

ENGLAND	O	M	R	W	Wd	Nb		O	M	R	W	Wd	Nb
DeFreitas	31	6	93	2	-	-	DeFreitas	3	2	1	1	-	-
Malcolm	19	3	76	1	-	-	Malcolm	2.5	0	9	1	-	-
Watkin	15	2	60	0	-	-							
Pringle	35.1	6	100	5	-	-							
Hick	18	4	77	2	-	-							
Gooch	2	0	3	0	-	-							

ENGLAND	1ST INNINGS	R	B	2ND INNINGS	R	B
*GA Gooch	b Walsh	37	115			
MA Atherton	b Ambrose	5	8			
GA Hick	c Richardson b Ambrose	0	10			
AJ Lamb	c Haynes b Marshall	1	3			
MR Ramprakash	c Richards b Allen	24	48			
RA Smith	not out	148	271			
+RC Russell	c Dujon b Hooper	46	111			
DR Pringle	c Simmons b Allen	35	86			
PAJ DeFreitas	c Dujon b Marshall	29	48			
SL Watkin	b Ambrose	6	32			
DE Malcolm	b Ambrose	0	4			
Extras	(1 lb, 22 nb)	23				
Total	(all out, 118 overs)	354				

Fall of wickets: 1-5 (Atherton), 2-6 (Hick), 3-16 (Lamb), 4-60 (Ramprakash), 5-84 (Gooch), 6-180 (Russell), 7-269 (Pringle), 8-316 (DeFreitas), 9-353 (Watkin), 10-354 (Malcolm, 118 ov)

WEST INDIES	O	M	R	W	Wd	Nb		O	M	R	W	Wd	Nb
Ambrose	34	10	87	4	-	-							
Marshall	30	4	78	2	-	-							
Walsh	26	4	90	1	-	-							
Allen	23	2	88	2	-	-							
Hooper	5	2	10	1	-	-							

HAMPSHIRE v WEST INDIANS

Venue: County Ground, Southampton
Toss: Hampshire won the toss and decided to bat
Umpires: B Dudleston, R Julian

Date: 29th, 30th, 1st July 1991
Result: Match drawn
Scorers: VH Isaacs (Hampshire), AEJ Weld (West Indies)

HAMPSHIRE	1ST INNINGS	R	B	2ND INNINGS	R	B
VP Terry	c Anthony b Patterson	12		(2) c Dujon b Ambrose	2	
TC Middleton	c Richardson b Walsh	20		(1) not out	76	
*MCJ Nicholas	c Simmons b Hooper	37		not out	59	
RA Smith	retired hurt	62				
DI Gower	b Hooper	10				
KD James	not out	11				
+AN Aymes	c Hooper b Walsh	5				
RJ Maru	c Haynes b Ambrose	23				
SD Udal	c Hooper b Ambrose	0				
CA Connor	c Dujon b Ambrose	0				
KJ Shine	c sub b Ambrose	12				
Extras	(4 b, 2 lb, 4 nb)	10		(7 lb, 4 nb, 4 w)	15	
Total	(all out, 78 overs)	202		(1 wicket, 57 overs)	152	

Fall of wickets: 1-21, 2-42, 3-144, 4-151, 5-158, 6-186, 7-186, 8-190, 9-202 (78 ov)
Fall of wickets: 1-9 (Terry)

WEST INDIANS	O	M	R	W	Wd	Nb		O	M	R	W	Wd	Nb
Ambrose	19	7	70	4	-	-	Ambrose	12	5	22	1	-	-
Patterson	7	2	19	1	-	-	Walsh	13	3	22	0	-	-
Walsh	18	7	41	2	-	-	Anthony	14	1	57	0	-	-
Anthony	10	2	30	0	-	-	Hooper	12	1	28	0	-	-
Hooper	24	10	36	2	-	-	Richards	4	1	13	0	-	-
							Simmons	2	0	3	0	-	-

WEST INDIANS	1ST INNINGS	R	B	2ND INNINGS	R	B
PV Simmons	c Nicholas b Shine	0				
DL Haynes	b Connor	44				
RB Richardson	c Aymes b James	33				
BC Lara	b Udal	75				
CL Hooper	c Maru b Udal	196				
+PJL Dujon	c Aymes b Connor	68				
*IVA Richards	not out	15				
HAG Anthony						
CEL Ambrose						
CA Walsh						
BP Patterson						
Extras	(3 b, 5 lb, 9 nb, 1 w)	18				
Total	(6 wickets, dec, 104 overs)	449				

Fall of wickets: 1-7, 2-67, 3-102, 4-212, 5-396, 6-449 (104 ov)

HAMPSHIRE	O	M	R	W	Wd	Nb		O	M	R	W	Wd	Nb
Shine	27	4	104	1	-	-							
Connor	28	2	100	2	-	-							
James	19	2	77	1	-	-							
Udal	22	3	117	2	-	-							
Maru	8	2	43	0	-	-							

ENGLAND v WEST INDIES, THIRD TEST

Venue: Trent Bridge, Nottingham
Toss: England won the toss and decided to bat
Umpires: JH Hampshire, MJ Kitchen

Date: 4th, 5th, 6th, 8th, 9th July 1991
Result: West Indies won by 9 wickets

ENGLAND	1ST INNINGS	R	B	2ND INNINGS	R	B
*GA Gooch	lbw b Marshall	68	110	b Ambrose	13	42
MA Atherton	lbw b Ambrose	32	80	b Marshall	4	6
GA Hick	c Dujon b Ambrose	43	113	c Dujon b Ambrose	0	5
AJ Lamb	lbw b Ambrose	13	21	lbw b Marshall	29	82
MR Ramprakash	b Ambrose	13	64	c Dujon b Ambrose	21	118
RA Smith	not out	64	150	c Richards b Walsh	15	37
+RC Russell	c Logie b Allen	3	22	b Walsh	3	19
DR Pringle	c sub (CB Lambert) b Allen	0	6	c Simmons b Walsh	3	33
PAJ DeFreitas	b Walsh	8	12	not out	55	86
RK Illingworth	c Hooper b Ambrose	13	46	c Simmons b Walsh	13	16
DV Lawrence	c Allen b Marshall	4	24	c Hooper b Allen	34	38
Extras	(17 lb, 21 nb, 1 w)	39		(14 lb, 4 nb, 3 w)	21	
Total	(all out, 103.5 overs)	300		(all out, 79 overs)	211	

Fall of wickets: 1-108 (Atherton), 2-113 (Gooch), 3-138 (Lamb), 4-186 (Ramprakash), 5-192 (Hick), 6-212 (Russell), 7-217 (Pringle), 8-228 (DeFreitas), 9-270 (Illingworth), 10-300 (Lawrence, 103.5 ov)
Fall of wickets: 1-4 (Atherton), 2-8 (Hick), 3-25 (Gooch), 4-67 (Lamb), 5-100 (Smith), 6-106 (Ramprakash), 7-106 (Russell), 8-115 (Pringle), 9-153 (Illingworth), 10-211 (Lawrence, 79 ov)

WEST INDIES	O	M	R	W	Wd	Nb		O	M	R	W	Wd	Nb
Ambrose	34	7	74	5	-	-	Ambrose	27	7	61	3	-	-
Marshall	21.5	6	54	2	-	-	Marshall	21	6	49	2	-	-
Walsh	24	4	75	1	-	-	Allen	7	2	23	1	-	-
Allen	17	0	69	2	-	-	Walsh	24	7	64	4	-	-
Hooper	6	4	10	0	-	-							
Richards	1	0	1	0	-	-							

WEST INDIES	1ST INNINGS	R	B	2ND INNINGS	R	B
PV Simmons	b Illingworth	12	25	c Russell b Lawrence	1	3
DL Haynes	c Smith b Lawrence	18	26	not out	57	97
RB Richardson	b Lawrence	43	76	not out	52	100
CL Hooper	c Russell b DeFreitas	11	22			
*IVA Richards	b Illingworth	80	155			
AL Logie	c Ramprakash b DeFreitas	78	132			
+PJL Dujon	c Hick b Pringle	19	79			
MD Marshall	c Illingworth b DeFreitas	67	133			
CEL Ambrose	b Illingworth	17	44			
CA Walsh	lbw b Pringle	12	35			
IBA Allen	not out	4	4			
Extras	(2 b, 13 lb, 20 nb, 1 w)	36		(5 nb)	5	
Total	(all out, 118.1 overs)	397		(1 wicket, 32.2 overs)	115	

Fall of wickets: 1-32 (Haynes), 2-32 (Simmons), 3-45 (Hooper), 4-118 (Richardson), 5-239 (Richards), 6-272 (Logie), 7-324 (Dujon), 8-358 (Ambrose), 9-392 (Walsh), 10-397 (Marshall), 118.1 ov)
Fall of wickets: 1-1 (Simmons)

ENGLAND	O	M	R	W	Wd	Nb		O	M	R	W	Wd	Nb
DeFreitas	31.1	9	67	3	-	-	DeFreitas	11	3	29	0	-	-
Lawrence	24	2	116	2	-	-	Lawrence	12.2	0	61	1	-	-
Illingworth	33	8	110	3	-	-	Pringle	7	2	20	0	-	-
Pringle	25	6	71	2	-	-	Illingworth	2	0	5	0	-	-
Hick	5	0	18	0	-	-							

MINOR COUNTIES v WEST INDIANS

Venue: Feethams Cricket Ground, Darlington
Toss: West Indians won the toss and decided to bat
Umpires: GA Stickley, TG Wilson

Date: 10th, 11th July 1991
Result: Match drawn
Scorers: B Hunt, AEJ Weld

WEST INDIANS	1ST INNINGS	R	B	2ND INNINGS	R	B
PV Simmons	c Roberts b Greensword	33		not out	78	
CB Lambert	c Greensword b Evans	50		c Love b Taylor	23	
RB Richardson	st Fothergill b Evans	29		c Fothergill b Arnold	0	
BC Lara	c Greensword b Arnold	82		b Arnold	13	
CL Hooper	c Arnold b Plumb	21		not out	41	
+D Williams	run out	3				
HAG Anthony	not out	63				
IBA Allen	b Taylor	1				
*IVA Richards	c Dean b Taylor	4				
CA Walsh	not out	9				
BP Patterson						
Extras	(2 lb, 2 nb, 1 w)	5		(4 b, 4 lb)	8	
Total	(8 wickets, dec, 94.5 overs)	300		(3 wickets, 33 overs)	163	

Fall of wickets: 1-87, 2-87, 3-139, 4-204, 5-219, 6-223, 7-235, 8-282
Fall of wickets: 1-34, 2-39, 3-55

MINOR COUNTIES	O	M	R	W	Wd	Nb		O	M	R	W	Wd	Nb
Taylor	18	5	59	2	-	-	Arnold	10	1	48	2	-	-
Arnold	19.5	1	69	1	-	-	Taylor	8	2	43	1	-	-
Greensword	21	7	53	1	-	-	Plumb	5	0	22	0	-	-
Evans	24	7	67	2	-	-	Evans	4	1	17	0	-	-
Plumb	12	2	50	1	-	-	Brown	3	0	15	0	-	-
							Love	3	0	10	0	-	-

MINOR COUNTIES	1ST INNINGS	R	B	2ND INNINGS	R	B
GK Brown	c Williams b Patterson	10				
MJ Roberts	c Richards b Anthony	63				
NA Folland	c Lambert b Allen	6				
JD Love	b Allen	2				
SJ Dean	b Patterson	6				
SG Plumb	c Williams b Anthony	5				
*S Greensword	c Williams b Anthony	10				
+AR Fothergill	c Richards b Anthony	7				
RA Evans	not out	50				
KA Arnold	c Williams b Anthony	9				
NR Taylor	not out	52				
Extras	(5 b, 2 lb, 22 nb, 7 w)	36				
Total	(9 wickets, dec, 70.3 overs)	256				

Fall of wickets: 1-14, 2-34, 3-38, 4-68, 5-87, 6-111, 7-121, 8-134, 9-155

WEST INDIANS	O	M	R	W	Wd	Nb		O	M	R	W	Wd	Nb
Patterson	10	2	49	2	-	-							
Allen	11	0	32	2	-	-							
Anthony	17	4	45	5	-	-							
Lara	22.3	1	104	0	-	-							
Hooper	8	2	15	0	-	-							
Richards	2	1	4	0	-	-							

GLAMORGAN v WEST INDIANS

Venue: St Helen's, Swansea
Toss: Glamorgan won the toss and decided to bat
Umpires: D Fawkner-Corbett, JW Holder

Date: 16th, 17th, 18th July 1991
Result: Match drawn

GLAMORGAN	1ST INNINGS	R	B	2ND INNINGS	R	B
SP James	c Williams b Patterson	8		c Richardson b Ambrose	24	
H Morris	c Lara b Ambrose	0		c Williams b Ambrose	0	
A Dale	c Richardson b Ambrose	62		(4) not out	51	
MP Maynard	c Williams b Marshall	8		(5) not out	7	
PA Cottey	c Richardson b Marshall	8				
*AR Butcher	b Anthony	94				
RDB Croft	c Williams b Ambrose	0				
+CP Metson	c and b Hooper	27		(3) b Ambrose	5	
SL Watkin	c Williams b Ambrose	5				
SR Barwick	c Williams b Ambrose	0				
M Frost	not out	0				
Extras	(6 lb, 32 nb, 2 w)	40		(8 b, 3 lb, 3 nb, 1 w)	15	
Total	(all out, 83.1 overs)	252		(3 wickets, 46.2 overs)	102	

Fall of wickets: 1-1, 2-16, 3-38, 4-60, 5-186, 6-191, 7-217, 8-243, 9-252, 10-252 (83.1 ov)
Fall of wickets: 1-1, 2-14, 3-87

WEST INDIANS	O	M	R	W	Wd	Nb		O	M	R	W	Wd	Nb
Ambrose	22.1	6	56	5	-	-	Ambrose	12	6	14	3	-	-
Patterson	19	5	61	1	-	-	Patterson	13	7	14	0	-	-
Marshall	10	2	34	2	-	-	Anthony	9.2	2	30	0	-	-
Anthony	15	3	59	1	-	-	Hooper	10	2	22	0	-	-
Hooper	17	4	36	1	-	-	Lara	2	0	11	0	-	-

WEST INDIANS	1ST INNINGS	R	B	2ND INNINGS	R	B
CB Lambert	lbw b Barwick	99				
*DL Haynes	b Watkin	45				
RB Richardson	st Metson b Croft	109				
BC Lara	c Maynard b Frost	6				
CL Hooper	c Croft b Barwick	80				
AL Logie	b Dale	8				
+D Williams	c Maynard b Dale	6				
MD Marshall	not out	46				
HAG Anthony	not out	4				
CEL Ambrose						
BP Patterson						
Extras	(6 lb, 5 nb, 2 w)	13				
Total	(7 wickets, dec, 114 overs)	416				

Fall of wickets: 1-92, 2-208, 3-221, 4-280, 5-297, 6-323, 7-408

GLAMORGAN	O	M	R	W	Wd	Nb		O	M	R	W	Wd	Nb
Watkin	23	7	86	1	-	-							
Frost	19	1	111	1	-	-							
Croft	37	8	116	1	-	-							
Barwick	21	7	41	2	-	-							
Dale	14	2	56	2	-	-							

KENT v WEST INDIANS

Venue: St Lawrence Ground, Canterbury
Toss: West Indians won the toss and decided to bat
Umpires: DJ Constant, MJ Harris

Date: 20th, 21st, 22nd July 1991
Result: West Indians won by 4 runs

WEST INDIANS	1ST INNINGS	R	B	2ND INNINGS	R	B
PV Simmons	c Ellison b Davis	77		c and b Merrick	107	97
DL Haynes	c Igglesden b Merrick	4		c Marsh b Igglesden	4	
BC Lara	lbw b Ellison	19		b Davis	18	
AL Logie	c Marsh b Igglesden	70		c Ellison b Merrick	26	
*IVA Richards	c Marsh b Fleming	29		c Marsh b Davis	56	
CL Hooper	not out	61		not out	54	
+PJL Dujon	c Ward b Ellison	22				
HAG Anthony	b Fleming	7		(7) not out	6	
IBA Allen	not out	3				
CA Walsh						
BP Patterson						
Extras	(4 lb, 14 nb)	18		(4 lb, 1 nb, 2 w)	7	
Total	(7 wickets, dec, 87 overs)	310		(5 wickets, dec, 50 overs)	278	

Fall of wickets: 1-20, 2-79, 3-147, 4-207, 5-213, 6-270, 7-281
Fall of wickets: 1-29, 2-106, 3-145, 4-174, 5-263

KENT	O	M	R	W	Wd	Nb		O	M	R	W	Wd	Nb
Merrick	12	1	48	1	-	-	Merrick	10	0	51	2	-	-
Igglesden	14	6	20	1	-	-	Igglesden	8	2	43	1	-	-
Ellison	18	2	55	2	-	-	Ellison	9	1	50	0	-	-
Penn	10	2	46	0	-	-	Penn	12	1	61	0	-	-
Davis	16	1	87	1	-	-	Davis	11	1	69	2	-	-
Fleming	17	3	50	2	-	-							

KENT	1ST INNINGS	R	B	2ND INNINGS	R	B
TR Ward	c Lara b Patterson	0		c sub b Patterson	2	
SG Hinks	c Lara b Patterson	8		c Richards b Hooper	31	
NR Taylor	not out	138	228	c Richards b Allen	21	
GR Cowdrey	c Patterson b Anthony	7		c +Lara b Patterson	104	174
MV Fleming	c Allen b Walsh	7		b Walsh	116	122
*+SA Marsh	b Patterson	22		run out	8	
RM Ellison	c Simmons b Allen	14		b Anthony	4	
RP Davis	c Hooper b Patterson	27		(9) b Anthony	10	
C Penn	c +Lara b Anthony	9		(8) c +Lara b Anthony	3	
TA Merrick				c Logie b Patterson	6	
AP Igglesden				not out	1	
Extras	(1 b, 8 lb, 5 nb, 1 w)	15		(9 b, 18 lb, 1 nb, 3 w)	31	
Total	(8 wickets, dec, 75.1 overs)	247		(all out, 69.4 overs)	337	

Fall of wickets: 1-0, 2-30, 3-45, 4-56, 5-125, 6-150, 7-220, 8-247 (75.1 ov)
Fall of wickets: 1-6, 2-46, 3-80, 4-272, 5-293, 6-301, 7-311, 8-327, 9-331, 10-337 (69.4 ov)

WEST INDIANS	O	M	R	W	Wd	Nb		O	M	R	W	Wd	Nb
Patterson	20	4	70	4	-	-	Patterson	9.4	2	57	3	-	-
Allen	19	5	57	1	-	-	Allen	8	2	24	1	-	-
Anthony	14.1	2	47	2	-	-	Anthony	13	0	65	3	-	-
Walsh	12	1	45	1	-	-	Walsh	16	3	57	1	-	-
Hooper	10	1	19	0	-	-	Hooper	14	2	64	1	-	-
							Richards	9	1	43	0	-	-

Photographs courtesy of Brian Lara, Nasser Khan, Alamy, Getty Images, Graham Morris, Roger Wootton and Warwickshire CCC

Padding up and ready to go!

A very early trophy; my first overseas tour, to India in
1983 with Trinidad & Tobago schoolboys

Watching the cricket, deep in concentration

Celebrating a milestone at Fatima College

Flicking it away for runs

Bigger than the Champions Trophy!

Getting the sweep out with my beloved Gray-Nicolls; Bunty bought
me that bat to dissuade me from going on a football tour!

With nephew Marvin (left) in Cantaro, Santa Cruz – as kids we were inseparable;
with Bunty, having been named schools cricketer of the year

My very own road! With sister Agnes, daughter Tyla and brother Lyndon

My mum and sister cheering me on

An honorary doctorate from the University of Sheffield

With my beloved mentor Joey Carew, having been awarded
Trinidad's highest award, the Trinity Cross, after my 375

Back to Fatima in 1994. "Cricket will only get you so far, you
need your education..." Wise words from my teachers

My mother Pearl was the rock of our family

Back in Cantaro in 1994; a rare breather in the midst of the madness

Batting on my tour of England in 1991. It was a tough summer
for me, but an immensely valuable learning experience

Antigua, 1994: hunting down a record...

The shot that changed my life

Planting a kiss on my all-time favourite slab of 22 yards

I felt that Sir Garfield Sobers wanted me to join him at the summit; he backed me right from the very start

The respect of your teammates is a priceless thing

It was destiny that Sobers should be at Antigua to see it happen. At that moment, it felt like we were the only people in the ground

A few days off and back into it! Those early days at
Warwickshire were chaotic but immensely enjoyable

Treble winners, '94 vintage

501*

It was a joy to have my friend Keith Piper with me at the end

The shot that echoed around the world; when we called my mother
Pearl from the dressing room that night, she refused to believe it!

Our captain Dermot Reeve enjoyed the spotlight being on the club

Pure joy; note how I'm still protecting my bat!

CHAPTER 5

1994

SHOULD WE BE TALKING ABOUT *DESTINY* HERE?

*'People might find it strange to say,
but it all seemed so inevitable'*

MICHAEL ATHERTON

THE YEAR DAWNS huge on my horizon. It's 1994, my first home series against England, and this time I'm guaranteed to play. For any West Indian, this is the big one. Australia during my early years might have been the second-best team behind us, but the historical relationship we have with England demands more of the public attention. That's how it was, and how it always will be.

Still, the year doesn't start too great. Even though I'm with the West Indies team and I have my own apartment, I'm still spending time at Joey Carew's place, I have my own room there from schooldays. One day myself and Joey's son Michael are driving by the house, I need to pick up some clothes, so Michael stays in the car as I run inside to get my stuff. On coming out, I see Michael running towards me back into the house, shouting. "Get inside, they have a gun! They have a gun!" From the doorway I see my car speeding away, with everything inside going with it. Including my kitbag and my Gray-Nicolls bat.

Now, I'm due to go on tour with the national team the next day, and there I am with no kit. A few hours later the phone goes at the house. God knows how they got the number, it doesn't pay to ask too many questions, but they must realise whose car they stole because they're telling us down the line that I can get my cricket gear picked up on the Beetham Highway. So we drive down there, Michael and me, and there's my kitbag on the side of the road! "Well, Brian can do without his car," they must have thought. "But his *bat*? We need to get that back to him."

Look, I'm glad they did. Because that bat would come in useful over the next few weeks. And anyway, it was a rental car...

* * *

I was hungry. Three years I was around the team. Three years for two Tests. I felt like I'd done nothing but watch and learn and bite my lip and bide my time. I'd still not played a Test match against the English.

You need to serve your time, I got that, and I understand I'm learning all the way. But man, did it make me appreciate what it is to play for the West Indies. And not just myself – so much other young players around the Caribbean. Being on the outskirts was tough, but it strengthened me. Made me value what it meant.

The minute I got in, I was gonna make sure my name be pencilled in whenever the West Indies was putting together a team. By then Viv and Gordon were retired, and their absence left a few spots open, but that just stepped up the competition.

There was some talent kicking around. Carlisle Best, Jimmy Adams, Keith Arthurton. I didn't want to be left out. Couldn't bear the thought. I played with a few amazing young cricketers that were scoring first-class runs and had to do the waiting like I did and they weren't coming in for me.

My first Test match on home soil, 1992, was that one-off Test match with South Africa coming back into cricket that we almost lost. The next few Test matches I played in the Caribbean, against Pakistan, came off the back of that Australia tour where I got 277 at Sydney. I performed OK, scoring a 96 in Trinidad and giving it away, but I didn't score a hundred in that series, so I had to establish myself in the eyes of the Caribbean people.

I had to be the best batsman in the England series. The person to score the most runs and walk away as the Man of the Series with the West Indies winning. Not performing was not an option.

The expectation was huge. Before England, I'd played 11 Tests, for just the one hundred. Just one, single monster score. I was intensely focused to make it a series that established me not just in the West Indies, but as a premier batsman around the world.

England came into it feeling that they should have won, or at least not lost, last time out in 1990. Coming back to the West Indies and not seeing a few familiar faces would have given them hope. They had seven players returning from the previous tour and while I was confident we would win, I didn't expect a walkover. I knew what close encounters were but I didn't know what losing a Test series was. The West Indies just didn't lose a whole series.

Nasser Hussain, Chris Lewis, the captain Michael Atherton, they all represented England at the 1988 Youth World Cup in Australia, so there was a little bond that was already established. And even though I was just a passenger in 1990, being back in the presence of the likes of Alec Stewart, Angus Fraser, Jack Russell and Robin Smith, all returning for more, meant that I was comfortable.

I'd sat through numerous Test matches against England, carrying drinks, running errands, trying to walk the line. I'd had enough of it.

* * *

Just facing these West Indies fast bowlers in the nets, you get a sense of their threat. Of course we had the world-renowned Ambrose and Walsh, and all the respect afforded to them because of their performances over time.

But the Benjamins, Kenny and Winston, not brothers but namesakes, were two bowlers who really impressed me. I remember playing against them in a four-day game in Montserrat before the series, and on the first morning we couldn't really identify the pitch, the whole square was green. We had a very young Trinidad & Tobago team and I could see the fright in everyone's faces because the Leeward Islands had both Benjamins, Ambrose and a guy called Vaughn Walsh who bowled faster than them all. Something I learned very early on, that when it came to facing our quicks, fear was never far from the surface, even for some very good players.

For me, it wasn't fear. But facing up to both Benjamins was a heavy task. They had amazing talent. They could both move the ball at pace, and at deceptive pace as well. And they were hungry to play. Not carrying the name, and maybe not being as relaxed as Ambrose was, where most of the times while playing first-class cricket he would take it easy, these two guys were on the periphery of West Indies cricket so they always had something to prove.

I still made runs against them, and in truth I was in the form of my life. What a first-class season I was having: 715 runs in five matches. Before making a hundred against Guyana, and a double against Barbados, I hit a special 180 against Jamaica at the Queen's

Park Oval that will stay with me forever. I walked out to bat at 38-2 and of the next 219 runs we put on, I swept, cut and chipped 180 of them. Farming the strike, not allowing Courtney Walsh, Franklyn Rose or their other quicks to get at my batting partners, I was in that rare state of mind where I was dancing to my own music. Courtney would deliver the ball in the early part of the over and if I couldn't hit a boundary, I would chip the ball over the infield for a couple to retain the strike. I was in complete control. It was ominous for England ahead of the first Test.

I'm not sure how much they would have seen of Kenny Benjamin, but him doing the business with six wickets in the first innings at Jamaica after such a great start by the English openers was no surprise to me. Atherton and Stewart played well, but Kenny just blew the rest away. Going under the radar of Walsh and Ambrose sometimes worked in his favour, while other times he would try a little too hard in certain situations, but it was a wonderful spell and brought us back into it.

We were under a lot of pressure in that game with the quick dismissals of Simmons, Haynes and Richie, leaving us three down for not much. I was batting four, with Arthurton and Jimmy behind me. That's a pretty raw middle order, and for a time the English were all over us.

I suffer from something called pterygiums. It covers the cornea and grows in the eye, and when there's an excess of sun it gets inflamed and feels like I have a piece of grit or a small particle in there, and I have to keep blinking to get my eyes watery. I was suffering from that in that match. I remember on a couple of occasions Devon Malcolm roughed me up because I wasn't able to focus properly. The physio, Dennis Waight, ran out to apply some special eye drops to calm the affected area and keep the eye's surface as moist as possible. Trust me you don't want to be dealing with Devon Malcolm if you've got an eye problem.

I survived that and started to settle, passing fifty in good shape. When I came up against a tough bowling attack, I always tried to pounce on the weaker side of the attack. Now, Graeme Hick would not have been one of their frontline bowlers, and a little bit of carelessness and overconfidence trying to propel myself to a hundred was my undoing. My mindset would have been about getting to my hundred while England are resting their main guys. I fell for 83, playing across the line, beating up on myself for not scoring my first hundred in the Caribbean.

My mind went back to that 96 against Pakistan and the 60-odd against South Africa. Those close calls, getting set and not carrying on, was something I didn't like at all. After experiencing that 277 I fell in love with long innings and I felt like any time I got set, the only person that could get me out was myself. And when I say set, I'm talking about facing 50 balls or scoring 30 runs, where I've seen the majority of the bowling attack. I was in that frame of mind where getting out for anything above those numbers, I would be mad as hell. Still, runs for Jimmy, Arthurton and myself put us back on top, contributing in excess of 300 between us. With a decent lead, the quicks did the rest, with only Hick showing any sort of resistance. We knocked it off for the loss of a couple of wickets, one of which was mine, getting carried away when the game was almost done.

I remember quite clearly Hick's innings, he would have been under loads of pressure, being all at sea during the '91 series in England. At the beginning of the tour he would've been a target for our bowlers, and at Sabina, when the match is in the hands of the West Indies, to put up a fighting effort meant that they could take away positives in the batting. He showed a lot of fight making 96, something we may not have seen in the past.

* * *

The build-up to Guyana was mixed. I was feeling good, and looking forward to having a hit on that batting paradise but I was very upset for my countryman Phil Simmons missing out after just one Test match. It's not about regional insularity. I hate that way of thinking and there's too much of it in West Indies cricket. Instead, it stems from love for your countryman.

So, Richie moved up to open and they called up this boy Chanderpaul into the team. I didn't have much knowledge of him as I would have been travelling and he might've only played one or two first-class seasons. My awareness? Young, upcoming and suddenly given an opportunity in his home country. What struck me immediately was his tenacity and staying power. He had major determination to succeed. It was a great decision by the West Indies as he went on to become one of our greats.

The Bourda pitch and the size of the outfield was definitely something I enjoyed. You pass the infield and you have a boundary. Look, if Michael Atherton can strike at close to 50, you know the outfield is fast. Bourda was one of my favourite grounds. The cricket atmosphere was amazing, good people filling the ground right in the heart of the city where everyone turned out. Atherton's 144 showed that there was always value for shots, but England's 322 was never enough.

I *loved* batting with Jimmy Adams. I always loved the battle when we were side by side. We played at the Youth World Cup together, and against each other when we were both coming through and Jamaica came up against Trinidad & Tobago. He was always so patient. In those early days he had endless concentration and if he was often subdued in the middle, it never seemed to affect him.

I first realised in Australia that we were the perfect foils for each other. It's no secret I batted better with a Jimmy Adams than say a Carl Hooper. If there were times I needed to scuttle back and stay away from a bowler he was good at holding the strike but if one needed to be taken down he would allow me the space to do so.

I played his entire career with him and we got on very well. Off the pitch we had a very different lifestyle, I was not his cup of tea when it came to the nightlife. Jimmy was someone who knew a few people around the place, he was very friendly and made friends in Australia and England. He was quite happy to be more reserved and just go about his business.

We worked well together and at Guyana, just as at Jamaica, we batted nicely in partnership. After posting a century stand with Desmond Haynes, I was joined by Jimmy who helped me ease my way to a first hundred in the Caribbean.

Truth is, England's attack was totally ineffective on that surface, as was the case with most bowling attacks at Guyana in the first innings.

First half of a match, Bourda is a batting paradise. Then it crumbles. You came to expect serious low bounce in the second innings and as England faced up to us they had nowhere to go.

Curtly on a track with unpredictable bounce was a nightmare. He went at under two an over across the whole Test match. That sort of bowler, 6ft 7in and the hand is coming down from 8ft, ramming the ball into the wicket – you're naturally expecting bounce as a batter, your bat's raised-up ready for the bounce, and then that ball keeps *low*? That was Guyana on the fourth and fifth days. If you're a batsman you need to be playing out of your crease, even if the ball is short you still need to be moving forward, playing off your front foot towards the ball just in case. These were the challenges England were facing.

Two matches, and we've won them both. For me I've got a home Test hundred, a monkey off my back, Curtly's loose and we're up in the series. But even in the closing stages at Bourda my mind's racing on. I'm already thinking about Trinidad.

* * *

I'm anxious to get home. The adrenaline is flowing coming off the win at Guyana, the expectation is great and the atmosphere at the Queen's Park Oval is abuzz – the members pavilion is abuzz, the net sessions are abuzz, everything is alive and it's *palpable*, you can feel it and taste it. It's a very loyal crowd at Trinidad. I feel like I owe it to them to put on a show.

I've been around for about eight years, from youth cricket, gaining followers right through my three years of youth cricket, making a hundred against India's tourists, doing well against the Australians and then the English in 1990, so I've created a huge fanbase at home. The expectation is great and yes, it does make me anxious. Not anxious about failing, that never comes into it. It's more an anxiety, an impatience, to get out to the middle. Until it's on and happening, I can't think straight.

So I walk out to bat early in the afternoon session on the first day, and I'm buzzing but I can't fully relax. This is the English, on my home ground in front of my own people, and I'm so desperate to put a flag in the ground at the Queen's Park Oval that I turn cautious, I'm circumspect, much too watchful, more on the defensive side than I was at Bourda. Sure, Trinidad is a different track to Guyana, it's not as batsman-friendly, so the strike rate is gonna be lower. But I'm still over-cautious.

I'm on 43 when it happens, and it's *never* out, by the way. This ball from Chris Lewis from round the wicket hits me very high on the tip of my pads, it's going over the stumps and it isn't even straight anyway. No matter. I'm done. The entire cricket ground goes quiet. Everyone's come to see me bat, to get at least a fifty, so to fall short, LBW to Chris Lewis, is a deep dejection. Having to walk back towards the pavilion on your home ground having failed is the worst feeling in the game.

I love my bats too much to throw them around. They're much too precious and beautiful. And it's not like I have an endless supply, I can't just walk into a store in Trinidad and pick up another. But this day I get close to launching it across the dressing room. For a few minutes I'm furious. I have to remind myself that if you want to survive in cricket you have to know how the game *is*. I can't stay in that frame of mind for very long. It doesn't help anyone.

Sometimes, especially when the team was doing well, I would feel like I *had* to still be out there, and it would hurt me to think that I wasn't. That was the mindset I had. I never had enough. I was never sated. I'd be sitting there, enjoying the guys who were scoring runs but always in the back of my mind thinking, 'Why did you play *that* shot? How could you let *that* happen?'.

England took a decent lead on first innings but again our young pups step up, Adams and Chanderpaul showing their mettle to pull us back in front. For such an inexperienced guy, Chanderpaul shows great maturity to stick it out, while Jimmy is a guy with a one-track mind. He is going to bore you into the ground. Those boys give us something to work with.

We're confident. It's Trinidad, the last innings of the match. The pitch is deteriorating. Run-chases at the Queen's Park Oval are generally won by the team bowling. It's the fourth evening, England need 194, and we've got about 90 minutes to bowl before the close.

Ambrose is on it, right from ball one. A nip-backer smacks into Atherton's front pad. One down. Then almost immediately Mark Ramprakash runs himself out and Ambi's into the middle order. They can forget about it. Smith: bowled. Stewart: bowled. Thorpe: bowled. He picks up six wickets that night, two to nicks and four to straight balls. It's incredible.

With not much more than an hour to bowl, us being in a precarious position and batters being vulnerable in the late evening session, Ambrose pounces on the opportunity to light the world afire, and I mean it's *wild*, pandemonium in the stands, people going crazy. Pan music is playing, it's a packed house, and we're just in awe of him, every single ball.

I'd seen it before, when something just flicks inside of him. There was always something that had to tick him off. Perth in '93, seven for *one*. An eight-for at Bridgetown against the English last time they were here. Even that one-off Test against South Africa, when he just says, "If we're losing the match we're losing it with the ball in *my* hand."

For someone who picked up the game late and liked basketball more than cricket his skill levels were unbelievable. His rhythm and natural ability to run in and bowl fast was something to behold, and which came from deep inside. Curtly was someone who went about his business. Nothing much bothered him unless you challenged him and that's when it happened. The warrior spirit was in him and that night he blew the place apart.

Yeah, I painted the town red that night. You know, heading to the Coconuts nightclub most likely, Pelican was also a place we visited a lot, a little pub around the savannah close to the Hilton Hotel where we stayed. That would have been a big buzz, everyone who was out would have headed there, spectators and players and whoever was in town. That would have been the hotspot, nowhere else better to be.

So the place was buzzing, but would we be celebrating as a whole team, all the big guys together? That would be unlikely. Most of the time, 75 per cent of that team wouldn't be out. Curtly didn't venture out too much, Richie would play his music in his room. Sherwin Campbell, Stuart Williams, those would be the two main guys back then. Every now and then you'd try and get Courtney out, twisting the old pro's arm to have a look. But Shiv? No. Jimmy? No.

One of the things we suffered from was how detached we were from island to island, so it was hard to get eight of our guys together in a hotel bar. I was always envious of that with other teams. You'd play the Australians, and you'd go downstairs to the hotel bar and they'd all be in there together. Same with the English guys, if one of them is getting into trouble, they'd all be getting into trouble together. And the English, they'd always be asking me, "Brian, where to next? Where's the best spots to go?"

It was just something our team never cultivated. I don't know what it was like back in the day, but for us, it wasn't like that. Only when we had a big win would we really come together.

That night, there were a few other people absent. With a scorecard saying 40-8 overnight, the England boys would be licking their wounds somewhere quiet.

* * *

I liked them, the English. They were a good bunch. Atherton in particular, we went way back. Even though we'd won the series, we knew they could compete with us. We weren't licking them like we used to. The English players weren't bad. Weren't bad at all.

I noticed how they seemed in good spirits in Barbados. This happens with touring teams to the Caribbean, they get their wives and girlfriends over for the Barbados leg and it brightens them up. They seemed a much better unit at Bridgetown, in a much better frame of mind. The series was gone, so in a way they could relax. And anything's better than 46 all out.

The stands were heaving with tourists, it seemed like they each had their own flag, you know? The ground was plastered with them. They gave the English team a lift, and when Atherton and Stewart got to 47 without loss on the first morning and they all cheered and jumped for joy it was just amazing to watch.

When we looked at the track on that first morning we saw a pitch devoid of moisture. And look, we got it, a lot of cricket boards made their money from gate receipts. We could see the pitch was made to last five days. It wasn't a major topic for us but we just felt that the way the pitch played early on, that it'll be difficult for us to get 20 wickets across the match. You do your damage in Barbados at the beginning with pace and bounce and there was none of that. England capitalised with Atherton and Stewart. Those two were good all series and they got away from us on the first day.

I had a lot of respect for Alec Stewart as a batter. He was one of the English players who was willing to take on the West Indies with the short ball, he was a good puller, and a good driver off the back foot. Real respect for him. I had a lot of liking for his style of play, the confidence and the first approach being to attack and the second line being defence, unlike a lot of English players, who would be defensive first. Your margin of error was very slim against him. He showed on maybe the best batting surface in the series how good he was. Hundreds in both innings at Bridgetown, not many have done that.

For his second hundred he got good support from Graham Thorpe, who showed us again that England's young brigade could play. I later learnt that he'd watched me that series and added some bits to his own style, picking the bat up higher and cocking the wrists and so on.

The backlift for me was never a conscious thing. It was never something I changed *to*. It was there from the beginning, and you know what, there's so many different things that could have caused it. Playing cricket in the garage at home and facing your brother bowling quickly in the space of 15 yards was one reason. I could attribute it to street cricket, using bats that are bigger than you, trying to get it up as quickly as possible to get it back down. The most overriding thing is that no one really tried to change it. It doesn't matter how out of the ordinary it looked. No one ever tried to change the way I picked the bat up. It had a bit of flair and class in it, I was getting the job done, so why change it, why do just the norm?

Leaving this Barbados Test I was jealous of Stewart's performance. I'd been the leading series runscorer going into that match and Stewart went past me. I'd two scores and three failures, I was coming off four average scores, two in Trinidad and two in Barbados. Coming off a hundred in Guyana I should have been in a much better position. I made 64 in the second innings at Barbados but I would consider that a failure because we lost.

Yes, we were 3-1 up but I was not happy with how the series had gone. Compared to what I set out to achieve at the beginning of the series, I was nowhere near. I had to score runs at Antigua.

* * *

I'll never forget the first time I met him. Funny thing was, I hadn't even wanted to go to Barbados for this tournament. What I really wanted was to play football in Venezuela with Trinidad & Tobago under 16s. It was my dad who had other ideas.

"What's your plan?" he says to me.

"Of course I'm going with the football team," I say, trying to sound defiant.

"And I suppose you have the money to buy all the gear you need for that trip?"

I'm saddened by his response, but I can't say I'm surprised. I'm not sure how much football matches he watched, whereas with cricket, he never missed a match.

"What do you mean, Dad?"

"Exactly what I said," he says. "But look, if you *are* interested in going to Barbados I *may* just have enough money to buy you your favourite Gray-Nicolls bat."

Well, I couldn't argue with that. Throwing in the bat, he made a compelling case. He always knew how to play me.

So, the Sir Garfield Sobers International Schools Cricket Tournament was held on the island every year and that year, 1986, our Harvard Cricket Coaching Clinic, of which I was the captain, was entering a team. We would be coming up against English schoolboy cricketers and teams from all over the Caribbean.

Bryan Davis was one of the school coaches at Fatima and he – or maybe it was his younger brother Charlie, they had both played with Sobers for the West Indies back in the day – sent a message to him ahead of our visit, something along the lines of, "If you're on the island there is a little boy coming to play in your schools tournament and you should go and have a look at him".

Of course I knew of him, Sir Garfield St Aubrun Sobers, world record holder, the 365 man, the greatest allrounder the game has ever seen. I had never seen him play but my mind was alive with the stories. "Is Sir Garfield Sobers here?" I asked one of the officials as soon as we landed. "No son, but he will be at the matches."

I couldn't wait to meet the greatest. I was praying it would happen, and sure enough he did come, as one morning before we went out to play we all lined up and he moved down the line shaking our hands.

I was always an inquisitive kid, at least when it came to sports. My academic teachers may have wished it was the same in the classroom, not that there was any chance of that happening. Instinctively, I blurted out: "Are you really Sir Sobers, the world record holder?"

I say it quietly, for not much people to hear, and so not to look stupid.

"Yes, I'm... are you Brian Lara?"

"Yes! Yes I am!" My heart is going at a thousand beats a minute. I'm a kid and the great man knows who I am. "How do you know my name?"

"Oh, don't worry about that," he says. "I just came to see you bat, young man."

I will never forget that day. Nor will I ever forget the day he went on record to say this: "The West Indies selectors can keep this young man Brian Lara out of the team for as long as they want but take it from me, he is going to be one of our greatest batsmen."

* * *

Was it preordained? That he should be there at the Rec? And that it should come to pass that as the crowds finally dispersed, having made their own piece of history, he is there standing opposite me in the middle, the two of us alone in all the madness?

I don't know. What I do know: I tend to see it as everything falling into place. The scorecard, 3-1 up in the series, a world record, Sir Garfield being there at the ground, the magic of Antigua, the crazy atmosphere of that place, a coming together of all these elements. Should we be talking about *destiny* here? Perhaps. But it was still my job to do it.

I always prepared for a cricket match by working my ass off to make sure I was in the best position mentally and physically, so anything positive that happened to me, I was prepared for it.

But still, looking at that week, that day and that moment, Sir Garry and me, there was something else at play, something magical beyond all logic and reason. Call it what you like. That's how it felt for me.

I didn't know it at the time, but various friends and family had jumped on an early flight from Trinidad to Antigua that morning, just to witness it. It was probably for the best that I didn't know, but what a joy to see them when it was all over. When did you get in?

I'd be asking, and they would say, "Oh, this morning – I knew you were gonna score those runs and I just had to see it." That was just so lovely. If only Dad could have been there with them. The one man who would have made my innings truly worth it.

The rest of the game passes in a blur. I can remember Robin Smith and Michael Atherton piling on to a draw. I was definitely tired physically and mentally. I felt it during the game. There were periods I went off and on the field. I didn't want to make it look like I couldn't field after I batted, but if we had lunch or tea I came out a couple of overs later. The umpires never really questioned it.

I went into the city every night. I just wanted to be a part of it, to feel it, taste it. I'd have dinner with different people, go back to the hotel and get ready for the next day's play. I accommodated every one of my friends and family who'd flown in from home. It was a tremendous feeling.

* * *

After the match they put on a special flight to take us all back home, my mother and me, and some of the spectators.

There was a stop in Grenada, which is not normal, but I think there was a request from their prime minister, who was friendly with our prime minister. Only when I got on that flight did I find out we were heading for Grenada. My job was to get out onto the platform at the top of the plane's staircase and meet some officials and wave to a massive crowd in the airport in Grenada, and then we'd be on our way to Trinidad.

The euphoria, man. The whole feeling and atmosphere was new to me. It was a whole nation showing its appreciation of one of their sons. My mind went back to going to Piarco Airport as a seven-year-old with my dad and my brothers when our great sprinter Hasely Crawford won that Olympic gold medal in 1976. I remember feeling even from that early age that this was something I would love for myself.

I'm a sportsperson. I was a sports boy, and the adulation showed to Hasely Crawford, I started to dream about it. Eighteen years later there it was, at the same airport in Piarco with thousands of people coming to celebrate and welcome me home. To emulate that was just a wonderful feeling. All the celebrations and functions that were put on in haste – and only for a short period of time, as I had to go to England to play for Warwickshire – yeah, I was exhausted. But I was happy to have Chanderpaul with me on these parades, a guy who came into the team for a fellow Trinidadian and was now celebrating with me back home.

Those few days were wild. A motorcade through downtown Port of Spain, and being given the key to the city. A parade through the Eastern Borough to an event at Arima Town Hall, where I got see my old godfather, Joe Ragoobarsingh, among the well-wishers. Seeing two of my early coaches, Hugo Day and Rex Dewhurst, beautiful guys who ran the clinics at Harvard Club when I was a boy. A reception at President's House where I was given an award from the president, Noor Hassanali. The prime minister, Patrick Manning, declaring it to be one of the best days of his life. I was given lots of awards that week. But nothing could top the Trinity Cross, then considered the highest honour in the country. All the while, my mother was there in the background, smiling on.

I'd played five days of cricket, broken a record, and suddenly the place is going crazy, the whole island's off the hook. Every newspaper you picked up, you're on the front, middle and back pages. *The Express* ran a 24-page special souvenir supplement, and later that week named me the '*Express* Individual of the Year'. Some soft drinks company took out an advert saying 'Congratulations Brian!' with a photo of me positioned next to their product. The papers must have made a killing. Of course I enjoyed it but looking back now, you could say they got away with murder.

* * *

I was too naïve to fully grasp what was happening around me. I was just riding it. I understood that people had high expectations for me to be a West Indies cricketer, but to be transformed overnight from someone trying to establish themselves at the beginning of a series to now being seen as a superstar, I couldn't be aware of all the obstacles and pressures that would come with it. If you're not sure what's around the corner, it's hard to set yourself for when it hits you.

Viv helped. He'd put me on to Jonathan Barnett, told me that he would get me the right deals. Jonathan became my manager, and I introduced him to David Manasseh, who I knew through horse racing and who wanted a job in sports management. Jonathan took him on board and they became a force, and between them they protected me. They were tough to the outside world when at times I couldn't be tough. When I was tired, exhausted, they put everything on their shoulders for me.

In a funny kind of way, that innings at Antigua also firmed up my chances with the girl I was courting, Leasel Rovedas, now the mother of my kids. A very beautiful woman and hard to get, and during that time I was still courting and trying to see if I could get a relationship with her. After the 375 she had no choice! I even interrupted a motorcade in my honour, which was rolling down the street past the bank she was working in, just so I could drop her in a bunch of flowers.

It was a wonderful period, if all too brief. They put me up in a suite at the Hilton Hotel and I celebrated hard, clubbing, partying, all the time with police security protection. I had to be on my toes because Trinidad was swamped with British press, I guess they had permission from their London editors to follow me around.

I had all this protection but after four days, when it came for me to leave for London, I stepped outside the hotel and it suddenly struck me that I was on my own. That was the day I was going to the airport, and the security detail had just disappeared. I swiftly had to call someone to get them to take me to the airport. I thought, 'So this is what life's gonna be like now'. They get what they want, and when they're done, you're left alone on the side of the street.

I raced to the airport. The flight had to wait for me. And who was on it? The boys from the British press.

Together we headed to London. Seven days after the end of the Antigua Test I would play my first match for Warwickshire. *Seven days.*

LEEWARD ISLANDS v TRINIDAD & TOBAGO

Venue: Sturge Park, Plymouth
Toss: Trinidad and Tobago won the toss and decided to bat
Points: Leeward Islands 16; Trinidad and Tobago 0

Date: 14th, 15th, 16th January 1994
Result: Leeward Islands won by an innings and 110 runs
Umpires: LH f, BEW Morgan

TRINIDAD & TOBAGO	1ST INNINGS	R	B	2ND INNINGS	R	B
A Balliram	lbw b Ambrose	2		(7) st Jacobs b Phillip	11	
R Mangallie	b KCG Benjamin	10		(1) b Ambrose	1	
+D Williams	c Jacobs b WKM Benjamin	23		(2) lbw b KCG Benjamin	0	
*BC Lara	c and b KCG Benjamin	2		(3) b Phillip	84	
RAM Smith	c Phillip b KCG Benjamin	0		(4) lbw b WKM Benjamin	21	
KA Mason	lbw b Ambrose	24		(5) lbw b Walsh	8	
A Lawrence	lbw b Ambrose	20		(6) c KCG Benjamin b Phillip	9	
D Ramnarine	b KCG Benjamin	7		st Jacobs b Arthurton	12	
NB Francis	b Ambrose	0		c Walsh b Arthurton	13	
R Dhanraj	not out	8		c Arthurton b Phillip	9	
S Mahabir	b KCG Benjamin	2		not out	1	
Extras	(1 nb)	1		(5 b, 9 lb)	14	
Total	(all out, 46.5 overs)	99		(all out, 76 overs)	183	

Fall of wickets: 1-12 (Balliram), 2-12 (Mangallie), 3-14 (Lara), 4-14 (Smith), 5-56, 6-73, 7-82, 8-82, 9-88, 10-99 (46.5 ov)
Fall of wickets: 1-2 (Williams), 2-6 (Mangallie), 3-63 (Smith), 4-91, 5-120, 6-141, 7-160, 8-160, 9-182, 10-183 (76 ov)

LEEWARD ISLANDS	O	M	R	W	Wd	Nb		O	M	R	W	Wd	Nb
Ambrose	14	7	12	4	-	-	Ambrose	13	7	10	1	-	-
KCG Benjamin	11.5	3	19	5	-	-	KCG Benjamin	15	4	44	1	-	-
WKM Benjamin	8	1	33	1	-	1	WKM Benjamin	16	8	26	1	-	-
Walsh	6	1	25	0	-	-	Walsh	10	5	24	1	-	-
Phillip	7	2	10	0	-	-	Phillip	18	3	55	4	-	-
							Arthurton	4	1	10	2	-	-

LEEWARD ISLANDS	1ST INNINGS	R	B	2ND INNINGS	R	B
SC Williams	c Lara b Ramnarine	13				
LA Harrigan	b Mahabir	51				
CW Walwyn	lbw b Francis	80				
*KLT Arthurton	c and b Dhanraj	93				
+RD Jacobs	c Smith b Dhanraj	14				
LL Lawrence	b Lara	56				
WKM Benjamin	b Francis	16				
CEL Ambrose	c Williams b Dhanraj	28				
KCG Benjamin	b Ramnarine	14				
WD Phillip	c sub (PV Simmons) b Ramnarine	7				
VA Walsh	not out	0				
Extras	(1 b, 16 lb, 3 nb)	20				
Total	(all out, 104.4 overs)	392				

Fall of wickets: 1-25 (Williams), 2-132 (Harrigan), 3-198 (Walwyn), 4-224 (Jacobs), 5-281 (Arthurton), 6-310 (WKM Benjamin), 7-359 (Lawrence), 8-381 (Ambrose), 9-392 (Phillip), 10-392 (KCG Benjamin, 104.4 ov)

TRINIDAD AND TOBAGO	O	M	R	W	Wd	Nb		O	M	R	W	Wd	Nb
Francis	24	2	83	2	-	-							
Lawrence	2	0	3	0	-	-							
Dhanraj	30	1	122	3	-	-							
Ramnarine	17.4	0	49	3	-	-							
Mahabir	26	1	96	1	-	-							
Lara	5	0	22	1	-	-							

TRINIDAD & TOBAGO v JAMAICA

Venue: Queen's Park Oval, Port of Spain
Toss: Trinidad and Tobago won the toss and decided to field
and Tobago 16; Jamaica 0

Date: 21st, 22nd, 23rd, 24th January 1994
Result: Trinidad and Tobago won by 3 wickets **Points:** Trinidad
Umpires: LH Barker, Z Maccum

JAMAICA	1ST INNINGS	R	B	2ND INNINGS	R	B
DS Morgan	c Ragoonath b Elvin	18		c Williams b Elvin	0	
RG Samuels	c Elvin b Antoine	7		c Lara b Elvin	19	
JC Adams	c Mason b Antoine	4		run out (Ramnarine)	0	
RW Staple	c Balliram b Ramnarine	30		st Williams b Dhanraj	32	
TO Powell	c Lara b Ramnarine	49		b Ramnarine	7	
RC Haynes	b Elvin	21		(7) c Lara b Bodoe	43	
FR Redwood	b Ramnarine	28		(6) c Lara b Antoine	57	
NO Perry	st Williams b Ramnarine	0		c Ramnarine b Dhanraj	34	
+PA Gayle	c Lara b Ramnarine	2		c Lara b Dhanraj	0	
FA Rose	b Dhanraj	24		not out	7	
*CA Walsh	not out	11		c Bodoe b Dhanraj	1	
Extras	(4 b, 2 lb, 6 nb)	12		(5 b, 4 lb, 8 nb)	17	
Total	(all out, 56.2 overs)	206		(all out, 71.2 overs)	217	

Fall of wickets: 1-24 (Samuels), 2-29 (Adams), 3-56 (Morgan), 4-68 (Staple), 5-95 (Haynes), 6-164 (Powell), 7-164 (Perry), 8-165 (Redwood), 9-167 (Gayle), 10-206 (Rose, 56.2 ov)
Fall of wickets: 1-1 (Morgan), 2-14 (Adams), 3-33 (Samuels), 4-46 (Powell), 5-89 (Staple), 6-151 (Redwood), 7-206 (Perry), 8-207 (Gayle), 9-210 (Haynes), 10-217 (Walsh, 71.2 ov)

TRINIDAD AND TOBAGO	O	M	R	W	Wd	Nb		O	M	R	W	Wd	Nb
Antoine	16	2	54	2	-	3	Antoine	17	5	47	1	-	6
Elvin	12	3	50	2	-	3	Elvin	15	3	40	2	-	2
Ramnarine	14	2	48	5	-	-	Dhanraj	11.2	1	40	4	-	-
Dhanraj	4.2	0	14	1	-	-	Ramnarine	10	1	47	1	-	-
Bodoe	10	1	34	0	-	-	Bodoe	18	4	34	1	-	-

TRINIDAD AND TOBAGO	1ST INNINGS	R	B	2ND INNINGS	R	B
S Ragoonath	c Powell b Rose	21		(2) c Gayle b Rose	8	
A Balliram	b Haynes	17		(1) run out	12	
RAM Smith	c Samuels b Rose	0		lbw b Walsh	25	
*BC Lara	c Staple b Haynes	180		lbw b Perry	23	
+D Williams	c Powell b Rose	4		(6) c sub (AJ Andrews) b Walsh	14	
KA Mason	c Powell b Haynes	0		(5) not out	52	
M Bodoe	c Powell b Haynes	0		lbw b Rose	4	
D Ramnarine	b Rose	1		b Walsh	7	
R Dhanraj	c Powell b Haynes	11		not out	5	
RE Elvin	lbw b Haynes	0				
EC Antoine	not out	0				
Extras	(2 b, 2 lb, 17 nb, 2 w)	23		(9 b, 2 lb, 6 nb)	17	
Total	(all out, 78.5 overs)	257		(7 wickets, 77.3 overs)	167	

Fall of wickets: 1-38 (Ragoonath), 2-38 (Smith), 3-45 (Balliram), 4-59 (Williams), 5-60 (Mason), 6-83 (Bodoe), 7-123 (Ramnarine), 8-228 (Dhanraj), 9-228 (Elvin), 10-257 (Lara, 78.5 ov)
Fall of wickets: 1-17 (Ragoonath), 2-31 (Balliram), 3-68 (Lara), 4-77 (Smith), 5-107 (Williams), 6-121 (Bodoe), 7-135 (Ramnarine)

JAMAICA	O	M	R	W	Wd	Nb		O	M	R	W	Wd	Nb
Rose	19	1	74	4	1	10	Walsh	24	7	40	3	-	3
Walsh	20	5	75	0	-	7	Rose	12.3	4	29	2	-	1
Haynes	26.5	5	82	6	1	-	Redwood	10	5	13	0	-	-
Perry	13	4	22	0	-	-	Haynes	15	1	37	0	-	-
							Perry	16	2	37	1	-	2

WEST INDIES v ENGLAND, FIRST TEST

Venue: Sabina Park, Kingston
Toss: England won the toss and decided to bat
Umpires: SA Bucknor, ID Robinson

Date: 19th, 20th, 21st, 23rd, 24th February 1994
Result: West Indies won by 8 wickets
Referee: SM Gavaskar

ENGLAND	1ST INNINGS	R	B	2ND INNINGS	R	B
†MA Atherton	c Murray b KCG Benjamin	55	189	c Adams b Walsh	28	78
AJ Stewart	c Murray b KCG Benjamin	70	118	run out (KCG Benjamin)	19	27
GP Thorpe	b KCG Benjamin	16	69	(7) b WKM Benjamin	14	41
RA Smith	b Walsh	0	6	(3) c Adams b Walsh	2	12
GA Hick	b Adams	23	65	(4) c sub (RA Harper) b KCG Benjamin	96	187
MP Maynard	lbw b KCG Benjamin	35	68	(5) c Murray b WKM Benjamin	0	3
+RC Russell	lbw b KCG Benjamin	0	4	(6) c Adams b WKM Benjamin	32	55
CC Lewis	c Adams b Ambrose	8	27	lbw b Ambrose	21	69
AR Caddick	c Adams b KCG Benjamin	3	27	not out	29	50
AP Igglesden	not out	3	16	c Adams b KCG Benjamin	0	10
DE Malcolm	run out	6	5	b Walsh	18	22
Extras	(2 b, 5 lb, 4 nb, 4 w)	15		(1 b, 3 lb, 2 nb, 2 w)	8	
Total	(all out, 98.1 overs)	234		(all out, 91.5 overs)	267	

Fall of wickets: 1-121 (Stewart), 2-133 (Atherton), 3-134 (Smith), 4-172 (Hick), 5-172 (Thorpe), 6-172 (Russell), 7-194 (Lewis), 8-209 (Caddick), 9-227 (Maynard), 10-234 (Malcolm)
Fall of wickets: 1-34 (Stewart), 2-39 (Smith), 3-58 (Atherton), 4-63 (Maynard), 5-126 (Russell), 6-155 (Thorpe), 7-213 (Lewis), 8-226 (Hick), 9-228 (Igglesden), 10-267 (Malcolm)

WEST INDIES	O	M	R	W	Wd	Nb		O	M	R	W	Wd	Nb
Ambrose	22	8	46	1	-	-	Ambrose	24	4	67	1	1	1
Walsh	23	6	41	1	-	-	Walsh	24.5	6	67	3	-	-
KCG Benjamin	24	7	66	6	4	3	WKM Benjamin	20	3	56	3	-	-
WKM Benjamin	19.1	7	43	0	-	-	KCG Benjamin	18	2	60	2	1	1
Adams	10	1	31	1	-	1	Adams	2	0	9	0	-	-
							Simmons	3	1	4	0	-	-

WEST INDIES	1ST INNINGS	R	B	2ND INNINGS	R	B
DL Haynes	c Thorpe b Malcolm	4	13	not out	43	77
PV Simmons	c Russell b Caddick	8	10	lbw b Igglesden	12	27
*RB Richardson	c Maynard b Malcolm	5	13	(4) not out	4	20
BC Lara	b Hick	83	131	(3) b Caddick	28	35
KLT Arthurton	c Lewis b Malcolm	126	232			
JC Adams	not out	95	226			
+JR Murray	lbw b Igglesden	34	47			
WKM Benjamin	b Caddick	38	58			
CEL Ambrose	b Caddick	0	4			
KCG Benjamin	b Lewis	0	1			
CA Walsh	lbw b Lewis	0	8			
Extras	(10 lb, 3 nb, 1 w)	14		(5 b, 3 lb)	8	
Total	(all out, 123 overs)	407		(2 wickets, 26.2 overs)	95	

Fall of wickets: 1-12 (Haynes), 2-12 (Simmons), 3-23 (Richardson), 4-167 (Lara), 5-256 (Arthurton), 6-319 (Murray), 7-389 (WKM Benjamin), 8-389 (Ambrose), 9-390 (KCG Benjamin), 10-407 (Walsh)
Fall of wickets: 1-38 (Simmons), 2-87 (Lara)

ENGLAND	O	M	R	W	Wd	Nb		O	M	R	W	Wd	Nb
Malcolm	23	3	113	3	-	-	Malcolm	5	1	19	0	-	-
Caddick	29	5	94	3	-	3	Caddick	6	1	19	1	-	-
Lewis	26	4	82	2	1	-	Lewis	3	0	6	0	-	-
Igglesden	24	5	53	1	-	-	Igglesden	7	0	36	1	-	-
Hick	21	4	55	1	-	-	Hick	3	1	2	0	-	-
							Stewart	2.2	0	5	0	-	-

WEST INDIES v ENGLAND, SECOND TEST

Venue: Bourda, Georgetown
Toss: West Indies won the toss and decided to field
Umpires: CR Duncan, S Venkataraghavan

Date: 17th, 18th, 19th, 20th, 22nd March 1994
Result: West Indies won by an innings and 44 runs
Referee: JR Reid

ENGLAND	1ST INNINGS	R	B	2ND INNINGS	R	B
*MA Atherton	c Murray b Ambrose	144	296	b Ambrose	0	4
AJ Stewart	b Walsh	0	4	b KCG Benjamin	79	137
MR Ramprakash	lbw b Walsh	2	6	b Ambrose	5	27
RA Smith	c Lara b KCG Benjamin	84	160	c Richardson b Ambrose	24	52
GA Hick	c Richardson b Ambrose	33	77	b KCG Benjamin	5	5
GP Thorpe	b Ambrose	0	13	b Walsh	20	61
IDK Salisbury	lbw b WKM Benjamin	8	60	(9) b Walsh	19	82
+RC Russell	c Richardson b Ambrose	13	72	(7) c Murray b Ambrose	6	38
CC Lewis	c Richardson b KCG Benjamin	17	63	(8) c Adams b KCG Benjamin	24	102
ARC Fraser	not out	0	4	b KCG Benjamin	0	1
AP Igglesden	b KCG Benjamin	0	2	not out	1	3
Extras	(14 lb, 7 nb)	21		(2 b, 2 lb, 2 nb, 1 w)	7	
Total	(all out, 124.5 overs)	322		(all out, 85 overs)	190	

Fall of wickets: 1-0 (Stewart), 2-2 (Ramprakash), 3-173 (Smith), 4-245 (Hick), 5-253 (Thorpe), 6-276 (Atherton), 7-281 (Salisbury), 8-322 (Russell), 9-322 (Lewis), 10-322 (Igglesden)
Fall of wickets: 1-0 (Atherton), 2-30 (Ramprakash), 3-91 (Smith), 4-96 (Hick), 5-129 (Stewart), 6-140 (Thorpe), 7-150 (Russell), 8-185 (Lewis), 9-186 (Fraser), 10-190 (Salisbury)

WEST INDIES	O	M	R	W	Wd	Nb		O	M	R	W	Wd	Nb
Ambrose	30	8	58	4	-	-	Ambrose	23	5	37	4	-	-
Walsh	26	7	69	2	-	2	Walsh	25	4	71	2	-	1
KCG Benjamin	23.5	5	60	3	-	3	WKM Benjamin	16	4	44	0	-	-
WKM Benjamin	26	9	62	1	-	-	KCG Benjamin	19	6	34	4	1	1
Adams	3	1	10	0	-	2	Adams	2	2	0	0	-	-
Chanderpaul	16	2	49	0	-	-							

WEST INDIES	1ST INNINGS	R	B	2ND INNINGS	R	B
DL Haynes	c Russell b Salisbury	63	135			
*RB Richardson	c Lewis b Fraser	35	86			
BC Lara	c Atherton b Lewis	167	210			
KLT Arthurton	c Thorpe b Salisbury	5	16			
JC Adams	lbw b Igglesden	137	262			
S Chanderpaul	b Salisbury	62	135			
+JR Murray	lbw b Salisbury	0	1			
WKM Benjamin	b Fraser	44	53			
CEL Ambrose	c Russell b Lewis	10	14			
KCG Benjamin	c Russell b Lewis	1	15			
CA Walsh	not out	10	10			
Extras	(2 b, 6 lb, 13 nb, 1 w)	22				
Total	(all out, 153.3 overs)	556				

Fall of wickets: 1-63 (Richardson), 2-177 (Haynes), 3-203 (Arthurton), 4-315 (Lara), 5-441 (Chanderpaul), 6-441 (Murray), 7-505 (WKM Benjamin), 8-520 (Ambrose), 9-532 (KCG Benjamin), 10-556 (Adams, 153.3 ov)

ENGLAND	O	M	R	W	Wd	Nb		O	M	R	W	Wd	Nb
Lewis	28	1	110	3	-	7							
Igglesden	24.3	3	94	1	-	-							
Fraser	29	5	85	2	-	3							
Salisbury	37	4	163	4	-	-							
Hick	20	1	61	0	-	-							
Ramprakash	15	1	35	0	1	3							

WEST INDIES v ENGLAND, THIRD TEST

Venue: Queen's Park Oval, Port of Spain
Toss: West Indies won the toss and decided to bat
Umpires: SA Bucknor, S Venkataraghavan

Date: 25th, 26th, 27th, 29th, 30th March 1994
Result: West Indies won by 147 runs
Referee: JR Reid

WEST INDIES	1ST INNINGS	R	B	2ND INNINGS	R	B
DL Haynes	b Salisbury	38	98	b Lewis	19	68
*RB Richardson	lbw b Salisbury	63	172	c and b Caddick	3	28
BC Lara	lbw b Lewis	43	104	c Salisbury b Caddick	12	18
KLT Arthurton	lbw b Lewis	1	17	c Stewart b Caddick	42	88
JC Adams	c Smith b Lewis	2	10	c Russell b Salisbury	43	97
S Chanderpaul	b Fraser	19	52	c Fraser b Caddick	50	124
+JR Murray	not out	27	77	c Russell b Caddick	14	37
WKM Benjamin	b Fraser	10	15	c Fraser b Lewis	35	51
CEL Ambrose	c Thorpe b Fraser	13	31	b Caddick	12	13
KCG Benjamin	b Fraser	9	9	not out	5	19
CA Walsh	lbw b Lewis	0	1	lbw b Lewis	1	4
Extras	(1 b, 13 lb, 12 nb, 1 w)	27		(8 b, 13 lb, 12 nb)	33	
Total	(all out, 95.2 overs)	252		(all out, 87.5 overs)	269	

Fall of wickets: 1-66 (Haynes), 2-158 (Richardson), 3-158 (Lara), 4-163 (Adams), 5-164 (Arthurton), 6-201 (Chanderpaul), 7-212 (WKM Benjamin), 8-241 (Ambrose), 9-251 (KCG Benjamin), 10-252 (Walsh)
Fall of wickets: 1-15 (Richardson), 2-37 (Lara), 3-51 (Haynes), 4-131 (Arthurton), 5-143 (Adams), 6-167 (Murray), 7-227 (WKM Benjamin), 8-247 (Ambrose), 9-267 (Chanderpaul), 10-269 (Walsh, 87.5 ov)

ENGLAND	O	M	R	W	Wd	Nb		O	M	R	W	Wd	Nb
Fraser	24	9	49	4	-	3	Fraser	25	6	71	0	-	2
Caddick	19	5	43	0	1	2	Caddick	26	5	65	6	-	1
Lewis	25.2	3	61	4	-	4	Lewis	27.5	6	71	3	-	9
Salisbury	22	4	72	2	-	3	Salisbury	9	1	41	1	-	-
Ramprakash	2	1	8	0	-	-							
Hick	3	1	5	0	-	-							

ENGLAND	1ST INNINGS	R	B	2ND INNINGS	R	B
*MA Atherton	c Murray b WKM Benjamin	48	103	lbw b Ambrose	0	1
AJ Stewart	b Ambrose	6	13	b Ambrose	18	23
MR Ramprakash	c and b WKM Benjamin	23	55	run out	1	4
RA Smith	lbw b Ambrose	12	34	b Ambrose	0	2
GA Hick	lbw b Walsh	40	70	c Murray b Ambrose	6	14
GP Thorpe	c Lara b Ambrose	86	167	b Ambrose	3	28
+RC Russell	b Ambrose	23	108	(8) c sub (PV Simmons) b Ambrose	4	12
CC Lewis	b Ambrose	9	21	(9) c WKM Benjamin b Walsh	6	17
IDK Salisbury	c Lara b Walsh	36	65	(7) c Lara b Walsh	0	3
AR Caddick	c Lara b WKM Benjamin	6	24	c Lara b Walsh	1	12
ARC Fraser	not out	8	32	not out	0	0
Extras	(10 b, 9 lb, 11 nb, 1 w)	31		(6 lb, 1 nb)	7	
Total	(all out, 112.2 overs)	328		(all out, 19.1 overs)	46	

Fall of wickets: 1-16 (Stewart), 2-82 (Ramprakash), 3-87 (Atherton), 4-115 (Smith), 5-167 (Hick), 6-249 (Russell), 7-273 (Lewis), 8-281 (Thorpe), 9-294 (Caddick), 10-328 (Salisbury, 112.2 ov)
Fall of wickets: 1-0 (Atherton), 2-1 (Ramprakash), 3-5 (Smith), 4-21 (Hick), 5-26 (Stewart), 6-27 (Salisbury), 7-37 (Russell), 8-40 (Thorpe), 9-45 (Caddick), 10-46 (Lewis, 19.1 ov)

WEST INDIES	O	M	R	W	Wd	Nb		O	M	R	W	Wd	Nb
Ambrose	29	6	60	5	-	-	Ambrose	10	1	24	6	-	-
Walsh	27.2	3	77	2	-	7	Walsh	9.1	1	16	3	-	1
KCG Benjamin	20	5	70	0	1	-							
WKM Benjamin	24	3	66	3	-	2							
Adams	4	0	18	0	-	-							
Chanderpaul	5	0	13	0	-	2							
Arthurton	3	0	5	0	-	-							

WEST INDIES v ENGLAND, FOURTH TEST

Venue: Kensington Oval, Bridgetown
Toss: West Indies won the toss and decided to field
Umpires: LH Barker, DB Hair

Date: 8th, 9th, 10th, 12th, 13th April 1994
Result: England won by 208 runs
Referee: JR Reid

ENGLAND	1ST INNINGS	R	B	2ND INNINGS	R	B
*MA Atherton	c Lara b KCG Benjamin	85	165	c Lara b Walsh	15	43
AJ Stewart	b WKM Benjamin	118	221	b Walsh	143	319
MR Ramprakash	c Murray b WKM Benjamin	20	52	c Chanderpaul b Walsh	3	12
RA Smith	c Murray b WKM Benjamin	10	17	lbw b KCG Benjamin	13	41
GA Hick	c Murray b Ambrose	34	58	c Lara b Walsh	59	126
GP Thorpe	c sub (PV Simmons) b KCG Benjamin	7	21	c Arthurton b Walsh	84	129
+RC Russell	c Chanderpaul b Ambrose	38	56	not out	17	17
CC Lewis	c Murray b Ambrose	0	2	c Walsh b Adams	10	7
AR Caddick	b Ambrose	8	24			
ARC Fraser	c Chanderpaul b Walsh	3	15			
PCR Tufnell	not out	0	0			
Extras	(8 lb, 24 nb)	32		(8 b, 6 lb, 36 nb)	50	
Total	(all out, 100.2 overs)	355		(7 wickets, dec, 108.5 overs)	394	

Fall of wickets: 1-171 (Atherton), 2-223 (Ramprakash), 3-242 (Smith), 4-265 (Stewart), 5-290 (Thorpe), 6-307 (Hick), 7-307 (Lewis), 8-327 (Caddick), 9-351 (Fraser), 10-355 (Russell, 100.2 ov)
Fall of wickets: 1-33 (Atherton), 2-43 (Ramprakash), 3-79 (Smith), 4-194 (Hick), 5-344 (Stewart), 6-382 (Thorpe), 7-394 (Lewis, 108.5 ov)

WEST INDIES	O	M	R	W	Wd	Nb		O	M	R	W	Wd	Nb
Ambrose	24.2	5	86	4	-	6	Ambrose	22	4	75	0	-	13
Walsh	24	3	88	1	-	14	Walsh	28	5	94	5	-	8
WKM Benjamin	22	4	76	3	-	1	WKM Benjamin	22	3	58	0	-	3
KCG Benjamin	20	5	74	2	-	3	KCG Benjamin	20	1	92	1	-	11
Chanderpaul	10	4	23	0	-	-	Chanderpaul	10	3	30	0	-	-
							Adams	6.5	0	31	1	-	1

WEST INDIES	1ST INNINGS	R	B	2ND INNINGS	R	B
DL Haynes	c Atherton b Fraser	35	51	(8) c Thorpe b Tufnell	15	42
*RB Richardson	c Atherton b Fraser	20	30	(1) c Ramprakash b Caddick	33	94
BC Lara	c sub (N Hussain) b Lewis	26	45	c Tufnell b Caddick	64	89
KLT Arthurton	c Russell b Fraser	0	3	(5) b Tufnell	52	116
JC Adams	c Thorpe b Fraser	26	68	(2) c Russell b Caddick	12	49
S Chanderpaul	c Ramprakash b Tufnell	77	231	c sub (N Hussain) b Hick	5	29
+JR Murray	c Thorpe b Fraser	0	2	c Thorpe b Caddick	5	21
WKM Benjamin	c Hick b Fraser	8	13	(9) c Tufnell b Tufnell	3	8
CEL Ambrose	c Hick b Fraser	44	74	(10) b Lewis	12	30
KCG Benjamin	not out	43	82	(4) c Hick b Caddick	0	5
CA Walsh	c Tufnell b Fraser	13	17	not out	18	18
Extras	(1 lb, 11 nb)	12		(1 b, 7 lb, 10 nb)	18	
Total	(all out, 101.5 overs)	304		(all out, 82.2 overs)	237	

Fall of wickets: 1-55 (Richardson), 2-55 (Arthurton), 3-95 (Lara), 4-126 (Adams), 5-126 (Haynes), 6-126 (Murray), 7-134 (WKM Benjamin), 8-205 (Ambrose), 9-263 (Chanderpaul), 10-304 (Walsh, 101.5 ov)
Fall of wickets: 1-43 (Adams), 2-43 (KCG Benjamin), 3-128 (Lara), 4-150 (Chanderpaul), 5-164 (Arthurton), 6-179 (Murray), 7-195 (Richardson), 8-199 (WKM Benjamin), 9-216 (Haynes), 10-237 (Ambrose, 82.2 ov)

ENGLAND	O	M	R	W	Wd	Nb		O	M	R	W	Wd	Nb
Fraser	28.5	7	75	8	-	-	Fraser	17	7	40	0	-	-
Caddick	24	2	92	0	-	2	Caddick	17	3	63	5	-	1
Lewis	17	2	60	1	-	6	Tufnell	36	12	100	3	-	3
Tufnell	32	12	76	1	-	3	Lewis	8.2	1	23	1	-	6
							Hick	4	2	3	1	-	-

WEST INDIES v ENGLAND, FIFTH TEST

Venue: Antigua Recreation Ground, St John's
Toss: West Indies won the toss and decided to bat
Umpires: SA Bucknor, DB Hair

Date: 16th, 17th, 18th, 20th, 21st April 1994
Result: Match drawn
Referee: JR Reid

WEST INDIES	1ST INNINGS	R	B	2ND INNINGS	R	B
PV Simmons	lbw b Caddick	8	27	not out	22	71
SC Williams	c Caddick b Fraser	3	17	not out	21	73
BC Lara	c Russell b Caddick	375	538			
JC Adams	c sub (N Hussain) b Fraser	59	164			
KLT Arthurton	c Russell b Caddick	47	184			
S Chanderpaul	not out	75	182			
+JR Murray						
WKM Benjamin						
CEL Ambrose						
KCG Benjamin						
*CA Walsh						
Extras	(3 lb, 23 nb)	26			0	
Total	(5 wickets, dec, 180.2 overs)	593		(no wicket, 24 overs)	43	

Fall of wickets: 1-11 (Williams), 2-12 (Simmons), 3-191 (Adams), 4-374 (Arthurton), 5-593 (Lara)

ENGLAND	O	M	R	W	Wd	Nb		O	M	R	W	Wd	Nb
Fraser	43	4	121	2	-	12	Fraser	2	1	2	0	-	-
Caddick	47.2	8	158	3	-	2	Caddick	2	1	11	0	-	-
Tufnell	39	8	110	0	-	1	Tufnell	6	4	5	0	-	-
Lewis	33	1	140	0	-	8	Hick	8	2	11	0	-	-
Hick	18	3	61	0	-	-	Ramprakash	3	1	5	0	-	-
							Thorpe	2	1	1	0	-	-
							Stewart	1	0	8	0	-	-

ENGLAND	1ST INNINGS	R	B	2ND INNINGS	R	B
*MA Atherton	c Murray b Ambrose	135	383			
AJ Stewart	c Ambrose b KCG Benjamin	24	41			
MR Ramprakash	lbw b KCG Benjamin	19	29			
RA Smith	lbw b KCG Benjamin	175	315			
GA Hick	b KCG Benjamin	20	28			
GP Thorpe	c Adams b Chanderpaul	9	30			
+RC Russell	c Murray b WKM Benjamin	62	161			
CC Lewis	not out	75	175			
AR Caddick	c WKM Benjamin b Adams	22	83			
ARC Fraser	b Adams	0	9			
PCR Tufnell	lbw b WKM Benjamin	0	9			
Extras	(9 b, 20 lb, 23 nb)	52				
Total	(all out, 206.1 overs)	593				

Fall of wickets: 1-40 (Stewart), 2-70 (Ramprakash), 3-373 (Smith), 4-393 (Atherton), 5-401 (Hick), 6-417 (Thorpe), 7-535 (Russell), 8-585 (Caddick), 9-589 (Fraser), 10-593 (Tufnell, 206.1 ov)

WEST INDIES	O	M	R	W	Wd	Nb		O	M	R	W	Wd	Nb
Ambrose	40	18	66	1	-	-							
Walsh	40	9	123	0	-	13							
WKM Benjamin	41.1	15	93	2	-	3							
KCG Benjamin	37	7	110	4	-	1							
Chanderpaul	24	1	94	1	-	6							
Adams	22	4	74	2	-	-							
Arthurton	2	1	4	0	-	-							

Page 4 EXPRESS Thursday, April 21, 1994

NEWS

He's off to England Monday

• TRIBUTE from Page 1.

Central Bank Towers yesterday, Draper said the country needed to develop "a new culture which acknowledges existence and achievement.

the matinee ends at the Port-of-Spain City Hall where Lara will be presented with the keys to the city by Mayor Telly Paul.

Speaking at a news conference at

Saying there was a tendency in this country to "prey on the negative," Draper country to "prey on the negative," Draper We need to help particularly the young people understand what their heroes are, to recognise them and pay tribute to them.

School children will therefore form an integral part of the activity tomorrow.

Tomorrow's motorcade will also pass Harvard Sports Club where Lara's skill as a batsman was nurtured.

On Saturday another motorcade will go through Chaguanas and San Fernando and the respective mayors will greet the group. It will also pass through

things happen we hear to honour them.

Government, however is still considering what kind of gift or assistance it should give to Lara. "We certainly want to discuss it with him before we arrive at any conclusions," Draper said.

Asked whether Government recognised Lara's contractual obligations, it would also discuss with him how he could be involved in the development of young people and cricket in Trinidad and Tobago.

Lara will be met by Prime Minister Patrick Manning and members of the Cabinet and the national football team.

He will be serenaded by San Sebastien steelband, Fist Jamettes and WITCO Desperadoes at a small open-air function.

Manning will formally welcome and congratulate him. Other dignitaries expected to be present are Opposition Leader Basdeo Panday, several of Lara's friends (whom he asked to be present) and his family.

Lara: Enjoy it but forget about me

• LARA from Page 1

body to just enjoy it, you know. I've looked the record but forget about me. I think Trinidad and Tobago needs to be happy and be proud and just enjoy themselves.

Describing himself as "very tired but very happy to be in this position," Lara passed on his thanks to his family and how to Santa Cruz.

"I just want to say I'm happy for everyone—my mother who is very proud of me, my family, my entire way who put me into cricket. Agnes, and everybody in Santa Cruz, you know? I mean they'll all be happy. I'm not sure how much sleep they've got in the last week...

said, I'd like them to forget about me. Enjoy it, you know, just body to forget about me. Enjoy it, you know, just enjoy it, just be happy and enjoy the whole week.

First things first: Home sweet home

BY SHERIFF ANN DE LEON

STREETS decorated with coloured bulbs, a steering group made up of his cousins, and a greet of neighbours greeted Brian Lara as he returned to his after-midnight welcome back party in his hometown Cantaro village, Santa Cruz.

A tired, frustrated looking Lara left Piarco International Airport with heavily armed police escort, after insisting he intended to proceed to his home for his night's

Villagers of Santa Cruz, where their hero Brian Lara was born, came out to greet him on his record-breaking feat of scoring 375 in a Test match.

GREAT INNINGS!

Trinidad goes wild

$2 million for Lara

Cricketer buys a Mercedes and seeks house on a hi...

EXPRESS Tuesday, April 26, 1994 Page 3

Newsday $1
TUESDAY APRIL 19, 1994

KING LARA
Conqueror of World cricket

Tobago hails Brian Lara

By JAMES D. ANDREWS

EVEN the Trinidad and Tobago Electricity Commission's inanimate transformers opposite the House of Assembly building paid tribute to Brian Lara, as Tobagonians flocked to Scarborough on Sunday to greet the world champion batsman.

On the pole stood three transformers numbered 50, flanked by two bearing the magic number 375. It was serendipity of th

But that is by the

Trinidad Guardian
the Guardian of democracy
Wednesday, April 20, 1994

TT star rules the world — English Press

Lara back tomorrow

Daily Express
The National Newspaper of Trinidad & Tobago
SATURDAY, APRIL 23, 1994

LARAMA

EVERYBODY wanted a berth, and some actually came close to getting large chunks. Like the man who grabbed on to the record breaking left arm and wouldn't let go.

ABOUTIQUE
FOR CLOTHI

Brian Lara waves to the crowd during a motorcade in downtown Port-of-Spain after his world record score of 375 in 1994. Shivnarine Chanderpaul (right) who part... Lara when he broke the record joins in the mome...

Sports Extra
April 24, 1994

Trinidad Guardian
(the Guardian of democracy)
Saturday, April 23, 1994

New
WEDNESDAY

Lara comes

Natio

THE GOVERNMENT last night de...
Friday- April 22, a "National Day of Ac...
ment" in honour of the world record...
ing performance of young cricketer...
Lara, and other recent successes in...
All schools will get the day off.

Lara on Monday at the Antigua Recreation...
broke the 36 year old record of Sir Gary So...
scoring 375 runs - the highest individual Te...
a batsman. Sir Gary scored 365.

Lara
Lottery Bonus
Daily Bonus Draw
68857

ay $1

ANIA

All hail King Lara
TT batting hero gets nation's highest award

Daily Express
The National Newspaper of Trinidad & Tobago

Paying tribute to
the king of cricket

LARA DAY

Govt declares Friday
Day of Achievement

Haitian footballer
opts to stay in T&T

Page 22 SPORTS EXTRA Sunday, April 24, 1994

ad Guardian

se of his choice'
menade, national award for Lara

of attention at a reception in honour
team hosted by their Excellencie

BRIAN LARA waves to
adoring fans at Pia
International Airport

Two Grannies Die In Fire

Lottery Bonus
Daily Bonus Draw
49614

Trinidad & Tobago's

Newsday $1
No.213 FRIDAY APRIL 22, 1994

OUR HERO RETURNS
See Page 2

For Brian Lara:
National Award
House of choice
75,000 free travel
City Promenade
Pages: 6, 7, 14, 37, 30, 39, 41, 42, 47, 48

NEWS

Return of a hometown hero
By KIM JOHNSON

BRIAN LARA'S WEEKEND ITINERARY

WITH LOVE, MOM

Chaguanas honours a role model
By DAVID BREWSTER

Fans mob Lara on Harris Promenade
By AZARD ALI

Lara holds the key

.

1994

THE INTIMIDATOR

*'I knew something was on the cards when
I saw him in the nets at 8.30am'*

TIM MUNTON

I'LL NEVER FORGET the walk. Moving through customs, into the madness, my mind goes back to Sir Viv, being pushed aside as a youngster by the mob at Heathrow, all of them awestruck by this man. A little over a week ago I was just another kid trying to make his name. Now, I'm *this* person. Or something like him, at least.

The first chance I get to lie down, I think about my poor performances in the past, how different the conditions are in England to the Caribbean, how my last trial over here was a failure. I'm coming back with this big reputation, but back to a place I haven't got close to mastering. I've pulled off this massive achievement yet it feels a world away.

The first press conference, the first of many in those early days, happens almost immediately in London. It's packed. Thankfully Dwight is there with me, along with the Warwickshire captain Dermot Reeve and Dennis Amiss, the chief exec who brokered the deal for me.

Over the next few months I'll come to learn just how good Dennis was. He'd played for England so he understood the game, but I could see he got the administrative side better than most too. He sure had an eye for a deal. We signed that first contract for £40,000 for the season, with negotiations thrashed out before the 375 – had we talked *after* it, we might have had a bit more bargaining power. Not that I was bothered about the money. I was a little boy, with just a couple of Test hundreds, and they were offering me the chance to play county cricket, to follow in the footsteps of all the greats to have played in it. That was everything for me.

It's funny to think I wasn't even their first choice. When Allan Donald confirmed he'd be touring England with South Africa that summer, the Indian allrounder Manoj Prabhakar had been their guy and they only turned to me when he had to pull out.

I didn't need any convincing. Remember, this is 1994. County cricket is the most sought after, scrutinised first-class competition in the world. Even if you're good, even if you're *very* good, you're still not guaranteed to play in it. You may have a good agent, but there are so many players available. There's nothing else on the landscape, even for the world's best players. When the 18 counties went looking for overseas players, you had to be in the upper echelons just to be considered.

The money aspect was not a factor. It was to put myself in this small group. Look at some of the names from that summer: Mohammad Azharuddin, Wasim Akram, Mushtaq Ahmed, Carl Hooper, Courtney Walsh, Desmond Haynes. I was keen to join that list. And the second thing in our favour was Warwickshire's location. Dennis may have felt he'd got a good deal with the £40k. But with my best friend living just up the road, I'd have happily signed for half that.

* * *

The first few days were tough but fun. Constant meet-and-greets, press conferences, events, and then I had to fit in some practice sessions. On my arrival at Edgbaston I walked in to meet the staff and was given a couple of boxes of fan mail to sort through. Warwickshire was in a wonderful position at the time. Membership was going up, there was a buzz around the place. I was given a Peugeot for the summer with the number plate L375 ARA and I was handed my county cap, which players don't normally get until they play a few matches.

Sure I was a little wired, but I'm on a high, riding it for as long as I can stay upright. I want to do everything, and I'm no introvert. Of an evening, I'll be out with Dwight for drinks, I'm gonna see what Birmingham is like at night. I wouldn't want to call it burning the candle at both ends, but I'm certainly wide-eyed.

Dwight was making a name for himself at Aston Villa and I tapped into that. When I was first in England in 1991 he was still a rookie living in this little attic in someone's house. I remember spending some time with him up there, the two of us squeezed into this little box. In 1994 he would have been 22. We were still kids.

It was so important for me that he was there. It was a shame I couldn't live with him but I remember his apartment, it wasn't that big. Bedrooms in England are tiny, and I wouldn't have been able to survive there. We needed our own space. It was smart for him to be living close to where his training was, a little outside of the city, up near the Belfry golf course.

Even in those early days we still managed to fit in a few evenings of golf. In England in the summer you could leave at 6pm and still get nine holes in and that became our course. First time I arrived, there were 375 golf balls waiting for me at the club, a gift from one of the brands. It soon became our private place, where we could just play and take it easy. By then my golf obsession had properly taken hold. Though I'd only picked it up that year, I was already hooked.

I'd only played my first round in January in Montserrat, following a furious blow-up at Antigua. I was 24, captaining our Trinidad & Tobago side at St. John's in a one-dayer against a good Leeward Islands side and we were cruising to victory, needing not that many to win with six wickets in hand and plenty of overs to get them. First I got out, then my teammate Kenneth Williams got hit in the eye and had to retire hurt, and from there we somehow lost the game, still with wickets in hand. Afterwards I locked the door in the changing room and let my teammates have it. Some of those players still recall it to that day.

Anyway, we went to Montserrat the next day and turned up at Sturge Park for a four-dayer to find a square that was all green. We couldn't see a pitch, but we had no trouble identifying Ambrose and the Benjamin boys. We lost in two-and-a-half days, but we couldn't leave the island, as it was one of those tiny places with only a single plane a day. We had the best part of two days to kill waiting for our flight.

It hadn't been a great few days, so Phil Simmons said that seeing as there wasn't much else to do, why shouldn't we have a round of golf. Reluctantly, I agreed. There were only right-handed clubs, so I had no choice which way to pick them up. I played a very bad round and didn't think much of it until I got to the 18th hole, hit a driver up onto the green and sunk it for a birdie. That was it. Suddenly, I understood the obsession. I played the next day, and the next. I've been fixated since.

Back in Trinidad there were no left-handed clubs so I figured if I was going to pursue this, I'd best learn how to play right-handed. Soon enough the conversation gets around that I'm playing golf and it's going to affect my batting, so I decide to stick to playing right-handed. All the pros back then seemed to be right-handed. There were no left-handed golfers to emulate, so it looked like that was how you played the game. I was never going to go back.

All of this brought into focus what I thought were strange ideas around what constitutes 'left-handers' and 'right-handers' in batting. Naturally, I am right-handed, and very much so. But I would not be able to pick a bat up in the 'right-handed' style, because my left hand is weak. The way I understand it, when you're a 'right-hander', and you're a top-handed player, you need your left hand to be strong. And of course the same must apply the other way round. My top hand – my right – controlled my game, so that was where my strength was. That just seemed natural and logical to me. By contrast in golf, my weak left hand breaks down all the time. In golf I swing much better as a 'left-hander', but I have no orientation, and so I'm stuck being a right-hander.

* * *

I have three days from the time I land in England to the first ball of the season. I'm focusing hard at practice because I need to learn fast. Those days in between are as hectic as anyone could imagine but I'm still focused during nets. Whatever minutes I got, I spend them trying to understand how to play the moving ball, and to get to grips with the challenges ahead. On a technical level I was telling myself to watch the ball and delay my strokeplay, to delay, delay, and delay some more. It was one thing I learned, coming out of my 1991 tour of English conditions, that I was batting like I was still in the Caribbean. Playing through the line of deliveries at home, you could trust the pace and bounce. I'd played enough cricket in the Caribbean to know what not to do here. It was April in England. I needed to understand that the pitches would have moisture, live grass, and a softness underfoot.

Mentally, I was trying to make this leap. From one world, which every unknown kid lives in, where no one knows who you are and you're falling under the radar, to three years later, when there's an expectation to do extraordinary things. Fortunately, I love that stuff. Challenges don't intimidate me. They never have. Doing well in county cricket was a major part of my career.

It was good to be coming up against Glamorgan in our first game, and a West Indian quick in Ottis Gibson. It's fresh and immediate, the competition, and you're in there telling yourself that a fellow West Indian is not going to get you out. I'd destroyed Ottis that year against Barbados, hitting a double century, so I was feeling good anyway. Whatever happens, I won't allow him to get me out.

There wasn't much time to get to know my teammates before we took the field but I got a sense of things when I first walked in and there was a note pinned on the wall: 'Welcome to the second-best left-hander in the world'. I could see it was a no-nonsense kind of dressing room, full of big characters with an air of competition inside the team as well as out of it. It didn't take long to work out the joker, our opening batter, Roger Twose. At least I think it was a joke. Either way, it wore thin when he went out in the first match and scored a big double century. Then, you know, the comparison becomes real.

It was good fun to share a partnership with him, and for us both to register important scores as we racked up a huge winning total. My 147, a first hundred in England, a first at Edgbaston, felt like a big reward for keeping on top of the chaos of that week.

It was a fast education. I believe that facing Ottis – good pace, swinging the ball much more than he did back home – and combatting that spell from him, helped me understand what the rest of the bowlers were doing. What I took away from dealing with him, this top-class county cricketer, was my capacity to adjust and learn. For all the madness, my switch was on. And it'd be on for a while yet.

* * *

The guys were saying they'd never seen anything like it. It was a 'Lara-mania' kind of thing. I couldn't do much without a lot of eyes on me. People were in my garden in the morning and the evening. I'd be followed when I was driving home. Apparently, according to a BBC documentary they later did on me, the one person in England who was photographed more than Princess Diana in 1994 was me. Sure we played on it, but it was a ridiculous amount of attention for a guy from overseas with a few Test hundreds. I didn't have any security, I just had to learn how to manage it.

I would do a few autographs a day, and then a few more when the dressing room attendant brought the next load of letters. Thing was, I played cricket in part for the adulation it brought. I make no bones about that. People who say it's not important to them aren't giving the full truth. In the Caribbean you play sport for enjoyment and to bring smiles to people's faces. Satisfying my dad – seeing him sitting there in the shade under his tree, smiling to himself – so much flows from that feeling. Which young man of 24, with his world turned upside down for the better, wouldn't like what was going on? For a time, everything was favourable. As I say, for a *time*.

We hit the road. Leicestershire next, Phil Simmons' team. I was looking forward to getting stuck into another West Indian, someone I considered a friend. They had the better of the game but I scored a hundred in both innings. No one else got runs because everyone was scared of a guy called David Millns. He was strong and quick and my guys were shying away from him. I felt like I was back in school cricket, coming up against a real quick and all your schoolmates know you're going to be down that end batting. Millns and Alan Mullally were firing, and I had to see us through to a draw. We got to the close seven down for 206. I was 120 not out.

I'd made four hundreds back-to-back. The 375, the 147, and now these two against Leicester. I headed to Taunton feeling good and ready for more. I'd made a 90-odd there in 1991 and my recollection was of a pitch with a hardness to it.

It was a rain-affected game so we only got to bat properly once, chasing 322 in a contrived chase. Mushtaq Ahmed was their trump card but I loved facing legspin and I'd faced him before. He wasn't going to be a problem. I can't remember all the other bowlers but I was in such rich form that it didn't matter. It was an innings where I'm not thinking anything, one of those where you feel you can do anything. I was most likely willing one of my teammates out so I could go bat. Again, that's just the truth, and anyone who's properly played the game can't pretend they haven't occasionally felt that themselves. We chased it comfortably, and I hit 136 from 84 balls. In fairness, Mushtaq did get me in the end.

That game also threw up the first sign of trouble.

* * *

I was enjoying myself, feeling like I was a part of things. Gladstone Small had taken me under his wing in those early weeks, trying his best to shield me from the outside stuff. Being West Indian and an international cricketer, he knew his way around the place, and where you could get a good Caribbean meal. He came forward as more of a protective friend than anything else. I got the feeling that Gladstone could relax with me because he'd already played international cricket, been around the block, and had nothing more to prove.

Keith Piper, who was an outstanding wicketkeeper, was another who had become a good friend, as had Michael Bell, our left-arm fast bowler. Both Bell and Piper kept a connection with their West Indian roots and we had a lot to talk about.

OK, so I'd been given a phone by some company or other. That was how it was back then. You'd just randomly get given stuff. Rain is falling in the game and there's a bit of a break. I'm in the dressing room setting my phone up, and then it's time to get back on the field. Dermot Reeve, who wasn't playing in the game, says to me, "Take it on the field, I'll give you a call". Apparently Ian Botham and Allan Lamb had done something similar in a Test match, and Piper and Gladstone were both egging me on. Anyway it's overcast, dark, we're only gonna be out there for a few minutes, so why not? It's just for fun. I popped my phone in my whites pocket. Dermot called and I answered on the field. We all had a quick laugh about it, then the phone goes back in the pocket and we're off the field again soon after. I don't think anything more of it.

A few days later that image of me speaking on the phone out on the pitch gets plastered all over the press. And look, if you see a photo of me taking a call on the field, it doesn't look good, does it? The media took me to pieces, turning a joke into a negative, framed in a way that Lara was making so much money that he's taking calls on the field. People took that joke and turned it into something else.

I was pissed off. I didn't feel supported by the Warwickshire players. It was around that point in time that I started to identify one or two of the guys who saw an opportunity to get their own names out. There's one thing that gets stuck on successful sportspeople – Kohli, Tendulkar, Michael Jordan, Tiger Woods – this personal drive that they have is looked upon in a different way, you know?

After all, everyone's trying to get to the top. It's just that for some people who don't have the skills, they have to find other ways to promote themselves.

I felt that some of my teammates were talking to the press. Where I lived, what I was doing, who I was seeing, what was happening in the dressing room. This really got to me. Some of the people around me weren't friends or family, they were strangers. They didn't say, "Let's put a blanket over the whole thing because he needs a bit of protection". They were in a position where getting their brand out there was easy and they were part of the madness going on.

* * *

The days either side of the Taunton game I spent in London. I was really starting to weave my way into the city. There was lots of promotional work to do – I was with Joe Bloggs, the clothing brand, and was even 'immortalised' at Madame Tussauds! – and I was eagerly learning the best restaurants and checking out the clubs. There was always something to do, and I went out nightly to find it. I loved the time away, loved those bright lights. Kai on Mayfair's South Audley Street was fast becoming my favourite Chinese restaurant. I'd go there with my agents, David Manasseh and Jonathan Barnett, and after dinner Jonathan would head home and David would take me to Café de Paris to have some fun, while Tramp was another club that was top of my list. I became friends with the late Johnny Gold and the late Robert Sangster, the guys who owned Tramp, and I always felt welcome there. It was discreet, you could do your thing at that place and be sure it wouldn't be in the papers the next day. Mick Jagger would often be there, wanting to talk cricket. Another night you might bump into Boy George. I became good friends with Ben Goldsmith and Ade, the big guy who played the getaway driver in *Snatch*.

By the time of the Middlesex match at Lord's I was well entrenched in the west-end scene. It was one vast celebrity hangout. If one night it was Tramp, the next it might be Ten Rooms or Browns.

I loved Ten Rooms, especially on a Sunday when you'd hear the best R&B and reggae, while Browns was my favourite spot for a while. Jake the owner became one of my best friends in London after we met at Lord's and hit it off.

Many a night I'd sit at his table, just watching the shenanigans taking place. On any one night you might have Elton John, Prince or some other superstar just turning up. Supermodels would be there, Kate Moss, Naomi Campbell. And then there was me, Dwight and a few other footballers like Stan Collymore.

I even ended up with my own pizza, named 'Trinidad Hot', at another place that I still love frequenting, Ciro's Pizza Pomodoro in Knightsbridge. My friendship with the fanciful, eccentric Ciro is even stronger today, and often after our careers were over, Shane Warne and myself would join Ciro at the underground restaurant for a merry time of singing and dancing, eating pizzas and sipping a few drinks.

I was no longer some starry-eyed kid. While I may have walked close to those clubs in 1991, I would have stood outside. Back then I was just a little cricketer who anybody would push away on the side of the road, and then three years later you're the talk of the town. Who wouldn't enjoy that? I can't lie, I loved to lap up the attention. I loved the attention of the girls. I did enjoy that part of it, but I was still very focused on Leasel Rovedas back home.

The other thing, it didn't affect my scores. I remember there was some talk about the prospect of hitting six hundreds on the trot and a few names and dates came up. It was exciting and I was looking forward to the match. I did my usual, I wasn't rolling in at two in the morning, I was back home having dinner and if I did stop off somewhere before or during that match I made sure to keep a lid on things.

I did actually need my sleep. I was always making decisions based on how much I needed. I had this routine of going to sleep at about 6pm straight after play, getting up at 9pm, going out until 1am-ish – as long as we didn't have a curfew – and then back to sleep in order to be at the ground for the morning. It just made sense. I couldn't really sleep through the whole night. I liked going out, and I still felt that if I was picking up a few hours here and there, I was getting enough.

Everywhere I went, everything I did was being recorded. I was followed a *lot*. These photographers would be outside the clubs all through the night. Even a couple of days before Lord's, it was being reported that I was out on the town enjoying myself. I hated any suggestion that I wasn't as focused on my game as I should be.

I could start to feel the press coverage getting to me a little. There were one or two little hiccups, a couple of negative things that I felt were unnecessary. When the intrusive behaviour came in and started to rub me the wrong way, I started getting very defensive.

Anyway, it didn't happen. First innings, I got 26. Caught down the legside from a guy called Richard Johnson, so that ended any chance of that record. I failed to get six straight.

I still went out in the second innings and scored 140. There was a prize of something like £20,000 for anyone who could hit one over the Pavilion. That second innings, I hit one very near to the old guy who sits on top of the building. Honestly, I was *that* close…

* * *

After a couple of games away from home we went back up to Edgbaston. Durham was next up.

We lost the toss and they piled on a big total stretching into the second day, so it was well into Friday afternoon by the time we got to bat. I was out there early, for the second over, but I didn't walk out like myself. I could feel that something was wrong, and the first few balls I faced I looked all at sea. My feet felt heavy, my movements not so fluid. I couldn't say why, but I didn't feel like my old self. I remember taking a single, going up to the non-striker's end and telling the umpire that it'd come to an end. The run. It was finished.

Soon after I was bowled behind my legs by Anderson Cummins, their Bajan overseas, only reprieved by the no-ball call. Minutes later I nicked the left-armer Simon Brown to the keeper behind the stumps, the catch going at knee height. I took two steps towards the pavilion, but I caught sight of the bowler's arms go up in joy and then down onto his head. I looked back, saw the ball on the ground, and darted back into my crease.

I scratched to 111 by the end of the day, easily my worst hundred of the streak and the year. Then the game stopped, the whole of Saturday rained off. I felt the poor form, lived with it all weekend. I didn't score much in the Sunday League game.

Something wasn't right. I wasn't happy with my technique. I wondered if perhaps I was picking up my bat too wide, and that it needed to come back a little straighter.

Tim Munton was always the first man at the ground. He'd get in early, walk across the car park, past the nets and up to the dressing room. He turned up on that morning to find me in the nets with our coach Bob Woolmer. Bob had put a set of spring-loaded stumps behind me, another set just outside my eyeline in front of me, and he was throwing balls down. The drill was forcing me to pick my bat up straighter behind me and then to bring it down straight, because if I didn't, it would clatter into one or both sets of stumps. Tim did a double take when he saw us, looked at his watch and smiled. He wasn't used to seeing me arriving on time, let alone early. He later said he knew something special was on the cards when he found me in the nets at 8:30am.

We all sat down and spoke about the different equations that we would accept, how far they were ahead, and what they should give us. My personal thinking was that I already had a hundred on the board, and I thought it'd be nice to take my pads off and come back to score another hundred later in the day if I had to. They'd already put up 556, and we were 210-2 going into the final day. We were thinking of declaring, giving their openers a free hit up to an agreed target, and then we'd be back out there trying to chase it down.

It didn't play out like that. Dermot Reeve came back into the room and said they wanted to set us something ridiculous. They said that we had Lara, and they knew what had happened at Taunton, and they had a couple of injuries which could give away the game, so what do you guys think? We would be running the risk of giving up first innings batting points for an unreachable total. We figured that if they're not gonna play the game how it's supposed to be, then we won't either. And there was something else to consider. We were very bad on our over rates for the year, and over-rate penalties were calculated at the end of the season. So part of our thinking was getting our first-innings points, declaring and then rushing through the afternoon session to bring our over rate down.

So that was that. Nothing doing. With both teams settling in for the long haul, I come to realise what might be out there for me. Just before I go out, I mention to Dermot that if I'm going strong, I'd like to get another double hundred, as it wasn't so long ago that I'd hit the 277. He says he's cool with that.

By the time I see him next, at lunch, I'm on about 280 – I've scored 170-odd in a session – and I look at him again and say, "So, skipper, I just scored a triple hundred, right? It'd be nice, you know, to score another one of those too." "Yeah, you go," he says. "We'll find the right time to declare."

Between lunch and tea, that's when it starts getting serious. It becomes clear that something big is bubbling away. The crowd starts to grow, first a trickle, then a flood. Dennis Amiss goes to find Dermot and says to him, "Don't even think about it". More and more people keep coming through the gates.

We don't have an electric scoreboard updating us, but it's pretty audible on the mic, the guy shouting out different names and numbers as they come and go. There's one number I'm listening out for. Viv's number, 322. I'm doing whatever I can to knock that number down, to get that score, the highest in county cricket by a West Indian, that's a serious motivation. There's no talk of declarations now. Dennis Amiss has already used his power.

After 375 I'm thinking about the big one. I'm thinking Hanif Mohammad. I get to 376, I say, "Brian, man, it's time to *go*".

By tea, I'm really motoring. Records are falling all around me. It's on.

I'm focused, but to focus too much on what's happening, the *size* of it, would take me into a different frame of mind, and I don't want to get away from the fun of it. I know my next milestone is going to be 400, I'm thinking it's cool to have a one, a two, a three and a four.

Again the guy on the mic comes on to shout something else and by now I'm on a different plane, batting with ultra-aggressiveness, taking the attack to every bowler as more names start to fall. Graeme Hick's name is mentioned. A guy called MacLaren, the man with the highest score in English cricket. Then, well, *Bradman*.

Trevor Penney is with me through the afternoon, we put on 315 together, all the while he's giving me flak for nicking the strike on the fifth and sixth ball, I'm saying to him too right I'm having the strike, we're here to entertain! He still likes to say that without his 44, we'd be nowhere. After him, Keith Piper joins me, and it's great having him next to me as he goes looking for his own hundred.

I remember one point, just before tea. I've just passed 400, and they're short of players with injuries and a couple of our guys are on the field. I flick a ball to square leg and Mike Burns, our 12th man, hesitates momentarily, then runs in and dives forward but the ball drops just short. He tells me later that he was so nervous about taking a screamer to get rid of me that he "hurtled in at 50 percent". Again, it's destiny, right? If a Durham fielder is there, then there's a chance it could have been a different story, but it just so happens to go up to one of our guys who, in that second, calculates in his head how bad he would feel if he takes that catch. Just to complete the passage, a few shots later I hit a big straight drive, he's at deep mid-off and he dives brilliantly to stop the boundary and save face. The whole thing is *outstanding*.

By then the bowling's very pedestrian, a couple are missing, their main spinner David Graveney might've been off the field. They have John Morris bowling medium pace and a young left-arm spinner, David Cox. Not much else. But the clock's ticking down, and it's not clear how long we've got till the close.

The last moments are just beautiful. Morris is bowling. I don't realise it's the last scheduled over of the match so I'm calm against the first three balls, no worries. Then out of nowhere Morris bounces me and hits me on the helmet, which sharpens me up! Piper comes down to tell me that actually I've only got two balls left to get it done. That sharpens me up too. Next ball I lick one through the covers to bring it up. The crowd converges and again it's just joy, pure magical joy.

Back in the dressing room someone gets hold of my home number and calls my mother. She asks who it is and then hangs up, says that some guy reckons Brian scored 501 or some nonsense score. Eventually, my brothers tune in to the radio to hear the news. Amid all the pandemonium in the dressing room, I'm still asking myself, whenever I have a quiet moment, what just happened? *How* did this happen? And why *me?*

I'm constantly trying to make sense of it. I'd always put so much pressure on myself to be the best. At school, in the streets, even in the garage, I was always thinking I had to be the best. It was my dream to play for the West Indies. But to be what some people were calling *The First Superstar of Cricket*, to be talked about in that way, where did *that* come from?

That six weeks of cricket, 375 to 501, is maybe the most invincible I ever felt. I prepared for it, I practised for it, and I lived to succeed. It was the most amazing period in my career. I came in feeling hesitant, apprehensive, because I'd had such a bad 1991 tour, but everything came off the middle of the bat. It was a mentally mature pursuit of excellence. I wanted to defeat everybody. I saw bowlers who didn't want to bowl anymore, I saw captains who just wanted to get off the field. That was the war I knew I was winning. I became an intimidator. Not with words, but with my game.

Afterwards it starts to hit me. And I come to see that it's really about desire, about channelling something deep inside. It's like I've been given these two golden tickets with the numbers 375 and 501 written on them, and I have to hold onto them tight, because they give us all a standing. These tickets give the whole of the West Indies a standing.

* * *

The evening of the 501 was chaotic. A lot of signings, a mass of media to do, taking pictures with the head groundsman and his team. Back in the dressing room there was champagne flowing, the entire team throwing it all over me, the doors constantly swinging open with well-wishers. The phone calls came in – the Trinidad prime minister, Patrick Manning, called me. My agents were on the line. I'd had them busy since 375 and they just became busier.

Some time that night I think I was driven down to the hotel – I was in no state to drive myself. I was going back home in two days for a short break, back to see my family. It had been agreed even before the 501 that I would take a few days off as we had a window in our season, but we still had this semi-final to play in the B&H Cup down at The Oval, the very next day after the Durham game.

I got to London very late. There was an early morning assortment of things to do. I was being driven all over the city doing interviews with TV and radio, I'd not had much sleep, and it's not much more than 12 hours since I hit that final ball. I was told to keep off my feet, to rest when I could. If it was an ordinary game, a Sunday League game away from home, then maybe I would not have played, although that rarely went down well, because counties were selling out their seats because I was coming. But this was a semi-final. A big game. There was no question of missing it.

The plan was all talked about and effected. I started fielding, came up with an excuse, and came off the field to rest ahead of our run chase. But me being off the field for some time meant I couldn't bat early in our reply, I was only allowed to bat at No.6.

My record in the one-day game was OK but not brilliant so there wasn't too much reliance on me in those types of games. Other guys were scoring runs. I came in at 120-4, 268 the target. I felt like I was in cruise control, like I was just continuing from 501, a different bowling attack but the same rhythm. I didn't feel under pressure at all. The Oval pitch was always considered a good one for batting where the ball comes on to the bat. It was the most similar to those West Indian pitches of old, those tracks you used to get at Barbados. I didn't wanna do much running, I was sure of that. We got it done, I hit 70, and though I got out before the close, Reeve and Penney saw us home.

Exhausted perhaps, but I still went out. It was London, after all. I couldn't get enough of that city.

I believe the flight back home was sold out after the 501. English journalists were everywhere. Photographers shouting and snapping at me all the way down the tunnel to the plane. What was supposed to be a quiet time back home would turn into another media frenzy, just like with 375. But look, to me, it was still satisfying. I wasn't too bothered by it. At times of course it could be tiring – you go to find a little peace and find it's not on the table – but it wasn't something I felt intimidated by. I'm 25. It's already more than anything I could have dreamed of.

* * *

Something shifted after I got back to England. The relentlessness of the season started to bite. The mood got gloomier. Cracks appeared in places where they shouldn't.

First game back we played Kent, I didn't get many. And then it was to Northants, Curtly's team. That game was billed as the best versus the best, and I laughed at that idea because the battle they were talking about was the kind I would be staying well away from. As a batter, why would you go looking for a battle with the best bowler in the world? It didn't make any sense. I was always looking to make runs against bowlers I knew I could dominate and no one in the world ever dominated Curtly Ambrose. I was smart enough to know that I needed to stay away from him and pick up my singles where I could. I didn't score much against him but I got through it, and he hit me on the head, so I imagine he was happy with that. I scored 197, my seventh hundred of the season.

After Curtly hit me, the next few balls of that over were pitched up as he tried to get me caught behind or LBW. That was a totally sensible tactic and I'd seen him do it many times, but I remember walking into the dressing room and seeing that some of my team were unhappy with what had happened. Some of them were saying that if it was one of them, then the rest of the over would have been short balls. I wasn't too happy that some of my teammates seemed to want to see me get peppered.

All this limelight around me was becoming a problem. I was being seen as special, and some people didn't like it. Tim Munton captained a fair chunk of that four-day season, Dermot Reeve captained the one-day stuff, and I remember not feeling very comfortable with him because I was more trying to take a break during some of those matches.

The schedule was Thursday, Friday, Saturday of the four-day game, then Sunday League, then finishing the four-day game on the Monday, then a knockout game, and then you start again. I tried to push back because I was close to being done. Physically I could deal with it but I was finding it very difficult mentally to stay focused.

It was new for everybody. Neither myself nor Warwickshire had any experience of it. Everywhere we went, the guy who was having his benefit at Kent or Glamorgan or wherever would have 50 pieces for me to sign, photographs of 375 and books and replica shirts so they could sell them. It got to a point where I had no time for myself. My life was not my own.

Away from the cricket it was very hectic too. There was money to be made, and people around me who wanted to make it, so if I did get a day off I'd probably be off somewhere doing a shoot or whatever, and that wouldn't go down too well, and people would be saying his priorities weren't right.

Looking back, I can understand how important it was for me not to miss the matches. People were paying to come see you. Clubs were selling out their games. But at the time I was too tired to see it.

* * *

One thing I do regret. There was a four-day game against Lancashire at Edgbaston. I wanted to take a break. Dwight was flying back to Trinidad, and I said to him I was gonna take this game off and go with him. It didn't matter what I told Warwickshire leading up to the game, saying I wasn't fully fit and I was exhausted and so on, they said I had to play that game. I pleaded to have that week off but they were adamant. Get some physiotherapy, get some help, and be ready to play. It got to the morning of the match and they asked me to come in to do a fitness test. Dwight was there with me, and I was already packed and ready to go with him. Leasel Rovedas was back home too, and I wanted to see her.

I told them I couldn't make the fitness test. Dwight was waiting. He came into the players area to ask me what I was doing and I said to him that I'd be coming. Before I left they said, "Well, you've got to be fit for the Sunday League. You have to play in that game." But you know, I'm not going to Scotland, I'm going to the Caribbean.

Anyway, I left. On the morning of the game. My agent called me and said, "Go, enjoy yourself, come back and I will deal with it". I got back a few days later and we had a meeting with the club. I think the management had come round to understanding the state of mind I was in, but some of the players weren't happy.

Dermot didn't feel great about it, and I get that now. He was having the season of his life, and he was pissed off. Bob Woolmer, the coach, was another who was having a great season. I regret that I upset them. I didn't need to go to Trinidad just to have a break. If that was what I needed, I could have had that break in my apartment in Birmingham. And it wasn't like I was going back home to sleep for a week. It was the middle of the season. If you really need a break, have it in Birmingham. At the end of the day, if I sign a five-month contract I've got to honour it.

Truth was, I'd got to a stage where my mind wasn't there. Before Warwickshire, the longest season I'd played was five weeks. A county season, such as we were having, involved the best part of 50 games across five months.

The last two months are a blur. I remember we won the B&H Cup at Lord's in July, our first silverware. And then against Hampshire, I made 191 in the match that clinched the Championship. More champagne, more pictures, and then literally the day after we were back at Lord's for the NatWest Trophy Final. It was very overcast, Tom Moody was bowling using the slope, and I was playing at balls that pitched outside leg stump, holding my shape, and watching the ball be taken in front of first slip. The game was rain affected so it went into a second day, which meant we ended up batting in early morning conditions *twice*. We got the bad end of the luck twice over. I made 81 but I got out at a crucial time, and we lost badly. So the quadruple bid was over, but we were still well placed in the Sunday League. I chipped in with a few scores in the final weeks as the boys got it done to clinch the treble.

Great success, but a testing year. I was playing for the West Indies, so I knew all about team dynamics and the fact that it wasn't going to be great all the time. Yes, we won three trophies, but there was a bittersweet taste in my mouth. What I failed to realise at the time, or maybe failed to communicate to people, was that for those latter months I was burnt out. My state of mind wasn't good. I had nothing left to give, so I pushed people away.

There were others, beyond Gladstone Small and Keith Piper, that I truly valued. Tim Munton, I had the greatest respect for. A true workhorse and hero for Warwickshire. I give a lot of credit for our success to him. He resembled Angus Fraser as a bowler, which maybe explained why he only played a couple of Tests, but a true professional and one of the guys who, with a mature head, helped me get through the season. I think he understood my situation. I believe he has a lot of empathy inside him. Dennis Amiss too was tremendous with me all year.

I always felt comfortable in their company and never doubted they had my back. I'll always be so thankful to them for that.

* * *

The craziest year would end at least on a beautiful note. That December, we're in India on tour when Sobers turns up. I see him around the hotel at Mumbai, we chat a little, I just think it's one of those things, you know? He's here for an event maybe, or a little media work. Well, one morning, before the Test match in Mumbai, the captain and coach call the team together and Sobers comes out holding this big trophy. Suddenly a TV camera emerges, and he starts to speak, saying what an honour it is, on behalf of the BBC, to present me with this award.

I don't even know what it's for, to be honest. I'd not heard it before. The *BBC Overseas Sports Personality of the Year*. It's only when Sobers says that he himself is a former recipient, and he starts mentioning other winners, Muhammad Ali, Pelé, Eusébio, that it starts hitting home, the size and *scale* of it. This is for one person chosen across the whole of the sporting world. It's an incredible honour.

That trophy, up there in my bar at home in Trinidad, remains one of my most prized possessions.

WARWICKSHIRE v GLAMORGAN

Venue: Edgbaston, Birmingham
Toss: Glamorgan won the toss and decided to bat
Points: Warwickshire 22; Glamorgan 4

Date: 28th, 29th, 30th April, 1st May 1994
Result: Warwickshire won by an innings and 103 runs
Umpires: JH Hampshire, JW Holder

GLAMORGAN	1ST INNINGS	R	B	2ND INNINGS	R	B
SP James	c Asif Din b NMK Smith	19		lbw b Small	61	
*H Morris	lbw b Munton	24		b Munton	0	
A Dale	c Piper b Munton	32		c Reeve b Small	0	
MP Maynard	lbw b Reeve	5		c PA Smith b Small	34	
DL Hemp	c NMK Smith b Munton	127		c Twose b Small	2	
PA Cottey	lbw b PA Smith	18		c Reeve b Davis	33	
RDB Croft	b Reeve	30		c Davis b Munton	5	
OD Gibson	b Small	61		c Reeve b Davis	15	
RP Lefebvre	c Twose b Munton	20		b Davis	32	
+CP Metson	lbw b PA Smith	2		c PA Smith b Small	0	
SL Watkin	not out	0		not out	0	
Extras	(9 b, 13 lb, 4 nb, 1 w)	27		(4 b, 3 lb)	7	
Total	(all out, 130.4 overs)	365		(all out, 67.3 overs)	189	

Fall of wickets: 1-31, 2-53, 3-64, 4-118, 5-158, 6-222, 7-327, 8-354, 9-365, 10-365 (130.4 ov)
Fall of wickets: 1-4, 2-9, 3-89, 4-93, 5-104, 6-126, 7-155, 8-170, 9-189, 10-189 (67.3 ov)

WARWICKSHIRE	O	M	R	W	Wd	Nb		O	M	R	W	Wd	Nb
Small	27	6	75	1	-	-	Small	17.3	3	46	5	-	-
Munton	23.4	5	57	4	-	-	Munton	21	5	73	2	-	-
NMK Smith	18	3	46	1	-	-	NMK Smith	15	4	25	0	-	-
Reeve	23	5	61	2	-	-	Davis	12	7	24	3	-	-
Davis	21	7	51	0	-	-	PA Smith	2	0	14	0	-	-
PA Smith	12	2	35	2	-	-							
Lara	1	0	7	0	-	-							
Twose	5	1	11	0	-	-							

WARWICKSHIRE	1ST INNINGS	R	B	2ND INNINGS	R	B
DP Ostler	b Gibson	42				
RG Twose	not out	277				
BC Lara	c Maynard b Croft	147				
Asif Din	st Metson b Croft	42				
*DA Reeve	lbw b Gibson	18				
PA Smith	b Watkin	38				
NMK Smith	c Gibson b Dale	15				
+KJ Piper	run out	12				
RP Davis	not out	35				
GC Small						
TA Munton						
Extras	(7 b, 9 lb, 14 nb, 1 w)	31				
Total	(7 wickets, dec, 176 overs)	657				

Fall of wickets: 1-50, 2-265, 3-372, 4-439, 5-535, 6-561, 7-596

GLAMORGAN	O	M	R	W	Wd	Nb		O	M	R	W	Wd	Nb
Watkin	32	7	99	1	-	-							
Gibson	30	4	134	2	-	-							
Croft	51	13	173	2	-	-							
Lefebvre	39	11	122	0	-	-							
Dale	24	3	113	1	-	-							

WARWICKSHIRE v LEICESTERSHIRE

Venue: Edgbaston, Birmingham
Toss: Warwickshire won the toss and decided to field
Points: Warwickshire 5; Leicestershire 8

Date: 5th, 6th, 7th, 9th May 1994
Result: Match drawn
Umpires: B Dudleston, DR Shepherd

LEICESTERSHIRE	1ST INNINGS	R	B	2ND INNINGS	R	B
PV Simmons	c Reeve b Bell	9		c Reeve b PA Smith	39	
*NE Briers	c Ostler b Reeve	154		c sub b NMK Smith	22	
TJ Boon	c Ostler b Small	42		(8) did not bat		
JJ Whitaker	c Reeve b Bell	25		(3) b PA Smith	4	
VJ Wells	c Piper b PA Smith	21		(4) b NMK Smith	2	
BF Smith	b Small	78		(5) not out	25	
+PA Nixon	c Reeve b Small	7		(6) c Piper b NMK Smith	19	
GJ Parsons	lbw b Bell	6		(7) not out	11	
ARK Pierson	not out	26				
DJ Millns	lbw b PA Smith	10				
AD Mullally	c Bell b Munton	1				
Extras	(8 b, 6 lb, 10 nb)	24		(4 b, 8 lb, 1 w)	13	
Total	(all out, 123.2 overs)	403		(5 wickets, dec, 42 overs)	135	

Fall of wickets: 1-11, 2-100, 3-162, 4-212, 5-320, 6-341, 7-348, 8-378, 9-402, 10-403 (123.2 ov)
Fall of wickets: 1-73, 2-76, 3-79, 4-79, 5-108

WARWICKSHIRE	O	M	R	W	Wd	Nb		O	M	R	W	Wd	Nb
Small	27	3	77	3	-	-	Bell	5	0	19	0	-	-
Bell	26	5	89	3	-	-	Munton	11	3	25	0	-	-
Munton	27.2	6	78	1	-	-	PA Smith	9	2	27	2	-	-
PA Smith	16	2	67	2	-	-	NMK Smith	17	5	52	3	-	-
NMK Smith	13	3	35	0	-	-							
Reeve	14	5	43	1	-	-							

WARWICKSHIRE	1ST INNINGS	R	B	2ND INNINGS	R	B
DP Ostler	c Nixon b Millns	17		lbw b Millns	14	
RG Twose	c Nixon b Parsons	51		c Simmons b Millns	12	
BC Lara	c and b Pierson	106		not out	120	
Asif Din	b Pierson	14		(7) run out	9	
*DA Reeve	c sub b Pierson	0		(4) c Parsons b Millns	3	
PA Smith	c sub b Pierson	13		(5) c Whitaker b Millns	0	
+KJ Piper	c sub b Pierson	0		(6) b Pierson	8	
NMK Smith	c Simmons b Pierson	18		c sub b Simmons	20	
GC Small	c Millns b Pierson	5		not out	0	
MAV Bell	not out	4				
TA Munton	c sub b Pierson	5				
Extras	(14 b, 5 lb, 2 nb)	21		(7 b, 3 lb, 10 nb)	20	
Total	(all out, 71.5 overs)	254		(7 wickets, 56.4 overs)	206	

Fall of wickets: 1-27, 2-129, 3-201, 4-201, 5-206, 6-210, 7-229, 8-238, 9-247, 10-254 (71.5 ov)
Fall of wickets: 1-32, 2-45, 3-61, 4-61, 5-91, 6-120, 7-187

LEICESTERSHIRE	O	M	R	W	Wd	Nb		O	M	R	W	Wd	Nb
Mullally	20	6	55	0	-	-	Mullally	12	1	57	0	-	-
Millns	13	3	52	1	-	-	Millns	15	4	54	4	-	-
Wells	6	1	29	0	-	-	Parsons	13	4	41	0	-	-
Parsons	15	3	57	1	-	-	Pierson	13	2	23	1	-	-
Pierson	17.5	5	42	8	-	-	Simmons	3.4	1	21	1	-	-

SOMERSET v WARWICKSHIRE

Venue: County Ground, Taunton
Toss: Somerset won the toss and decided to bat
Points: Somerset 2; Warwickshire 18

Date: 19th, 20th, 21st, 23rd May 1994
Result: Warwickshire won by 6 wickets
Umpires: R Julian, KJ Lyons

SOMERSET	1ST INNINGS	R	B	2ND INNINGS	R	B
MN Lathwell	c Davis b PA Smith	86				
I Fletcher	c Davis b PA Smith	17				
RJ Harden	c Davis b PA Smith	0				
NA Folland	c Piper b Davis	21				
*AN Hayhurst	not out	111				
+RJ Turner	c Lara b Munton	40				
HRJ Trump	c Davis b Small	15				
GD Rose	c Lara b Munton	1		(2) not out	13	
Mushtaq Ahmed	c Davis b Munton	2		(1) not out	9	
A Payne	c Munton b Davis	34				
PJ Bird	not out	0				
Extras	(6 b, 19 lb, 2 nb, 1 w)	28			0	
Total	(9 wickets, dec, 147.2 overs)	355		(no wicket, dec, 3.1 overs)	22	

Fall of wickets: 1-36, 2-36, 3-76, 4-149, 5-249, 6-272, 7-295, 8-299, 9-349

WARWICKSHIRE	O	M	R	W	Wd	Nb		O	M	R	W	Wd	Nb
Small	36.2	6	104	1	-	-	Asif Din	2	0	9	0	-	-
Munton	42	17	77	3	-	-	Ostler	1.1	0	13	0	-	-
PA Smith	16	7	24	3	-	-							
Twose	13	1	42	0	-	-							
Davis	25	9	59	2	-	-							
NMK Smith	15	6	24	0	-	-							

WARWICKSHIRE	1ST INNINGS	R	B	2ND INNINGS	R	B
DP Ostler	not out	41		run out	51	
RG Twose	not out	13		c Turner b Mushtaq Ahmed	33	
BC Lara				b Mushtaq Ahmed	136	
PA Smith				c Lathwell b Hayhurst	39	
Asif Din				not out	42	
TL Penney				not out	9	
+KJ Piper			.			
NMK Smith						
GC Small						
RP Davis						
*TA Munton						
Extras	(3 lb)	3		(1 b, 4 lb, 6 nb, 1 w)	12	
Total	(no wicket, dec, 21 overs)	57		(4 wickets, 53.4 overs)	322	

Fall of wickets:
Fall of wickets: 1-71, 2-96, 3-170, 4-296

SOMERSET	O	M	R	W	Wd	Nb		O	M	R	W	Wd	Nb
Bird	7	1	32	0	-	-	Bird	9	0	53	0	-	-
Payne	4	1	13	0	-	-	Payne	8	1	41	0	-	-
Mushtaq Ahmed	6	3	9	0	-	-	Mushtaq Ahmed	14	0	65	2	-	-
Rose	2	2	0	0	-	-	Rose	18.4	1	117	0	-	-
Trump	2	2	0	0	-	-	Hayhurst	4	0	41	1	-	-

MIDDLESEX v WARWICKSHIRE

Venue: Lord's Cricket Ground, St John's Wood
Toss: Middlesex won the toss and decided to field
Points: Middlesex 5; Warwickshire 5

Date: 26th, 27th, 28th, 30th May 1994
Result: Match drawn
Umpires: JD Bond, DJ Constant

WARWICKSHIRE	1ST INNINGS	R	B	2ND INNINGS	R	B
DP Ostler	c Brown b Fraser	17		lbw b Johnson	26	
RG Twose	b Williams	10		lbw b Fraser	1	
BC Lara	c Brown b Johnson	26		c and b Emburey	140	
TL Penney	lbw b Williams	43		c Ramprakash b Fraser	11	
*DA Reeve	c Gatting b Johnson	4				
PA Smith	c and b Johnson	24		(5) c Gatting b Weekes	65	
+KJ Piper	c Ramprakash b Williams	22		(6) not out	32	
NMK Smith	c Brown b Fraser	20		(7) not out	22	
RP Davis	c Carr b Emburey	7				
GC Small	b Williams	13				
TA Munton	not out	5				
Extras	(10 lb, 10 nb)	20		(2 b, 3 lb, 4 nb)	9	
Total	(all out, 89 overs)	211		(5 wickets, dec, 75 overs)	306	

Fall of wickets: 1-21, 2-47, 3-66, 4-78, 5-125, 6-164, 7-166, 8-193, 9-193, 10-211 (89 ov)
Fall of wickets: 1-2, 2-50, 3-129, 4-224, 5-278

MIDDLESEX	O	M	R	W	Wd	Nb		O	M	R	W	Wd	Nb
Williams	24	4	71	4	-	-	Williams	10	0	55	0	-	-
Fraser	24	10	43	2	-	-	Fraser	17	4	60	2	-	-
Johnson	22	9	45	3	-	-	Johnson	17	2	64	1	-	-
Emburey	14	5	37	1	-	-	Emburey	20	3	79	1	-	-
Gatting	5	1	5	0	-	-	Weekes	11	1	43	1	-	-

MIDDLESEX	1ST INNINGS	R	B	2ND INNINGS	R	B
DL Haynes	c and b Small	0		(7) lbw b Munton	24	
MA Roseberry	lbw b Twose	119		c Piper b Munton	73	
*MW Gatting	lbw b Munton	52		lbw b Munton	18	
MR Ramprakash	c Lara b Small	37		b Munton	0	
JD Carr	lbw b Small	0		(1) lbw b PA Smith	32	
PN Weekes	c Lara b PA Smith	3		(5) c Piper b PA Smith	29	
+KR Brown	c Piper b Small	0		(6) b Small	46	
RL Johnson	lbw b Reeve	4		(9) c NMK Smith b Munton	0	
NF Williams	b Reeve	7		(8) lbw b Small	10	
JE Emburey	not out	9		not out	4	
ARC Fraser	c Piper b Munton	3		not out	0	
Extras	(1 b, 10 lb, 2 nb, 2 w)	15		(3 b, 6 lb)	9	
Total	(all out, 100 overs)	249		(9 wickets, 50 overs)	245	

Fall of wickets: 1-0, 2-77, 3-156, 4-156, 5-163, 6-174, 7-185, 8-201, 9-246, 10-249 (100 ov)
Fall of wickets: 1-84, 2-129, 3-129, 4-132, 5-206, 6-221, 7-239, 8-239, 9-245

WARWICKSHIRE	O	M	R	W	Wd	Nb		O	M	R	W	Wd	Nb
Small	28	5	70	4	-	-	Small	14	2	41	2	-	-
Munton	35	12	68	2	-	-	Munton	17	3	76	5	-	-
PA Smith	12	2	35	1	-	-	PA Smith	5	0	36	2	-	-
Reeve	17	4	31	2	-	-	NMK Smith	8	0	33	0	-	-
NMK Smith	3	1	15	0	-	-	Davis	4	0	19	0	-	-
Twose	5	0	19	1	-	-	Lara	2	0	31	0	-	-

WARWICKSHIRE v DURHAM

Venue: Edgbaston, Birmingham
Toss: Durham won the toss and decided to bat
Points: Warwickshire 6; Durham 5

Date: 2nd, 3rd, 4th, 6th June 1994
Result: Match drawn
Umpires: TE Jesty, PB Wight

DURHAM	1ST INNINGS	R	B	2ND INNINGS	R	B
W Larkins	c Penney b Munton	13	36			
M Saxelby	b Small	19	55			
JE Morris	c Lara b PA Smith	204	287			
S Hutton	b Davis	61	202			
*P Bainbridge	c Reeve b NMK Smith	67	126			
JI Longley	lbw b NMK Smith	24	35			
+CW Scott	lbw b Small	13	21			
AC Cummins	lbw b Twose	62	98			
DA Graveney	not out	65	96			
DM Cox						
SJE Brown						
Extras	(2 b, 17 lb, 6 nb, 3 w)	28				
Total	(8 wickets, dec, 158.5 overs)	556				

Fall of wickets: 1-35, 2-39, 3-225, 4-365, 5-393, 6-420, 7-422, 8-556 (158.5 ov)

WARWICKSHIRE	O	M	R	W	Wd	Nb		O	M	R	W	Wd	Nb
Small	22	8	80	2	1	-							
Munton	28	4	103	1	1	-							
Reeve	5	2	12	0	1	-							
PA Smith	15	5	51	1	-	1							
Davis	36	12	105	1	-	-							
NMK Smith	32	6	97	2	-	-							
Twose	9.5	1	42	1	-	2							
Lara	11	1	47	0	-	-							

WARWICKSHIRE	1ST INNINGS	R	B	2ND INNINGS (F/O)	R	B
DP Ostler	c Scott b Cummins	8	6			
RG Twose	c Cox b Brown	51	35			
BC Lara	not out	501	427			
TL Penney	c Hutton b Bainbridge	44	126			
PA Smith	lbw b Cummins	12	31			
+KJ Piper	not out	116	151			
*DA Reeve						
NMK Smith						
RP Davis						
GC Small						
TA Munton						
Extras	(28 b, 22 lb, 26 nb, 2 w)	78				
Total	(4 wickets, dec, 135.5 overs)	810				

Fall of wickets: 1-8 (Ostler), 2-123 (Twose), 3-437 (Penney), 4-488 (PA Smith)

DURHAM	O	M	R	W	Wd	Nb		O	M	R	W	Wd	Nb
Cummins	28	1	158	2	-	11							
Brown	27	1	164	1	-	1							
Bainbridge	33	4	169	1	-	-							
Graveney	7	1	34	0	-	-							
Cox	30	5	163	0	-	-							
Larkins	5	0	39	0	-	1							
Morris	5.5	1	33	0	2	-							

SURREY v WARWICKSHIRE

Venue: The Foster's Oval, Kennington
Toss: Warwickshire won the toss and decided to field
Umpires: DJ Constant, B Dudleston

Date: 7th June 1994
Result: Warwickshire won by 4 wickets

SURREY		R	B	WARWICKSHIRE		R	B
DJ Bicknell	c and b Reeve	39		DP Ostler	b Pigott	44	
*+AJ Stewart	c Burns b Twose	24		+M Burns	c Thorpe b Benjamin	18	
GP Thorpe	c and b NMK Smith	87		RG Twose	c Stewart b Pigott	46	
DM Ward	b NMK Smith	61		PA Smith	lbw b Pigott	8	
AD Brown	c Penney b NMK Smith	8		Asif Din	c Cuffy b Boiling	19	
AJ Hollioake	lbw b Reeve	3		BC Lara	b Hollioake	70	
MA Butcher	c Munton b Reeve	4		*DA Reeve	not out	46	
ACS Pigott	not out	13		TL Penney	not out	12	
J Boiling	not out	9		NMK Smith			
JE Benjamin				GC Small			
CE Cuffy				TA Munton			
Extras	(11 lb, 2 nb, 6 w)	19		Extras	(3 lb, 4 nb)	7	
Total	(7 wickets, 55 overs)	267		Total	(6 wickets, 54.1 overs)	270	

Fall of wickets: 1-59, 2-92, 3-210, 4-232, 5-236, 6-242, 7-254
Fall of wickets: 1-28, 2-106, 3-117, 4-120, 5-158, 6-251

WARWICKSHIRE	O	M	R	W	Wd	Nb	SURREY	O	M	R	W	Wd	Nb
Small	11	2	38	0	-	-	Cuffy	11	0	66	0	-	-
Munton	11	2	36	0	-	-	Benjamin	11	0	41	1	-	-
Reeve	11	0	48	3	-	-	Butcher	3.1	0	26	0	-	-
Twose	5	0	33	1	-	-	Pigott	11	0	43	3	-	-
NMK Smith	8	0	54	3	-	-	Hollioake	7	0	49	1	-	-
PA Smith	9	0	47	0	-	-	Boiling	11	1	42	1	-	-

NORTHAMPTONSHIRE v WARWICKSHIRE

Venue: County Ground, Northampton
Toss: Warwickshire won the toss and decided to bat
Points: Northamptonshire 6; Warwickshire 24
Date: 23rd, 24th, 25th, 27th June 1994
Result: Warwickshire won by 4 wickets
Umpires: AA Jones, B Leadbeater

WARWICKSHIRE	1ST INNINGS	R	B	2ND INNINGS	R	B
AJ Moles	c Lamb b Penberthy	32		(6) b Ambrose	10	
RG Twose	c Ripley b Penberthy	35		b Curran	39	
BC Lara	c Loye b Taylor	197		(7) c Lamb b Cook	2	
DP Ostler	c Ripley b Taylor	17		(1) b Cook	87	
TL Penney	c Ripley b Ambrose	39		(3) c sub b Ambrose	43	
PA Smith	b Taylor	1		(4) st Ripley b Cook	4	
*DA Reeve	c Felton b Taylor	5		(5) not out	15	
+KJ Piper	st Ripley b Cook	11		not out	7	
NMK Smith	c Penberthy b Curran	28				
G Welch	not out	35				
TA Munton	c Lamb b Ambrose	36				
Extras	(6 b, 14 lb, 6 nb, 1 w)	27		(1 b, 11 lb, 10 nb, 1 w)	23	
Total	(all out, 115.4 overs)	463		(6 wickets, 37.3 overs)	230	

Fall of wickets: 1-71, 2-86, 3-124, 4-292, 5-303, 6-319, 7-348, 8-365, 9-395, 10-463 (115.4 ov)
Fall of wickets: 1-107 (Twose), 2-168 (Ostler), 3-190 (Penney), 4-191 (PA Smith), 5-208 (Moles), 6-213 (Lara)

NORTHAMPTONSHIRE	O	M	R	W	Wd	Nb		O	M	R	W	Wd	Nb
Ambrose	27.4	10	49	2	-	-	Ambrose	13	1	56	2	-	-
Taylor	32	4	139	4	-	-	Taylor	3	0	20	0	-	-
Curran	18	4	53	1	-	-	Curran	6	0	52	1	-	-
Penberthy	19	2	105	2	-	-	Penberthy	6	0	39	0	-	-
Cook	13	3	69	1	-	-	Cook	9.3	2	51	3	-	-
Bailey	6	0	28	0	-	-							

NORTHAMPTONSHIRE	1ST INNINGS	R	B	2ND INNINGS (F/O)	R	B
RJ Warren	lbw b Munton	10		(9) not out	94	
NA Felton	c Reeve b Munton	5		c Penney b PA Smith	23	
RJ Bailey	c Piper b Welch	54		c Piper b Munton	2	
*AJ Lamb	c Penney b Welch	81		b NMK Smith	22	
MB Loye	c Reeve b Welch	3		c Penney b Welch	113	
KM Curran	b PA Smith	23		c Penney b NMK Smith	56	
AL Penberthy	c Piper b Munton	21		c Penney b Munton	19	
+D Ripley	lbw b Munton	4		(1) c Piper b Munton	16	
CEL Ambrose	lbw b Reeve	2		(11) b Munton	0	
NGB Cook	c Piper b Munton	8		(8) c Reeve b PA Smith	1	
JP Taylor	not out	4		(10) c Reeve b Munton	26	
Extras	(9 b, 4 lb, 34 nb, 5 w)	52		(7 b, 11 lb, 32 nb, 1 w)	51	
Total	(all out, 92.1 overs)	267		(all out, 175.4 overs)	423	

Fall of wickets: 1-11, 2-32, 3-169, 4-181, 5-194, 6-240, 7-252, 8-255, 9-257, 10-267 (92.1 ov)
Fall of wickets: 1-43 (Felton), 2-43 (Ripley), 3-48 (Bailey), 4-83 (Lamb), 5-205 (Curran), 6-249 (Penberthy), 7-256 (Cook), 8-341 (Loye), 9-423 (Taylor), 10-423 (Ambrose, 175.4 ov)

WARWICKSHIRE	O	M	R	W	Wd	Nb		O	M	R	W	Wd	Nb
Munton	25.1	4	53	5	-	-	Munton	41.4	12	79	5	-	-
Reeve	20	8	29	1	-	-	Reeve	17	8	24	0	-	-
Welch	12	1	58	3	-	-	Welch	26	8	81	1	-	-
PA Smith	14	2	53	1	-	-	PA Smith	30	8	90	2	-	-
NMK Smith	12	3	33	0	-	-	NMK Smith	51	18	118	2	-	-
Twose	9	0	28	0	-	-	Twose	10	5	13	0	-	-

WARWICKSHIRE v HAMPSHIRE

Venue: Edgbaston, Birmingham
Toss: Hampshire won the toss and decided to bat
Points: Warwickshire 24; Hampshire 6

Date: 30th, 31st August, 1st, 2nd September 1994
Result: Warwickshire won by an innings and 95 runs
Umpires: KJ Lyons, R Palmer

HAMPSHIRE	1ST INNINGS	R	B	2ND INNINGS	R	B
TC Middleton	c Moles b Smith	18		c Moles b Munton	2	
VP Terry	c and b Davis	71		c Piper b Munton	36	
GW White	b Munton	30		b Smith	18	
RA Smith	c Twose b Davis	5		c Munton b Davis	34	
*MCJ Nicholas	c Small b Munton	2		not out	36	
KD James	c Smith b Welch	25		c Lara b Davis	0	
+AN Aymes	c Lara b Munton	0		c Penney b Davis	0	
SD Udal	c Moles b Davis	64		b Smith	1	
RJ Maru	c Ostler b Small	32		c Piper b Smith	6	
CA Connor	c Moles b Munton	21		lbw b Smith	14	
JNB Bovill	not out	0		lbw b Smith	4	
Extras	(8 lb, 2 nb)	10		(5 b, 7 lb)	12	
Total	(all out, 108.2 overs)	278		(all out, 50.2 overs)	163	

Fall of wickets: 1-74, 2-129, 3-133, 4-136, 5-136, 6-139, 7-208, 8-240, 9-277, 10-278 (108.2 ov)
Fall of wickets: 1-27, 2-60, 3-76, 4-120, 5-120, 6-120, 7-121, 8-129, 9-149, 10-163 (50.2 ov)

WARWICKSHIRE	O	M	R	W	Wd	Nb		O	M	R	W	Wd	Nb
Small	20.2	7	49	1	-	-	Small	6	4	2	0	-	-
Munton	23	5	44	4	-	-	Munton	14	5	34	2	-	-
Twose	5	1	19	0	-	-	Smith	19.2	4	65	5	-	-
Welch	16	6	45	1	-	-	Davis	11	1	50	3	-	-
Smith	18	5	36	1	-	-							
Davis	26	7	77	3	-	-							

WARWICKSHIRE	1ST INNINGS	R	B	2ND INNINGS	R	B
AJ Moles	c Aymes b Connor	24				
RG Twose	st Aymes b Udal	137				
BC Lara	c Smith b Udal	191				
DP Ostler	c Nicholas b Bovill	25				
TL Penney	b Bovill	20				
G Welch	c Aymes b Connor	43				
+KJ Piper	lbw b Bovill	16				
NMK Smith	not out	29				
RP Davis	c Connor b Udal	17				
GC Small	c Udal b Connor	2				
*TA Munton	b Connor	7				
Extras	(1 b, 10 lb, 14 nb)	25				
Total	(all out, 119 overs)	536				

Fall of wickets: 1-54, 2-349, 3-384, 4-403, 5-434, 6-474, 7-484, 8-519, 9-521, 10-536 (119 ov)

HAMPSHIRE	O	M	R	W	Wd	Nb		O	M	R	W	Wd	Nb
Connor	31	3	124	4	-	-							
Bovill	27	4	99	3	-	-							
James	19	1	86	0	-	-							
Udal	28	1	142	3	-	-							
Maru	14	0	74	0	-	-							

...ra rips apart
...cord books

...AD and Tobago were yesterday...
...ng over news that the cricketing...
...world record for another record...
...class cricket, with 501 not out for...
...club Warwicks.

(remaining body text illegible)

Brian's record brightens day

by MARLON MULLER Sports Writer

A BATTING record Monday turned...
...into joyful celebration yesterday...
...throughout the areas he had that...
...hosted out, Brian Lara, must adds...
...yet another world record to his...
...already bulging bag.

...in controlled to 501 for...
...Warwickshire reduced the 408 run...
...scored by Pakistan's Hanif Mohammed...

TOP 10

'Warwicks Wonder' du[e]
home for a short break

LONDON, Reuter —
RECORD-SETTING
West Indies prolific batsman Brian Lara is re-
ported to be flying home
to the Caribbean this
week for a short break.

The "Warwicks
Wonder," who last week
became the first man to
score seven centuries in
eight first-class innings,
is quoted in the Mail yesterday as saying he wants
a rest.

He has reportedly been
released by Warwickshire
to fly to Trinidad, where
he is still a pet of four days
with his mother.

The Mail On Sunday
quotes him as saying "To
be honest, I need a rest.
I'm enjoying my cricket,
but it's been tough and
I'm feeling the wear and
tear of the season."

"I'm happy to get some

good rest when we have
eight or nine days' break
after tomorrow's Benson
and Hedges Cup semi-fi-
nal against Sussex."

Lara's agent, Jonathan
Barnett, was reported as
telling the paper: "Brian's
very homesick and is tra-
velling his mother. He's 25,
but not used to being
away from home for a
long period like this.

"Brian's a one of 11 children and they are all very
close, very protective of
their mother since his father died. He's missing
her badly."

Lara has been in phe-
nomenal form this year,
scoring 2,199 from 14
First Class innings at an
average of 184.90 with
nine single centuries, a
double and a triple.

He started the year by
establishing a new West

Indies record for the highest aggregate in a regional season when he scored
715 runs at an average of
79.44 from nine innings,
including scores of 180,
169 and 206.

The free-scoring left-
hander hit the West
Indies record for the highest Test hook on for
700 runs in eight innings

including the world
record Test score of 375 in
Antigua during the recent
five Test series in the
Caribbean when he ave-
raged 99.75 per innings.

Lara continued his
rec-gal when he joined
Warwickshire for his
maiden County season.

Juventus 2-2

BRIAN LARA
profile 71 bouree

ENFORCER 200 ALARM (advertisement)

Warwicks $$$ woes...
Lara or lo[se]

Trinidad & Tobago's
Newsday $1
THURSDAY JUNE 2, 1994

LONDON: Warwickshire chief ex-
ecutive Dennis Amiss said on
Wednesday the county faced a "huge
dilemma" over whether to try and
persuade world record-breaker
Brian Lara to re-sign in two years'

Donald, who has given the county ster-
ling service over seven years, or if not,
who also holds the world record not
score of 375.

Amiss said: "Brian is a great player
and obviously we don't want him to feel
being slips through our fingers.

(remaining text illegible)

Newsday $1
TUESDAY JUNE 7, 1994

...cordbreaker Lara
...ONE 500 CLUB MEMBER

LONDON: Brian Lara rewrote the
...ket record books on Monday
...the world's highest first-class

Edgbaston, Birmingham, West Indies batsman Lara
beat the previous mark of 499 by Pakistani
Hanif Mohammed for Karachi against
Bahawalpur in the 1958-59 season.

second day of the rain-hit game on Friday, Lara
reached the landmark by cover driving occasional bowler John Morris for four.
Trinidadian left-hander Lara, who holds the
world's highest
Test score of 375, has now hit seven centuries in

said there were only two deliveries left."
The Trinidadian, who batted in total for nearly
eight hours and struck 10 sixes and 62 fours,
added: "Records are there to be broken and I'm
happy to be the one doing it.

"If the records I have set are broken I hope I am
the one doing it. It's hard to compare my test 375
...501 here... you just have to cherish both of

The National Newspaper of Trinidad &
TUESDAY, JUNE 7, 1994

ADVANTAGE
LARA 501

Brian to tell how he did it

BIRMINGHAM, (AFP)— West Indies batting sensation Brian Lara smashed the most coveted world cricket record at Edgbaston here yesterday —and then insisted he ought to be more consistent.

The remarkable 25-year-old left-hander amassed an unbeaten 501 for Warwickshire against Durham—the great individual first class innings in the history of the game.

501 breaks 36-year record

Privy Council to sit on amnesty today

• PLEASE turn to RECORD on Page 6.

• PLEASE turn to AMNESTY on Page 4

n Cup final July 9

Trinidad Guardian
the Guardian of democracy
Tuesday, June 7, 1994

	NO 7	TOTAL	NO 3
	8 1 0	5 0 1
	WICKETS 4
	AN	BOWLER
		3

Lara — 501 not out!
Batting star hits cricket's highest first class score

BIRMINGHAM, AP — WEST INDIAN batsman Brian Lara's majestic reign took cricket to new heights Monday when he became the first player to score 500 runs in a first-class innings.

Recor
after
recor

alty

CHAPTER 7

1995

THE FASTER IT COMES, THE FASTER IT GOES

'No player in the history of West Indies cricket had faced such an accumulation of adulation and pressure so suddenly and in such proportions as now threatened to overwhelm him'

MICHAEL MANLEY, *A HISTORY OF WEST INDIES CRICKET*

THE 1995 TOUR came on the back of our first series defeat in 15 years. In May of that year, Australia beat us in Jamaica to win the series 2-1. It was a crushing moment, seeing it and experiencing it. We weren't accustomed to that feeling. I was not accustomed to that feeling. We were in disarray. The whole of the Caribbean was in a frenzy.

I knew as a little boy that West Indies dominated cricket. My dream was to play for the best team in the world. That was my father's dream, that was my brothers' dream. I got into a team that knew nothing about losing. The contentious defeat to New Zealand in 1980 would not have factored in a young man's brain. We'd maybe give up the odd Test match but never a series. Our purpose was to win, and to do it in a way that showed ourselves to the world.

It couldn't last. Nothing ever does. What happened in 1995 was inevitable, but the inevitable happened faster than it should have. We hadn't paid attention to the progress of the game and how cricket was evolving. We'd lost sight of what was important to stay that step ahead and continue to be the best. We paid zero attention to that. We got complacent. We put everything down to the fact that we had talent when it came to cricket. Everybody who played the game to a good level can tell you that they were born with a certain amount of talent. Well, that's not enough. Not nearly enough.

I believe that the West Indies Cricket Board (WICB) didn't understand the importance of county cricket to our cricketers. They didn't understand how Richards, Greenidge and Haynes kept themselves sharp in those conditions. English cricket had a lot to do with the success of the West Indies team. Our first-class season back in those days was literally five weeks; you start in the first week of January and finish the second week of February. That was not enough cricket. It was inevitable that we were going to be beaten.

I know money was an issue but as a cricket team and a cricketing region we were at the height of our marketability at a time when big companies were recognising the benefits of associating with sports and successful sporting teams. Better coaches, facilities, academies should have been established for our young cricketers to play all year round under proper guidance. I remember our country's first indoor cricket facility – it was built by some private group to play fun, indoor cricket but many a times they would allow me to bring some bowlers along to have a net session outside of business hours. This was back in the late Eighties. We didn't build on those ideas.

It was always likely to be Australia who got there first. They'd been on our tail for a while and by 1995 they were ready. The disappointment was deafening. It was felt throughout the world, wherever cricket was appreciated. We all felt it. West Indians in America, West Indians in England. It will never stop hurting, being a player on the field that day. People remember that series, when the world tilted on its axis. They remember Courtney Browne dropping Steve Waugh in Jamaica and Waugh going on to score a double hundred. They remember Ambrose and Waugh squaring up to each other, and then that last Test match slipping through our fingers. They remember seeing the crown falling from our heads.

Defeat cut us deep. We didn't have the same confidence that we had before. We were never the same again.

* * *

England, too, were after us. We weren't scared, but we knew they were confident, perhaps for the first time in 20 years. That draw against us in 1991 had them fancied to win this series. Back then we'd had guys with 100 Test matches to their name. This time, Richie Richardson the captain, Carl Hooper and myself would've been the three most senior batters. Desmond Haynes, the last of the big guns from the era of dominance, was no longer part of the team. Here we had another great cricketer unceremoniously cut from a team he gave his all for and at a time when we may have needed him most. I had deep respect for the man, he'd personally guided me through the 1992 World Cup when I was forced to open the batting. He had more to give, no doubt, but unfortunately the men in charge didn't think so. Clearly all that experience in England, all that knowledge built up over the years, all those stints at Middlesex and battles on the frontline of those magnificent West Indies teams, none of that was important after all. We still had Ambrose and Walsh, but the rest of the attack was touring England for the first time. This team was pretty raw.

You've got to remember they hadn't beaten the West Indies since the Sixties. That is a lot of history. It would have been the same feeling that Allan Border had in 1992 when we arrived with an inexperienced batting line-up in Australia, and they nearly pulled it off.

Personally, I was looking forward to the challenge. I'd be going there in a different capacity. I knew I'd be playing all the Test matches. I went to England as a rookie in 1991. I went back to England as a rookie in county cricket with one world record and left with a second. There was a number on my back now. I'd be the man everybody is focusing on.

In 1991 I'd been eager to play every game to impress the selectors. Here I was more eager to manage myself across a brutally long tour. My experience of county cricket was great but the sheer amount we played left me jaded. A four-month tour of England, knowing all the games we had to play, would have to be managed properly.

I was determined to make this series something to remember. As a young man, you can score as much runs as you want in the West Indies. To be truly recognised you have to score runs away from home. For people to really rate you, you have to perform in England. You have to make scores in India, Pakistan. You have to stand tall on the bouncy tracks in Australia.

I had more confidence going into that summer than I'd had when I pitched up at Edgbaston for Warwickshire. I arrived for this one fully equipped with the knowledge. I had a reputation, but I was used to that. And now I was used to England, and their conditions. I was so ready.

I was focused. Perhaps, I don't know, a little too focused.

* * *

We started off in Arundel, the perfect place to begin a tour. It's beautiful there, with a lovely, relaxed atmosphere. The Duke of Norfolk's XI vs the West Indies. I was stood down from the game and watched from the sidelines, which was fine by me. I was happy to walk around and chat to the villagers. Those matches might not have much significance in stats but it's good to go out to a village and interact with the people. We all sat on the mound with some chairs as there's no major pavilion.

The Arundel concept, much like the Bradman Oval in Bowral, was something I tried to get my own government to set up. A few years ago, I was asked what I could advise them on, and I said I'd love to see a facility in our Santa Cruz village. There was a sporting ground in my name there from the 375, and I had this dream where international teams could start their tours of the Caribbean there.

Those types of facilities in the Caribbean start off good but end up being run down. I wanted it turned into something that the government had to maintain. The idea was endorsed by the late Patrick Manning, our prime minister between 2001 and 2010, and the job was being done – underground drainage, turf grass not the normal Savannah grass, installing a big PA system. We catered for everybody, with facilities for other sports like basketball and netball. The one thing that we were all proud of in the village was our pan-around-the-neck musicians. We won the national competition a few times and they needed a home as well. All this was being put into place right there at the recreation ground in my name.

Then in 2010 the government lost power, and the incoming government stopped it immediately. They would only see the bad in that project. It was just left to rot. I got a lot of flak from the villagers because I was front and centre with it and I saw it. I had a dream. But I was helpless to keep it running.

Something else from Arundel, man. One of the boys in the bleachers let something go; it was *bad*. Our manager Sir Wes Hall actually called a meeting and said, "I tasted it guys, I tasted it." Who was the culprit? It was Kenny, Kenny Benjamin. Looking back, Sir Wes was up against it from the very start!

Sir Wes had a tough job keeping the show on the road, but he was great. I loved him. Great character, a genius with words. He was outstanding. A true ambassador. You felt proud to be alongside him when you walked into a room with the West Indies team, and you knew he was gonna get up and talk. Sometimes you worry in those moments, but with a guy like Sir Wes Hall, you knew you'd get some laughs first of all, but then he would represent us. All of us. The whole of the West Indies. None of that factional rubbish. And he'd do it in an articulate and beautiful way.

Managerial skills? Sure, he did his work. But Sir Wes leant a little bit more to *cricket* management, you know? He was a part of team meetings, part of selection, everything. For most of my time, our manager was a former cricketer. I had Lance Gibbs when I started out, and then Clive Lloyd. Later on, it shifted to guys who had more managerial skills, the kind of men who worked in big offices, and you started to feel that something was missing. I treated everybody the same, but when you're growing up and you have a great ex-cricketer as a manager, you have deep respect for them and their position. When Sir Wes spoke, you always listened.

From Arundel, we got down to business. We played a one-dayer in Hampshire, and then a couple of first-class games to tune up for the ODI series. I hit a half-century in a rain-affected game against Worcestershire to get my eye in.

England won that ODI series. They were the better team, and in Michael Atherton they had an unlikely Man of the Series. It was a little surprising to see him doing so well in one-day cricket, because he was a staunchly Test cricketer, someone who compiled his runs very slowly. Batting back in those days of one-day cricket, played across 55 overs in England, there was a propensity to have a lot of Test cricketers building a foundation. Going at six runs an over, you would have felt like you had an unassailable score. Athers batted very well, scoring a hundred in the decider at Lord's. He even looked like he might be enjoying himself for once. But my mind is on the Test matches. Nothing else comes close.

* * *

For all our worries, we still had some formidable players. The feeling after the Australia series was that we struggled a little in the opening positions but had a lot of talent in the middle order. We had Richie and myself, we had Jimmy Adams and Carl Hooper, we had Arthurton, we had Chanderpaul, all players who love to play in the middle order.

The selectors landed on the idea of Carl opening the batting, because of his technical brilliance, but would he accept the job? They felt that his slightly lackadaisical approach to batting might be tightened up if he's facing the new ball, with three slips and a gully, but more gaps in the field. Management felt they could entrust him with the opening position, and with Greenidge, Haynes and, to a lesser extent, Phil Simmons missing, we were now playing around in that opening position with the likes of Sherwin Campbell and Stuart Williams. Carl accepted the challenge, and duly scored a couple of brilliant hundreds as an opener in the warm-up games. He looked in good form going into Leeds.

And of course, with the ball, we still had Walsh and Ambrose, plus Ian Bishop and Kenny Benjamin. That is a serious attack.

Bish was a special talent who I was thrilled to see back after two years out of the team. I knew *of* him before I got to know him properly. We played school cricket against each other, he for Belmont Secondary. Tall, raw, had pace. School pace, but he could still get it down there. Let's just say he created a lot of fear in our school.

In 1986 we played in the same youth tournament back home, but then the following year he chose to go to England to play club cricket, which meant he missed out on selection for the 1988 Youth World Cup. I was surprised, but still kind of impressed that he'd gone to England so early in his career, and it didn't hold him back. A year later he was in the West Indies team.

Not going to the same school meant we weren't immediately friends but as time drew closer to Trinidad & Tobago trials, we had more interactions with each other. He bowled me a ball once after we'd both been confirmed in the team. I got up to play it and it climbed on me, took my glove and flew over the keeper's head. When I looked down at my glove all the padding had been ripped apart and I could see the back of my hand. I said, "Listen, man, we're already both in the team together, you don't need to try to kill me..."

He was a big presence on the field, but off it Bish was very quiet. I wouldn't say he kept to himself, but he had the demeanour of someone who was not pushy, not loud. If Michael Holding was 'Whispering Death', you'd have to get a nickname very close to that for Ian Bishop. I think he has a very soft heart inside. He is a people person, where you feel very comfortable hanging around Ian Bishop. Negative thoughts about other people are not something he tolerates. A very genuine, God-fearing guy.

Speak to anyone, Ian Bishop was destined for greatness as a fast bowler. Cruel luck with injuries stopped that process. There was one really sad game when I knew it was not working out for him. We were playing a four-day game against the Leeward Islands, and Bish came back for us, and he could literally not find the pitch. Some balls were going to second slip, others wide down the legside for four. Even completing an over was difficult for him. That's when I knew he had to redo his action, and after that he was not quite the same bowler. He came back as a more conventional swing bowler, bowling with his fingers up, the ball hardly in his hand, trying to get it to swing. All of this, compared to the serious pace we'd become accustomed to.

What a career he could have had. Those stress fractures changed him as a bowler. Coming back in '95, it had been two years since he'd played Test cricket, and hardly any first-class cricket at all. So, a different kind of bowler, but still a force on that tour. You look at his dismissals that summer, he still had enough pace, swinging it big away from right-handers. That was his forte: huge outswing, pace and bounce and that outswing would be angled in at the stumps for left-handers.

He was exactly what we needed in that first Test at Leeds. Headingley's a good ground for swing and he got massive movement and was unplayable at times in England's first innings. You look at Atherton getting out for 80-odd, caught behind, and a huge inswinger to hit Graham Thorpe in front of the stumps. England were bundled out inside 60 overs, with Bish picking up five.

Typically, having looked so good, it didn't work out for Carl in our reply, poking his first ball to slip off Devon Malcolm, which brought me in to face the second ball of the innings. Immediately I go on the attack, upper-cutting Malcolm to get myself going.

He is the sort of bowler you don't try to get behind the line, you do not defend your position. Put it this way: Devon Malcolm is coming to attack you and he doesn't know where it's going, so you're gonna get some good stuff, and some stuff you can pounce on. I rush to a run-a-ball fifty in little over an hour before my adrenaline gets me out. The left-arm spinner Richard Illingworth comes on, he tosses one up outside off stump, maybe it's an arm ball, I take a swing at it, and I'm caught at first slip by Graeme Hick.

I'm disappointed. This is not how I play. I'm a player who likes to get into a rhythm first and *then* take the attack to the bowlers. Initially, I like to pick up singles to get away from the strike. I'm happy spending time at the non-striker's end. It's a general approach to my batting when I'm playing at my best, but at Leeds I take the attack to the bowlers early and look, I know why, it's because Devon Malcolm is not someone who everyone is comfortable with. I know I need to win that battle and I do, but it's not my natural way and that leads to my dismissal. I'm unable to throttle back and pace my innings. My hot-headedness gets me out. They're stunned, the English, to see the back of me, giving my wicket away.

It's my first innings against them since the 375. In nine Tests since Antigua, I've made one Test hundred – against New Zealand at Wellington – either side of a poor series in India and then the Australia series, where I hit three fifties in four Tests but again no hundred. For much of the last year I've felt shot, exhausted, and now, in this showdown with the English, I'm twitchy and overly aggressive.

On this occasion, it's just about enough. Useful runs from Campbell, Adams and Arthurton give us a good first-innings lead, from where our quicks step up to leave us chasing just 126 to win. I join Carl early in the chase and we get it done easily, the two of us finishing unbeaten, with Carl, after that first-baller in the first innings, looking totally in control.

Across both innings, no Englishman gets too many runs except for Atherton. He stood alone in that game. But for all that it augurs well for us, with our two main weapons, Ambrose and Walsh, not having to do too much, I've sensed that England can't be so poor again as they were at Leeds.

On paper it looked like a dominant win, but it happened in such a way that made you feel it wasn't solid. We didn't wear the opposition down in such a way that they played at their best, yet we still dominated them. They didn't bowl well, and as expected our bowlers were on song. But I felt that our ultra-aggressive approach with the bat was going to be difficult to maintain, and that I batted out of character with my two innings. I had close to a hundred runs in the match for once out, but it all happened too frenetically.

I liked looking at any innings I played like I was telling a story, the build-up would tend to be slow and of a survivalist nature, eventually blossoming into full-on aggression and excitement. At Headingley it wasn't that I batted with a point to prove. It was more like I was playing a role, inhabiting some persona that wasn't quite me.

* * *

My first Test match at Lord's. It's so hard to explain what that place means to a team, and to us as individuals. It's like you're plugged into history. I remember in 1991 staring up at the wooden board in the visitors' dressing room, marvelling at it. As a young man, you look up and see those names: Sobers, Greenidge, Haynes, Richards, and catch sight of a couple of great Trinidadian ones – Charlie Davis, Bernard Julien – and that becomes an immediate dream and goal. It didn't present itself in 1991. I played that ODI, and made that hundred there for Warwickshire, but this is different. This is the Lord's Test.

I feel like this is my time. The 375 has gone, the first Test match has gone. This is the present. The Lord's drama is right in front of me. A Test hundred is all I can think about.

The first thing as a batter you have to reckon with is the strange slope. Batting at the Nursery End as a left-hander, balls pitching outside leg stump will be passing the outside edge of your bat and vice versa from the Pavilion End; coming back down the slope, balls will be straightening back *into* me. I'm still playing these angles and equations out in my head when Angus Fraser, on his home ground, pitches one up from the Nursery End to trap me LBW for 6.

And again, a familiar problem: I've let the place get to me, and I've lost sight of what motivates me. I thought too much about my own score, of my own name up on that board, and it took me away from the state of mind where I play my best. I allowed my motivation to shift away from the team situation to the mystery and desire of scoring runs at Lord's. It happened also at the MCG – again, you look at my scores and they're not there. My attention and motivation shifts to something else, I get caught up in my own story instead of the story of the team, and it affects my ability to score runs.

Despite my failure, Arthurton, Richardson and Adams all make useful runs to give ourselves a small lead, but again we aren't dominating like we're used to doing, and in their second innings the English get stuck in. Robin Smith plays our quicks very well for 90, and Hick looks much more at home against us than he did in 1991. Eventually they set us 296 to win in four sessions.

Chasing that kind of total in the fourth innings, the bowling side are always the favourites, but we start well and are only one down at the close on the fourth day. We're confident going into the final day and though I know it'll be difficult to win the game, with myself and Campbell at the crease I feel like we have a good chance.

In the event, that morning session bends the game back to England. Again. I've gone off quickly, hitting 10 fours in my 54, before Darren Gough gets one to angle across me down the slope. Gough was the most difficult England bowler I faced in the Nineties. Fortunately, I didn't play much against him, and I'd be happy with that because he was short and skiddy, he swung it, he was smart with the ball and he had a lot of guts. I watched many Ashes series where he wore his heart on his sleeve, and I admired that. He was a true icon of English cricket and while he wasn't the player that Botham was, he had the same kind of persona, the same big personality. From that shorter height, with that angle, he was a Malcolm Marshall type of bowler, and with a slippery bouncer. I always found those bowlers more difficult. I felt more comfortable against taller bowlers because you knew how the ball was going to bounce. Gough used the slope bowling from the Pavilion End, took my outside edge through to Alec Stewart, and that was my Lord's Test done.

England went on to win without much fight from us. Our hopes had rested on the captain who was coming in at No.5, but when Richie bagged his second nought of the series, and then Keith Arthurton also fell for no score, that signalled the end. Where was the fight? That's what I couldn't understand. I just couldn't get my head around the way Keith approached his innings – a 40-ball nought! We needed to shift the opposition away from pushing for a win to being much more defensive. It was mind-boggling that someone could be in that frame of mind chasing a total; this was a critical moment, we were in a predicament, and we needed to stay on the front foot. He didn't take 40 balls to get off the mark only to end up playing a pivotal role, he took 40 balls to get nothing. It didn't lead to anything. The whole effort was too soft. It wasn't how we should be playing our cricket. This wasn't the real West Indies.

What a turnaround. I'm sure the English would have come away from Leeds wondering, as it happened, what had hit them. But that feeling I had, that how England played up there wasn't a true reflection of what they were capable of, was put into reality at Lord's. I guess they showed their fighting spirit. There were a lot more West Indians at Lord's than at Leeds, but it came to fruition that the English weren't a pushover. As a squad, we knew after Lord's that we were engaged in a fight.

* * *

If I put a lot of pressure on myself to score runs at Lord's, imagine how I'm feeling returning to my English home. Walking into Edgbaston, past the guys on the gate and the dressing room attendants, popping up to see Dennis Amiss, the nostalgia from being back at that venue where I had such an amazing five months, I felt so comfortable. This was my home, my people. The only difference was walking into the opposition dressing room.

I'd also signed a five-year contract for Warwickshire. I don't know how my agent did it (or why, to be honest) but he brokered a deal that included the 1995 season. He told them that if they wanted me for five years, they'd have to pay me for the 1995 season, even though I wouldn't be playing for them. Crazy, really. But the club weren't going to let me go, and I guess we had bargaining power.

It was a six-figure sum, and six-figure sums for a yearly contract weren't too common in those days.

In '94 I played on a surface that produced a lot of runs for me. It's a massive square, and I'd have played from far left to far right that season. But when we rocked up for that Test, there was something about the surface that didn't look right. It had a lot of cracks, and some were running *across* the pitch, which is not a good sight for any batter. You can accept cracks that get the ball moving from side to side. Cracks running across the pitch leading to uneven bounce, no chance.

England won the toss and chose to bat, thinking that the pitch was only likely to get worse, so at least they'd give us something tough to chase in the fourth innings. It was sound thinking, I guess. But that week at Edgbaston nothing followed the norm. We could see even before a ball was bowled that it wouldn't be a long Test match. We didn't want to be chasing too much in the fourth innings, so we needed to bowl well to make that the case.

When the first ball from Curtly Ambrose flew over Michael Atherton's head and then over the keeper Junior Murray's outstretched gloves for four byes, we knew that this was not going to be a no-result Test. The state of the pitch, with the height and ability of our bowlers, meant that England had no chance. They were blown away inside half a day's play.

The pitch settled down a little after that and we battled hard to put a few runs on the board, taking many knocks to get up to 300. Richie played a very good, responsible captain's innings, taking a lot of blows for the cause, while the way Sherwin Campbell played was just brilliant. He hung in there and battled with the bowlers and with the pitch throughout and was deservedly made Man of the Match. You'd think the eight wickets from Courtney Walsh would normally have won it, but Sherwin's 79 on that wicket was well-deserving.

There might've been more talented players, but post the halcyon days, you could always count on Sherwin Campbell to do his best. Coming from Barbados he wasn't scared of pace and stood up to the best of them. A funny guy, he's one of my favourite teammates. He had a professional side when it came to his cricket, but what a wonderful person.

Once we'd secured a good lead, it was all over. England were there to be shot at. They were helpless on that pitch. I actually felt kind of sorry for them. There was nowhere to hide.

An innings victory put us 2-1 up and in far better spirits but we didn't have much time to celebrate or really enjoy it because, amazingly, following the early finish of this game, we played a makeshift one-day game against Warwickshire on what would have been the final day of the Test. Dennis Amiss used his marketing skills to put in the request, and the boys agreed to it. It was my county, so I had a bit of sympathy and was happy to play, but just imagine that happening now. I was actually given the honour of captaining the West Indies team in the match, which was a special moment for me, the first time I'd done the job in a competitive match.

Aside from that, my return was another anti-climax. I made 21 in our only innings, out LBW to Dominic Cork. Bad pitch or not, this was nowhere near good enough. Three Tests and a highest score of 54 was not what I'd planned for a tour of England. My average wasn't bad, but I was *way* out. With half the series gone I was looking for answers.

* * *

In the gap between Tests, I'm given the honour to captain the West Indies in a first-class match for the first time, taking charge against Middlesex at Lord's. Eager to get some batting practice, and with Richie and Courtney choosing to rest, I'm thrilled to take on the role. I take these things very seriously, and although the match is a draw, it gives me a new jolt of energy going into the Old Trafford Test, as does the presence of my mother, who's travelled over with my sister, Agnes, to watch me in England for the first time.

Halfway through the summer, I'm way behind where I want to be, so I set my mind to truly get my game going. By that stage of the tour, I was finding batting in the nets a little frustrating. I wasn't getting the best out of it. The main bowlers weren't pulling their weight, and you'd often end up facing someone like a Sherwin Campbell or some young English net bowlers.

That aside, I started working extra hard on my game, batting longer in the nets, taking throwdowns from anyone who was around.

I wanted to feel the bat in my hands at all times, so that it became a part of me again. I set my mind to big things in Manchester.

On first glance, the pitch looked dry and devoid of moisture, underprepared or even doctored. England had invited a couple of spinners up to Manchester in their squad and seeing the pitch we knew why. We were happy to win the toss and bat, but our application was poor. I got to 87, thinking I'd get to my first hundred of the series only to be cut down by Cork again, and again leg-before.

We had no significant contribution from anybody else. Richie had played bravely at Edgbaston, showing great fight, and we hoped he was running into some form, but his horror tour continued in Manchester, as we were shot out for 216.

England now had the advantage. It was a dry pitch, but we didn't emphasise spin as much as them. Carl Hooper, our best offspinner, was injured in the first innings so he didn't bowl, and Arthurton and Adams only bowled a few overs between them. The pacers struggled to get their batters out. They set out to bat time and scored at a painfully slow run rate. They took the best part of two days out of the Test match, knowing that the pitch would deteriorate. It was slow going, but look, it's a Test match, they did what they had to do. After they got up to 437, the only realistic chance we had was to bat big and go past England's lead of 221. We both knew that batting last was going to be difficult.

With Carl injured, I'm prepared to open, because I'm batting at No.3 and I assume it's natural that I move up, but instead Arthurton is pushed out to open as it's felt that I'm too important a wicket to lose up top.

Facing a deficit of 200-plus is always a huge mountain to climb but there was still a lot of time in the game. After we lose Arthurton early, Sherwin and I put on a decent partnership to get us going, and we were optimistic going into day four. Overnight, I was calculating what we needed to make a match out of it. We were three wickets down, Richie and me were the not out batters, and the deficit was just 62 runs.

From there I'm looking for a way to win the match. That would've been my thought process and Richie's too. If we could bat through the first hour or so on that fourth morning and carry on from there,

England had a couple of spinners, and with my ability to play spin, we could apply some pressure.

Enter Cork again. It was the first over of the day and five minutes that changed the entire game. From a situation where England had a precarious advantage, one we could really eat into, he turned it all in their favour in a matter of three balls, as 161-3 turned into 161-6. Richie went first, unluckily bowled off the pad and inside edge as he tried to leave it, a one in a hundred dismissal, and then Junior Murray and finally Carl, both trapped in front. Cork had a hat-trick in the day's first over.

Now we're in a true battle. As the last recognised batter, you have to start thinking differently. I started that day 59 not out. I'd added a single before the hat-trick. My thoughts switched to how I could shepherd the strike and score big. Mentally, it didn't take away from the fact that I was still looking for a big score but navigating my way to one just got more complicated.

This would be one of my better innings. I cut loose. Attacking the spinners, I remember hitting the offspinner Mike Watkinson over extra cover, playing all the shots. I took control of the innings. Any chance of the match relied on me staying out in the middle. I needed to get to three figures and then keep scoring, getting us to a target our bowlers could bowl at. I put on partnerships with Bishop, Kenny Benjamin, Ambrose.

These situations where you're batting with the tail and your job is to score, it baffles me that some batters see it as an opportunity to get a little 'not out' next to their name. I just can't comprehend it. I've seen it so many times. Score quickly, get as many runs as possible. Sometimes I'd get a single off the last ball, sometimes I'd hit the last two balls for boundaries with the field in, as eight runs is as good as me being on strike the next over. It is not productive to not pick up runs off the first four balls when they're spread out wide. It was the first time all summer I fully cut loose and showed English audiences what I could do. I was motoring on 145 when I picked out Nick Knight in the deep at midwicket, who took a good catch. I was the ninth man out, tantalisingly close to a target that our bowlers could really bowl at.

We have a lot of history. That 46 all out in Trinidad was in everybody's minds. Mentally we felt like we could potentially get one over on England. I was able to put 70 or so runs on them batting with the tail, and after I left, and the last pair added a further 31, we set them 94 to win. Walsh, Ambrose, Bishop, Benjamin and the team have too much pride to throw in the towel. We wanted to make them work for it.

They started well and looked like they were going to cruise to the target. With the score on 39, Atherton, who would be the bane of our existence throughout the series, needlessly ran himself out, and with his dismissal came the mini collapse. Suddenly we were back in the game. From nowhere they were four down for 48, and even worse than that, with Robin Smith off to hospital after being struck in the face by a short ball from Bishop.

They were on the back foot. Old memories came flooding back, all those great results we'd had in the past against the run of things. We felt good and like we could pull it off, but it wasn't to be. Jack Russell and John Crawley edged England to the win. The bottom line says they won by six wickets. The reality was it was much tighter. Still, no complaints. The better team won. All the damage had been done in the first innings. If we'd gone on to win that game it would've been a great victory, but an undeserved one.

* * *

In the year since Antigua, I'd become accustomed to the good and bad things that went with it. I knew the expectations. I knew the knives were out in some places, and that I had support in others. I didn't know it then, but looking back now, it was a case of people wanting to target people who are at the top. It happens to every superstar. I'd grown numb to many of the things that might have affected me a year earlier. Yet still it was there, this temper, under the surface, slowly burning up.

With defeat coming late on the fourth day, I spend what would have been the final day with Mum and Agnes. There are no naughty-boy net sessions, and that evening Clive Lloyd invites the team to his home in Sale for a barbecue. It's a good night, the drink's flowing and we're chatting away as a team, obviously disappointed by the result but reminding each other that it's still an even series.

A conversation starts up between me, Jimmy and Shiv about the state of our team. We talk about how we aren't being productive enough in the nets, how it's hard to get a proper 15-20-minute session because the fast bowlers tend to bowl for a short while and then they're done. We've come to expect it, but it's still a problem. In present day cricket, you may have your slingers and net bowlers but back then we had none of that. A few Lancashire staffers might get sent down, but you're very dependent on your squad. That night I say to the boys that I feel like we aren't getting full productivity out of our sessions, and the same sentiments are mentioned by Jimmy and Shiv.

Looking back now, I can understand better that guys are bowling through a full Test match, so they need to rest up during practice. But at that point in time, I was just desperate for our batters to get some proper practice, and it wasn't happening. Anyway, we're at Clive's place, and I'm hearing what everyone has to say and it's in tune with what I'm saying.

The next morning we're travelling to Somerset to play another practice game, a second match of the summer against them. I have breakfast with my family ahead of a team meeting at 10am, with the bus due to leave for Taunton soon after. Richie opens the meeting. He asks if anyone wants to say anything coming off the back of a defeat. I'm a senior player, I feel like what I say should be respected for the position I'm in. I want what I'm about to say to be taken as it's meant, and not in any negative way.

I say what I feel I have to say. I believe our practice sessions should be a little more serious, and that the discipline in the nets isn't there. I say we have guys who are batting, searching for form, and can't get any quality bowling. I'm not calling names, but everyone knows what I'm saying, and I guess it's indirectly attacking somebody or some people. There was a long silence after I spoke. I saw the heads of those players I thought understood and agreed with what I was saying slowly drop.

Richie says, "Does anybody else share that view?" And everybody keeps quiet. Silence. Eventually Ian Bishop stands up. "I don't think I would have said it like Brian said it," he says, "but I agree that we could be a little more productive in practice sessions." He's always been more diplomatic than me.

Silence falls over the room again. Richie then says to me, "It looks like you're alone in sharing this opinion, and I don't know who you think you are, but I'm in charge of this team, and I don't see anything going wrong."

Then it all goes off. There's a big confrontation. He tries to put me in my place, attacking me, calling me egotistical and saying I'm in it for myself and all this rubbish, and by now I'm boiling up and I just flip, and I flip because I care about this team more than anything in the world and it destroys me when someone, anyone, even my captain, says that I don't. "If you think I have any agenda, I am *done*. I've had enough of this." In that moment I'm prepared to walk away from the whole thing for good. And I leave the room.

I go upstairs to Mum's room and tell her and Agnes to pack. She asks me why. I tell her we're finished, we're going home, and she asks, quietly, if we can pray. That stops me in my tracks but still my head's spinning. Next thing I know we're all kneeling next to the bed and she's asking the Big Man to guide her son.

I'm still hot. I pay the bill, and jump in the car before Sir Wes can get to me, and I'm gone. Down the M1 towards Heathrow, not that I have any flight to catch, but I'm heading there regardless. All the while, the president of the West Indies board, a man called Peter Short, is trying to get hold of me. He's in London for some reason – they always find a reason to spend the board's money for a nice old time whenever we play in England – and he wants to talk to me. I get a call from my agent who asks me what the hell's going on, saying that he's been contacted because I'm not picking up my phone and the president wants to speak to me. My agent tells me to come into London and meet up with him, seeing as I've got no flight to board anyway. I figure that's a fair point.

So, I go to meet the president – Sir Wes is there too, by now – and say, listen, this is the situation, I can't take it anymore. I confide in Sir Wes, not for the first time, that cricket is ruining my life. It's not the game itself but the scrutiny and pressure around me that is getting me down, breaking my spirit. The president says there is no way I can leave this tour. He says he wants me to reconsider my actions and that this mustn't get out. Sir Wes speaks beautifully about my responsibilities and resolves to offer me his support. I'm calming down now, and I say I can understand where they're coming from, and that whatever has happened is done. I say that I'm happy to go home and face the consequences of whatever they want to throw at me, but if I *do* rejoin the team then it's done, finished, no fallout, we move on. I say I'm prepared to rejoin. The president says that he can *guarantee* that it's done. The one thing he wants me to do is to apologise to my team and my captain. "For what I said? No way am I doing that!" "No Brian, for walking out of the team meeting and leaving the room without permission." OK, fair enough, I say. I have no problem with that.

After being given a couple of days to get my head together, I rejoin the team for the back end of that Taunton game. The game itself is awful. We lose the services of Jimmy for the rest of the tour after he suffers a bad one, his cheekbone shattered to pieces by a bouncer from the Somerset quick, Andre van Troost. I'm not there to see it but it's a pretty horrific accident. It leaves a nasty feeling for all of us.

Everyone's on edge. I apologise to the captain and my team for my outburst, and I assume that's it. We shake hands and as far as I'm concerned everything can go back to normal. In the days after Taunton, I feel that the players who understood where I was coming from are pretty comfortable with me. But this is the start of an uncomfortable relationship with Curtly Ambrose, and maybe a few of the other guys who feel slighted by what I said.

With these long overseas tours, there are always flashpoints. Everyone has their breaking point, but the show goes on. After Taunton, we all get on a coach and go to Gloucester, play another practice game, and then it's up to Nottingham for the next Test.

* * *

The series stands at 2-2. We've played on four result pitches, with one team dominating and then the other. The final two games will be played on two flat tracks. Forcing a win will be tough.

Trent Bridge, especially, is a batting paradise. We lose the toss and England have first use, Atherton and Hick both making hundreds as they pile on a big total. It's such a good batting track from ball one that it's difficult to dislodge them.

We play a legspinner called Rajindra Dhanraj. Now, Dhanraj and I had grown up at the same time. He came from deep south Trinidad, and at the end of every school season Dhanraj would have the most wickets and I'd have the most runs. In 1986 he was a top bowler for our youth team and again in 1987 when I became captain. Legspinners in youth cricket were a rarity in the Caribbean. The northern side – Barbados, the Windward Islands, the Leewards and Jamaica – were better players of pace than spin. Only really in Guyana and Trinidad could youth players play spin well.

Dhanraj went to the Youth World Cup with me in 1988 in Australia and started playing for Trinidad & Tobago's senior team. It took him a bit of time, as what you'd deliver as a legspinner in junior cricket – two leg-breaks and a googly and you get a wicket – wasn't gonna cut it in first-class cricket in the Caribbean. Come up against Greenidge and Haynes and it's a different story. So, it took him a bit of time to get into first-class cricket, but he was still one of the best young spinners in the Caribbean, and I always felt he had a future.

He got his opportunity at Trent Bridge but sadly he didn't produce anything. It was his first match, and he was very nervous. Against top-class players, he was easily readable; you could pick the leg-break and the googly from his fingers. But still, he had talent, he just wasn't backed. We were still fixating on our fast bowlers and thinking that the only way you can bowl spin for the West Indies is if you bat like Carl Hooper first. It took my mind back to Rangy Nanan, the great Trinidad & Tobago offspinner – now, *that* man could bowl offspin. Rangy took four wickets on debut for West Indies and never played again.

Personally, I was now feeling good. I made some runs with Campbell, we put on 140, and I could see that on this pitch, and with the attack England had, this was a help-yourself kind of day. All I was thinking about was scoring runs quickly to put us into a good position with some kind of lead.

I was flying. I batted beautifully and expressed myself. It was one of those innings that I truly enjoyed because at no point did I feel in any trouble. Cork basically surrendered and moved to a legside attack, bowling well outside leg stump and I was like, 'What's this?' and I'd still get the ball away. I got out late on the third evening, playing a little paddle shot to one of those filthy waist-high legside deliveries and feathering it to the keeper. It was one of those days when I felt like I was never gonna get out. I would take 152, but man, it could have been double that.

We gave up a small deficit on first innings with the intention of really going after them, and on the final day we kept putting pressure on them, taking regular wickets through the morning session. Throughout it I was calculating how many overs were left and by which point we'd have needed to bowl them out, to keep the game alive.

At one stage we had them at 176-8, a lead of 200, and we're thinking we're well in the game, with the run rate for a chase not much more than a run-a-ball. But then Watkinson, who's dropped early in the piece by Sherwin, and the tail put together some runs to make the game safe. When they finally declared, the target was out of reach. The game was dead.

Late on that final afternoon, England nine wickets down, a very strange thing happened. I noticed it immediately. Stuart Williams waved to the captain and said he had to go off the field. The match was drifting to nothing, and suddenly our opening batsman has had to go off the field. This was not the case when we were still in the match. Time spent off the field is time you have to wait to bat – unless there is a physical injury – so we all knew that when we came to bat, he wouldn't be opening.

Eventually England declared, and I'm told to put my pads on and go out to open. Not many players would want to bat in a dead situation like that, when all you can do is get out. I smiled but I was not happy. I was on a good run. And I couldn't understand the logic. Just the previous Test at Old Trafford I was held back from opening, my wicket deemed too valuable to lose and Keith Arthurton was thrown into the opening spot after Carl Hooper's injury. Now that idea has suddenly lost its importance and I'm thrown out there. Again I smiled but I was burning up inside.

I got out with minutes to go, got back to the dressing room and slammed my bat into my bag. I'm coming off that big argument with Richie and we've patched things up but again I've blown up, saying this is rubbish. Nobody said anything. Richie didn't retaliate.

Poor old Wes Hall tried to calm me down, but I was pissed off. I felt that Stuart Williams went off the field because he didn't want to bat. So, I vented.

I don't know if Ambrose tried to put me in my place, as he was capable of doing that. I can't remember, but he probably did. It was that kind of summer.

Things are even more strained with Richie after that. I had nothing against him as a man, but I thought he was not a strong leader. No doubt in my mind Desmond Haynes should have been the captain of the West Indies team after Viv Richards. I believe that the board favoured Richie because when you've had strong personalities like Clive Lloyd and Viv Richards, who is ultra-alpha and did his own thing in the eyes of the bosses, they didn't want to go down the road of appointing the most senior and vocal player, so they bypassed Haynes and gave it to someone they felt that would not rock the boat.

The job just wasn't Richie's forte. He put what happened that summer down to me being anxious to be the captain. I put it down to poor leadership. I don't regret much, but maybe we could have done things differently. Maybe I had too much passion for the cause. But I tell you, there was no ulterior motive.

* * *

So, to The Oval for the finale. Two apiece, with one to play. The pitches were hard and fast by late summer, much more like Caribbean surfaces. My only prior experience of The Oval would have been Warwickshire the year before. It didn't have the same amount of moisture as other English pitches, and with the majority of Tests there tending to happen at the end of a summer, it had good pace and even bounce. In short, it had runs.

England won the toss and used it well, with contributions through the innings and 90s for Hick and Jack Russell, who both had good summers. Their total of 454 made it hard for us to find a way to defeat them.

I was in prime form by then. I'd had a below average start to the series but after hundreds in the last two Tests, and on a good track at a quick scoring ground with time to bat, I was ready to go again. Devon Malcolm was back and again I wouldn't be poking around and bobbing and weaving. He was gonna bowl fast and the faster it comes, the faster it goes. That was how I looked at it. Similar to Headingley, where I went ultra-aggressive, I did the same here, but the pitch was more conducive to strokeplay so I didn't play recklessly. I played their spinner Watkinson very well, I used the cut shot a lot, I was aggressive to the fast bowlers. In all I took 206 balls for my 179, a third hundred in a row to give me 765 runs for the series.

I was thrilled, too, to see Carl get a hundred in our innings, and from No.6 in the order. He could bat in any position, but there is always something special about watching a great player walk out to bat by himself. Viv could bat anywhere, but would I ever want to see him walking out with someone else, opening the batting? No chance. Carl Hooper, I hoped would never have to open again. The whole majestic thing of him walking out in a floppy hat and no thigh pad to face guys bowling at 90mph, I needed to see that by itself.

We posted 692-8 before declaring, but there was nothing in the pitch. Atherton was solid again, and the game and series finished up as a draw.

For me, it was a strong end to a far from ideal summer. From being in strife with my batting early on, I'd found some form. My final numbers, three fifties, three tons, were pretty good. But all the while, something else was distracting me. I couldn't shake it.

We were fallible, fading. We were not the force we used to be. And that knowledge kept eating away at me.

* * *

There's always something else. Soon after I got home, I received a letter, saying I needed to appear in front of a disciplinary committee. I immediately armed myself with my lawyer, explaining what happened and that I'd been promised by the president that the matter at Manchester was done with and finished. When my lawyer explained to them that the president had said this to me, they responded that the president himself had no authority to make decisions such as those and sorry, Lara would have to answer to these claims.

Again, I'm burning up inside. What was supposed to be a dead matter and something to be swept under the rug is now public information, and I have to explain my position. I was fined or whatever the case may be. It turned out that Peter Short's words had no power, and I was disciplined and ridiculed. Inevitably, opinions were flying around in public. Everyone wanted a piece of it. I was considered fair game.

I'd been told in London that the tour would be in jeopardy, a shambles, a national humiliation, if I made that decision to leave it, and so I stayed. If I could stick by my decision, then they should have stuck by theirs.

ENGLAND v WEST INDIES, FIRST TEST

Venue: Headingley, Leeds
Toss: West Indies won the toss and decided to field
Umpires: HD Bird, S Venkataraghavan
Referee: JR Reid

Date: 8th, 9th, 10th, 11th June 1995
Result: West Indies won by 9 wickets
TV Umpire: P Willey
Scorers: JT Potter (England), AEJ Weld (West Indies)

ENGLAND	1ST INNINGS	R	B	2ND INNINGS	R	B
RA Smith	c Richardson b Benjamin	16	48	c Arthurton b Ambrose	6	10
*MA Atherton	c Murray b Bishop	81	145	c Murray b Walsh	17	42
GA Hick	c Campbell b Benjamin	18	24	c Walsh b Bishop	27	47
GP Thorpe	lbw b Bishop	20	68	c Campbell b Walsh	61	119
+AJ Stewart	c Hooper b Bishop	2	17	c Murray b Benjamin	4	11
MR Ramprakash	c Campbell b Bishop	4	10	b Walsh	18	55
PAJ DeFreitas	c Murray b Benjamin	23	27	c sub (S Chanderpaul) b Walsh	1	5
D Gough	c Ambrose b Bishop	0	1	c sub (SC Williams) b Ambrose	29	50
PJ Martin	c Murray b Ambrose	2	5	c Lara b Bishop	19	39
RK Illingworth	not out	17	28	not out	10	27
DE Malcolm	b Benjamin	0	4	b Ambrose	5	7
Extras	(1 b, 15 nb)	16		(1 b, 3 lb, 7 nb)	11	
Total	(all out, 59.5 overs)	199		(all out, 67.2 overs)	208	

Fall of wickets: 1-52 (Smith), 2-91 (Hick), 3-142 (Thorpe), 4-148 (Atherton), 5-153 (Ramprakash), 6-154 (Stewart), 7-154 (Gough), 8-157 (Martin), 9-199 (DeFreitas), 10-199 (Malcolm, 59.5 ov)
Fall of wickets: 1-6 (Smith), 2-55 (Atherton), 3-55 (Hick), 4-82 (Stewart), 5-130 (Ramprakash), 6-136 (DeFreitas), 7-152 (Thorpe), 8-193 (Gough), 9-193 (Martin), 10-208 (Malcolm, 67.2 ov)

WEST INDIES	O	M	R	W	Wd	Nb		O	M	R	W	Wd	Nb
Ambrose	17	4	56	1	-	6	Ambrose	20.2	6	44	3	-	3
Walsh	13	2	50	0	-	2	Walsh	22	4	60	4	-	3
Bishop	16	2	32	5	-	1	Bishop	19	3	81	2	-	2
Benjamin	13.5	2	60	4	-	6	Benjamin	6	1	19	1	-	-

WEST INDIES	1ST INNINGS	R	B	2ND INNINGS	R	B
CL Hooper	c Thorpe b Malcolm	0	1	not out	73	72
SL Campbell	run out	69	101	c Atherton b Martin	2	5
BC Lara	c Hick b Illingworth	53	55	not out	48	40
JC Adams	c Martin b Hick	58	109			
KLT Arthurton	c Stewart b DeFreitas	42	153			
*RB Richardson	lbw b Martin	0	7			
+JR Murray	c Illingworth b DeFreitas	20	50			
IR Bishop	run out	5	19			
CEL Ambrose	c Gough b Malcolm	15	31			
CA Walsh	c Stewart b Gough	4	13			
KCG Benjamin	not out	0	5			
Extras	(4 b, 11 lb, 1 nb)	16		(1 b, 3 lb, 2 nb)	6	
Total	(all out, 90.3 overs)	282		(1 wicket, 19 overs)	129	

Fall of wickets: 1-0 (Hooper), 2-95 (Lara), 3-141 (Campbell), 4-216 (Adams), 5-219 (Richardson), 6-243 (Murray), 7-254 (Arthurton), 8-254 (Bishop), 9-275 (Walsh), 10-282 (Ambrose, 90.3 ov)
Fall of wickets: 1-11 (Campbell)

ENGLAND	O	M	R	W	Wd	Nb		O	M	R	W	Wd	Nb
Malcolm	7.3	0	48	2	-	-	Martin	8	2	49	1	-	-
Gough	5	1	24	1	-	-	DeFreitas	4	0	33	0	-	1
DeFreitas	23	3	82	2	-	1	Illingworth	3	0	31	0	-	-
Martin	27	9	48	1	-	-	Malcolm	4	0	12	0	-	1
Illingworth	24	9	50	1	-	-							
Hick	4	0	15	1	-	-							

ENGLAND v WEST INDIES, SECOND TEST

Venue: Lord's Cricket Ground, St John's Wood
Toss: England won the toss and decided to bat
Umpires: DR Shepherd, S Venkataraghavan
Referee: JR Reid

Date: 22nd, 23rd, 24th, 25th, 26th June 1995
Result: England won by 72 runs
TV Umpire: AGT Whitehead
Scorers: DC Kendix (England), AEJ Weld (West Indies)

ENGLAND	1ST INNINGS	R	B	2ND INNINGS	R	B
*MA Atherton	b Ambrose	21	41	c Murray b Walsh	9	26
+AJ Stewart	c Arthurton b Gibson	34	85	c Murray b Walsh	36	37
GA Hick	c Lara b Bishop	13	44	b Bishop	67	92
GP Thorpe	c Lara b Ambrose	52	108	c Richardson b Ambrose	42	99
RA Smith	b Hooper	61	107	lbw b Ambrose	90	227
MR Ramprakash	c Campbell b Hooper	0	14	c sub (SC Williams) b Bishop	0	10
DG Cork	b Walsh	30	77	c Murray b Bishop	23	50
D Gough	c Campbell b Gibson	11	19	b Ambrose	20	44
PJ Martin	b Walsh	29	63	c Arthurton b Ambrose	1	6
RK Illingworth	not out	16	39	lbw b Walsh	4	10
ARC Fraser	lbw b Walsh	1	6	not out	2	4
Extras	(1 b, 10 lb, 4 nb)	15		(6 b, 27 lb, 7 nb, 2 w)	42	
Total	(all out, 99.4 overs)	283		(all out, 99.1 overs)	336	

Fall of wickets: 1-29 (Atherton), 2-70 (Hick), 3-74 (Stewart), 4-185 (Smith), 5-187 (Ramprakash), 6-191 (Thorpe), 7-205 (Gough), 8-255 (Cork), 9-281 (Martin), 10-283 (Fraser, 99.4 ov)
Fall of wickets: 1-32 (Atherton), 2-51 (Stewart), 3-150 (Hick), 4-155 (Ramprakash), 5-240 (Thorpe), 6-290 (Cork), 7-320 (Smith), 8-329 (Gough), 9-334 (Martin), 10-336 (Illingworth, 99.1 ov)

WEST INDIES	O	M	R	W	Wd	Nb		O	M	R	W	Wd	Nb
Ambrose	26	6	72	2	-	1	Ambrose	24	5	70	4	1	2
Walsh	22.4	6	50	3	-	1	Walsh	28.1	10	91	3	-	2
Gibson	20	2	81	2	-	1	Gibson	14	1	51	0	-	-
Bishop	17	4	33	1	-	-	Bishop	22	5	56	3	1	3
Hooper	14	3	36	2	-	-	Hooper	9	1	31	0	-	-
							Adams	2	0	4	0	-	-

WEST INDIES	1ST INNINGS	R	B	2ND INNINGS	R	B
SL Campbell	c Stewart b Gough	5	4	(2) c Stewart b Cork	93	222
CL Hooper	b Martin	40	107	(1) c Martin b Gough	14	18
BC Lara	lbw b Fraser	6	31	c Stewart b Gough	54	62
JC Adams	lbw b Fraser	54	165	c Hick b Cork	13	21
*RB Richardson	c Stewart b Fraser	49	71	lbw b Cork	0	9
KLT Arthurton	c Gough b Fraser	75	169	c sub (PN Weekes) b Cork	0	40
+JR Murray	c and b Martin	16	22	c sub (PN Weekes) b Gough	9	26
OD Gibson	lbw b Gough	29	40	lbw b Cork	14	22
IR Bishop	b Cork	8	15	not out	10	19
CEL Ambrose	c Ramprakash b Fraser	12	38	c Illingworth b Cork	11	30
CA Walsh	not out	11	10	c Stewart b Cork	0	2
Extras	(8 b, 11 lb)	19		(5 lb)	5	
Total	(all out, 112 overs)	324		(all out, 78.3 overs)	223	

Fall of wickets: 1-6 (Campbell), 2-23 (Lara), 3-88 (Hooper), 4-166 (Richardson), 5-169 (Adams), 6-197 (Murray), 7-246 (Gibson), 8-272 (Bishop), 9-305 (Ambrose), 10-324 (Arthurton, 112 ov)
Fall of wickets: 1-15 (Hooper), 2-99 (Lara), 3-124 (Adams), 4-130 (Richardson), 5-138 (Arthurton), 6-177 (Murray), 7-198 (Gibson), 8-201 (Campbell), 9-223 (Ambrose), 10-223 (Walsh, 78.3 ov)

ENGLAND	O	M	R	W	Wd	Nb		O	M	R	W	Wd	Nb
Gough	27	2	84	2	-	-	Fraser	25	9	57	0	-	-
Fraser	33	13	66	5	-	-	Gough	20	0	79	3	-	-
Cork	22	4	72	1	-	-	Illingworth	7	4	9	0	-	-
Martin	23	5	65	2	-	-	Martin	7	0	30	0	-	-
Illingworth	7	2	18	0	-	-	Cork	19.3	5	43	7	-	-

ENGLAND v WEST INDIES, THIRD TEST

Venue: Edgbaston, Birmingham
Toss: England won the toss and decided to bat
Umpires: MJ Kitchen, ID Robinson
Referee: JR Reid

Date: 6th, 7th, 8th July 1995
Result: West Indies won by an innings and 64 runs
TV Umpire: JW Holder

ENGLAND	1ST INNINGS	R	B	2ND INNINGS	R	B
*MA Atherton	c Murray b Ambrose	0	3	b Walsh	4	21
+AJ Stewart	lbw b Benjamin	37	70	(11) absent hurt		
GA Hick	c Richardson b Walsh	3	5	c Hooper b Bishop	3	2
GP Thorpe	c Campbell b Ambrose	30	33	c Murray b Bishop	0	6
RA Smith	c Arthurton b Bishop	46	92	(2) b Bishop	41	84
JER Gallian	b Benjamin	7	20	(7) c Murray b Walsh	0	2
DG Cork	lbw b Walsh	4	18	(5) c sub (SC Williams) b Walsh	16	33
D Gough	c Arthurton b Bishop	1	17	c Campbell b Walsh	12	30
PJ Martin	c sub (SC Williams) b Walsh	1	12	(6) lbw b Walsh	0	5
RK Illingworth	b Bishop	0	7	(9) c Hooper b Bishop	0	8
ARC Fraser	not out	0	2	(10) not out	1	1
Extras	(4 lb, 10 nb, 4 w)	18		(12 nb)	12	
Total	(all out, 44.2 overs)	147		(all out, 30 overs)	89	

Fall of wickets: 1-4 (Atherton), 2-9 (Hick), 3-53 (Thorpe), 4-84 (Stewart), 5-100 (Gallian), 6-109 (Cork), 7-124 (Gough), 8-141 (Smith), 9-147 (Martin), 10-147 (Illingworth), 44.2 ov)
Fall of wickets: 1-17 (Atherton), 2-20 (Hick), 3-26 (Thorpe), 4-61 (Cork), 5-62 (Martin), 6-63 (Gallian), 7-88 (Gough), 8-88 (Smith), 9-89 (Illingworth), 30 ov)

WEST INDIES	O	M	R	W	Wd	Nb		O	M	R	W	Wd	Nb
Ambrose	7.5	1	26	2	-	2	Walsh	15	2	45	5	-	5
Walsh	17.1	4	54	3	-	1	Bishop	13	3	29	4	-	5
Bishop	6.2	0	18	3	-	7	Benjamin	2	0	15	0	-	2
Benjamin	13	4	45	2	-	3							

WEST INDIES	1ST INNINGS	R	B	2ND INNINGS	R	B
CL Hooper	c Stewart b Cork	40	71			
SL Campbell	b Cork	79	140			
BC Lara	lbw b Cork	21	42			
JC Adams	lbw b Cork	10	25			
*RB Richardson	b Fraser	69	174			
KLT Arthurton	lbw b Fraser	8	21			
+JR Murray	c Stewart b Martin	26	24			
IR Bishop	c Martin b Illingworth	16	59			
KCG Benjamin	run out	11	34			
CA Walsh	run out	0	0			
CEL Ambrose	not out	4	6			
Extras	(5 b, 5 lb, 6 nb)	16				
Total	(all out, 98 overs)	300				

Fall of wickets: 1-73 (Hooper), 2-105 (Lara), 3-141 (Adams), 4-156 (Campbell), 5-171 (Arthurton), 6-198 (Murray), 7-260 (Bishop), 8-292 (Benjamin), 9-292 (Walsh), 10-300 (Richardson, 98 ov)

ENGLAND	O	M	R	W	Wd	Nb		O	M	R	W	Wd	Nb
Fraser	31	7	93	2	-	2							
Gough	18	3	68	0	-	3							
Cork	22	5	69	4	-	3							
Martin	19	5	49	1	-	-							
Illingworth	8	4	11	1	-	-							

MIDDLESEX v WEST INDIANS

Venue: Lord's Cricket Ground, St John's Wood
Toss: West Indians won the toss and decided to bat
Umpires: A Clarkson, KJ Lyons

Date: 22nd, 23rd, 24th July 1995
Result: Match drawn

WEST INDIANS	1ST INNINGS	R	B	2ND INNINGS	R	B
CL Hooper	lbw b Shine	24		c Weekes b Feltham	53	
SL Campbell	b Tufnell	102				
S Chanderpaul	b Tufnell	71		lbw b Feltham	4	
*BC Lara	b Tufnell	62		st Brown b Weekes	17	
KLT Arthurton	c Radford b Tufnell	83		not out	55	
JC Adams	c Weekes b Nash	27		lbw b Feltham	8	
+JR Murray	lbw b Shine	1		(2) c Feltham b Shine	21	
OD Gibson	c Carr b Tufnell	33		c Weekes b Feltham	3	
CEL Ambrose	c Nash b Tufnell	11		c Carr b Feltham	2	
KCG Benjamin	not out	26		b Ramprakash	44	
R Dhanraj	run out	6		(7) b Feltham	0	
Extras	(10 lb)	10		(6 lb)	6	
Total	(all out, 131.5 overs)	456		(9 wickets, dec, 54.2 overs)	213	

Fall of wickets: 1-68, 2-161, 3-261, 4-268, 5-338, 6-339, 7-390, 8-410, 9-441, 10-456 (131.5 ov)
Fall of wickets: 1-60, 2-76, 3-83, 4-113, 5-132, 6-132, 7-142, 8-148, 9-213 (54.2 ov)

MIDDLESEX	O	M	R	W	Wd	Nb		O	M	R	W	Wd	Nb
Nash	24.5	4	93	1	-	-	Johnson	8	2	33	0	-	-
Johnson	24	3	84	0	-	-	Shine	6	0	42	1	-	-
Shine	14	1	65	2	-	-	Feltham	19	5	41	6	-	-
Feltham	5	1	22	0	-	-	Weekes	19	2	74	1	-	-
Tufnell	40	8	111	6	-	-	Ramprakash	2.2	0	17	1	-	-
Weekes	24	4	71	0	-	-							

MIDDLESEX	1ST INNINGS	R	B	2ND INNINGS	R	B
PN Weekes	b Ambrose	0		not out	23	
TA Radford	lbw b Gibson	12		not out	26	
MR Ramprakash	c Ambrose b Benjamin	10				
JC Harrison	c Murray b Gibson	5				
*JD Carr	st Murray b Dhanraj	115				
+KR Brown	c Chanderpaul b Dhanraj	6				
DJ Nash	c Adams b Hooper	29				
MA Feltham	lbw b Gibson	10				
RL Johnson	c Ambrose b Dhanraj	29				
KJ Shine	c Hooper b Dhanraj	6				
PCR Tufnell	not out	0				
Extras	(1 b, 2 lb, 12 nb)	15		(1 lb, 2 nb)	3	
Total	(all out, 73.5 overs)	237		(no wicket, 18 overs)	52	

Fall of wickets: 1-0, 2-15, 3-27, 4-59, 5-78, 6-135, 7-146, 8-215, 9-229, 10-237 (73.5 ov)

WEST INDIANS	O	M	R	W	Wd	Nb		O	M	R	W	Wd	Nb
Ambrose	10	6	20	1	-	-	Ambrose	4	3	1	0	-	-
Benjamin	16	8	31	1	-	-	Benjamin	4	2	11	0	-	-
Gibson	14	5	45	3	-	-	Dhanraj	5	1	16	0	-	-
Hooper	15	0	60	1	-	-	Chanderpaul	4	1	18	0	-	-
Dhanraj	17.5	1	66	4	-	-	Lara	1	0	5	0	-	-
Adams	1	0	12	0	-	-							

ENGLAND v WEST INDIES, FOURTH TEST

Venue: Old Trafford, Manchester
Toss: West Indies won the toss and decided to bat
Umpires: HD Bird, CJ Mitchley
Referee: JR Reid

Date: 27th, 28th, 29th, 30th July 1995
Result: England won by 6 wickets
TV Umpire: JC Balderstone

WEST INDIES	1ST INNINGS	R	B	2ND INNINGS	R	B
CL Hooper	c Crawley b Cork	16	50	(7) lbw b Cork	0	1
SL Campbell	c Russell b Fraser	10	23	(1) c Russell b Watkinson	44	102
BC Lara	lbw b Cork	87	118	c Knight b Fraser	145	226
JC Adams	c Knight b Fraser	24	39	c and b Watkinson	1	3
*RB Richardson	c Thorpe b Fraser	2	7	b Cork	22	57
KLT Arthurton	c Cork b Watkinson	17	48	(2) run out (Fraser->Russell)	17	74
+JR Murray	c Embury b Watkinson	13	21	(6) lbw b Cork	0	1
IR Bishop	c Russell b Cork	9	18	c Crawley b Watkinson	9	23
CEL Ambrose	not out	7	18	(10) not out	23	43
KCG Benjamin	b Cork	14	11	(9) c Knight b Fraser	15	22
CA Walsh	c Knight b Fraser	11	14	b Cork	16	18
Extras	(1 lb, 5 nb)	6		(5 b, 9 lb, 8 nb)	22	
Total	(all out, 60.2 overs)	216		(all out, 91.5 overs)	314	

Fall of wickets: 1-21 (Campbell), 2-35 (Hooper), 3-86 (Adams), 4-94 (Richardson), 5-150 (Arthurton), 6-166 (Lara), 7-184 (Murray), 8-185 (Bishop), 9-205 (Benjamin), 10-216 (Walsh, 60.2 ov)
Fall of wickets: 1-36 (Arthurton), 2-93 (Campbell), 3-97 (Adams), 4-161 (Richardson), 5-161 (Murray), 6-161 (Hooper), 7-191 (Bishop), 8-234 (Benjamin), 9-283 (Lara), 10-314 (Walsh, 91.5 ov)

ENGLAND	O	M	R	W	Wd	Nb		O	M	R	W	Wd	Nb
Fraser	16.2	5	45	4	-	2	Fraser	19	5	53	2	-	-
Cork	20	1	86	4	-	3	Cork	23.5	2	111	4	-	5
White	5	0	23	0	-	-	Embury	20	5	49	0	-	3
Embury	10	2	33	0	-	-	White	6	0	23	0	-	1
Watkinson	9	2	28	2	-	-	Watkinson	23	4	64	3	-	-

ENGLAND	1ST INNINGS	R	B	2ND INNINGS	R	B
NV Knight	b Walsh	17	45	c sub (S Chanderpaul) b Bishop	13	64
*MA Atherton	c Murray b Ambrose	47	130	run out (Benjamin->Murray)	22	40
JP Crawley	b Walsh	8	26	not out	15	62
GP Thorpe	c Murray b Bishop	94	147	c Ambrose b Benjamin	0	6
RA Smith	c sub (SC Williams) b Ambrose	44	106	retired hurt	1	8
C White	c Murray b Benjamin	23	52	c sub (S Chanderpaul) b Benjamin	1	5
+RC Russell	run out (Campbell->Arthurton)	35	86	not out	31	39
M Watkinson	c sub (SC Williams) b Walsh	37	107			
DG Cork	not out	56	91			
JE Embury	b Bishop	8	43			
ARC Fraser	c Adams b Walsh	4	23			
Extras	(18 b, 11 lb, 34 nb, 1 w)	64		(2 lb, 8 nb, 1 w)	11	
Total	(all out, 136 overs)	437		(4 wickets, 35.5 overs)	94	

Fall of wickets: 1-45 (Knight), 2-65 (Crawley), 3-122 (Atherton), 4-226 (Smith), 5-264 (Thorpe), 6-293 (White), 7-337 (Russell), 8-378 (Watkinson), 9-418 (Embury), 10-437 (Fraser, 136 ov)
Fall of wickets: 1-39 (Atherton), 2-41 (Knight), 3-45 (Thorpe), 4-48 (White)

WEST INDIES	O	M	R	W	Wd	Nb		O	M	R	W	Wd	Nb
Ambrose	24	4	91	2	-	13	Ambrose	5	1	16	0	-	-
Walsh	38	5	92	4	-	7	Walsh	5	0	17	0	-	2
Bishop	29	3	103	2	-	11	Bishop	12	6	18	1	1	-
Benjamin	28	4	83	1	-	5	Benjamin	9	1	29	2	-	7
Adams	8	1	21	0	-	2	Arthurton	2.5	1	5	0	-	-
Arthurton	9	2	18	0	-	2	Adams	2	0	7	0	-	-

SOMERSET v WEST INDIANS

Venue: County Ground, Taunton
Toss: West Indians won the toss and decided to bat
Umpires: VA Holder, AGT Whitehead

Date: 2nd, 3rd, 4th August 1995
Result: West Indians won by 155 runs

WEST INDIANS	1ST INNINGS	R	B	2ND INNINGS	R	B
SC Williams	c and b Kerr	0		c Ecclestone b van Troost	119	
JR Murray	c Turner b Ecclestone	19		lbw b Ecclestone	6	
*RB Richardson	c Turner b Kerr	33		b van Troost	88	
JC Adams	c Turner b van Troost	7		retired hurt	0	
KLT Arthurton	c Batty b Kerr	0		c Turner b van Troost	1	
S Chanderpaul	lbw b Ecclestone	100		c Turner b van Troost	26	
+CO Browne	c Turner b Kerr	19		c Bowler b Trump	1	
VC Drakes	c Turner b Kerr	0		c Holloway b van Troost	4	
OD Gibson	c Turner b van Troost	17		not out	101	
IR Bishop	b Trump	5		c Parsons b Trump	25	
R Dhanraj	not out	13		c Lathwell b Batty	1	
Extras	(4 b, 2 lb, 6 nb, 5 w)	17		(5 lb, 6 nb, 3 w)	14	
Total	(all out, 63.4 overs)	230		(all out, 79 overs)	386	

Fall of wickets: 1-7, 2-43, 3-58, 4-60, 5-71, 6-138, 7-138, 8-184, 9-211, 10-230 (63.4 ov)
Fall of wickets: 1-12, 2-218, 3-219, 4-224, 5-231, 6-237, 7-292, 8-347, 9-386 (79 ov)

SOMERSET	O	M	R	W	Wd	Nb		O	M	R	W	Wd	Nb
van Troost	19	5	53	2	-	-	van Troost	19	1	120	5	-	-
Kerr	14	1	82	5	-	-	Kerr	6	0	45	0	-	-
Ecclestone	14	4	31	2	-	-	Ecclestone	3	0	17	1	-	-
Parsons	3	2	8	0	-	-	Trump	34	10	95	2	-	-
Trump	11.4	3	38	1	-	-	Batty	17	2	104	1	-	-
Hayhurst	2	1	12	0	-	-							

SOMERSET	1ST INNINGS	R	B	2ND INNINGS	R	B
MN Lathwell	b Drakes	23		c Browne b Gibson	17	
PD Bowler	c Bishop b Gibson	19		c Murray b Gibson	1	
*AN Hayhurst	c Adams b Gibson	10		c Browne b Gibson	5	
PCL Holloway	c Bishop b Drakes	5		not out	16	
KA Parsons	c Browne b Dhanraj	1		c Williams b Gibson	6	
SC Ecclestone	c Williams b Dhanraj	37		run out	12	
+RJ Turner	c Browne b Bishop	72		b Bishop	0	
JID Kerr	b Arthurton	80		c sub (BC Lara) b Drakes	2	
JD Batty	not out	45		c Drakes b Dhanraj	13	
HRJ Trump	lbw b Arthurton	4		c Chanderpaul b Dhanraj	5	
AP van Troost	c Bishop b Drakes	9		st Browne b Dhanraj	0	
Extras	(1 b, 10 lb, 57 nb, 1 w)	69		(2 b, 4 lb, 4 nb)	10	
Total	(all out, 76.2 overs)	374		(all out, 33 overs)	87	

Fall of wickets: 1-48, 2-58, 3-65, 4-81, 5-83, 6-149, 7-285, 8-347, 9-363, 10-374 (76.2 ov)
Fall of wickets: 1-12, 2-23, 3-24, 4-33, 5-45, 6-45, 7-58, 8-81, 9-87, 10-87 (33 ov)

WEST INDIANS	O	M	R	W	Wd	Nb		O	M	R	W	Wd	Nb
Bishop	16	2	86	1	-	-	Bishop	10	2	24	1	-	-
Gibson	19	0	100	2	-	-	Gibson	11	2	32	4	-	-
Drakes	16.2	0	75	3	-	-	Drakes	9	3	23	1	-	-
Dhanraj	20	3	83	2	-	-	Dhanraj	3	1	2	3	-	-
Arthurton	5	0	19	2	-	-							

ENGLAND v WEST INDIES, FIFTH TEST

Venue: Trent Bridge, Nottingham
Toss: England won the toss and decided to bat
Umpires: CJ Mitchley, NT Plews
Referee: JR Reid

Date: 10th, 11th, 12th, 13th, 14th August 1995
Result: Match drawn
TV Umpire: G Sharp
Scorers: GA Stringfellow (England), AEJ Weld (West Indies)

ENGLAND	1ST INNINGS	R	B	2ND INNINGS	R	B
NV Knight	lbw b Benjamin	57	191	(7) c Browne b Benjamin	2	13
*MA Atherton	run out	113	247	(1) c Browne b Bishop	43	152
JP Crawley	c Williams b Benjamin	14	32	(2) b Walsh	11	18
GP Thorpe	c Browne b Bishop	19	37	c Browne b Walsh	76	183
RK Illingworth	retired hurt	8	28	(11) not out	14	52
GA Hick	not out	118	213	(3) b Benjamin	7	25
C White	c Browne b Bishop	1	13	(5) c Campbell b Bishop	1	17
+RC Russell	c Browne b Bishop	35	76	(6) c Browne b Benjamin	7	16
M Watkinson	lbw b Benjamin	24	40	(8) not out	82	137
DG Cork	c Browne b Benjamin	31	48	(9) c Browne b Benjamin	4	6
ARC Fraser	b Benjamin	0	1	(10) c Arthurton b Benjamin	4	22
Extras	(4 b, 8 lb, 8 nb)	20		(4 lb, 14 nb)	18	
Total	(all out, 152.4 overs)	440		(9 wickets, dec, 104 overs)	269	

Fall of wickets: 1-148 (Knight), 2-179 (Crawley), 3-206 (Atherton), 4-211 (Thorpe), 5-239 (White), 6-323 (Russell), 7-380 (Watkinson), 8-440 (Cork), 9-440 (Fraser, 152.4 ov)
Fall of wickets: 1-17 (Crawley), 2-36 (Hick), 3-117 (Atherton), 4-125 (White), 5-139 (Russell), 6-148 (Knight), 7-171 (Thorpe), 8-176 (Cork), 9-189 (Fraser)

WEST INDIES	O	M	R	W	Wd	Nb		O	M	R	W	Wd	Nb
Walsh	39	5	93	0	-	4	Walsh	30	6	70	2	-	9
Bishop	30.1	6	62	3	-	6	Bishop	21	8	50	2	-	4
Benjamin	34.3	7	105	5	-	-	Benjamin	25	8	69	5	-	4
Dhanraj	40	7	137	0	-	-	Dhanraj	15	1	54	0	-	-
Arthurton	9	0	31	0	-	-	Arthurton	13	3	22	0	-	-

WEST INDIES	1ST INNINGS	R	B	2ND INNINGS	R	B
SC Williams	c Atherton b Illingworth	62	143	(5) did not bat		
SL Campbell	c Crawley b Watkinson	47	225	c Russell b Cork	16	22
BC Lara	c Russell b Cork	152	182	(1) c Russell b Fraser	20	30
*RB Richardson	c Hick b Illingworth	40	45			
KLT Arthurton	b Illingworth	13	28			
R Dhanraj	c Knight b Cork	3	46			
S Chanderpaul	c Crawley b Watkinson	18	101	(3) not out	5	8
+CO Browne	st Russell b Illingworth	34	67	(4) not out	1	6
IR Bishop	c Hick b Watkinson	4	11			
KCG Benjamin	not out	14	21			
CA Walsh	b Fraser	19	24			
Extras	(2 b, 7 lb, 2 nb)	11			0	
Total	(all out, 148.3 overs)	417		(2 wickets, 11 overs)	42	

Fall of wickets: 1-77 (Williams), 2-217 (Campbell), 3-273 (Richardson), 4-319 (Arthurton), 5-323 (Lara), 6-338 (Dhanraj), 7-366 (Chanderpaul), 8-374 (Bishop), 9-384 (Browne), 10-417 (Walsh, 148.3 ov)
Fall of wickets: 1-36 (Lara), 2-36 (Campbell)

ENGLAND	O	M	R	W	Wd	Nb		O	M	R	W	Wd	Nb
Fraser	17.3	6	77	1	-	1	Fraser	6	1	17	1	-	-
Cork	36	9	110	2	-	1	Cork	5	1	25	1	-	-
Watkinson	35	12	84	3	-	-							
Illingworth	51	21	96	4	-	-							
Hick	4	1	11	0	-	-							
White	5	0	30	0	-	-							

ENGLAND v WEST INDIES, SIXTH TEST

Venue: The Oval, Kennington
Toss: England won the toss and decided to bat
Umpires: VK Ramaswamy, DR Shepherd
Referee: JR Reid

Date: 24th, 25th, 26th, 27th, 28th August 1995
Result: Match drawn
TV Umpire: JH Hampshire
Scorers: KR Booth, AEJ Weld

ENGLAND	1ST INNINGS	R	B	2ND INNINGS	R	B
*MA Atherton	c Williams b Benjamin	36	85	(2) c Browne b Bishop	95	269
JER Gallian	c Hooper b Ambrose	0	8	(1) c Williams b Ambrose	25	97
JP Crawley	c Richardson b Hooper	50	159	c Browne b Ambrose	2	11
GP Thorpe	c Browne b Ambrose	74	177	c Williams b Walsh	38	67
GA Hick	c Williams b Benjamin	96	164	not out	51	114
AP Wells	c Campbell b Ambrose	0	1	not out	3	39
+RC Russell	b Ambrose	91	221			
M Watkinson	c Browne b Walsh	13	55			
DG Cork	b Ambrose	33	63			
ARC Fraser	not out	10	35			
DE Malcolm	c Lara b Benjamin	10	7			
Extras	(15 b, 11 lb, 15 nb)	41		(4 lb, 5 nb)	9	
Total	(all out, 159 overs)	454		(4 wickets, 98 overs)	223	

Fall of wickets: 1-9 (Gallian), 2-60 (Atherton), 3-149 (Crawley), 4-192 (Thorpe), 5-192 (Wells), 6-336 (Hick), 7-372 (Watkinson), 8-419 (Russell), 9-443 (Cork), 10-454 (Malcolm, 159 ov)
Fall of wickets: 1-60 (Gallian), 2-64 (Crawley), 3-132 (Thorpe), 4-212 (Atherton)

WEST INDIES	O	M	R	W	Wd	Nb		O	M	R	W	Wd	Nb
Ambrose	42	10	96	5	-	4	Ambrose	19	8	35	2	-	-
Walsh	32	6	84	1	-	5	Walsh	28	7	80	1	-	6
Benjamin	27	6	81	3	-	4	Bishop	22	4	56	1	-	2
Bishop	35	5	111	0	-	8	Hooper	22	11	26	0	-	-
Hooper	23	7	56	1	-	-	Chanderpaul	6	0	22	0	-	-
							Lara	1	1	0	0	-	-

WEST INDIES	1ST INNINGS	R	B	2ND INNINGS	R	B
SC Williams	c Russell b Malcolm	30	40			
SL Campbell	c Russell b Fraser	89	152			
KCG Benjamin	c Atherton b Cork	20	44			
BC Lara	c Fraser b Malcolm	179	206			
*RB Richardson	c Hick b Cork	93	156			
CL Hooper	c Russell b Malcolm	127	180			
S Chanderpaul	c Gallian b Cork	80	146			
+CO Browne	not out	27	32			
IR Bishop	run out	10	18			
CEL Ambrose	not out	5	8			
CA Walsh						
Extras	(5 b, 20 lb, 2 nb, 5 w)	32				
Total	(8 wickets, dec, 163 overs)	692				

Fall of wickets: 1-40 (Williams), 2-94 (Benjamin), 3-202 (Campbell), 4-390 (Lara), 5-435 (Richardson), 6-631 (Chanderpaul), 7-653 (Hooper), 8-686 (Bishop)

ENGLAND	O	M	R	W	Wd	Nb		O	M	R	W	Wd	Nb
Malcolm	39	7	160	3	1	-							
Fraser	40	6	155	1	-	-							
Watkinson	26	3	113	0	-	-							
Cork	36	3	145	3	4	2							
Gallian	12	1	56	0	-	1							
Hick	10	3	38	0	-	-							

CHAPTER 8

1998

THE OUTSTRETCHED HAND

'Trinidad Intercolonial cricketers have a slogan about local umpiring. "They do not do such things in England and in Barbados…" It is a tradition that Trinidad umpires are severe with Trinidad players'

CLR JAMES, *BEYOND A BOUNDARY*

I'D JUST TURNED 18 when I first came up against Malcolm Marshall. It was early 1988. Life was happening fast. I'd just been named captain of the West Indies Under 19 team and was due to fly to Australia for the Youth World Cup.

Just before we left for Australia, I was selected to play for Trinidad & Tobago in the Red Stripe Cup, the Caribbean's first-class competition, for the first time. It was a massive moment, the next step on my path to fulfilling the dream with which I had been fixated since I was a little boy. I was able to play three games before we left and the second one, and the only one at the Queen's Park Oval, came against Barbados.

They were a mighty team back then, undoubtedly the toughest team in our first-class competition. This was *Barbados*. The island that's produced more great cricketers per capita than any other place in the world. The names form much of the folklore of Caribbean cricket. The three Ws – Sir Everton Weekes, Sir Frank Worrell, Sir Clyde Walcott. Sir Garfield Sobers. Seymour Nurse. Sir Wes Hall, Charlie Griffith. And they all came long before my time. Gordon Greenidge, Desmond Haynes, Joel Garner, Carlisle Best and many others, they were the names I was most familiar with. These were the guys I watched and revered as a boy.

There was one name that was extra special to me. Malcolm Denzil Marshall was to my mind the greatest fast bowler the West Indies ever produced. He was quick, seriously quick on occasion, but he never relied solely on pace to intimidate batters out. He was clever, a master tactician, almost always bowling within himself to think batters out. He could swing it, seam it, he had an incredible slower ball that seemed to swerve into the right-hander, and they ducked for cover when he unleashed his devastating bouncer. Man, he was a genius. A total genius with the red ball in his hand.

A couple of days before the first-class game, we played a one-dayer against them. I'd never played a senior game of cricket for my home country at the Queen's Park Oval before. My debut the week before against the Leeward Islands had taken place at Guaracara Park in south Trinidad, so this felt like the big one. My home ground. My own people. Dad watching, Malcolm playing.

I wouldn't be telling the truth if I said I wasn't scared walking out to bat. Malcolm had just taken a wicket, so my very first ball would be bowled by him. Walking out to bat and passing Joel Garner talking to Malcolm, I felt like a midget in his presence. Garner? The man is something like seven-foot tall. I take guard. Helmet, but no grille, just those Perspex side pieces. I look up. He's at the top of his mark. Malcolm Marshall.

He turns smoothly and starts galloping in and all I can say to myself is to keep looking at the ball, keep looking at the ball. Down it comes and I barely have time to fend it off my body as the ball flies down the legside and their keeper Thelston Payne dives to his right to grab it low to the ground.

I'm gone.

I have to make my way back to the pavilion, dejected and embarrassed. I must have felt like this before somewhere, maybe at school or in the streets. But definitely not in front of a packed Queen's Park Oval.

A large crowd had come to see me against these two great fast bowlers and I've failed them. So many of my fellow students at Fatima College, and our teachers, had been there to watch me that day, which made me scared of going to school the next day. I may have had a four-day game that started on the Friday of that week, but I still had to be in school. This was Fatima, after all.

I was the laughing stock of the school the next day. As if they wouldn't have dirtied their underwear facing one of the most feared fast bowlers in the world! That's just how it had to be. I took the chastising. I knew they were secretly in awe and proud that their schoolmate was living his dream, and a dream that a lot of them shared.

* * *

The four-day game came round fast. And truthfully? I was itching to get back out there, to face the fear. The longer version of the game has always been more important to me. I looked forward to it much more, especially back then. To play for the West Indies, to even be *considered*, that was the only arena that truly mattered.

I walked out to bat not thinking about my last score, only about keeping those two legends out. I just wanted to bat. To bat and bat and bat. I wanted to feel the atmosphere of playing against such a great team. I wanted to get *inside* that atmosphere, so I could truly start to touch it. Yes, I was still shaking, my palms still sweating as they had been earlier in the week, but I wanted it.

I batted better than I felt I was capable of. Everything they threw at me, I had an answer for. I was still diminutive, still lacking the big muscles, but I kept a straight bat, deflecting the ball here and there and picking up my ones and twos. I batted long, for the best part of six hours. My concentration was strong. I never allowed the moment to get the better of me.

I was on 92 when I was given out LBW to Joel Garner. I couldn't believe it. The ball hit me on the highest tip of my pad and with Joel's height surely it was going over the stumps. And to be given out by a Trinidad umpire as well! The crowd were as much in shock as I was, and we felt the disappointment together. I wanted to bat forever. *They* wanted me to bat forever.

Just as I'd done a few days earlier, I made the slow, sad stroll back to the pavilion. The dejection was similar. In those first terrible moments after a dismissal it's always the same, but I was soon feeling a lot better than I had a few days earlier.

Afterwards it hit me. And it stays with me to this day. I'm often asked when I felt I had the ability to make it. Well, *this* was the moment. The moment when belief turned to truth. There wasn't a better bowling attack in the West Indies to test my ability and I'd come through it.

Two years later, I was chosen to *captain* the Trinidad & Tobago senior team. I was no kind of age. There were a couple of West Indies players in our squad and a few veteran players like Rangy Nanan and Kelvin Williams so I was shocked when I was given the job. But I guess our selectors knew what they were doing, they wanted to get me ready, to groom me, for the really big job some time down the line.

That year, 1990, we had a horrific four-day tournament but we got to the finals of the limited-overs tournament, again to face Barbados at the Queen's Park Oval.

We fielded first and held them to 178-9, our fast bowler Tony Gray bowling well. I walked out at No.3 with the score on 40 and again to face Malcolm. I'll never forget it. He bowled one delivery, I moved down the wicket and it was wide outside the off stump. I gestured to the umpire that it looked like a wide, the umpire agreed and signalled it. Malcolm, and what felt like the whole of his team, rounded on me, suggesting I should just bat and leave the umpiring to the umpires.

I didn't really understand their anger but I decide to apologise to Malcolm at the water break and with a smile on his face he says the next time he bowls to me he will lick me down. We won that game to lift the trophy, but I never forgot my exchange with the great Marshall, and neither did he.

A year later I'm lying flat on my back at the Kensington Oval. It's a fast and bouncy pitch, pace like fire, and before I can duck, the ball's slammed into my temple. Thankfully those plastic side pieces cushion the blow but I'm down, spreadeagled on the turf. I look up to see an outstretched hand. Helping me to my feet, Malcolm looks me right in the eye and says, that smile again all over his face, "I *told* you I would lick you down..." Fast bowlers have long memories.

* * *

Malcolm against England was unplayable. In all he took 127 wickets at 19, with six five-wicket hauls in 26 matches. Only Curtly's record – 164 from 34 games – could compare. In my mind they stand alone as the greatest of my time. I can't split them. And nor can the numbers: their Test bowling averages are virtually identical.

I got to know Malcolm on the 1991 tour of England, being lucky enough to share a room with him, and what an education. I just couldn't shut up, the questions would just tumble out of me, and I think I was thankful too; because until then I'd been thrown in with Jeffrey Dujon, a cool guy but one who smoked and smoked and smoked in his room like it was going out of fashion, which I guess it was. But with Malcolm? With Malcolm I was in *awe*.

Throughout my career, I found that with Bajan cricketers, their appetite for this game of ours was so great that they'd be open to talking about it anytime, anywhere. It's like it's in their blood, you know? In my experience it's more the case with Bajans than with any other region in the Caribbean. I wasn't playing that Test series, but no matter to Malcolm, he would still go through the day's play with me, all the details, the unseen things, what went right and wrong. It was like I'd enrolled at my own cricket university. How I wished I could be out there sweating for 90 overs. But what a privilege just to sit with him and take in as much as I could.

It's an exceptional sight to watch a great West Indian fast bowler working outside of the tough, hot conditions of the Caribbean and honestly, in cosy, overcast English conditions with his Windies sweater on, pushing off on that angled run, across the lush chequered grass, hardly a bead of sweat on his brow – Marshall was the *epitome* of fast bowling. It was poetry. Pure poetry in motion. At times I'd wake up in the morning and look across the room and have to pinch myself.

It turned out that those Tests in England in 1991 would be his final acts in Test cricket. He was only 33. Here's what I think: he had more to give. He was a knowledgeable man, and he deserved better.

As cricketers, we can be petty. At times, even cruel. Sometimes, I think that we allow our doubts about ourselves to spread outwards to wanting to see others fall. I've seen it a lot, how destructive it can be. I feel that some of us take enjoyment from seeing other great ones cut down to size.

OK, let me put it this way: Malcolm Marshall did not leave West Indies cricket in the ceremonial manner he should have been afforded.

No question he was having a rough World Cup in 1992. No question he was not as penetrative as we knew him to be. But there's also no question that everyone goes through these periods. This was *Malcolm Marshall* we were talking about. There was disharmony in the camp and Richie Richardson was unable to control it. A decision was taken to leave Malcolm out for our make-or-break match against the Australians. I was astounded.

Great players don't stay out of the limelight very long. As a fellow player, you feel like his next game is gonna be *his* game. I was shocked by it, and of course it affected the opposition in a positive way. No West Indies team should *ever* have left Malcolm Marshall on the sidelines for a big game.

He was distraught. When that decision was taken, that was it for him. His time was done, just like that. Thanks for everything, now who's up next? It was sad to see it end like that.

He continued playing for Hampshire and spent a few seasons with Durban in South Africa's first-class season post-apartheid, playing professional cricket, still plying his trade at 35, still fit, but lost to the West Indies, forced instead to guide players for the benefit of other countries.

Malcolm only resurfaced with Richie's departure, becoming coach when Courtney Walsh took over, and he seemed settled in the role when the call came to put me in charge. I believe he welcomed the decision. That was the sense I had from the way he was with me.

The tragedy – and there's no other word for it – is that we never got the chance to see it through.

* * *

I captained every school team I played in. I captained Trinidad & Tobago Under 19s at 17. I captained the West Indies youth team at the Youth World Cup in Australia. When I was 19, I captained the West Indies Under 23s against Pakistan. A year later, at 20, I was made captain of the Trinidad & Tobago senior team and West Indies A.

Captaining against that Pakistan side when we had Keith Arthurton on our team, 23 and on the verge of a Test debut, or when your own country's selectors push you up ahead of a Test player like Gus Logie, it tells you something.

I was burnt by Logie in 1990 when I was given the national team captaincy, but looking back, I get it, I can understand his position. He was a big Test player by then, a man who thought the job should be his. When I asked him if he'd be my vice-captain he shut me off. Perhaps, I don't know, he resented me for taking the job, but I never coveted it. You think at the age of 20 I'm pushing myself up to anybody to say that I should be captain, given the leadership of the Trinidad & Tobago cricket team? No chance.

Captaincy was just one of those things I was entrusted with. There was never any question of it. Every team I ever played for, I was either made captain immediately or I took over at some point in time. And so, mentally you start to prepare yourself for the job, and I guess some people took that the wrong way. Richie Richardson certainly did in 1995. He thought I wanted his job, and evidently so did a few others. Curtly Ambrose has said words to that effect.

Well, I don't agree with that. But what I could *not* do was keep quiet when I felt, as in '95, that something needed to be said. I shared my experiences and ideas, which could be intimidating, but a strong leader should welcome that. Ultimately, the most important thing as a captain is to make your team successful. If you fail, you're out. I learned the hard way that if you're not successful you're going to be replaced regardless. Or you should get out quick, before they get to you.

* * *

Let me tell you where the West Indies board went wrong. At the start of 1998 I was summoned to a meeting in Antigua, the headquarters of West Indies cricket. I had no clue who else was going to be there. I walk into the office at 10am and I'm being asked certain questions, and I can't remember all of them but it was mainly about leadership, whether I felt ready, moving forward and stuff like that.

I wasn't sure if other players were going to be there. I certainly had no inkling that Courtney, still officially the team captain, might be there at the same time. So we finish this meeting, I leave the room and as I'm walking down the corridor I run into Courtney, which was very uncomfortable for both of us.

We nod and pass each other and as I turn back, I see Courtney walking into the room I've just exited. Just imagine how Courtney would be feeling. He didn't know what was said in my meeting, but he knew how it looked. Who could blame him if he thought I was saying give me the job in there and saying bad stuff about his captaincy? It was so badly handled by the board, and it created a lot of unnecessary tension. Worse, a few days later came the official announcement. They were replacing Courtney with me.

What the West Indies board did to Courtney and me was a disservice to both of us. It definitely put a cloud over my future relationship with some of our players because Courtney Walsh was, rightly, one of the most-loved players in the game. As a player, as a captain, he was a very humble man, and the idea that I tried to push him out made things very difficult.

Courtney was a professional, and a man of great pride who truly had West Indies cricket in his soul. But I think that was the beginning of the end. I captained the West Indies on three separate occasions but from that very first moment, I believe that my captaincy had little room to grow.

A difficult situation was made harder by Richie Richardson, who chose to go to the press to question me, saying that it would be difficult for "so controversial a character" to pull the team together "when he doesn't have too much support from all the players". He was clearly trying to whip up as much anti-feeling towards me, and all this on the eve of a Test series against England.

At least my leadership was welcomed by Clive Lloyd, who was manager at the time, and Malcolm. I felt very comfortable with them both, I knew they had my back. It was a joy to resume our roommate discussions with Malcolm but this time on a different level, no longer the great fast bowler and sub batter, now as coach and captain.

A funny thing happened in the very first practice session. Curtly Ambrose never batted in the nets. Many times, I would hear him jokingly say, "I would take my chance in the middle!" I must confess the West Indies nets is a dangerous place. I felt like I had to change that because it wasn't like in the past where the top order did all the batting. We were no longer that strong, so I asked Curtly to put his pads on. "Where the hell were you for the last 10 years? Didn't you hear? I don't bat in the nets!" And off I went, never to be discussed again. He did slip his pads on when he felt in the mood, though…

Curtly would have seen the disappointment felt by his great friend and naturally sided with him. But it's important to say that they both did their jobs professionally, and that Courtney and Curtly's dedication on the pitch was second to none. They wouldn't have known how to give half-hearted effort, they had too much class for that. I knew I could count on them on the field. Out there, it was always a professional unit. It was off the field where things were tough.

In those first weeks and months I never properly reached out to Courtney as I should have done. I think that was one of the things I was afraid to do, or perhaps, I just didn't know how to do it.

I regret that.

* * *

It had to begin at Sabina Park, Courtney's back yard, and against the English, in scenes of utter chaos.

I'd captained once before in a Test match, against India in Barbados in 1997 when Courtney was injured and we'd successfully defended 120, but this was my first official game as captain. Despite the noise around my appointment, I was still optimistic. It was the proudest moment of my career, after all. I was desperate for it to go well.

Two days before the series was due to start, we went down to Sabina to check on the pitch and we could not believe the state of it. How best to describe? It was so uneven, the hills and valleys on that pitch, that when someone tied some string from the base of both sets of stumps, in certain areas you could roll a cricket ball underneath that piece of string. There was still a couple of days to go before the game had to start and we were told that it was all gonna be fine, and not to worry. Yeah, I didn't buy that. I thought it could be dangerous, but what could we do? We had a Test match to start.

Judging pitches is a tricky business though, so I was trying to keep an open mind when myself and Michael Atherton tossed up. We couldn't know for sure how it would play. Atherton won it and decided to bat. I could understand that. They didn't want to be batting last on that surface. Or first on it, as it would happen.

The first few balls were carnage. Half an hour in, England were two wickets down with no sign of the pitch settling down. The sun was beating down on it, hardening the surface, and the harder it got, the more the ball would take off and fly.

At the first water break, England were three wickets down and in serious trouble. Players were being hit about the body and on the gloves. Somehow, Alec Stewart was still there, his fingers all smashed up. Atherton, who was already out, came onto the field. We had a conversation – Atherton, myself, the umpires Steve Bucknor and Venkat. I could see that this was an unplayable pitch, and I said so. This was not how a Test match should be played and decided. My feeling was that players were at risk of serious injury. You know, it's still a sport, and it was a situation where we all felt we should discontinue this game.

As far as I could see, everybody was in agreement. It didn't matter what palpitations were taking place upstairs in the plush President's Box. Nothing up there could have affected the decision. The politics of it and the ramifications beyond us players didn't mean anything, and as captain it wasn't a worry for me. This was about the players. That Test pitch was dangerous, so we abandoned it. I remember speaking to the officials, suggesting that we reschedule an extra Test match somewhere else, so we could still get five full games in the series.

I felt that if we were going to Trinidad to play the second Test anyway, and we had this period between the scheduled games, then the officials at Port of Spain might be capable of preparing an extra game on a different pitch. One quick call to Joey Carew and it was on. We packed up our things at Sabina and made our way to Trinidad to play two back-to-back Test matches.

We shared a Test match apiece at Port of Spain before wins at Georgetown and Antigua sealed a 3-1 victory for us. Our first run chase at Trinidad was held together by a brilliant unbeaten innings by Carl Hooper, who hung in there with our keeper David Williams through some tight moments to claim a three-wicket win, and then in Guyana it was Shiv Chanderpaul making a hundred on his home turf. The series was still alive going into Antigua, but more class from Carl, and runs elsewhere, saw us home by an innings to clinch the series.

I was disappointed not to score a hundred myself but very happy with how we went about the series. After the unprecedented embarrassment of Jamaica, we'd gotten back on track. Ambrose took 30 wickets, Walsh got 22, the main players were doing what they should do. On the field, I was trying to create and make things happen. If the players didn't know it already, I was *not* a defensive captain. My conversations around the series with Malcolm were riveting and our planning had been exceptional. It was a great start. I felt good. It couldn't last. Then the unthinkable happened.

* * *

During that winter, on the eve of our tour of South Africa, a huge impasse between the West Indies board and the players' association over pay and conditions blew up and sent debris flying in all directions. As captain, I was at the heart of it. For a time it looked unlikely that we would tour, or that I would keep my job. In the event, with the help of a note written by Mandela himself, we did tour under my captaincy. That story is for another time, but it inevitably created a strain between myself and Malcolm. He sat on the fence during that dispute, as he should have. After all, he was an employee of the board. But from being so close, there was now a disconnect between us.

After just about surviving that South Africa tour, myself and Malcolm reunited to produce one of the greatest Test series ever played, against Australia in early 1999, and that series pepped us up going into the 1999 World Cup in England. We strategised and planned well for that tournament, with a clear idea how we wanted to play our cricket in the knockout stages.

One morning midway through the tournament, Clive Lloyd came to see the team to tell us that Malcolm wasn't feeling well and would be staying back at the hotel. We didn't think too much of it. Only after the game, when Malcolm didn't travel with us, did I start to get a little worried. Still, you don't think the worst. You don't allow those kinds of thoughts to creep in.

A few days later, Clive and Rudi Webster, our team psychologist, told us that Malcolm would be unable to continue for the rest of the World Cup. And then, we did start to worry. There were no outward signs, he just disappeared. I wondered if he'd been suffering in silence. Still, you don't allow your mind to go there.

Then came the news. Cancer of the colon. We'd only celebrated his 41st birthday the previous month. We were told it wasn't yet terminal, that he'd have all the best treatment. He began chemotherapy in England.

It failed. He couldn't respond to it. This wasn't just an illness.

As time went by, more information was given. I was told, confidentially, that Malcolm did not have long to live. He went back to Barbados to marry his girlfriend Connie and prepare to die.

My dad's death had been sudden. Heart attack. This was long, drawn out. How do you comprehend a young, beautiful man at the age of 41 being given months to live?

I saw him once, maybe weeks before his death. "I'll be back with you shortly," he said. "I'm gonna beat this." When he said that to me, I already knew.

I tell you, Sir Wes Hall is a true preacher. He said to me, Malcolm Marshall accepted his fate and came to peace with God.

In New Zealand that winter, in the shadow of Malcolm's death, things fell apart.

TRINIDAD & TOBAGO v BARBADOS

Venue: Queen's Park Oval, Port of Spain
Toss: Barbados won the toss and decided to field

Date: 27th January 1988
Result: Barbados won by 8 wickets (Run rate) **Points:** Trinidad and Tobago 0; Barbados 2
Umpires: M Hosein, Z Maccum

TRINIDAD & TOBAGO		R	B	BARBADOS		R	B
+CR Rampersad	c Payne b Garner	0		CA Best	not out	53	
CG Yorke	c Walcott b Springer	24		AS Gilkes	c Lara b Gilman	1	
A Rajah	c Springer b Greene	19		PJC Alleyne	lbw b Nanan	30	
KA Williams	run out	25		+TRO Payne	not out	20	
*HA Gomes	not out	38		AL Grant			
BC Lara	c Payne b Marshall	0		LN Reifer			
AH Gray	c Payne b Marshall	4		*MD Marshall			
R Nanan	not out	9		VS Greene			
IR Bishop				J Garner			
H Joseph				HWD Springer			
GH Gilman				VD Walcott			
Extras	(1 lb, 11 nb, 1 w)	13		Extras	(6 b, 9 lb)	15	
Total	(6 wickets, innings closed, 40 overs)	132		Total	(2 wickets, 31.4 overs)	119	

Fall of wickets: 1-2 (Rampersad), 2-48 (Yorke), 3-54 (Rajah), 4-101 (Williams), 5-103 (Lara), 6-109 (Gray)
Fall of wickets: 1-4 (Gilkes), 2-66 (Alleyne)

BARBADOS	O	M	R	W	Wd	Nb	TRINIDAD AND TOBAGO	O	M	R	W	Wd	Nb
Garner	9	0	26	1	-	6	Gray	5	0	11	0	-	-
Walcott	4	0	25	0	1	-	Gilman	5	0	15	1	-	-
Marshall	8	3	12	2	-	1	Bishop	5	1	23	0	-	-
Greene	10	0	35	1	-	4	Joseph	8	1	24	0	-	-
Springer	9	0	33	1	-	-	Nanan	7	0	21	1	-	-
							Gomes	1	0	3	0	-	-
							Lara	0.4	0	7	0	-	-

TRINIDAD & TOBAGO v BARBADOS

Venue: Queen's Park Oval, Port of Spain
Toss: Barbados won the toss and decided to bat
Points: Trinidad and Tobago 8; Barbados 4

Date: 29th, 30th, 31st January, 1st February 1988
Result: Match drawn
Umpires: CE Cumberbatch, S Mohammed

BARBADOS	1ST INNINGS	R	B	2ND INNINGS	R	B
CA Best	c Rajah b Bishop	15		b Gray	77	
AS Gilkes	lbw b Bishop	15		c Rampersad b Dhanraj	20	
RIC Holder	c Lara b Dhanraj	33		c Lara b Bishop	25	
PJC Alleyne	lbw b Bishop	0		(6) lbw b Gray	0	
+TRO Payne	lbw b Gray	31		run out	20	
AL Grant	c Lara b Dhanraj	10		(7) not out	32	
*MD Marshall	c Williams b Nanan	71		(8) b Gray	2	
HWD Springer	c Williams b Nanan	0		(11) not out	0	
J Garner	c Bishop b Dhanraj	29		lbw b Gray	0	
VS Greene	c Lara b Dhanraj	16		c Yorke b Nanan	2	
WE Reid	not out	6		(4) lbw b Nanan	9	
Extras	(2 b, 8 lb, 7 nb, 7 w)	24		(9 b, 4 lb, 5 nb)	18	
Total	(all out, 93.2 overs)	250		(9 wickets, 99 overs)	205	

Fall of wickets: 1-37 (Best), 2-46 (Gilkes), 3-46 (Alleyne), 4-100 (Payne), 5-113 (Holder), 6-149 (Grant), 7-150 (Springer), 8-226 (Marshall), 9-233 (Garner), 10-250 (Greene, 93.2 ov)
Fall of wickets: 1-48 (Gilkes), 2-105 (Holder), 3-138 (Reid), 4-154 (Best), 5-154 (Alleyne), 6-173 (Payne), 7-182 (Marshall), 8-183 (Garner), 9-201 (Greene)

TRINIDAD AND TOBAGO	O	M	R	W	Wd	Nb		O	M	R	W	Wd	Nb
Gray	16	2	50	1	-	5	Gray	15	2	54	4	-	5
Bishop	13	2	48	3	7	2	Bishop	16	2	32	1	-	-
Nanan	27	9	41	2	-	-	Dhanraj	16	4	42	1	-	-
Joseph	12	2	34	0	-	-	Nanan	38	14	39	2	-	-
Dhanraj	25.2	4	67	4	-	-	Joseph	14	3	25	0	-	-

TRINIDAD & TOBAGO	1ST INNINGS	R	B	2ND INNINGS	R	B
+CR Rampersad	c Payne b Garner	4				
CG Yorke	lbw b Springer	23				
A Rajah	c Marshall b Garner	0				
BC Lara	lbw b Garner	92				
*HA Gomes	lbw b Best	36				
KA Williams	b Reid	19				
AH Gray	lbw b Marshall	15				
R Nanan	not out	46				
IR Bishop	c and b Marshall	6				
H Joseph	c Alleyne b Reid	13				
R Dhanraj	lbw b Reid	1				
Extras	(5 b, 5 lb, 27 nb)	37				
Total	(all out, 105 overs)	292				

Fall of wickets: 1-4 (Rampersad), 2-14 (Rajah), 3-51 (Yorke), 4-126 (Gomes), 5-177 (Williams), 6-202 (Gray), 7-230 (Lara), 8-250 (Bishop), 9-277 (Joseph), 10-292 (Dhanraj, 105 ov)

BARBADOS	O	M	R	W	Wd	Nb		O	M	R	W	Wd	Nb
Garner	24	3	71	3	-	10							
Marshall	24	2	60	2	-	15							
Greene	14	3	31	0	-	2							
Springer	24	5	61	1	-	-							
Reid	14	1	42	3	-	-							
Best	5	1	17	1	-	-							

TRINIDAD & TOBAGO v BARBADOS

Venue: Queen's Park Oval, Port of Spain
Toss: Trinidad and Tobago won the toss and decided to field
Umpires: CE Cumberbatch, M Hosein

Date: 10th February 1990
Result: Trinidad and Tobago won by 5 wickets

BARBADOS		R	B	TRINIDAD AND TOBAGO		R	B
*DL Haynes	b Sieuchan	12	48	PV Simmons	lbw b Walcott	23	31
PA Wallace	c KC Williams b Gray	15	31	DI Mohammed	b Walcott	57	106
CA Best	c D Williams b Sieuchan	12	26	*BC Lara	b Marshall	41	56
CG Greenidge	c Gray b Sieuchan	22	41	AL Logie	c Springer b Stephenson	33	41
+TRO Payne	c Bishop b Nanan	16	27	N Bidhesi	lbw b Stephenson	10	24
RIC Holder	c Simmons b Gray	17	17	+D Williams	not out	5	5
MD Marshall	lbw b Bishop	24	24	KC Williams	not out	3	3
EA Moseley	run out	1	3	R Sieuchan			
FD Stephenson	c Nanan b Gray	21	40	R Nanan			
HWD Springer	not out	14	19	IR Bishop			
VD Walcott	not out	2	6	AH Gray			
Extras	(2 b, 17 lb, 3 w)	22		Extras	(3 lb, 2 nb, 3 w)	8	
Total	(9 wickets, 47 overs)	178		Total	(5 wickets, 44.2 overs)	180	

Fall of wickets: 1-27 (Wallace, 10 ov), 2-44 (Haynes, 16 ov), 3-55 (Best, 20 ov), 4-87 (Greenidge, 28 ov), 5-94 (Payne, 31 ov), 6-119 (Holder, 34 ov), 7-122 (Moseley, 35 ov), 8-144 (Marshall, 40 ov), 9-173 (Stephenson, 46 ov)
Fall of wickets: 1-40 (Simmons, 12 ov), 2-121 (Lara, 30 ov), 3-147 (Mohammed, 36 ov), 4-168 (Bidhesi, 42 ov), 5-171 (Logie, 44 ov)

TRINIDAD AND TOBAGO	O	M	R	W	Wd	Nb	BARBADOS	O	M	R	W	Wd	Nb
Bishop	10	0	39	1	1	-	Marshall	10	2	33	1	1	1
Gray	9	3	22	3	1	-	Moseley	8.2	0	46	0	1	-
Nanan	10	0	33	1	-	-	Walcott	8	0	31	2	-	1
Sieuchan	10	1	34	3	-	-	Stephenson	8	0	34	2	1	-
KC Williams	8	0	31	0	-	-	Springer	10	0	33	0	-	-

BARBADOS v TRINIDAD & TOBAGO

Venue: Kensington Oval, Bridgetown
Toss: Barbados won the toss and decided to field
Points: Barbados 16; Trinidad and Tobago 5

Date: 25th, 26th, 27th, 28th January 1991
Result: Barbados won by 9 wickets
Umpires: DM Archer, CE Mack

TRINIDAD & TOBAGO	1ST INNINGS	R	B	2ND INNINGS	R	B
PV Simmons	b Skeete	31		b Skeete	58	
S Ragoonath	c Browne b Cummins	9		lbw b Cummins	9	
DI Mohammed	c Best b Marshall	3		b Marshall	8	
BC Lara	c Browne b Cummins	67		c Best b Skeete	24	
*AL Logie	c Skeete b Marshall	0		c Browne b Cummins	60	
N Bidhesi	b Skeete	36		lbw b Marshall	14	
+D Williams	c Campbell b Skeete	17		c Browne b Marshall	1	
AH Gray	c Browne b Marshall	30		(9) c sub (HWD Springer) b Skeete	2	
R Nanan	b Skeete	4		(10) c Wallace b Skeete	9	
R Sieuchan	c Cummins b Marshall	45		(8) run out	10	
R Dhanraj	not out	2		not out	0	
Extras	(1 b, 10 lb, 11 nb, 1 w)	23		(7 lb, 9 nb, 1 w)	17	
Total	(all out, 77.4 overs)	267		(all out, 61 overs)	212	

Fall of wickets: 1-12 (Ragoonath), 2-41 (Mohammed), 3-58 (Simmons), 4-59 (Logie), 5-155 (Lara), 6-173 (Bidhesi), 7-186 (Williams), 8-194 (Nanan), 9-261 (Sieuchan), 10-267 (Gray, 77.4 ov)
Fall of wickets: 1-16 (Ragoonath), 2-52 (Mohammed), 3-102 (Simmons), 4-105 (Lara), 5-143 (Bidhesi), 6-150 (Williams), 7-181 (Sieuchan), 8-196 (Gray), 9-206 (Logie), 10-212 (Nanan, 61 ov)

BARBADOS	O	M	R	W	Wd	Nb		O	M	R	W	Wd	Nb
Moseley	19	3	49	0	1	5	Moseley	16	0	66	0	-	6
Cummins	17	1	58	2	-	2	Cummins	16	4	39	2	-	-
Marshall	21.4	4	76	4	-	3	Skeete	15	2	46	4	1	-
Skeete	18	2	68	4	-	1	Marshall	14	1	54	3	-	3
Best	2	0	5	0	-	-							

BARBADOS	1ST INNINGS	R	B	2ND INNINGS	R	B
PA Wallace	lbw b Dhanraj	69		lbw b Gray	24	
*DL Haynes	run out	21		not out	125	
CA Best	c Lara b Dhanraj	20		not out	119	
CG Greenidge	c Logie b Dhanraj	4				
RIC Holder	c Lara b Dhanraj	1				
SL Campbell	c Logie b Dhanraj	9				
MD Marshall	c Lara b Nanan	3				
+CO Browne	c Lara b Dhanraj	26				
AC Cummins	b Simmons	7				
EA Moseley	c Williams b Gray	23				
SM Skeete	not out	2				
Extras	(7 b, 6 lb, 1 nb)	14		(6 lb, 8 nb)	14	
Total	(all out, 75.2 overs)	199		(1 wicket, 95.4 overs)	282	

Fall of wickets: 1-78 (Haynes), 2-105 (Wallace), 3-111 (Greenidge), 4-127 (Best), 5-128 (Holder), 6-135 (Marshall), 7-143 (Campbell), 8-160 (Cummins), 9-197 (Moseley), 10-199 (Browne, 75.2 ov)
Fall of wickets: 1-45 (Wallace)

TRINIDAD AND TOBAGO	O	M	R	W	Wd	Nb		O	M	R	W	Wd	Nb
Gray	8	1	26	1	-	1	Gray	22	7	42	1	-	4
Sieuchan	5	1	25	0	-	-	Sieuchan	3	0	20	0	-	-
Nanan	29	13	47	1	-	-	Nanan	28	5	76	0	-	3
Dhanraj	25.2	7	64	6	-	-	Simmons	11	2	35	0	-	1
Simmons	8	1	24	1	-	-	Dhanraj	28	5	84	0	-	-
							Mohammed	3.4	0	19	0	-	-

WEST INDIES v ENGLAND, FIRST TEST

Venue: Sabina Park, Kingston
Toss: England won the toss and decided to bat
Umpires: SA Bucknor, S Venkataraghavan
Referee: BN Jarman

Date: 29th January 1998
Result: Game abandoned and match drawn
TV Umpire: JR Gayle

ENGLAND	1ST INNINGS	R	B	2ND INNINGS	R	B
*MA Atherton	c Campbell b Walsh	2	7			
+AJ Stewart	not out	9	26			
MA Butcher	c SC Williams b Walsh	0	1			
N Hussain	c Hooper b Ambrose	1	18			
GP Thorpe	not out	0	10			
JP Crawley						
AJ Hollioake						
AR Caddick						
DW Headley						
ARC Fraser						
PCR Tufnell						
Extras	(4 b, 1 nb)	5				
Total	(3 wickets, 10.1 overs)	17				

Fall of wickets: 1-4 (Atherton, 2.1 ov), 2-4 (Butcher, 2.2 ov), 3-9 (Hussain, 7.2 ov)

WEST INDIES	O	M	R	W	Wd	Nb		O	M	R	W	Wd	Nb
Walsh	5.1	1	10	2	-	-							
Ambrose	5	3	3	1	-	1							

WEST INDIES	1ST INNINGS	R	B	2ND INNINGS	R	B
SC Williams						
SL Campbell						
*BC Lara						
S Chanderpaul						
CL Hooper						
JC Adams						
+D Williams						
NAM McLean						
IR Bishop						
Extras						
Total						

Fall of wickets:

ENGLAND	O	M	R	W	Wd	Nb		O	M	R	W	Wd	Nb

WEST INDIES v ENGLAND, SECOND TEST

Venue: Queen's Park Oval, Port of Spain
Toss: England won the toss and decided to bat
Umpires: SA Bucknor, S Venkataraghavan
Referee: BN Jarman

Date: 5th, 6th, 7th, 8th, 9th February 1998
Result: West Indies won by 3 wickets
TV Umpire: CE Cumberbatch

ENGLAND	1ST INNINGS	R	B	2ND INNINGS	R	B
*MA Atherton	c Lara b Ambrose	11	52	b Walsh	31	95
AJ Stewart	lbw b Benjamin	50	126	c Hooper b McLean	73	154
JP Crawley	c SC Williams b Ambrose	17	100	lbw b McLean	22	78
N Hussain	not out	61	202	c and b Walsh	23	62
GP Thorpe	c D Williams b Hooper	8	18	c Lara b Walsh	39	108
AJ Hollioake	run out (Chanderpaul)	2	18	c Lara b Ambrose	12	23
+RC Russell	c SC Williams b McLean	0	2	lbw b Ambrose	8	14
AR Caddick	lbw b Walsh	8	23	c D Williams b Ambrose	0	7
DW Headley	c D Williams b Ambrose	11	57	not out	8	18
ARC Fraser	c D Williams b Benjamin	17	69	c Hooper b Ambrose	4	11
PCR Tufnell	c Lara b Benjamin	0	1	c D Williams b Ambrose	6	12
Extras	(6 b, 10 lb, 13 nb)	29		(5 b, 15 lb, 11 nb, 1 w)	32	
Total	(all out, 109 overs)	214		(all out, 94.5 overs)	258	

Fall of wickets: 1-26 (Atherton, 14.3 ov), 2-87 (Stewart, 39.5 ov), 3-105 (Crawley, 48.2 ov), 4-114 (Thorpe, 53.1 ov), 5-124 (Hollioake, 60.4 ov), 6-126 (Russell, 61.5 ov), 7-143 (Caddick, 70.6 ov), 8-172 (Headley, 86.4 ov), 9-214 (Fraser, 108.5 ov), 10-214 (Tufnell, 109 ov)
Fall of wickets: 1-91 (Atherton, 31.3 ov), 2-143 (Crawley, 52.3 ov), 3-148 (Stewart, 54.5 ov), 4-202 (Hussain, 71.6 ov), 5-228 (Hollioake, 82.2 ov), 6-238 (Russell, 86.2 ov), 7-239 (Thorpe, 87.5 ov), 8-239 (Caddick, 88.3 ov), 9-246 (Fraser, 92.2 ov), 10-258 (Tufnell, 94.5 ov)

WEST INDIES	O	M	R	W	Wd	Nb		O	M	R	W	Wd	Nb
Walsh	27	7	55	1	-	2	Benjamin	15	3	40	0	1	1
Ambrose	26	16	23	3	-	2	McLean	12	1	46	2	-	2
McLean	19	7	28	1	-	5	Ambrose	19.5	3	52	5	-	8
Benjamin	24	5	68	3	-	3	Walsh	29	5	67	3	-	1
Hooper	9	3	14	1	-	-	Hooper	19	8	33	0	-	-
Adams	3	0	8	0	-	1							
Chanderpaul	1	0	2	0	-	-							

WEST INDIES	1ST INNINGS	R	B	2ND INNINGS	R	B
SL Campbell	c Russell b Headley	1	43	c Stewart b Headley	10	12
SC Williams	c Atherton b Fraser	19	58	c Crawley b Fraser	62	120
*BC Lara	c Atherton b Fraser	55	100	c Russell b Fraser	17	53
CL Hooper	b Fraser	1	4	not out	94	203
S Chanderpaul	c Thorpe b Fraser	34	77	c Thorpe b Tufnell	0	10
JC Adams	lbw b Fraser	1	13	c Stewart b Fraser	2	7
+D Williams	lbw b Tufnell	16	45	c Thorpe b Headley	65	172
CEL Ambrose	c and b Fraser	31	83	c Russell b Headley	1	6
KCG Benjamin	b Fraser	0	22	not out	6	16
NAM McLean	c Caddick b Fraser	2	9			
CA Walsh	not out	0	2			
Extras	(12 b, 5 lb, 14 nb)	31		(10 b, 8 lb, 7 nb)	25	
Total	(all out, 73.1 overs)	191		(7 wickets, 98.2 overs)	282	

Fall of wickets: 1-16 (Campbell, 9.5 ov), 2-42 (SC Williams, 20.4 ov), 3-48 (Hooper, 22.3 ov), 4-126 (Chanderpaul, 43.6 ov), 5-134 (Lara, 45.4 ov), 6-135 (Adams, 47.6 ov), 7-167 (D Williams, 60.6 ov), 8-177 (Benjamin, 67.6 ov), 9-190 (McLean, 71.6 ov), 10-191 (Ambrose, 73.1 ov)
Fall of wickets: 1-10 (Campbell, 2.5 ov), 2-68 (Lara, 19.1 ov), 3-120 (SC Williams, 39.1 ov), 4-121 (Chanderpaul, 40.6 ov), 5-124 (Adams, 43.2 ov), 6-253 (D Williams, 91.6 ov), 7-259 (Ambrose, 93.3 ov)

ENGLAND	O	M	R	W	Wd	Nb		O	M	R	W	Wd	Nb
Headley	22	6	47	1	-	10	Headley	16	2	68	3	-	4
Caddick	14	4	41	0	-	3	Caddick	16	2	58	0	-	3
Fraser	16.1	2	53	8	-	3	Tufnell	34.2	9	69	1	-	2
Tufnell	21	8	33	1	-	2	Fraser	27	8	57	3	-	-
							Hollioake	5	0	12	0	-	-

WEST INDIES v ENGLAND, THIRD TEST

Venue: Queen's Park Oval, Port of Spain
Toss: England won the toss and decided to field
Umpires: DB Hair, EA Nicholls
Referee: BN Jarman

Date: 13th, 14th, 15th, 16th, 17th February 1998
Result: England won by 3 wickets
TV Umpire: CE Cumberbatch

WEST INDIES	1ST INNINGS	R	B	2ND INNINGS	R	B
SL Campbell	c Thorpe b Fraser	28	88	lbw b Fraser	13	64
SC Williams	c Thorpe b Caddick	24	48	c Atherton b Caddick	23	16
*BC Lara	c Russell b Fraser	42	53	lbw b Fraser	47	95
CL Hooper	c Butcher b Fraser	1	11	(5) lbw b Headley	5	36
S Chanderpaul	lbw b Fraser	28	111	(6) c Russell b Headley	39	92
JC Adams	c Atherton b Caddick	11	71	(7) c Atherton b Fraser	53	161
+D Williams	b Caddick	0	1	(8) lbw b Headley	0	5
CEL Ambrose	b Caddick	4	3	(9) b Headley	0	1
KCG Benjamin	lbw b Caddick	0	2	(4) c Russell b Fraser	1	11
NAM McLean	c Headley b Fraser	11	13	c Stewart b Caddick	2	34
CA Walsh	not out	5	9	not out	1	10
Extras	(5 nb)	5		(16 lb, 10 nb)	26	
Total	(all out, 67.4 overs)	159		(all out, 85.3 overs)	210	

Fall of wickets: 1-36 (SC Williams, 16.1 ov), 2-93 (Campbell, 29.3 ov), 3-95 (Hooper, 31.6 ov), 4-100 (Lara, 35.2 ov), 5-131 (Adams, 60.4 ov), 6-131 (D Williams, 60.5 ov), 7-140 (Ambrose, 62.2 ov), 8-140 (Benjamin, 62.4 ov), 9-150 (Chanderpaul, 65.1 ov), 10-159 (McLean, 67.4 ov)
Fall of wickets: 1-27 (SC Williams, 6.5 ov), 2-66 (Campbell, 23.1 ov), 3-82 (Benjamin, 27.2 ov), 4-92 (Lara, 33.1 ov), 5-102 (Hooper, 38.1 ov), 6-158 (Chanderpaul, 62.2 ov), 7-159 (D Williams, 62.6 ov), 8-159 (Ambrose, 64.1 ov), 9-189 (McLean, 78.3 ov), 10-210 (Adams, 85.3 ov)

ENGLAND	O	M	R	W	Wd	Nb		O	M	R	W	Wd	Nb
Headley	14	0	40	0	-	2	Caddick	19	6	64	2	-	-
Caddick	22	7	67	5	-	-	Fraser	25.3	11	40	4	-	1
Fraser	20.4	8	40	5	-	1	Headley	26	3	77	4	-	11
Tufnell	9	5	11	0	-	1	Tufnell	15	6	13	0	-	-
Butcher	2	1	1	0	-	-							

ENGLAND	1ST INNINGS	R	B	2ND INNINGS	R	B
*MA Atherton	lbw b Ambrose	2	11	c D Williams b Walsh	49	173
AJ Stewart	c D Williams b Hooper	44	112	c D Williams b Walsh	83	245
JP Crawley	b Ambrose	1	16	run out (Benjamin)	5	20
DW Headley	b Ambrose	1	17	(9) not out	7	11
N Hussain	c D Williams b Walsh	0	14	(4) lbw b Hooper	5	27
GP Thorpe	c D Williams b Hooper	32	88	(5) c D Williams b Ambrose	19	55
MA Butcher	c and b Adams	28	104	(6) not out	24	103
+RC Russell	not out	20	62	(7) c Hooper b Ambrose	4	25
AR Caddick	run out (Lara)	0	4	(8) c D Williams b Ambrose	0	1
ARC Fraser	c and b Ambrose	5	10			
PCR Tufnell	lbw b Ambrose	0	1			
Extras	(1 b, 4 lb, 7 nb)	12		(2 b, 15 lb, 12 nb)	29	
Total	(all out, 71.4 overs)	145		(7 wickets, 108 overs)	225	

Fall of wickets: 1-5 (Atherton, 3.3 ov), 2-15 (Crawley, 9.5 ov), 3-22 (Headley, 13.6 ov), 4-27 (Hussain, 18.5 ov), 5-71 (Stewart, 35.3 ov), 6-101 (Thorpe, 49.2 ov), 7-134 (Butcher, 66.6 ov), 8-135 (Caddick, 68.6 ov), 9-145 (Fraser, 71.3 ov), 10-145 (Tufnell, 71.4 ov)
Fall of wickets: 1-129 (Atherton, 58.2 ov), 2-145 (Crawley, 65.4 ov), 3-152 (Stewart, 72.6 ov), 4-167 (Hussain, 79.2 ov), 5-201 (Thorpe, 95.5 ov), 6-213 (Russell, 103.1 ov), 7-213 (Caddick, 103.2 ov)

WEST INDIES	O	M	R	W	Wd	Nb		O	M	R	W	Wd	Nb
Walsh	17	5	35	1	-	-	Walsh	38	11	69	2	-	1
Ambrose	15.4	5	25	5	-	6	Ambrose	33	6	62	3	-	7
McLean	9	2	23	0	-	-	Benjamin	11	3	24	0	-	2
Benjamin	13	3	34	0	-	2	McLean	4	0	17	0	-	1
Hooper	15	3	23	2	-	-	Adams	6	3	5	0	-	1
Adams	2	2	0	1	-	-	Hooper	16	3	31	1	-	-

WEST INDIES v ENGLAND, FOURTH TEST

Venue: Bourda, Georgetown
Toss: West Indies won the toss and decided to bat
Umpires: SA Bucknor, DB Hair
Referee: BN Jarman

Date: 27th, 28th February, 1st, 2nd March 1998
Result: West Indies won by 242 runs
TV Umpire: PT Montfort

WEST INDIES	1ST INNINGS	R	B	2ND INNINGS	R	B
SL Campbell	c Russell b Headley	10	48	c Ramprakash b Fraser	17	22
SC Williams	c Thorpe b Fraser	13	20	c Stewart b Headley	0	4
*BC Lara	c Thorpe b Croft	93	201	c Butcher b Tufnell	30	61
S Chanderpaul	c Thorpe b Fraser	118	263	run out (Hussain)	0	1
CL Hooper	c Hussain b Headley	43	78	lbw b Headley	34	72
JC Adams	lbw b Tufnell	28	78	lbw b Croft	18	48
+D Williams	c Croft b Headley	0	15	c Tufnell b Ramprakash	15	46
IR Bishop	c Butcher b Croft	14	64	not out	44	94
CEL Ambrose	c Headley b Tufnell	0	6	lbw b Croft	2	6
CA Walsh	not out	3	9	c Russell b Croft	0	6
D Ramnarine	c Russell b Croft	0	2	c Russell b Headley	19	80
Extras	(4 b, 14 lb, 12 nb)	30		(1 b, 11 lb, 6 nb)	18	
Total	(all out, 128.1 overs)	352		(all out, 72 overs)	197	

Fall of wickets: 1-16 (SC Williams, 7.1 ov), 2-38 (Campbell, 14.5 ov), 3-197 (Lara, 68.6 ov), 4-295 (Hooper, 97.4 ov), 5-316 (Chanderpaul, 102.2 ov), 6-320 (D Williams, 106.2 ov), 7-347 (Adams, 123.1 ov), 8-349 (Ambrose, 125.1 ov), 9-352 (Bishop, 126.5 ov), 10-352 (Ramnarine, 128.1 ov)
Fall of wickets: 1-4 (SC Williams, 1.4 ov), 2-32 (Campbell, 6.2 ov), 3-32 (Chanderpaul, 6.3 ov), 4-75 (Lara, 23.4 ov), 5-93 (Hooper, 27.1 ov), 6-123 (D Williams, 41.2 ov), 7-123 (Adams, 42.2 ov), 8-127 (Ambrose, 44.2 ov), 9-127 (Walsh, 46.2 ov), 10-197 (Ramnarine, 72 ov)

ENGLAND	O	M	R	W	Wd	Nb		O	M	R	W	Wd	Nb
Headley	31	7	90	3	-	6	Fraser	11	2	24	1	-	2
Fraser	33	8	77	2	-	4	Headley	13	5	37	3	-	1
Butcher	3	0	15	0	-	-	Croft	22	9	50	3	-	-
Croft	36.1	9	89	3	-	3	Tufnell	24	5	72	1	-	5
Tufnell	25	10	63	2	-	-	Ramprakash	2	1	2	1	-	-

ENGLAND	1ST INNINGS	R	B	2ND INNINGS	R	B
*MA Atherton	c Lara b Ambrose	0	10	lbw b Ambrose	1	10
AJ Stewart	c D Williams b Walsh	20	74	lbw b Walsh	12	29
MA Butcher	lbw b Bishop	11	42	lbw b Hooper	17	67
N Hussain	lbw b Walsh	11	52	c Adams b Walsh	0	2
GP Thorpe	c D Williams b Ramnarine	10	44	c Ramnarine b Ambrose	3	9
MR Ramprakash	not out	64	179	c D Williams b Walsh	34	110
+RC Russell	lbw b Ramnarine	0	4	c Lara b Ambrose	17	85
RDB Croft	c Lara b Hooper	26	91	c D Williams b Hooper	14	34
DW Headley	c D Williams b Hooper	0	4	c Chanderpaul b Ambrose	9	24
ARC Fraser	c Lara b Ramnarine	0	8	c Walsh b Hooper	2	7
PCR Tufnell	c Bishop b Ambrose	2	31	not out	0	9
Extras	(10 b, 2 lb, 14 nb)	26		(9 b, 2 lb, 16 nb, 1 w)	28	
Total	(all out, 87.1 overs)	170		(all out, 62.1 overs)	137	

Fall of wickets: 1-1 (Atherton, 3.1 ov), 2-37 (Butcher, 18.1 ov), 3-41 (Stewart, 21.5 ov), 4-65 (Hussain, 33.3 ov), 5-73 (Thorpe, 36.4 ov), 6-75 (Russell, 38.2 ov), 7-139 (Croft, 69.1 ov), 8-139 (Headley, 69.5 ov), 9-140 (Fraser, 72.4 ov), 10-170 (Tufnell, 87.1 ov)
Fall of wickets: 1-6 (Atherton, 2.5 ov), 2-22 (Stewart, 7.3 ov), 3-22 (Hussain, 7.5 ov), 4-28 (Thorpe, 10.4 ov), 5-58 (Butcher, 27.6 ov), 6-90 (Ramprakash, 42.6 ov), 7-118 (Croft, 55.2 ov), 8-125 (Russell, 56.3 ov), 9-135 (Fraser, 59.2 ov), 10-137 (Headley, 62.1 ov)

WEST INDIES	O	M	R	W	Wd	Nb		O	M	R	W	Wd	Nb
Walsh	27	7	47	2	-	5	Ambrose	14.1	3	38	4	-	11
Ambrose	12.1	5	21	2	-	8	Walsh	15	4	25	3	-	3
Ramnarine	17	8	26	3	-	-	Hooper	18	8	31	3	-	-
Bishop	13	4	34	1	-	3	Bishop	3	1	4	0	-	-
Adams	3	2	1	0	-	1	Ramnarine	11	5	23	0	1	-
Hooper	15	5	29	2	-	-	Adams	1	0	5	0	-	-

WEST INDIES v ENGLAND, FIFTH TEST

Venue: Kensington Oval, Bridgetown
Toss: West Indies won the toss and decided to field
Umpires: CJ Mitchley, EA Nicholls
Referee: BN Jarman

Date: 12th, 13th, 14th, 15th, 16th March 1998
Result: Match drawn
TV Umpire: HA Moore

ENGLAND	1ST INNINGS	R	B	2ND INNINGS	R	B
*MA Atherton	c Ambrose b Walsh	11	28	c Williams b Bishop	64	157
AJ Stewart	c Williams b Walsh	12	12	c Lara b Bishop	48	103
MA Butcher	c Hooper b Ambrose	19	52	c Lambert b Ambrose	26	69
N Hussain	c Lara b McLean	5	17	not out	46	72
GP Thorpe	c Lara b Hooper	103	268	not out	36	35
MR Ramprakash	c and b McLean	154	388			
+RC Russell	c Wallace b Hooper	32	71			
DW Headley	c Holder b Hooper	31	83			
AR Caddick	c Chanderpaul b Hooper	3	16			
ARC Fraser	c Walsh b Hooper	3	8			
PCR Tufnell	not out	1	1			
Extras	(10 lb, 17 nb, 2 w)	29		(1 b, 6 lb, 6 nb)	13	
Total	(all out, 153.5 overs)	403		(3 wickets, dec, 71 overs)	233	

Fall of wickets: 1-23 (Stewart, 4.4 ov), 2-24 (Atherton, 8.6 ov), 3-33 (Hussain, 13.4 ov), 4-53 (Butcher, 22.5 ov), 5-131 (Russell, 49.5 ov), 6-336 (Thorpe, 126.3 ov), 7-382 (Ramprakash, 145.4 ov), 8-392 (Caddick, 151.2 ov), 9-402 (Headley, 153.3 ov), 10-403 (Fraser, 153.5 ov)
Fall of wickets: 1-101 (Stewart, 38.1 ov), 2-128 (Atherton, 46.6 ov), 3-173 (Butcher, 60.6 ov)

WEST INDIES	O	M	R	W	Wd	Nb		O	M	R	W	Wd	Nb
Walsh	34	8	84	2	-	4	Walsh	12	1	40	0	-	-
Ambrose	31	6	62	1	-	10	Ambrose	12	4	48	1	-	7
McLean	27	5	73	2	-	-	Hooper	21	5	58	0	-	-
Hooper	37.5	7	80	5	-	-	Bishop	14	1	51	2	-	3
Bishop	20	1	74	0	-	8	Chanderpaul	5	3	13	0	-	-
Chanderpaul	4	0	20	0	-	-	McLean	7	0	16	0	-	-

WEST INDIES	1ST INNINGS	R	B	2ND INNINGS	R	B
CB Lambert	c Russell b Caddick	55	197	c Headley b Fraser	29	60
PA Wallace	lbw b Headley	45	51	lbw b Caddick	61	101
IR Bishop	c Russell b Tufnell	4	38			
*BC Lara	c Butcher b Headley	31	55	(3) not out	13	59
S Chanderpaul	c Stewart b Fraser	45	147	(4) not out	3	4
RIC Holder	b Ramprakash	10	33			
CL Hooper	lbw b Fraser	9	41			
+D Williams	c Ramprakash b Caddick	2	16			
NAM McLean	not out	7	35			
CEL Ambrose	st Russell b Tufnell	26	27			
CA Walsh	c and b Headley	6	14			
Extras	(13 b, 2 lb, 7 nb)	22		(1 b, 5 lb)	6	
Total	(all out, 107.3 overs)	262		(2 wickets, 37.3 overs)	112	

Fall of wickets: 1-82 (Wallace, 19.1 ov), 2-91 (Bishop, 30.1 ov), 3-134 (Lara, 45.2 ov), 4-164 (Lambert, 65.5 ov), 5-190 (Holder, 76.6 ov), 6-214 (Chanderpaul, 88.2 ov), 7-221 (Williams, 93.4 ov), 8-221 (Hooper, 96.1 ov), 9-255 (Ambrose, 104.2 ov), 10-262 (Walsh, 107.3 ov)
Fall of wickets: 1-72 (Lambert, 20.2 ov), 2-108 (Wallace, 34.4 ov)

ENGLAND	O	M	R	W	Wd	Nb		O	M	R	W	Wd	Nb
Headley	17.3	2	64	3	-	7	Caddick	6	1	19	1	-	-
Fraser	22	5	80	2	-	1	Headley	2	0	14	0	-	-
Caddick	17	8	28	2	-	-	Tufnell	16.3	3	37	0	-	1
Tufnell	33	15	43	2	-	1	Fraser	11	3	33	1	-	-
Ramprakash	18	7	32	1	-	-	Ramprakash	2	1	3	0	-	-

WEST INDIES v ENGLAND, SIXTH TEST

Venue: Antigua Recreation Ground, St John's
Toss: West Indies won the toss and decided to field
Umpires: SA Bucknor, CJ Mitchley
Referee: BN Jarman

Date: 20th, 21st, 22nd, 23rd, 24th March 1998
Result: West Indies won by an innings and 52 runs
TV Umpire: PC Whyte

ENGLAND	1ST INNINGS	R	B	2ND INNINGS	R	B
*MA Atherton	c Ramnarine b Ambrose	15	43	lbw b Ambrose	13	40
AJ Stewart	b Rose	22	95	c Wallace b Hooper	79	132
MA Butcher	c Lara b Ambrose	0	3	c Murray b Ambrose	0	6
DW Headley	c Lara b Ambrose	1	39	(8) c Murray b Ramnarine	1	9
N Hussain	c Holder b Ramnarine	37	124	(4) run out (Hooper->Murray)	106	318
GP Thorpe	lbw b Ramnarine	5	15	(5) not out	84	322
MR Ramprakash	c Chanderpaul b Walsh	14	62	(6) b Ramnarine	0	10
+RC Russell	c Lambert b Ramnarine	0	2	(7) lbw b Walsh	9	39
AR Caddick	c Walsh b Ramnarine	8	17	c Murray b Walsh	0	20
ARC Fraser	b Walsh	9	25	c Chanderpaul b Walsh	4	3
PCR Tufnell	not out	2	11	c Lambert b Walsh	0	4
Extras	(1 b, 2 lb, 11 nb)	14		(6 b, 4 lb, 14 nb, 1 w)	25	
Total	(all out, 70.5 overs)	127		(all out, 147.2 overs)	321	

Fall of wickets: 1-27 (Atherton, 13.1 ov), 2-27 (Butcher, 13.4 ov), 3-38 (Headley, 25.3 ov), 4-57 (Stewart, 34.4 ov), 5-66 (Thorpe, 39.5 ov), 6-105 (Hussain, 61.2 ov), 7-105 (Russell, 61.4 ov), 8-105 (Ramprakash, 62.4 ov), 9-117 (Caddick, 67.1 ov), 10-127 (Fraser, 70.5 ov)

Fall of wickets: 1-45 (Atherton, 14.1 ov), 2-49 (Butcher, 16.1 ov), 3-127 (Stewart, 42.4 ov), 4-295 (Hussain, 121.1 ov), 5-300 (Ramprakash, 125.2 ov), 6-312 (Russell, 136.2 ov), 7-313 (Headley, 137.5 ov), 8-316 (Caddick, 145.1 ov), 9-320 (Fraser, 145.4 ov), 10-321 (Tufnell, 147.2 ov)

WEST INDIES	O	M	R	W	Wd	Nb		O	M	R	W	Wd	Nb
Walsh	25.5	8	52	2	-	3	Walsh	31.2	7	80	4	-	4
Ambrose	17	6	28	3	-	5	Ambrose	20	5	66	2	1	7
Ramnarine	17	5	29	4	-	-	Rose	11	2	39	0	-	4
Hooper	1	1	0	0	-	-	Ramnarine	46	19	70	2	-	4
Rose	9	4	14	1	-	3	Hooper	39	18	56	1	-	2
Lambert	1	0	1	0	-	-							

WEST INDIES	1ST INNINGS	R	B	2ND INNINGS	R	B
CB Lambert	c Thorpe b Ramprakash	104	232			
PA Wallace	b Headley	92	135			
*BC Lara	c Stewart b Caddick	89	94			
S Chanderpaul	lbw b Fraser	5	40			
CL Hooper	not out	108	150			
RIC Holder	c and b Caddick	45	118			
+JR Murray	c Hussain b Headley	4	9			
FA Rose	lbw b Caddick	2	8			
CEL Ambrose	not out	19	23			
D Ramnarine						
CA Walsh						
Extras	(14 lb, 18 nb)	32				
Total	(7 wickets, dec, 131 overs)	500				

Fall of wickets: 1-167 (Wallace, 41.2 ov), 2-300 (Lara, 68.5 ov), 3-317 (Lambert, 79.1 ov), 4-324 (Chanderpaul, 81.6 ov), 5-451 (Holder, 116.5 ov), 6-458 (Murray, 119.6 ov), 7-465 (Rose, 124.1 ov)

ENGLAND	O	M	R	W	Wd	Nb		O	M	R	W	Wd	Nb
Caddick	26	3	111	3	-	-							
Fraser	21	3	88	1	-	-							
Headley	30	4	109	2	-	19							
Tufnell	35	6	97	0	-	4							
Ramprakash	19	0	81	1	-	-							

CHAPTER 9

1999-2000
I FELT FOR SWAGGY

'You need to set your own legacy.
When people look back to you, they'll want
to remember what you gave them.
They'll forget about results.
What they'll want to remember is
how you made them feel'

PSYCHIATRIST IN THE U.S.

I WAS STILL PRETTY NEW to the captaincy. In Test cricket we'd had that wonderful start against England, a horrific tour of South Africa where we lost 5-0, and an unbelievable time against Australia when we shared a series against the best team in the world. But for all that the Australia series briefly cleared the clouds above us, I knew that without Curtly Ambrose, who was coming to the end of his time, any talk of a revival in West Indies cricket was not gonna be possible.

We got down to New Zealand in late 1999 and it all went wrong. After a Test match we lost that we had no right losing, I went back to my hotel room. My bag was mid-air when my back hit the bed. I lay in silence but my brain was hot and racing. "Man, what happened?" Then the tears flowed uncontrollably.

I knew then that I needed to step away. I had to do something about it. Mentally, I was not capable of carrying on, so I asked for a break. I went to the board and asked them for some time away from the game. The board, and the president, Pat Rousseau, was happy about it and I suspected they had their own reasons. Eight months earlier they had me lined up to be sacked, putting me on a two-match probation only for it to blow up in their face with my performance at Sabina Park against the Australians.

I couldn't afford to care that I was showing my fragility in front of them; they were my employers and that was my only path to get the space I needed to heal. I said I will try to see someone professionally to help me through this period and I will be back when I am ready. They were happy to lose me as their captain but I don't think they were ready to lose me as a batter. Before I could breathe properly, they were throwing out names of people that they thought I could see. In my mind I'm shouting, "NO NO NO!"

But I'm more polite. "No, thank you."

These were all people either associated with the board, or who knew too much about cricket and my involvement. I needed to articulate my problems to someone totally devoid of anything to do with cricket. I no longer wanted to bottle up my feelings. I was good at that, but it always came back to bite me. I'd worked with Rudi Webster, our sometime team psychologist, and he was amazing during a couple of Test series. He is a fair man, and I thought of turning to him. But he loved West Indies cricket, and I couldn't see someone who had the West Indies at heart. It wouldn't be fair on them or me. I could tell that Pat Rousseau wanted to be in charge of this process and so, whether through genuine concern for me or not, some more suggestions were made.

We had a doctor who was part of our board's medical team who knew people in the United States and through him we reached out to an individual who they thought could help. This therapist was living in upstate New York, or perhaps it was New Jersey, the memories from that time are unclear. But importantly, he had no knowledge whatsoever of cricket. He said to me that the only reason he took my case was because he was interested in this game, about which he had no clue, so he thought, "Sure, why not?" I flew to America to spend four days in a psychiatric clinic.

It began with me filling out a form with about 300 questions on it. I spent hours and hours filling this thing out, writing in answers. On my second day, I was sent to a psychiatrist who asked me some very heavy questions. At one point, he asked if I'd ever felt suicidal. Now, I don't think I've ever, at any point in time, felt that way. I was never inclined to feel like the world, or my world, was coming to an end, or that I needed to end it. That was never in my thoughts. It was strange and unsettling, but I went along with it.

On my third day I was sent to a halfway house and I remember getting there and being surrounded in the gardens outside by some people who looked very uncomfortable in themselves, people who were really struggling. I watched them lighting cigarette after cigarette, just walking and talking to themselves. It was then that I started to wonder what I was doing there. I thought I was looking for answers just to get myself motivated to play cricket again.

My turn came up and I went back inside. The first question I was asked was, "What am I addicted to?" and I was like, "I don't understand your question". I must have been coming over quite defensive because I was advised to take a walk outside and to come back when I was ready.

"I don't know what you're talking about but I'm ready to answer anything that you want me to answer," I said. And he said it again: "What are you addicted to?" I said I don't smoke, I don't take drugs, and so you need to be more specific.

And he says, "Do you drink?"

"Of course I drink!"

How much, he says.

"I don't count my drinks, but I'm not a regular drinker, I don't have to have a glass with everything. I drink when I go out." He looks at me. "OK, look, when we win, or when I've had a good day, I go out, and no, I don't count my drinks."

"So you are a sporadic heavy drinker," he said. "You know there is a term for it. A sporadic alcoholic."

I left his office with this line, 'sporadic alcoholic', ringing in my ears. I had a long drive back to my hotel and I truly felt I needed to head straight to my room, pack my bag and get out of there. Maybe I could go see my sister Marlene in Queen's, New York. Three thousand US dollars an hour for *this* nonsense? Just before I pulled the trigger on that move I sat back in my seat and had another think.

I'd gotten defensive and I was upset, but this man knew more than I thought. I guess he'd have been given information of some very unfortunate behaviour from the 1996 World Cup, when we lost in the semi-finals against Australia in a game we should have won.

Chasing just 208, myself and Chanderpaul were *cruising*. Even when I got out we still only needed a little over 100 with eight wickets still in hand. At one point we were 165-2 with Shiv and Richie both going great, needing just 43 to win from nine overs.

It was *impossible* to lose. I had a little camcorder and was mock-interviewing our players in the dressing room about what it felt like to get to the World Cup final.

Then a wicket fell, then another, and then Shane Warne grabbed the ball. Before I knew it, we'd turned a certain victory into defeat. That was the World Cup that hurt me the most.

We got back to the hotel. I was really ticking. In the quarter-final against South Africa I'd been given a large bottle of champagne for the Man of the Match award, and there was also a bottle of vodka kicking around. Maybe my roommate, Courtney Browne, bought it, or maybe it was me. I can't remember.

So I'm in that room, ready to blow, and every time I pour another drink and pour one for Courtney he'll throw it on the floor behind his bed, right? By the time I'm finished I am *plastered*. I down the champagne and go for the vodka. It's pure booze depression. I keep asking myself, time after time, "How the hell could we lose this match?"

We're in Chandigarh and we need to take a train back to Delhi. On the train I knocked straight out after stumbling to my seat. When we arrived I woke up with my head spinning. Luckily, I didn't fit into that little gap that separated the train from the platform. Our manager Wes Hall recognised what was going on and instructed Courtney Browne to look after his roommate. Well, Courtney couldn't control me. I remember sliding down the arm of the escalator in my West Indies blazer. I think I ended up in a bin positioned at the bottom of the escalator. I have a confrontation with our team physio Dennis Waight, we're like two boxers face to face before the fight but he's twice my size, width-wise at least, so I'm in a losing battle there. Inside I'm screaming at myself: "Sober up, Brian! Sober up!" All in all, it's not the greatest. I get myself together by the time it comes to fly out, but by then the West Indies board have been told and soon enough I'm hauled in to see them. Another black mark slapped on the card. Our new manager for the next series, Clive Lloyd, had to get Dennis to withdraw his letter of complaint for me to be selected for the next tour. I suppose that was easy for Clive, since he knew Dennis from the days of Kerry Packer cricket in the Seventies.

The last conversation I had in the US with the psychiatrist went something like this: "You need to set your own legacy. When people look back to you, they want to remember what you gave them. They'll forget about results. What they'll want to remember is how you made them *feel*."

That line hit home. Something clicked inside of me. I got out of that place, four days away from home, and away from everyone, feeling like I wanted to get back into it. I wanted to leave something positive, I didn't want to leave West Indies cricket at this point in time.

And I was happy to be led. I just wanted to be a part of a team, to create a legacy we could all hold onto. My first attempt at captaining the West Indies cricket team was done. It had finished in a psychiatric clinic somewhere in the United States.

I had a lot to think about and seek clarity on. First up, that question: was my appointment to the captaincy rushed through by the West Indies Cricket Board? Or was I guilty of rushing it through myself? I don't go along with that. At no point in time did I say outright that I wanted to be West Indies captain, or that I *should* be West Indies captain.

I'd always been entrusted to lead older, more recognised players, and up and coming stars with big reputations themselves. I captained future stars like Jimmy Adams and Roland Holder in the Youth World Cup. At 20, I led a West Indies A team to Zimbabwe featuring the likes of Tony Gray, Patrick Patterson, Carl Hooper, Phil Simmons and Clayton Lambert. By 1998, 28 years old, it had reached the point where it was a natural progression to the job. Post-Viv, we'd had Richie from 1992-1995, and then Courtney for a couple of years. The West Indies selectors decided on a new captain and at the time I was Courtney's deputy and I was handed the job.

Regardless. No matter who did it, it was not an easy role. After me, Jimmy Adams, better known as Swaggy to us, would have a year of it before they got rid of him. After Jimmy, Carl Hooper came back from the abyss and captained for two years, before he disappeared again, and it came back round to me. The point is this: no one stays in it too long.

Why? Because it's the impossible job.

* * *

Anyway, Jimmy took over, and I was comfortable with that. We'd known each other since we were teenagers, we started out together as kids and shared a lot of good times on the field. I trusted and respected him.

He'd led us to victories over Zimbabwe – albeit barely at Trinidad, where they'd had 90-odd runs to win and got bowled out for 63 – and then staged a heist to beat Pakistan by one wicket in Antigua to take that series. So Jimmy had started fine. I was watching on from afar, trying to prepare mentally for England as best I could but knowing it wouldn't be easy. At the Queen's Park Oval for that match, I tried entering where the players normally entered and someone who had known me for years stood at the gate and outright told me I couldn't come in through that gate. I turned around and went home.

That summer, 2000, I arrived in England not fully fit. I'd put on a little weight and I had to get in shape physically, as well as into that competitive frame of mind.

I was coming back from something, trying to reinvent myself, and I could feel it was gonna take time. The 2000 tour was the first stop in my attempt to get back to where I used to be. It would happen eventually – Carl, who took over from Jimmy after that summer, would be captain for some of my best innings in Test cricket. But that tour of England was a new and different situation.

I had to find my fitness, physically and mentally, as the tour went on. We were up against a hungry team under Nasser Hussain; England were no pushovers and they were desperate.

You're talking 31 years since any England side had beaten the West Indies in a Test series. It had become an obsession for them.

I took a less imposing leadership role. For all of my career, certainly since 1994, I was pretty much considered a senior player, a voice that would come out, not necessarily being asked to speak but coming out when I felt there was something to say. But in 2000 I was in a more reserved position. It took time to calm some of that adrenaline rush, that urge to be near the centre of things, but I felt like I *wanted* to be led, I wanted someone to lead me. And it did help, it did. Because it materialised into good things in the few years that followed.

We won the first Test at Edgbaston quite easily and I was pleased for Jimmy because he made runs and it was a big win. But after England beat us at Lord's in a tight game we should've won, we went to Old Trafford for the third Test with the series in the balance.

It was here that I came up against Dominic Cork, who was on a buzz after playing well at Lord's and was never shy of a word at the best of times. Cork was a wonderful bowler, feisty and competitive, but he was exactly what I needed. Although I was working on more than just my batting, my game still hadn't clicked that series. The English bowlers knew they were on top, and Dominic decided to rub it in. "Come on lads, it's only a matter of time before he's back in the pavilion." I hear it loud and clear and a voice inside of me starts laughing at me. "So, this is what they think about you now." I dig my spikes in the turf and mark my territory, that intensity suddenly returning, and now my focus is on, immediate and impenetrable.

The umpires call lunch. I signal to the dressing room to send some bowlers to the nets. I head straight there, no food, nothing to drink, just a 30-minute hit before I'm back in the middle.

I may have been content to be subdued on that tour, to work my way back on my own terms. But I never liked the opposition having choice words when they felt they had the better of you. Steve Waugh, Michael Atherton and a few other captains would learn that very quickly: "Whatever you do, do not sledge Brian."

Well, that day I was provoked back to the old Brian. I went back out there like my old self again. I was on it. It was inevitable that I would hit my only hundred of the series.

It couldn't last. English pressure finally got to us at Leeds in the fourth Test, when we went down inside two days, skittled twice by a rampant English attack. We got to The Oval, scene of farewells, with England 2-1 to the good.

It wasn't just an important game for the rivalry. Curtly Ambrose had told the world that he was not going on after that tour. He'd been a great servant. A man who started cricket almost reluctantly but a bowler of great natural ability and a lot of pride, someone who served the West Indies in the best way possible. An awesome fast bowler, he was not the fastest but he could still rush you, and he *definitely* didn't give you any bad balls, and that was something I loved. I don't mind seeing a bowler with aggression because I know they're gonna get carried away and give you something to hit. Ambrose was never like that. He was a star, a natural star.

Curtly? I would call him a simple, fierce man. The way he treated me, he was fierce. The way he treated, I don't know, Graham Thorpe, he was fierce. He was *fierce*.

* * *

That match at The Oval had a lot of meaning bedded into it, beyond England's quest to stem the tide of three decades of being pushed around by us. Finally, they were ready. England was always playing the better cricket that summer. From the moment we took that first Test at Edgbaston, they had us under pressure. They were on us all the time.

We were dumped on the canvas in our first innings and we never recovered after that. I was bowled first ball round my legs by Craig White and we collapsed, all out for 125. We were done.

Ambrose and Walsh walked off arm in arm to a standing ovation. Echoes of Viv in '91. Their numbers from the series told a story, and one of concern for the future of the West Indies. Ambrose: 17 wickets at 18. Walsh: 34 at 13. The other bowlers were nowhere close.

We all knew the gap between the big two and the rest was vast. Yet it wasn't down to a big gulf in natural physical ability. Our other fast bowlers on that tour – Nixon Mclean, Reon King, Franklyn Rose – all bowled faster than Curtly and Courtney, but I felt that they didn't build on that natural ability. They weren't learning on the job. What they needed was to soak up the advice that was out there to hone their skills to become tougher Test match bowlers. This was the 21st century, you had to have discipline. The game was moving on fast and if you didn't move fast with it, you'd be left behind.

It was a poor series for me with the bat. That duck at The Oval capped a series in which I averaged under 30. I was the only one of our team to post a hundred in the series, but that wasn't enough. Truth was, I was not expecting great things. I was in a frame of adjustment. Leading the West Indies for two years had been disruptive and I was still emerging out the other side.

I am someone who never felt I had a flawless technique. I am a mind player who went into survival mode physically and technically when I entered the ring but the minute I sensed a weakening in their efforts, I pounced. Mentally, I'd then be in charge and it'd be tough for any opponent till the end.

My bat was never a broad bat. It was never Tendulkar's bat, where you look at it and go, "We *never* gettin' past that." Or Kallis' bat. Or Dravid's. That was never me. I am someone who, if you don't get me first, then I am in charge of everything. In England that year, I simply wasn't in that space. Jimmy always gave me 100 percent. I wish I could've given him more. He deserved the best of me. I just wasn't ready.

ENGLAND v WEST INDIES, FIRST TEST

Venue: Edgbaston, Birmingham
Toss: West Indies won the toss and decided to field
Umpires: DR Shepherd, S Venkataraghavan
Reserve Umpire: R Palmer
Date: 15th, 16th, 17th June 2000
Result: West Indies won by an innings and 93 runs
TV Umpire: B Dudleston
Referee: GT Dowling

ENGLAND	1ST INNINGS	R	B	2ND INNINGS	R	B
MA Atherton	c Jacobs b Walsh	20	52	b King	19	75
MR Ramprakash	c Hinds b Walsh	18	48	lbw b Walsh	0	3
*N Hussain	c Jacobs b Rose	15	82	c Jacobs b Walsh	8	26
GA Hick	c Campbell b Walsh	0	7	c Jacobs b Walsh	0	5
+AJ Stewart	b Ambrose	6	25	b Rose	8	12
NV Knight	c Lara b King	26	56	c Hinds b Adams	34	103
A Flintoff	c Lara b Walsh	16	20	b King	12	22
RDB Croft	c Jacobs b Walsh	18	19	c Hinds b King	1	14
AR Caddick	not out	21	67	c Hinds b Rose	4	27
D Gough	run out (Jacobs)	23	36	not out	23	52
ESH Giddins	c Jacobs b King	0	11	b Adams	0	17
Extras	(6 lb, 9 nb, 1 w)	16		(7 lb, 8 nb, 1 w)	16	
Total	(all out, 69 overs)	179		(all out, 58 overs)	125	

Fall of wickets: 1-26 (Ramprakash, 13.5 ov), 2-44 (Atherton, 17.4 ov), 3-45 (Hick, 19.4 ov), 4-57 (Stewart, 28.5 ov), 5-82 (Hussain, 39.5 ov), 6-112 (Knight, 46.4 ov), 7-112 (Flintoff, 47.2 ov), 8-134 (Croft, 53.5 ov), 9-173 (Gough, 65.4 ov), 10-179 (Giddins, 69 ov)
Fall of wickets: 1-0 (Ramprakash, 1.3 ov), 2-14 (Hussain, 9.4 ov), 3-14 (Hick, 11.4 ov), 4-24 (Stewart, 14.5 ov), 5-60 (Atherton, 25.2 ov), 6-78 (Flintoff, 29.4 ov), 7-83 (Croft, 33.2 ov), 8-94 (Caddick, 42.2 ov), 9-117 (Knight, 53.3 ov), 10-125 (Giddins, 58 ov)

WEST INDIES	O	M	R	W	Wd	Nb		O	M	R	W	Wd	Nb
Ambrose	20.5	10	32	1	-	2	Ambrose	14	8	16	0	-	2
Walsh	21	9	36	5	-	4	Walsh	19	10	22	3	-	-
King	14.1	2	60	2	1	2	Rose	10	1	43	2	-	5
Rose	13	3	45	1	-	1	King	9	4	28	3	-	1
							Gayle	3	0	4	0	-	-
							Adams	3	1	5	2	-	-

WEST INDIES	1ST INNINGS	R	B	2ND INNINGS	R	B
SL Campbell	b Gough	59	120			
CH Gayle	lbw b Gough	0	8			
WW Hinds	c Hussain b Caddick	12	11			
BC Lara	c Stewart b Gough	50	93			
S Chanderpaul	c Stewart b Flintoff	73	119			
*JC Adams	c Flintoff b Gough	98	299			
+RD Jacobs	c Stewart b Caddick	5	21			
CEL Ambrose	lbw b Croft	22	50			
FA Rose	lbw b Gough	48	54			
RD King	st Stewart b Croft	1	40			
CA Walsh	not out	3	12			
Extras	(6 b, 14 lb, 6 nb)	26				
Total	(all out, 136.5 overs)	397				

Fall of wickets: 1-5 (Gayle, 2.5 ov), 2-24 (Hinds, 7.4 ov), 3-123 (Campbell, 36.1 ov), 4-136 (Lara, 40.5 ov), 5-230 (Chanderpaul, 76.5 ov), 6-237 (Jacobs, 81.6 ov), 7-292 (Ambrose, 99.5 ov), 8-354 (Rose, 116.1 ov), 9-385 (King, 131.2 ov), 10-397 (Adams, 136.5 ov)

ENGLAND	O	M	R	W	Wd	Nb		O	M	R	W	Wd	Nb
Gough	36.5	6	109	5	-	3							
Caddick	30	6	94	2	-	-							
Giddins	18	4	73	0	-	3							
Croft	29	9	53	2	-	-							
Flintoff	23	8	48	1	-	-							

ENGLAND v WEST INDIES, SECOND TEST

Venue: Lord's Cricket Ground, St John's Wood
Toss: England won the toss and decided to field
Umpires: JH Hampshire, S Venkataraghavan
Referee: GT Dowling

Date: 29th, 30th June, 1st July 2000
Result: England won by 2 wickets
TV Umpire: R Julian
Scorers: LB Hewes (West Indies), DC Kendix (England)

WEST INDIES	1ST INNINGS	R	B	2ND INNINGS	R	B
SL Campbell	c Hoggard b Cork	82	155	c Gough b Caddick	4	8
AFG Griffith	run out (Caddick->Stewart)	27	91	c Stewart b Gough	1	27
WW Hinds	c Stewart b Cork	59	120	c Ramprakash b Caddick	0	2
BC Lara	c Stewart b Gough	6	17	c Cork b Caddick	5	19
S Chanderpaul	b Gough	22	61	c Ramprakash b Gough	9	16
*JC Adams	lbw b Gough	1	9	lbw b Cork	3	40
+RD Jacobs	c Stewart b Cork	10	28	c Atherton b Caddick	12	23
CEL Ambrose	c Ramprakash b Cork	5	12	c Ramprakash b Caddick	0	5
FA Rose	lbw b Gough	29	29	c and b Cork	1	4
RD King	not out	12	13	lbw b Cork	7	12
CA Walsh	lbw b Caddick	1	4	not out	3	5
Extras	(1 b, 8 lb, 2 nb, 2 w)	13		(8 lb, 1 nb)	9	
Total	(all out, 89.3 overs)	267		(all out, 26.4 overs)	54	

Fall of wickets: 1-80 (Griffith, 30.2 ov), 2-162 (Campbell, 55.2 ov), 3-175 (Lara, 62.3 ov), 4-185 (Hinds, 67.1 ov), 5-186 (Adams, 68.4 ov), 6-207 (Jacobs, 77.4 ov), 7-216 (Ambrose, 79.5 ov), 8-253 (Rose, 86.2 ov), 9-258 (Chanderpaul, 88.1 ov), 10-267 (Walsh, 89.3 ov)
Fall of wickets: 1-6 (Campbell, 3.3 ov), 2-6 (Hinds, 3.5 ov), 3-10 (Griffith, 8.1 ov), 4-24 (Lara, 11.2 ov), 5-24 (Chanderpaul, 12.3 ov), 6-39 (Jacobs, 21.2 ov), 7-39 (Adams, 22.6 ov), 8-39 (Ambrose, 23.1 ov), 9-41 (Rose, 24.3 ov), 10-54 (King, 26.4 ov)

ENGLAND	O	M	R	W	Wd	Nb		O	M	R	W	Wd	Nb
Gough	21	5	72	4	-	2	Gough	8	3	17	2	-	1
Caddick	20.3	3	58	1	-	-	Caddick	13	8	16	5	-	-
Hoggard	13	3	49	0	1	-	Cork	5.4	2	13	3	-	-
Cork	24	8	39	4	-	-							
White	8	1	30	0	-	-							
Vaughan	3	1	10	0	-	-							

ENGLAND	1ST INNINGS	R	B	2ND INNINGS	R	B
MA Atherton	c Lara b Walsh	1	7	lbw b Walsh	45	143
MR Ramprakash	c Lara b Ambrose	0	5	b Walsh	2	16
MP Vaughan	b Ambrose	4	24	c Jacobs b Walsh	41	93
GA Hick	b Ambrose	25	33	c Lara b Walsh	15	24
*+AJ Stewart	c Jacobs b Walsh	28	68	lbw b Walsh	18	25
NV Knight	c Campbell b King	6	17	c Jacobs b Rose	2	46
C White	run out (Adams)	27	59	c Jacobs b Walsh	0	3
DG Cork	c Jacobs b Walsh	4	24	not out	33	49
AR Caddick	c Campbell b Walsh	6	14	lbw b Ambrose	7	13
D Gough	c Lara b Ambrose	13	24	not out	4	19
MJ Hoggard	not out	12	18			
Extras	(5 lb, 3 nb)	8		(3 b, 8 lb, 12 nb, 1 w)	24	
Total	(all out, 48.2 overs)	134		(8 wickets, 69.5 overs)	191	

Fall of wickets: 1-1 (Ramprakash, 0.6 ov), 2-1 (Atherton, 1.6 ov), 3-9 (Vaughan, 8.5 ov), 4-37 (Hick, 14.2 ov), 5-50 (Knight, 20.1 ov), 6-85 (Stewart, 31.5 ov), 7-100 (White, 38.4 ov), 8-100 (Cork, 39.3 ov), 9-118 (Caddick, 43.4 ov), 10-134 (Gough, 48.2 ov)
Fall of wickets: 1-3 (Ramprakash, 5.3 ov), 2-95 (Vaughan, 36.3 ov), 3-119 (Hick, 44.3 ov), 4-120 (Atherton, 44.5 ov), 5-140 (Stewart, 54.2 ov), 6-140 (White, 54.5 ov), 7-149 (Knight, 57.5 ov), 8-160 (Caddick, 60.6 ov)

WEST INDIES	O	M	R	W	Wd	Nb		O	M	R	W	Wd	Nb
Ambrose	14.2	6	30	4	-	-	Ambrose	22	11	22	1	-	-
Walsh	17	6	43	4	-	1	Walsh	23.5	5	74	6	-	7
Rose	7	2	32	0	-	2	Rose	16	3	67	1	1	5
King	10	3	24	1	-	-	King	8	2	17	0	-	-

ENGLAND v WEST INDIES, THIRD TEST

Venue: Old Trafford, Manchester
Toss: West Indies won the toss and decided to bat
Umpires: DB Cowie, P Willey
Reserve Umpire: A Clarkson

Date: 3rd, 4th, 5th, 6th, 7th August 2000
Result: Match drawn
TV Umpire: KE Palmer
Referee: RS Madugalle

WEST INDIES	1ST INNINGS	R	B	2ND INNINGS	R	B
SL Campbell	c Thorpe b Gough	2	11	c Cork b White	55	101
AFG Griffith	lbw b Caddick	2	19	lbw b Croft	54	196
WW Hinds	c Stewart b Cork	26	70	c Stewart b Gough	25	58
BC Lara	c Thorpe b Gough	13	74	run out (Hussain)	112	158
*JC Adams	c Thorpe b White	24	92	lbw b Cork	53	215
RR Sarwan	lbw b Cork	36	100	lbw b Caddick	19	38
+RD Jacobs	b Caddick	5	20	not out	42	111
FA Rose	lbw b Cork	16	20	lbw b White	10	21
CEL Ambrose	c Hussain b Caddick	3	5	not out	36	45
RD King	not out	3	17			
CA Walsh	lbw b Cork	7	6			
Extras	(1 b, 12 lb, 7 nb)	20		(14 b, 4 lb, 12 nb, 2 w)	32	
Total	(all out, 71.1 overs)	157		(7 wickets, dec, 155 overs)	438	

Fall of wickets: 1-3 (Campbell, 2.5 ov), 2-12 (Griffith, 5.5 ov), 3-49 (Hinds, 27.3 ov), 4-49 (Lara, 28.5 ov), 5-118 (Sarwan, 57.1 ov), 6-126 (Jacobs, 63.1 ov), 7-130 (Adams, 64.1 ov), 8-135 (Ambrose, 65.3 ov), 9-148 (Rose, 69.1 ov), 10-157 (Walsh, 71.1 ov)
Fall of wickets: 1-96 (Campbell, 36.5 ov), 2-145 (Hinds, 54.5 ov), 3-164 (Griffith, 61.6 ov), 4-302 (Lara, 104.1 ov), 5-335 (Sarwan, 118.2 ov), 6-373 (Adams, 135.1 ov), 7-384 (Rose, 140.4 ov)

ENGLAND	O	M	R	W	Wd	Nb		O	M	R	W	Wd	Nb
Gough	21	3	58	2	-	4	Gough	27	5	96	1	-	11
Caddick	24	10	45	3	-	3	Caddick	23	4	64	1	-	1
Cork	17.1	8	23	4	-	-	Cork	28	9	64	1	-	-
White	9	1	18	1	-	-	Croft	47	8	124	1	-	-
							White	27	5	67	2	-	-
							Trescothick	1	0	2	0	2	-
							Vaughan	2	1	3	0	-	-

ENGLAND	1ST INNINGS	R	B	2ND INNINGS	R	B
MA Atherton	c Campbell b Walsh	1	16	c Jacobs b Walsh	28	63
ME Trescothick	b Walsh	66	163	not out	38	101
*N Hussain	c Adams b Walsh	10	36	not out	6	41
GP Thorpe	lbw b Walsh	0	1			
+AJ Stewart	c Jacobs b Ambrose	105	153			
MP Vaughan	c Lara b Ambrose	29	100			
C White	b King	6	30			
DG Cork	c Jacobs b Ambrose	16	35			
RDB Croft	not out	27	44			
AR Caddick	lbw b Ambrose	3	7			
D Gough	c Ambrose b King	12	11			
Extras	(10 b, 6 lb, 12 nb)	28		(4 b, 1 lb, 3 nb)	8	
Total	(all out, 97.2 overs)	303		(1 wicket, 33.4 overs)	80	

Fall of wickets: 1-1 (Atherton, 3.6 ov), 2-17 (Hussain, 13.4 ov), 3-17 (Thorpe, 13.5 ov), 4-196 (Stewart, 58.2 ov), 5-198 (Trescothick, 63.2 ov), 6-210 (White, 71.4 ov), 7-251 (Cork, 82.4 ov), 8-275 (Vaughan, 90.4 ov), 9-283 (Caddick, 92.3 ov), 10-303 (Gough, 97.2 ov)
Fall of wickets: 1-61 (Atherton, 21.1 ov)

WEST INDIES	O	M	R	W	Wd	Nb		O	M	R	W	Wd	Nb
Ambrose	27	7	70	4	-	1	Ambrose	12	2	31	0	-	2
Walsh	27	14	50	4	-	-	Walsh	14	6	19	1	-	-
Rose	20	3	83	0	-	7	King	2.4	0	15	0	-	-
King	12.2	3	52	2	-	3	Adams	5	1	10	0	-	1
Adams	11	4	32	0	-	1							

ENGLAND v WEST INDIES, FOURTH TEST

Venue: Headingley, Leeds
Toss: West Indies won the toss and decided to bat
Umpires: DB Cowie, G Sharp
Reserve Umpire: VA Holder
Scorers: LB Hewes (West Indies), JT Potter (England)

Date: 17th, 18th August 2000
Result: England won by an innings and 39 runs
TV Umpire: DJ Constant
Referee: RS Madugalle

WEST INDIES	1ST INNINGS	R	B	2ND INNINGS	R	B
SL Campbell	c Trescothick b Gough	8	11	c Hick b Gough	12	35
AFG Griffith	c Stewart b Gough	22	51	b Gough	0	1
WW Hinds	c Stewart b White	16	47	lbw b Gough	0	1
BC Lara	lbw b White	4	7	lbw b Gough	2	10
*JC Adams	b White	2	9	b Cork	19	43
RR Sarwan	not out	59	82	not out	17	56
+RD Jacobs	c Caddick b Cork	35	57	lbw b Caddick	1	5
NAM McLean	c Stewart b White	7	17	b Caddick	0	2
CEL Ambrose	b Cork	1	2	b Caddick	0	1
RD King	lbw b Gough	6	11	b Caddick	0	3
CA Walsh	c Caddick b White	1	6	b Caddick	3	5
Extras	(2 lb, 9 nb)	11		(3 lb, 4 nb)	7	
Total	(all out, 48.4 overs)	172		(all out, 26.2 overs)	61	

Fall of wickets: 1-11 (Campbell, 2.5 ov), 2-50 (Hinds, 16.1 ov), 3-54 (Lara, 18.2 ov), 4-56 (Griffith, 19.2 ov), 5-60 (Adams, 20.5 ov), 6-128 (Jacobs, 37.2 ov), 7-143 (McLean, 42.3 ov), 8-148 (Ambrose, 43.1 ov), 9-168 (King, 47.2 ov), 10-172 (Walsh, 48.4 ov)
Fall of wickets: 1-3 (Griffith, 2.1 ov), 2-3 (Hinds, 2.2 ov), 3-11 (Lara, 4.3 ov), 4-21 (Campbell, 10.4 ov), 5-49 (Adams, 19.5 ov), 6-52 (Jacobs, 22.1 ov), 7-52 (McLean, 22.3 ov), 8-52 (Ambrose, 22.4 ov), 9-53 (King, 22.6 ov), 10-61 (Walsh, 26.2 ov)

ENGLAND	O	M	R	W	Wd	Nb		O	M	R	W	Wd	Nb
Gough	17	2	59	3	-	6	Gough	10	3	30	4	-	3
Caddick	10	3	35	0	-	2	Caddick	11.2	5	14	5	-	1
White	14.4	4	57	5	-	-	Cork	5	0	14	1	-	-
Cork	7	0	19	2	-	-							

ENGLAND	1ST INNINGS	R	B	2ND INNINGS	R	B
MA Atherton	c Lara b Ambrose	6	18			
ME Trescothick	c Lara b Ambrose	1	7			
*N Hussain	lbw b Walsh	22	74			
GP Thorpe	lbw b Walsh	46	103			
+AJ Stewart	c Campbell b Walsh	5	18			
MP Vaughan	c Jacobs b Ambrose	76	132			
AR Caddick	c Jacobs b Ambrose	6	29			
GA Hick	st Jacobs b Adams	59	95			
C White	c Jacobs b McLean	0	7			
DG Cork	not out	11	19			
D Gough	c Griffith b Walsh	2	7			
Extras	(4 b, 13 lb, 18 nb, 3 w)	38				
Total	(all out, 81.5 overs)	272				

Fall of wickets: 1-7 (Trescothick, 2.5 ov), 2-10 (Atherton, 4.6 ov), 3-80 (Hussain, 28.3 ov), 4-93 (Thorpe, 34.4 ov), 5-96 (Stewart, 36.4 ov), 6-124 (Caddick, 47.3 ov), 7-222 (Hick, 72.2 ov), 8-223 (White, 73.4 ov), 9-269 (Vaughan, 80.1 ov), 10-272 (Gough, 81.5 ov)

WEST INDIES	O	M	R	W	Wd	Nb		O	M	R	W	Wd	Nb
Ambrose	18	3	42	4	-	5							
Walsh	24.5	9	51	4	-	6							
King	11	2	48	0	3	4							
McLean	22	5	93	1	-	3							
Adams	6	1	21	1	-	-							

ENGLAND v WEST INDIES, FIFTH TEST

Venue: The Oval, Kennington
Toss: West Indies won the toss and decided to field
Umpires: DJ Harper, DR Shepherd
Reserve Umpire: AGT Whitehead
Scorers: KR Booth, LB Hewes

Date: 31st August, 1st, 2nd, 3rd, 4th September 2000
Result: England won by 158 runs
TV Umpire: B Leadbeater
Referee: RS Madugalle

ENGLAND	1ST INNINGS	R	B	2ND INNINGS	R	B
MA Atherton	b McLean	83	214	c Jacobs b Walsh	108	331
ME Trescothick	c Campbell b Nagamootoo	78	192	c Lara b Ambrose	7	36
*N Hussain	c Jacobs b Nagamootoo	0	2	lbw b McLean	0	15
GP Thorpe	lbw b Walsh	40	158	c Griffith b Walsh	10	56
+AJ Stewart	lbw b McLean	0	3	c Campbell b Nagamootoo	25	104
MP Vaughan	lbw b Ambrose	10	26	lbw b Walsh	9	46
GA Hick	lbw b Ambrose	17	73	c Campbell b Walsh	0	2
C White	not out	11	40	run out (Griffith)	18	25
DG Cork	lbw b McLean	0	6	lbw b McLean	26	27
AR Caddick	c Hinds b Walsh	4	17	c Jacobs b McLean	0	3
D Gough	b Walsh	8	21	not out	1	8
Extras	(4 b, 15 lb, 10 nb, 1 w)	30		(1 b, 7 lb, 5 nb)	13	
Total	(all out, 123.4 overs)	281		(all out, 108 overs)	217	

Fall of wickets: 1-159 (Trescothick, 61.3 ov), 2-159 (Hussain, 61.5 ov), 3-184 (Atherton, 72.1 ov), 4-184 (Stewart, 72.4 ov), 5-214 (Vaughan, 82.3 ov), 6-254 (Hick, 108.6 ov), 7-254 (Thorpe, 109.5 ov), 8-255 (Cork, 112.5 ov), 9-264 (Caddick, 119.3 ov), 10-281 (Gough, 123.4 ov)
Fall of wickets: 1-21 (Trescothick, 12.5 ov), 2-29 (Hussain, 18.3 ov), 3-56 (Thorpe, 37.3 ov), 4-121 (Stewart, 71.1 ov), 5-139 (Vaughan, 85.2 ov), 6-139 (Hick, 85.4 ov), 7-163 (White, 93.1 ov), 8-207 (Cork, 104.3 ov), 9-207 (Caddick, 104.6 ov), 10-217 (Atherton, 108 ov)

WEST INDIES	O	M	R	W	Wd	Nb		O	M	R	W	Wd	Nb
Ambrose	31	8	38	2	-	5	Ambrose	22	8	36	1	-	4
Walsh	35.4	16	68	3	-	5	Walsh	38	17	73	4	-	1
McLean	29	6	80	3	1	-	McLean	22	5	60	3	-	-
Nagamootoo	24	7	63	2	-	-	Nagamootoo	19	7	29	1	-	-
Adams	4	0	13	0	-	-	Adams	7	3	11	0	-	-

WEST INDIES	1ST INNINGS	R	B	2ND INNINGS	R	B
SL Campbell	b Cork	20	74	c Hick b Gough	28	49
AFG Griffith	c Hick b White	6	64	c Stewart b Caddick	20	67
WW Hinds	lbw b Cork	2	7	(4) lbw b Caddick	7	15
BC Lara	b White	0	1	(3) lbw b Gough	47	104
*JC Adams	c Hick b Cork	5	17	c White b Caddick	15	58
RR Sarwan	c Trescothick b White	5	8	run out (Thorpe)	27	31
+RD Jacobs	not out	26	61	c Hick b Caddick	1	4
MV Nagamootoo	c Trescothick b Gough	18	22	lbw b Gough	13	15
CEL Ambrose	lbw b Caddick	0	1	(10) c Atherton b Cork	28	36
NAM McLean	b White	29	46	(9) not out	23	41
CA Walsh	b White	5	10	lbw b Cork	0	2
Extras	(3 lb, 6 nb)	9		(3 lb, 2 nb, 1 w)	6	
Total	(all out, 50.5 overs)	125		(all out, 70 overs)	215	

Fall of wickets: 1-32 (Campbell, 21.3 ov), 2-32 (Griffith, 22.4 ov), 3-32 (Lara, 22.5 ov), 4-34 (Hinds, 23.4 ov), 5-39 (Sarwan, 24.6 ov), 6-51 (Adams, 29.5 ov), 7-74 (Nagamootoo, 34.6 ov), 8-75 (Ambrose, 35.6 ov), 9-119 (McLean, 48.5 ov), 10-125 (Walsh, 50.5 ov)
Fall of wickets: 1-50 (Campbell, 18.3 ov), 2-50 (Griffith, 19.3 ov), 3-58 (Hinds, 25.1 ov), 4-94 (Adams, 43.4 ov), 5-140 (Sarwan, 52.2 ov), 6-142 (Jacobs, 53.2 ov), 7-150 (Lara, 54.3 ov), 8-167 (Nagamootoo, 58.5 ov), 9-215 (Ambrose, 69.4 ov), 10-215 (Walsh, 70 ov)

ENGLAND	O	M	R	W	Wd	Nb		O	M	R	W	Wd	Nb
Gough	13	3	25	1	-	4	Gough	20	3	64	3	1	2
Caddick	18	7	42	1	-	2	Caddick	21	7	54	4	-	-
White	11.5	1	32	5	-	-	White	11	2	32	0	-	-
Cork	8	3	23	3	-	-	Cork	15	1	50	2	-	-
							Vaughan	3	1	12	0	-	-

CHAPTER 10

2004
400 NOT OUT

'The most significant single in the history of Test cricket'

BOB WILLIS

THE KENSINGTON OVAL is a lively track and England's big guys are taking potshots at anyone who gets in their way.

It's been the story for weeks now, since the devastating fourth morning at Sabina Park when Steve Harmison shows himself as a fast bowler in the style of the great, old West Indians models, and it's the story again now. Harmison and his stablemate Andrew Flintoff are running riot and for us there's nowhere to hide. We lost in Jamaica. We lost in Trinidad. And now...

Flintoff is so hard to pick up. He has this wrist thing going on, whereby he's able to bend it backwards so far that you lose sight of the ball at the point of release. Harmison meanwhile is all arms and legs, banging it in short and smashing into the ribcage. He's too quick to hook with confidence and the bounce is on the uneven side, so that shot isn't really on the cards.

But here's a weird thing: I feel good for the first time in the series. My feet feel lighter. I'm ducking and weaving. It's as if the desperation of the situation and intensity of battle gives me more clarity. When my back's against the wall, something comes alive inside of me. I'm locked into the moment more than I have been for some time.

I was just taking the blows and hanging in there. I only face 71 balls for 36 before Flintoff gets one to climb on me and I'm caught in the gully. It's not much. It may sound like a small total for me. It *is* a small total for me. But I can feel as if something's on the horizon.

We're fighting for our lives in what was once the unbreachable fortress of West Indies cricket. After posting 224, we have them 155-8, before Graham Thorpe inches his way to a hundred and England to a two-run lead.

In our second innings we fall down *again*. Matthew Hoggard rips out our middle order with a hat-trick – Ronnie Sarwan, Shiv

Chanderpaul, Ryan Hinds – and we're sinking again, we're going under, we're going down in the match and going down in history.

My mind is bursting with terrible thoughts. We haven't lost a series at home to England since the year before I was born. It's 2004, a month shy of my 35th birthday, and I'm standing out there getting peppered, last man standing, knowing that I'll go down as the captain who let that record slip away.

* * *

Before Barbados, I'd managed 31 runs across the first two Test matches. Only Australia in 2000/01, when I bagged a duck apiece at Brisbane and Perth, had I started a series so badly, and I hit 182 at Adelaide immediately after that. So this is uncharted waters for me. And the job? The job is *hard*. I'd only returned to the captaincy 12 months earlier. We'd had some decent results – we won a series against Sri Lanka and broke the world record for a successful run chase against Australia, so even though we lost that series, and went down 3-0 in South Africa, I still felt pretty comfortable in the dressing room.

This experience against England, though, is tipping me over the edge. Captaining a struggling cricket team for five days on home soil? There's no other role in sport that puts as much mental, emotional and physical strain on an individual.

I couldn't get over the feeling that we'd swapped personalities. That the English now had these towering brutes bowling chin music and we had these raw, skiddy hopefuls looking to get a little swerve and movement. England's attack was totally different to their attacks of the past, and in some respects ours was too.

Harmison? *Revelation*. Tall, quick, awkward. He wasn't Ambrose-accurate but he didn't spray it around too much and that spell of 7-12 in Jamaica, in a match that was evenly poised, for me that must be the best bowling performance by an Englishman against a West Indies team that I played in. That spell put him on the map, and for a couple of years afterwards, he was as good a fast bowler as there was in the world.

Something else about this attack, and it came through at Trinidad in the second Test (0 and 8, don't wanna talk about it), was how deep their bowlers dug. It just wasn't something we were accustomed to. England now had bowlers that could come out after lunch with a ball 30 overs old and do real damage. Short stuff, reverse swing. That sort of threat belonged to very few teams and bowlers. This bunch had the lot.

The day before the final Test in Antigua I had a look at the runs chart. No one had run away with it. The bowlers had dominated. Only two hundreds had been registered – Thorpe's knock in Barbados and our opener Devon Smith for us, on the first day of the series.

I turned to Daren Ganga, a fellow Trinidadian who I was very close to and who I felt had a lot of talent, and told him I was going to score the most runs in the series. He laughed it off.

* * *

Getting to Antigua, the motivation was clear: avoid the whitewash.

There was some hesitation about what to do should I win the toss. Should we put ourselves in the firing line again with England going for the jugular, ready to make history? The pitch looked like a typical Recreation Ground surface, dry grass at the top and very hard, and we knew it would play well throughout. The dilemma: do I ask England to bat because we're scared of getting blown away, or do I take the bull by the horns and bat? I decided to take the positive option.

Chris Gayle and Ganga took care of the first hour but when I got to the crease Harmison was waiting. A few balls in, I'm still on nought, he angles a full ball across me, and as I go to punch it to mid-off, it leaves me late and flies through to Geraint Jones. There's a huge appeal. They're convinced I've nicked it.

There was a noise when the ball passed the bat, I don't dispute that. But I felt nothing on my bat. How much times have we seen in today's cricket where you hear something and there's no contact with the bat? The frustration that the English team showed, especially their captain Michael Vaughan, was maybe warranted. All I could tell them was the truth, which is that I am someone who walks. But I don't walk because *you* think I'm out, I walk because I *know* I'm out.

In Barbados I'd twice got through the initial assault, and once I'd done the same here I began to find my flow. A couple of loose deliveries from Hoggard were spanked to the fence, and Harmison was blunted. Once I'd cleared off those first 30 balls, I could start to expand my horizons a little. I duly registered my first fifty for the series and on a rain-affected first day, I went in 86 not out, knowing the hard work was to come.

The first hundred, which came inside the first half hour of day two, barely registered. My reaction told its own story. All I could think about was batting England out of the Test match.

From the moment I was out of that vulnerable period, starting again on day two, I had my eyes set on it, and once I've formed the picture, it starts to open out in front of me. That second spell from Harmison is not quite as penetrative as the first. I get through the second new ball either side of lunch. Some of the energy starts to drain out of them, and it's like we all settle into our roles. By late afternoon, they know as well as I do that the only person who can get Brian Lara out is Brian Lara. Nobody's expecting some magical delivery to emerge from nowhere. I bat through to the close, 313 not out.

There are no thoughts of declaring. If we declare on 595, our overnight score, there's a chance, especially with time being made up for the rain, that we'll be put under pressure on the final day. We had to make *sure* that England couldn't win the match. And besides, the crowd would have killed me if I'd declared. Our first concern was not being whitewashed, but I also felt that our best chance of winning the game was to bat on for another session – ensuring that we only have to bat once in the match – and *then* declare, bowl them out, make them follow-on, and see what day five has in store.

That morning, day three, I play golf, just like all those years ago. I guess by 2004 I'm more mature, because this time I get a little sleep beforehand.

* * *

In all my time, I never played a premeditated shot in a Test match. I'd *anticipate,* sure. All batters do that. The best ones have a sixth sense for what's coming down and mentally set themselves for the possibility. But I never premeditated. Like, against spinners, I never made up my mind to run down the pitch before the ball was released. I was sharp on my feet, and I was quick to pick up the trajectory of the ball, so I was able to make up my mind *after* the ball was in the air whether to jump out to play the big shot, or stay back in my crease and take it from there. It was the same against Warne, against Murali. I would wait to see it released from the hand before deciding where to go and what to do. The technique served me well. I went 12 years without being stumped in Test cricket.

So, the final few shots leading up to the landmark, all against England's offspinners, are controlled and calculated. I don't play a single false shot all morning. When Michael Vaughan tries to make things difficult, bringing mid-on up to Gareth Batty's off-breaks, hoping I'll play across the line trying to hit over mid-on, I launch him into the Players' Stand – over mid-on. That shot moves me from 374 onto 380, equal with Matthew Hayden's record. Next ball, I sweep for four to get to 384.

I never thought of taking the record back, of *reclaiming* it from Hayden. People like to say that I made it known that he'd only "borrowed" that record from me, as if it was on loan, or something. Truth was, I had enough on my plate without thinking about that stuff. There's a lot of rubbish spoken about it. That late night in Jamaica in 2003 when I got a call from my lawyer, giving me the number for the Perth dressing room to call up Hayden, I wasn't devastated or disappointed or anything of the kind, I just called him up, congratulated him and went back to sleep. It happens.

Anyway, I'm on 390 at lunch, with local boy Ridley Jacobs having just brought up his own hundred. We step out after the interval for one last dart and soon enough, with another sweep shot off Batty, I make it through. Make that a single, a double, a triple, a quadruple and a quintuple. The adrenaline propels me through to the non-striker's end and I fling myself in the air. Outwardly, my celebration is much more expressive than it was 10 years ago. But when the moment dies down and I'm left with just my thoughts, what's the overriding emotion? *Relief.*

The game ends in frustrating anti-climax. We make England follow-on and despite a good Vaughan hundred in their second innings, they're five down in the final session and there's still time to force a result. Sarwan is bowling his leg-breaks, Flintoff pushes one to my left hand at slip. I grab at it, but two of my fingers are strapped up so I can't get a proper grip, and in my momentum the ball rolls out of my hand. I backheel it like I'm playing for Spurs and make one last effort to grab it back, but it hits the turf. Our chance to win goes with that drop.

Funnily enough, and this is true, whenever I think back to Antigua 2004, that dropped catch comes through to me more vividly than anything else.

The aftermath is similar to '94 in that it has the prestige of a country celebrating one of its heroes, but the tone is slightly different. In 1994, it was a spontaneous outpouring. You're young and you speak from the heart. This time I remember having a written speech and being a little more political. I remember telling the government what I thought they needed to do to develop the game of cricket and sport in general. And I remember being more tired.

* * *

What had once felt impossible now feels inevitable.

Hard as it is to accept, we have to concede we're playing a very good side. They've put together a bowling attack that would go on to win back the Ashes. They have a world-class allrounder. Their back-up seamer is someone called Anderson, and they can bat. With something for them to achieve and the tools at their disposal, there is no respite. Just a few months on from Antigua, we'll face each other again, and this time on their turf.

I never started a series without optimism. It was never on my mind that just because we lost in the Caribbean it would be the same story in England. Every series is tough, but I was always optimistic. And our preparation was OK. We began with a win at Arundel against a good MCC side; I got a hundred as did Devon Smith, and Shiv Chanderpaul and Dwayne Bravo both made hundreds against Sri Lanka A at Shenley, so I felt that with the bat we were in a good space going into the first Test at Lord's.

I'd established in my mind what it was that irked me about that place. It's when you're walking in your pads around the perimeter of the ground to the nets at the nursery ground, and you look up to see these huge canvas photographs draped on these tall pillars behind each stand, each of them showing players who have done great things at the ground, these vast reminders of their feats, and I guess what I hadn't yet done myself. There are certain places where you feel that you belong and I felt like I belonged on one of those pillars, and on that wooden board in the dressing room. But in the days before the match I'm mindful of falling into the same trap which has caused me problems before. Thinking about milestones and honours boards gets me into trouble mentally.

Our attack is raw, but we have some pace. I believed that Tino Best and Fidel Edwards could get some joy. I'd seen Tino rough up a few of their guys in the West Indies and I thought that English conditions would suit his qualities – a pitch with moisture, with his pace, something *must* happen – and of course Fidel Edwards was a swing bowler. With some tight medium pace from Pedro Collins and Bravo backing them up, I felt we had a puncher's chance.

Our entire seam attack was playing there for the first time, and with the slope and the contours of the ground, the famous slanted pitch, we knew there was a danger of us getting overwhelmed if our lines were slightly off. Still, I was optimistic.

England won the toss and batted first. At the end of the first day they were 391-2.

* * *

I walked out to bat just after tea on day two. I had a clear head. My modus operandi was always to get set before expressing myself. I'd been batting for just over half an hour when I pushed forward to an Ashley Giles straighter delivery which beat my outside edge. I didn't touch it. Up goes Geraint Jones, the close fielders, and the umpire's finger. I took my time leaving the field.

I am upset, to say the least. I want to throw my entire kitbag over the balcony but as captain I have to compose myself. That night, I'm questioned about it in the press conference and I have one thing to say. "I still find it impossible not to walk when I am out." And I left it there. Chew on that.

Scrapping hard against a huge total, we at least got to see Shiv Chanderpaul at his best. Standing on the balcony to see him make his first hundred at Lord's, I was elated for him. From the scrawny boy who made his debut against England in 1994 to this, a decade later, one of the two steady hands in the batting line-up.

He was just a wonderful player. Coming in at No.5, often in difficult situations, he never dropped his guard. Bowlers like batters who come at them, because they believe they can be ruffled and dragged into a fight, but Chanderpaul was so single-minded that whatever situation he found himself in, he always had a plan. Speak to any opposition bowler, they hated bowling to him because defensively he was so strong. His temperament was incredible. He was never perturbed by anything.

He took his time to develop. When he came into the team you got the sense that socially he felt that he didn't belong, as if he was under observation, and it made him very reserved. He didn't look like your typical West Indian cricketer. Small, fidgety, he would touch his pads, touch his arm guard, he would shake his helmet; he had this uniqueness about him.

Quietly, in his own way, Shiv symbolised a large part of West Indies cricket which is not always represented at times, and that's the Indian community. He came to be loved throughout the Caribbean but especially, I felt, in Trinidad.

In 1994, he was side-on to the ball. Ten years later he was facing midwicket. He did things his way. In our cricket you were left alone. An occasional coach or former great player might come by to talk about any issues you may have, but generally we were left to do our own thing. Chanderpaul never compromised on his own ideas and, perhaps in part because of that, he got better with age. Our stories have always been tied up with each other's. I was so proud of him that day. And he followed it up in our second innings with another unbeaten score. He batted for more than 10 hours at Lord's and still they couldn't get him out.

We were beaten but we weren't dominated. If you score north of 650 runs in a Test match, you'd think you probably wouldn't lose. But what could we do? We had a pace attack which had never toured England, never bowled a ball at Lord's. We left that Test match knowing where our problems were.

* * *

A weakness of my captaincy was not understanding that the levels had dropped. Second time around in the job, I was actively trying to be more empathetic and understanding of the players around me, and I tried to work with them as much as possible, but I was still learning. For me, coming into the team as a kid, I didn't grow up having that empathy level. It just wasn't a part of the culture back then, so I didn't pick up those skills. The truth was, if your early performances didn't cut it, then you were disposed of, and someone else would step up.

I grew up seeing serious players who were amazing in first-class cricket but never got a look-in, so I struggled to process the fact that things had shifted. I should have been able to adjust to that, to adapt my leadership to take in this new reality. I was still partly of a mind that because you're playing for the West Indies, you should have what it takes, but it just wasn't the order of the day. The way I grew up, playing under Viv Richards, the attitude was such that if you got into his team you *had* to be a damn good player. And once you were in, there would be immediate responsibilities and expectations that came with it.

I had two years as an apprentice. This was what some of these youngsters needed, a proper learning phase, instead of being thrown in at the deep end.

I'd see them in the nets, I knew they had talent. I made my plans. Maybe those plans were meant for more experienced bowlers, battle-hardened campaigners who could execute, but I blame no one for our failures and I definitely don't blame my teammates. It was a combination of so much.

If I started with myself, it was a failure to appreciate the rawness of the talent we had. But my body language was a problem as well. I didn't use harsh words against my bowlers but, you know, a slumped head in the slips with a hand on my knee would indicate certain things, and I was guilty of that.

I'd get frustrated and my body language would give me away but I didn't mean anything by it. You just spend so much of your life watching the best team in the world play, and then, when you get into that team, you expect it to be a natural thing. And it wasn't.

We might also want to ask the West Indies board if the cricketers they were producing were given the right platform, the right foundation, to go out and perform at the top level. Were we harnessing their talent? Did we sufficiently value the academy system? Did we pay enough attention to the pathways through which young talented kids come through and the elite coaching methods that helped them improve? I stood at first slip at certain points that summer thinking that these kids were just lambs to the slaughter.

This was our reality. We were going through a cycle and now it was our turn to be punished. I just wasn't able to look it square in the face.

* * *

It's day two at Edgbaston, second Test, we're facing down another big score, and I'm batting as well as I've ever done in my life.

Matthew Hoggard is swinging it into my pads and I'm lacing him through mid-on, midwicket, square leg. Only against Harmison do I take a back step from time to time.

Honestly, it's right up there. I'm in such rhythm. A big score at Edgbaston would be a special thing. After encountering that horror pitch in '95, and not leaving too much of a mark on the 2000 Test, it was starting to feel a little like Trinidad, where it's my home ground and I'm fixated on doing well, but I'm running the risk of not concentrating on what really motivates me. Well, this match, this moment here, this is it.

There's nothing in front of me other than a big score. I'm not even thinking about a hundred, only about batting for as long as possible. I cruise into the nineties. Vaughan calls Flintoff back for another blast.

We'd first caught sight of Flintoff in 2000, when Ambrose and Walsh were still around. He wasn't quite the full deal back then. He was very young, played nicely off the back foot outside off stump, could hit a clean ball, bit loose. But as he gathered more experience he became a *magnificent* cricketer. His mindset I knew nothing about, but if we're talking about natural skill, he would be right up there. He was an instinctive player, never one to get bogged down by stats. He was fun to be on a cricket field with. He played to enjoy the game and you knew when he wasn't enjoying it. Well, he was enjoying himself that summer.

I'm on 95. I've been batting for over three hours. It's the 50th over of the innings. It's been a chanceless knock. In he comes, this vast unit pounding the turf, climbing into his delivery stride and in the same movement throwing his body wide of the crease to create his favoured angle across the left-hander, the arm reaching just past the perpendicular to release the ball from an immense altitude. I'm expecting to see something, a whirr of red maybe, but I've got nothing, I've lost it, I can't pick the thing up, his wrist has cocked so far back that the effect, accentuated with his height, is to hide the cherry at the point of release, so when he sends it down I only catch sight of it when it's halfway towards me. Flinching, as instincts of self-preservation kick in, I compute at the last split-second that it's full and straight and I squeeze my bat down to trap it in front of my stumps.

Right, OK. What happened there? My mind flashes back to Barbados, and getting battered back then by Flintoff. There's something murky about that wrist. It happened then and it's happening again now. It freaks me out. And the stands at Edgbaston, they're low, and I realise that somewhere in the distance, above the stands, *this* is where his hand is coming from. So I crouch a bit lower, ready to jab down on another full one or duck the bouncer, and I don't see this next one *at all*. Late pick-up, pushed drive, edged and a good catch by Graham Thorpe. Gone for 95 on my home ground. The despair is indescribable.

If you ask me what's my best innings, I wouldn't say that. But if you ask me how good I felt *during* an innings, this would be hard to top. I was thinking beyond. *Beyond.*

I don't think he did his 'Christ the Redeemer' celebration, perhaps that came later in the Flintoff story. I remember thinking during that later Ashes series, watching him roll it out every time he got a wicket, that it's great to see it when it's not you doing it. Imagine the flak I'd get back home if I ever got down on one knee and opened my arms like the Almighty, returned to save us all.

Flintoff's wrist, man. I'd never known a bowler like it. A few years later, batting at the same ground, facing the same bowler from the same end, Jacques Kallis would get the same result, losing sight of the ball, only picking it up mid-pitch, flinching and soon enough getting cleaned up. Forget the Redeemer. Fred's more like the devil.

* * *

We're well beaten at Edgbaston, just as at Lord's. I get another rough decision in the second innings, again off Giles, but so be it. The game hits hard when it wants to.

The next match at Old Trafford gives us brief reason for optimism. We bat first and are actually up in the match at the halfway stage thanks to some brilliant work from Dwayne Bravo, whose six wickets give us heart, before a third-innings collapse presents England with a manageable chase and Rob Key and Flintoff, fresh off his 167 at Edgbaston, see them home by seven wickets.

I'm now officially Flintoff's bunny, by the way. He nicks me off twice in the match. I can't see past that wrist.

I wouldn't say I'm willing it to end. But this epic and deeply scarring eight-Test marathon will come to a merciful end at The Oval. I play that Test match with the sort of freedom that comes from knowing that what will be, will be.

* * *

I'm not sure if enjoyment is quite the word, but my battle with Harmison on the second day of that match is up there with the most thrilling passages of play I can remember. He bowls seriously fast that day, and I guess it's only right that he will be the one to end this passage of Test cricket in the same way as he started it: by blowing us away.

In all, he takes eight wickets on that Friday spread across two innings; six in the first, and two more in our second innings after we follow-on. In amongst the carnage, I make 79 in quick time, taking him on before he gets me, eventually caught hooking to a very fine fine-leg. It was daredevil batting, maybe even devil-may-care. But look, we've been pummelled for months, we're gonna be whitewashed. At least throw a few back before the inevitable.

I think on that last afternoon of the series, I get the first unplayable delivery of my career.

Sure, I've been beaten by good balls and cleaned up, I've been beaten and it's taken the edge. What I'm talking about is a delivery that's swerving into my pads so I'm shaping up to hit through mid-on, the ball is telling me that I *have* to hit it there, so I get into position, and then it just, I don't know... it kind of *stops* and darts off the other way. Suddenly I'm going one way and the ball is going another and as I swivel round the ball is already with the slip fielder.

The kid who bowled it is in his early 20s. He's been kicking around the edges of the series, not doing much. This is only the ninth Test match of his career. In what turns out to be my final Test innings against England, Jimmy Anderson bowls me the best ball I will ever face in my life.

* * *

Oh, how we could have done with a Harmison or an Anderson that summer. Our attack – raw, inexperienced, thrown to the wolves – was massacred. We gave up 2,742 runs in four matches. In return we took 57 wickets, all at a cost of 48 runs per wicket. At no stage did we manage to take 20 wickets in a match. This was our reality.

As for my captaincy, I felt it was probably time to finish it, and besides, I figured I'd be sacked anyway. Certain things had come along to prolong it – the 400 was one – but this felt like the end. It had been a long and bruising year. We weren't exactly over-blessed with alternatives. But I guess, ultimately, I still found it impossible not to walk when I knew I was out.

Not quite yet though. We still had this one-day tournament to play at the end of the summer. Somehow, I'd need to find a way to get this tired, fractious team up for the next struggle. And to see if I could do the same for myself.

WEST INDIES v ENGLAND, FIRST TEST

Venue: Sabina Park, Kingston
Toss: West Indies won the toss and decided to bat
Umpires: BF Bowden, DJ Harper
Referee: MJ Procter

Date: 11th, 12th, 13th, 14th March 2004
Result: England won by 10 wickets
TV Umpire: EA Nicholls

WEST INDIES	1ST INNINGS	R	B	2ND INNINGS	R	B
CH Gayle	b Harmison	5	15	c Thorpe b Harmison	9	25
DS Smith	st Read b Giles	108	188	c and b Hoggard	12	42
RR Sarwan	lbw b Hoggard	0	11	lbw b Harmison	0	8
*BC Lara	c Flintoff b Jones	23	42	(5) c Flintoff b Hoggard	0	5
S Chanderpaul	b Hoggard	7	37	(4) b Harmison	0	7
RO Hinds	c Butcher b Giles	84	117	c Read b Jones	3	23
+RD Jacobs	c Vaughan b Jones	38	45	c Hussain b Harmison	15	22
TL Best	lbw b Harmison	20	29	c Read b Harmison	0	2
A Sanford	c Trescothick b Flintoff	1	17	c Trescothick b Harmison	1	8
CD Collymore	not out	3	21	not out	2	5
FH Edwards	c Flintoff b Hoggard	1	12	c Trescothick b Harmison	0	7
Extras	(6 lb, 14 nb, 1 w)	21		(4 lb, 1 nb)	5	
Total	(all out, 86.4 overs)	311		(all out, 25.3 overs)	47	

Fall of wickets: 1-17 (Gayle, 5.3 ov), 2-22 (Sarwan, 8.5 ov), 3-73 (Lara, 22.1 ov), 4-101 (Chanderpaul, 34.3 ov), 5-223 (Smith, 59.5 ov), 6-281 (Hinds, 71.5 ov), 7-289 (Jacobs, 74.5 ov), 8-300 (Sanford, 79.5 ov), 9-307 (Best, 83.3 ov), 10-311 (Edwards, 86.4 ov)
Fall of wickets: 1-13 (Gayle, 7.4 ov), 2-13 (Sarwan, 9.6 ov), 3-15 (Chanderpaul, 11.5 ov), 4-16 (Lara, 12.6 ov), 5-21 (Smith, 14.3 ov), 6-41 (Jacobs, 21.3 ov), 7-41 (Best, 21.5 ov), 8-43 (Hinds, 22.4 ov), 9-43 (Sanford, 23.5 ov), 10-47 (Edwards, 25.3 ov)

ENGLAND	O	M	R	W	Wd	Nb		O	M	R	W	Wd	Nb
Hoggard	18.4	3	68	3	-	3	Hoggard	9	2	21	2	-	-
Harmison	21	6	61	2	1	4	Harmison	12.3	8	12	7	-	-
Flintoff	16	3	45	1	-	6	Jones	4	1	10	1	-	1
Jones	18	2	62	2	-	-							
Giles	12	0	67	2	-	-							
Vaughan	1	0	2	0	-	1							

ENGLAND	1ST INNINGS	R	B	2ND INNINGS	R	B
ME Trescothick	b Edwards	7	21	not out	6	8
*MP Vaughan	c Lara b Edwards	15	28	not out	11	9
MA Butcher	c Jacobs b Edwards	58	139			
N Hussain	c sub (DE Bernard) b Best	58	158			
GP Thorpe	c Sanford b Best	19	39			
A Flintoff	c Hinds b Sarwan	46	50			
+CMW Read	c Hinds b Best	20	46			
AF Giles	b Sanford	27	61			
MJ Hoggard	not out	9	71			
SP Jones	c Sanford b Hinds	7	13			
SJ Harmison	run out (sub->Hinds)	13	12			
Extras	(7 b, 28 lb, 18 nb, 7 w)	60		(1 b, 2 nb)	3	
Total	(all out, 103.2 overs)	339		(no wicket, 2.3 overs)	20	

Fall of wickets: 1-28 (Trescothick, 7.2 ov), 2-33 (Vaughan, 9.2 ov), 3-152 (Butcher, 47.3 ov), 4-194 (Thorpe, 59.2 ov), 5-209 (Hussain, 63.2 ov), 6-268 (Flintoff, 74.4 ov), 7-278 (Read, 81.1 ov), 8-313 (Giles, 94.4 ov), 9-325 (Jones, 99.3 ov), 10-339 (Harmison, 103.2 ov)

WEST INDIES	O	M	R	W	Wd	Nb		O	M	R	W	Wd	Nb
Collymore	26	7	55	0	-	9	Best	1.3	0	8	0	-	1
Edwards	19.3	3	72	3	2	7	Hinds	1	0	11	0	-	1
Best	19	1	57	3	4	1							
Sanford	22	1	90	1	1	1							
Hinds	11.5	2	18	1	-	-							
Gayle	1	0	6	0	-	-							
Sarwan	4	1	6	1	-	-							

WEST INDIES v ENGLAND, SECOND TEST

Venue: Queen's Park Oval, Port of Spain
Toss: West Indies won the toss and decided to bat
Umpires: BF Bowden, DJ Harper
Referee: MJ Procter

Date: 19th, 20th, 21st, 22nd, 23rd March 2004
Result: England won by 7 wickets
TV Umpire: EA Nicholls

WEST INDIES	1ST INNINGS	R	B	2ND INNINGS	R	B
CH Gayle	c Read b Harmison	62	81	b Jones	16	38
DS Smith	lbw b Harmison	35	71	c Hoggard b Jones	17	43
RR Sarwan	c Flintoff b Harmison	21	30	lbw b Jones	13	24
*BC Lara	c Giles b Harmison	0	4	(6) lbw b Harmison	8	7
S Chanderpaul	c Read b Jones	2	13	c Hussain b Flintoff	42	147
DR Smith	c Hussain b Harmison	16	22	(7) c sub (PD Collingwood) b Flintoff	14	28
+RD Jacobs	run out (Giles->Read)	40	64	(4) c Flintoff b Jones	70	92
TL Best	c Read b Hoggard	1	15	lbw b Hoggard	2	7
A Sanford	run out (Vaughan->Read)	1	18	c Trescothick b Hoggard	1	13
PT Collins	b Harmison	10	30	b Jones	7	13
CD Collymore	not out	3	17	not out	0	0
Extras	(7 lb, 4 nb, 6 w)	17		(1 b, 3 lb, 10 nb, 5 w)	19	
Total	(all out, 60.1 overs)	208		(all out, 67 overs)	209	

Fall of wickets: 1-100 (Gayle, 24.4 ov), 2-110 (DS Smith, 26.1 ov), 3-110 (Lara, 26.5 ov), 4-113 (Chanderpaul, 29.4 ov), 5-142 (DR Smith, 36.1 ov), 6-143 (Sarwan, 36.6 ov), 7-148 (Best, 41.5 ov), 8-165 (Sanford, 48.1 ov), 9-202 (Jacobs, 56.2 ov), 10-208 (Collins, 60.1 ov)
Fall of wickets: 1-34 (Gayle, 12.1 ov), 2-45 (DS Smith, 14.4 ov), 3-56 (Sarwan, 18.3 ov), 4-158 (Jacobs, 50.3 ov), 5-171 (Lara, 53.1 ov), 6-194 (DR Smith, 60.6 ov), 7-195 (Chanderpaul, 62.1 ov), 8-200 (Best, 63.4 ov), 9-205 (Sanford, 65.6 ov), 10-209 (Collins, 67 ov)

ENGLAND	O	M	R	W	Wd	Nb		O	M	R	W	Wd	Nb
Hoggard	15	3	38	1	-	1	Hoggard	16	5	48	2	-	-
Harmison	20.1	5	61	6	-	1	Harmison	16	5	40	1	-	1
Flintoff	10	3	38	0	1	2	Jones	15	2	57	5	1	1
Giles	3	0	20	0	-	-	Flintoff	12	1	27	2	-	8
Jones	12	2	44	1	1	-	Giles	7	1	29	0	-	-
							Trescothick	1	0	4	0	-	-

ENGLAND	1ST INNINGS	R	B	2ND INNINGS	R	B
ME Trescothick	c Sanford b Best	1	13	b Best	4	3
*MP Vaughan	lbw b Collins	0	2	lbw b Sanford	23	24
MA Butcher	c Jacobs b Best	61	190	not out	46	45
N Hussain	b Best	58	223	c Jacobs b Sanford	5	8
GP Thorpe	c Gayle b Collins	90	228	not out	13	11
A Flintoff	c and b DR Smith	23	24			
+CMW Read	lbw b Collins	3	11			
AF Giles	c DS Smith b Collins	37	99			
MJ Hoggard	not out	0	15			
SP Jones	b Gayle	1	13			
SJ Harmison	b Gayle	0	2			
Extras	(5 b, 20 lb, 17 nb, 3 w)	45		(4 b, 3 lb, 1 nb)	8	
Total	(all out, 133.5 overs)	319		(3 wickets, 15 overs)	99	

Fall of wickets: 1-2 (Vaughan, 0.6 ov), 2-8 (Trescothick, 3.4 ov), 3-128 (Butcher, 61.2 ov), 4-186 (Hussain, 83.1 ov), 5-218 (Flintoff, 91.2 ov), 6-230 (Read, 94.2 ov), 7-315 (Giles, 126.4 ov), 8-318 (Thorpe, 130.1 ov), 9-319 (Jones, 133.3 ov), 10-319 (Harmison, 133.5 ov)
Fall of wickets: 1-8 (Trescothick, 0.3 ov), 2-59 (Vaughan, 8.2 ov), 3-71 (Hussain, 10.2 ov)

WEST INDIES	O	M	R	W	Wd	Nb		O	M	R	W	Wd	Nb
Collins	29	8	71	4	-	6	Best	4	0	27	1	-	-
Best	28	5	71	3	1	2	Collins	4	0	25	0	-	-
Sanford	26	6	60	0	1	2	Sanford	4	1	32	2	-	-
Collymore	24	7	39	0	-	4	Collymore	3	1	8	0	-	1
DR Smith	9	0	30	1	-	3							
Gayle	16.5	6	20	2	-	-							
Sarwan	1	0	3	0	-	-							

WEST INDIES v ENGLAND, THIRD TEST

Venue: Kensington Oval, Bridgetown
Toss: England won the toss and decided to field
Umpires: DB Hair, RE Koertzen
Referee: MJ Procter

Date: 1st, 2nd, 3rd April 2004
Result: England won by 8 wickets
TV Umpire: BR Doctrove

WEST INDIES	1ST INNINGS	R	B	2ND INNINGS	R	B
CH Gayle	lbw b Hoggard	6	18	b Harmison	15	14
D Ganga	lbw b Harmison	11	41	c Thorpe b Hoggard	11	43
*BC Lara	c Butcher b Flintoff	36	71	c Vaughan b Harmison	33	112
RR Sarwan	c Flintoff b Harmison	63	146	c Giles b Hoggard	5	20
S Chanderpaul	c Thorpe b Flintoff	50	99	lbw b Hoggard	0	1
RO Hinds	c Jones b Harmison	5	18	c Flintoff b Hoggard	0	1
+RD Jacobs	c sub (PD Collingwood) b Flintoff	6	14	c Butcher b Flintoff	1	6
TL Best	c Butcher b Flintoff	17	21	c Trescothick b Flintoff	12	30
PT Collins	c Trescothick b Jones	7	14	run out (Hussain)	1	7
CD Collymore	not out	1	12	not out	6	13
FH Edwards	c Read b Flintoff	0	1	c Hussain b Harmison	2	9
Extras	(14 lb, 7 nb, 1 w)	22		(5 lb, 3 nb)	8	
Total	(all out, 75.2 overs)	224		(all out, 42.1 overs)	94	

Fall of wickets: 1-6 (Gayle, 4.6 ov), 2-20 (Ganga, 11.5 ov), 3-88 (Lara, 31.6 ov), 4-167 (Sarwan, 57.4 ov), 5-179 (Hinds, 61.5 ov), 6-197 (Jacobs, 67.2 ov), 7-198 (Chanderpaul, 67.5 ov), 8-208 (Collins, 70.6 ov), 9-224 (Best, 75.1 ov), 10-224 (Edwards, 75.2 ov)
Fall of wickets: 1-19 (Gayle, 3.6 ov), 2-34 (Ganga, 14.2 ov), 3-45 (Sarwan, 20.4 ov), 4-45 (Chanderpaul, 20.5 ov), 5-45 (Hinds, 20.6 ov), 6-48 (Jacobs, 23.5 ov), 7-80 (Best, 35.5 ov), 8-81 (Collins, 37.6 ov), 9-85 (Lara, 38.4 ov), 10-94 (Edwards, 42.1 ov)

ENGLAND	O	M	R	W	Wd	Nb		O	M	R	W	Wd	Nb
Hoggard	16	5	34	1	-	-	Hoggard	14	4	35	4	-	1
Harmison	18	6	42	3	-	-	Harmison	15.1	5	34	3	-	-
Flintoff	16.2	2	58	5	-	3	Flintoff	13	4	20	2	-	2
Jones	16	1	55	1	1	-							
Giles	9	1	21	0	-	-							

ENGLAND	1ST INNINGS	R	B	2ND INNINGS	R	B
ME Trescothick	b Edwards	2	13	c Jacobs b Collymore	42	61
*MP Vaughan	c Jacobs b Edwards	17	69	c Jacobs b Collymore	32	33
MA Butcher	c Gayle b Edwards	5	31	not out	13	26
N Hussain	b Collymore	17	60	not out	0	2
GP Thorpe	not out	119	217			
A Flintoff	c Collymore b Best	15	28			
+CMW Read	lbw b Edwards	13	31			
AF Giles	c sub (AN Mayers) b Collins	11	24			
MJ Hoggard	lbw b Collins	0	13			
SP Jones	c Sarwan b Best	4	37			
SJ Harmison	b Collins	3	29			
Extras	(5 lb, 12 nb, 3 w)	20		(3 lb, 2 nb, 1 w)	6	
Total	(all out, 90 overs)	226		(2 wickets, 20 overs)	93	

Fall of wickets: 1-8 (Trescothick, 4.2 ov), 2-24 (Butcher, 15.1 ov), 3-33 (Vaughan, 21.6 ov), 4-65 (Hussain, 34.5 ov), 5-90 (Flintoff, 43.6 ov), 6-119 (Read, 53.6 ov), 7-147 (Giles, 61.2 ov), 8-155 (Hoggard, 63.5 ov), 9-187 (Jones, 77.6 ov), 10-226 (Harmison, 90 ov)
Fall of wickets: 1-57 (Vaughan, 11.2 ov), 2-91 (Trescothick, 19.4 ov)

WEST INDIES	O	M	R	W	Wd	Nb		O	M	R	W	Wd	Nb
Edwards	20	4	70	4	-	4	Edwards	6	0	32	0	-	-
Collins	23	6	60	3	1	5	Best	3	0	18	0	1	-
Collymore	16	3	26	1	1	3	Collymore	7	2	24	2	-	-
Hinds	4	1	7	0	-	-	Collins	4	0	16	0	-	2
Best	14	4	26	2	1	-							
Gayle	13	3	32	0	-	-							

WEST INDIES v ENGLAND, FOURTH TEST

Venue: Antigua Recreation Ground, St John's
Toss: West Indies won the toss and decided to bat
Umpires: Aleem Dar, DB Hair
Referee: MJ Procter

Date: 10th, 11th, 12th, 13th, 14th April 2004
Result: Match drawn
TV Umpire: BR Doctrove

WEST INDIES	1ST INNINGS	R	B	2ND INNINGS	R	B
CH Gayle	c and b Batty	69	80			
D Ganga	lbw b Flintoff	10	46			
*BC Lara	not out	400	582			
RR Sarwan	c Trescothick b Harmison	90	166			
RL Powell	c Hussain b SP Jones	23	39			
RO Hinds	c and b Batty	36	97			
+RD Jacobs	not out	107	207			
TL Best						
PT Collins						
CD Collymore						
FH Edwards						
Extras	(4 b, 5 lb, 5 nb, 2 w)	16				
Total	(5 wickets, dec, 202 overs)	751				

Fall of wickets: 1-33 (Ganga, 13.4 ov), 2-98 (Gayle, 25.5 ov), 3-330 (Sarwan, 83.4 ov), 4-380 (Powell, 95.5 ov), 5-469 (Hinds, 121.6 ov)

ENGLAND	O	M	R	W	Wd	Nb		O	M	R	W	Wd	Nb
Hoggard	18	2	82	0	-	2							
Harmison	37	6	92	1	2	-							
Flintoff	35	8	109	1	-	1							
SP Jones	29	0	146	1	-	-							
Batty	52	4	185	2	-	-							
Vaughan	13	0	60	0	-	2							
Trescothick	18	3	68	0	-	-							

ENGLAND	1ST INNINGS	R	B	2ND INNINGS (F/O)	R	B
ME Trescothick	c Jacobs b Best	16	34	c Sarwan b Edwards	88	188
*MP Vaughan	c Jacobs b Collins	7	17	c Jacobs b Sarwan	140	267
MA Butcher	b Collins	52	83	c Gayle b Hinds	61	164
N Hussain	b Best	3	15	b Hinds	56	107
GP Thorpe	c Collins b Edwards	10	35	not out	23	54
A Flintoff	not out	102	224	c Lara b Sarwan	14	37
+GO Jones	b Edwards	38	88	not out	10	21
GJ Batty	c Gayle b Collins	8	33			
MJ Hoggard	c Jacobs b Collins	1	33			
SP Jones	lbw b Hinds	11	50			
SJ Harmison	b Best	5	4			
Extras	(1 b, 5 lb, 22 nb, 4 w)	32		(4 b, 7 lb, 16 nb, 3 w)	30	
Total	(all out, 99 overs)	285		(5 wickets, 137 overs)	422	

Fall of wickets: 1-8 (Vaughan, 4.3 ov), 2-45 (Trescothick, 14.2 ov), 3-54 (Hussain, 18.5 ov), 4-98 (Butcher, 29.1 ov), 5-98 (Thorpe, 30.2 ov), 6-182 (GO Jones, 59.3 ov), 7-205 (Batty, 69.3 ov), 8-229 (Hoggard, 79.4 ov), 9-283 (Harmison, 96.1 ov), 10-285 (SP Jones, 99 ov)
Fall of wickets: 1-182 (Trescothick, 56.5 ov), 2-274 (Vaughan, 87.6 ov), 3-366 (Butcher, 113.3 ov), 4-387 (Hussain, 121.3 ov), 5-408 (Flintoff, 130.3 ov)

WEST INDIES	O	M	R	W	Wd	Nb		O	M	R	W	Wd	Nb
Collins	26	4	76	4	3	14	Best	16	1	57	0	2	-
Edwards	18	3	70	2	1	5	Edwards	20	2	81	1	1	8
Collymore	19	5	45	0	-	1	Collymore	18	3	58	0	-	-
Best	10.3	3	37	3	-	1	Powell	8	0	36	0	-	-
Hinds	17.3	7	29	1	-	1	Hinds	38	8	83	2	-	2
Sarwan	7	0	18	0	-	-	Gayle	17	6	36	0	-	2
Gayle	1	0	4	0	-	-	Sarwan	12	2	26	2	-	-
							Collins	8	2	34	0	-	4

ENGLAND v WEST INDIES, FIRST TEST

Venue: Lord's Cricket Ground, St John's Wood
Toss: West Indies won the toss and decided to field
Umpires: DJ Harper, RE Koertzen
Reserve Umpire: JH Evans

Date: 22nd, 23rd, 24th, 25th, 26th July 2004
Result: England won by 210 runs
TV Umpire: NJ Llong
Referee: RS Madugalle

ENGLAND	1ST INNINGS	R	B	2ND INNINGS	R	B
ME Trescothick	c Sarwan b Best	16	21	b Collins	45	93
AJ Strauss	c Jacobs b Banks	137	202	c Sarwan b Collins	35	103
RWT Key	c Lara b Bravo	221	288	run out (Chanderpaul)	15	20
*MP Vaughan	c Smith b Collins	103	154	not out	101	145
GP Thorpe	c Jacobs b Bravo	19	28	c and b Gayle	38	73
A Flintoff	b Banks	6	4	c Jacobs b Collins	58	42
+GO Jones	c Jacobs b Collins	4	13			
AF Giles	c Smith b Collins	5	10			
MJ Hoggard	not out	1	11			
SP Jones	lbw b Collins	4	7			
SJ Harmison	b Bravo	4	5			
Extras	(2 b, 20 lb, 13 nb, 13 w)	48		(3 b, 14 lb, 16 nb)	33	
Total	(all out, 121.4 overs)	568		(5 wickets, dec, 76.4 overs)	325	

Fall of wickets: 1-29 (Trescothick, 5.4 ov), 2-320 (Strauss, 65.2 ov), 3-485 (Key, 102.1 ov), 4-527 (Thorpe, 110.4 ov), 5-534 (Flintoff, 111.3 ov), 6-541 (GO Jones, 114.4 ov), 7-551 (Giles, 116.5 ov), 8-557 (Vaughan, 118.4 ov), 9-563 (SP Jones, 120.5 ov), 10-568 (Harmison, 121.4 ov)
Fall of wickets: 1-86 (Trescothick, 27.3 ov), 2-104 (Strauss, 33.4 ov), 3-117 (Key, 36.5 ov), 4-233 (Thorpe, 65.4 ov), 5-325 (Flintoff, 76.4 ov)

WEST INDIES	O	M	R	W	Wd	Nb		O	M	R	W	Wd	Nb
Collins	24	2	113	4	1	6	Best	3	1	14	0	-	-
Best	21	1	104	1	1	-	Collins	14.4	1	62	3	-	6
Edwards	21	2	96	0	3	6	Banks	26	1	92	0	-	-
Bravo	24.4	5	74	3	4	-	Edwards	13	0	47	0	-	8
Banks	22	3	131	2	-	1	Bravo	7	0	28	0	-	-
Sarwan	9	0	28	0	-	-	Gayle	9	0	45	1	-	2
							Sarwan	4	0	20	0	-	-

WEST INDIES	1ST INNINGS	R	B	2ND INNINGS	R	B
CH Gayle	lbw b Giles	66	82	b Harmison	81	88
DS Smith	b Giles	45	63	lbw b Giles	6	23
RR Sarwan	lbw b Hoggard	1	12	lbw b Hoggard	4	11
*BC Lara	c GO Jones b Giles	11	27	b Giles	44	95
S Chanderpaul	not out	128	270	not out	97	152
DJ Bravo	c GO Jones b SP Jones	44	105	c and b Giles	10	22
+RD Jacobs	c GO Jones b Hoggard	32	52	c Thorpe b Hoggard	1	4
OAC Banks	b Flintoff	45	70	b Harmison	0	16
TL Best	b Flintoff	0	1	st GO Jones b Giles	3	7
PT Collins	b Flintoff	0	11	st GO Jones b Giles	2	38
FH Edwards	b Giles	5	10	c GO Jones b Flintoff	2	24
Extras	(20 b, 11 lb, 3 nb, 5 w)	39		(5 b, 9 lb, 3 nb)	17	
Total	(all out, 116.4 overs)	416		(all out, 79.3 overs)	267	

Fall of wickets: 1-118 (Smith, 22.6 ov), 2-119 (Gayle, 24.3 ov), 3-127 (Sarwan, 27.5 ov), 4-139 (Lara, 32.2 ov), 5-264 (Bravo, 69.4 ov), 6-327 (Jacobs, 87.1 ov), 7-399 (Banks, 109.2 ov), 8-399 (Best, 109.3 ov), 9-401 (Collins, 113.2 ov), 10-416 (Edwards, 116.4 ov)
Fall of wickets: 1-24 (Smith, 5.5 ov), 2-35 (Sarwan, 10.1 ov), 3-102 (Gayle, 24.6 ov), 4-172 (Lara, 45.2 ov), 5-194 (Bravo, 51.3 ov), 6-195 (Jacobs, 52.1 ov), 7-200 (Banks, 56.4 ov), 8-203 (Best, 57.6 ov), 9-247 (Collins, 71.3 ov), 10-267 (Edwards, 79.3 ov)

ENGLAND	O	M	R	W	Wd	Nb		O	M	R	W	Wd	Nb
Hoggard	28	7	89	2	-	1	Hoggard	14	2	65	2	-	-
Harmison	21	6	72	0	-	-	Harmison	21	2	78	2	-	3
SP Jones	17	3	70	1	1	2	Giles	35	9	81	5	-	-
Giles	40.4	5	129	4	-	-	SP Jones	8	3	29	0	-	-
Flintoff	10	4	25	3	-	-	Flintoff	1.3	1	0	1	-	-

ENGLAND v WEST INDIES, SECOND TEST

Venue: Edgbaston, Birmingham
Toss: England won the toss and decided to bat
Umpires: DB Hair, SJA Taufel
Referee: RS Madugalle

Date: 29th, 30th, 31st July, 1st August 2004
Result: England won by 256 runs
TV Umpire: JW Lloyds

ENGLAND	1ST INNINGS	R	B	2ND INNINGS	R	B
ME Trescothick	c Lara b Bravo	105	182	run out (Sarwan)	107	158
AJ Strauss	c Jacobs b Lawson	24	40	c Jacobs b Lawson	5	22
RWT Key	c Lara b Collins	29	52	c Gayle b Lawson	4	7
*MP Vaughan	c and b Bravo	12	21	c Gayle b Lawson	3	17
GP Thorpe	c Jacobs b Collymore	61	116	st Jacobs b Gayle	54	89
A Flintoff	lbw b Bravo	167	191	c Bravo b Gayle	20	23
+GO Jones	c Jacobs b Collymore	74	97	b Lawson	4	21
AF Giles	c Chanderpaul b Bravo	24	47	b Gayle	15	31
MJ Hoggard	not out	15	42	c Smith b Gayle	6	17
JM Anderson	b Banks	2	13	(11) not out	8	7
SJ Harmison	not out	31	18	(10) lbw b Gayle	1	5
Extras	(6 lb, 15 nb, 1 w)	22		(8 b, 2 lb, 6 nb, 5 w)	21	
Total	(9 wickets, dec, 134 overs)	566		(all out, 65.1 overs)	248	

Fall of wickets: 1-77 (Strauss, 17.2 ov), 2-125 (Key, 31.3 ov), 3-150 (Vaughan, 38.1 ov), 4-210 (Trescothick, 59.1 ov), 5-262 (Thorpe, 73.5 ov), 6-432 (Jones, 104.4 ov), 7-478 (Giles, 118.2 ov), 8-522 (Flintoff, 124.3 ov), 9-525 (Anderson, 127.6 ov)
Fall of wickets: 1-24 (Strauss, 8.2 ov), 2-37 (Key, 10.3 ov), 3-52 (Vaughan, 16.3 ov), 4-184 (Trescothick, 44.6 ov), 5-195 (Thorpe, 49.4 ov), 6-214 (Jones, 54.4 ov), 7-226 (Flintoff, 57.3 ov), 8-234 (Giles, 61.4 ov), 9-239 (Harmison, 63.2 ov), 10-248 (Hoggard, 65.1 ov)

WEST INDIES	O	M	R	W	Wd	Nb		O	M	R	W	Wd	Nb
Collins	18	1	90	1	-	10	Collins	9	1	29	0	-	2
Collymore	30	6	126	2	-	2	Collymore	9	2	33	0	1	3
Lawson	23	4	111	1	-	2	Lawson	21	2	94	4	-	1
Bravo	24	6	76	4	1	1	Bravo	6	1	28	0	-	-
Banks	27	3	108	1	-	-	Banks	5	1	20	0	-	-
Sarwan	12	0	49	0	-	-	Gayle	15.1	4	34	5	-	-

WEST INDIES	1ST INNINGS	R	B	2ND INNINGS	R	B
CH Gayle	b Hoggard	7	9	c Strauss b Giles	82	102
DS Smith	c Giles b Hoggard	4	2	c Trescothick b Hoggard	11	21
RR Sarwan	b Flintoff	139	226	c Strauss b Giles	14	24
*BC Lara	c Thorpe b Flintoff	95	127	c Flintoff b Giles	13	21
S Chanderpaul	c Key b Giles	45	86	lbw b Giles	43	71
DJ Bravo	b Giles	13	47	b Giles	0	2
+RD Jacobs	c Trescothick b Hoggard	0	8	c Anderson b Hoggard	0	6
OAC Banks	c Jones b Harmison	4	19	not out	25	51
PT Collins	c Flintoff b Giles	6	22	lbw b Hoggard	0	9
CD Collymore	lbw b Giles	2	7	b Anderson	10	15
JJC Lawson	not out	0	2	b Anderson	2	12
Extras	(9 b, 5 lb, 6 nb, 1 w)	21		(17 b, 4 lb, 1 nb)	22	
Total	(all out, 91.3 overs)	336		(all out, 55.3 overs)	222	

Fall of wickets: 1-5 (Smith, 0.4 ov), 2-12 (Gayle, 2.6 ov), 3-221 (Lara, 49.4 ov), 4-297 (Sarwan, 70.4 ov), 5-323 (Bravo, 81.1 ov), 6-324 (Jacobs, 82.4 ov), 7-324 (Chanderpaul, 83.3 ov), 8-334 (Collins, 89.2 ov), 9-336 (Banks, 90.4 ov), 10-336 (Collymore, 91.3 ov)
Fall of wickets: 1-15 (Smith, 6.3 ov), 2-54 (Sarwan, 13.5 ov), 3-101 (Lara, 21.1 ov), 4-172 (Chanderpaul, 38.3 ov), 5-172 (Bravo, 38.5 ov), 6-177 (Gayle, 40.5 ov), 7-177 (Jacobs, 41.1 ov), 8-182 (Collins, 43.5 ov), 9-210 (Collymore, 51.2 ov), 10-222 (Lawson, 55.3 ov)

ENGLAND	O	M	R	W	Wd	Nb		O	M	R	W	Wd	Nb
Hoggard	18	0	89	3	-	2	Hoggard	16	5	64	3	-	-
Harmison	14	1	64	1	-	-	Harmison	5	1	29	0	-	-
Anderson	11	3	37	0	1	-	Flintoff	5	1	19	0	-	1
Giles	30.3	7	65	4	-	-	Giles	21	9	57	5	-	-
Flintoff	15	1	52	2	-	3	Anderson	5.3	1	23	2	-	-
Vaughan	1	0	8	0	-	1	Vaughan	3	0	9	0	-	-
Trescothick	2	0	7	0	-	-							

ENGLAND v WEST INDIES, THIRD TEST

Venue: Old Trafford, Manchester
Toss: West Indies won the toss and decided to bat
Umpires: Aleem Dar (Pakistan), SJA Taufel (Australia)
Reserve Umpire: PJ Hartley

Date: 12th, 13th, 14th, 15th, 16th August 2004
Result: England won by 7 wickets
TV Umpire: MR Benson
Referee: RS Madugalle (Sri Lanka)

WEST INDIES	1ST INNINGS	R	B	2ND INNINGS	R	B
CH Gayle	c Strauss b Hoggard	5	19	c Hoggard b Giles	42	73
SC Joseph	c Thorpe b Harmison	45	86	c Vaughan b Flintoff	15	41
RR Sarwan	b Flintoff	40	80	c Trescothick b Harmison	60	126
*BC Lara	b Flintoff	0	5	c Strauss b Flintoff	7	4
S Chanderpaul	c Jones b Hoggard	76	115	c Vaughan b Flintoff	2	10
DJ Bravo	c Jones b Hoggard	77	106	c Flintoff b Giles	6	18
+CS Baugh	c Vaughan b Anderson	68	84	c sub b Harmison	3	28
D Mohammed	c Strauss b Flintoff	23	36	c Key b Giles	9	27
PT Collins	retired hurt	19	22	b Harmison	8	16
CD Collymore	b Hoggard	5	14	not out	5	8
FH Edwards	not out	4	4	c Flintoff b Harmison	0	8
Extras	(9 b, 14 lb, 4 nb, 6 w)	33		(2 b, 4 lb, 1 nb, 1 w)	8	
Total	(all out, 94.3 overs)	395		(all out, 59.4 overs)	165	

Fall of wickets: 1-10 (Gayle, 4.3 ov), 2-85 (Sarwan, 26.6 ov), 3-97 (Lara, 28.5 ov), 4-108 (Joseph, 32.4 ov), 5-265 (Bravo, 67.4 ov), 6-266 (Chanderpaul, 69.1 ov), 7-308 (Mohammed, 78.3 ov), 8-383 (Collymore, 91.5 ov), 9-395 (Baugh, 94.3 ov)
Fall of wickets: 1-41 (Joseph, 10.4 ov), 2-88 (Gayle, 28.2 ov), 3-95 (Lara, 29.3 ov), 4-99 (Chanderpaul, 31.5 ov), 5-110 (Bravo, 36.3 ov), 6-121 (Baugh, 45.3 ov), 7-146 (Mohammed, 52.3 ov), 8-152 (Sarwan, 55.2 ov), 9-161 (Collins, 57.4 ov), 10-165 (Edwards, 59.4 ov)

ENGLAND	O	M	R	W	Wd	Nb		O	M	R	W	Wd	Nb
Hoggard	22	3	83	4	1	2	Hoggard	7	0	21	0	1	-
Harmison	26	5	94	1	-	1	Harmison	13.4	3	44	4	-	-
Flintoff	20	5	79	3	1	1	Flintoff	12	1	26	3	-	1
Anderson	11.3	1	49	1	-	-	Giles	22	6	46	3	-	-
Giles	15	0	67	0	-	-	Anderson	5	1	22	0	-	-

ENGLAND	1ST INNINGS	R	B	2ND INNINGS	R	B
ME Trescothick	c Sarwan b Edwards	0	2	b Collymore	12	13
AJ Strauss	b Bravo	90	227	c Chanderpaul b Collins	12	27
RWT Key	b Collymore	6	16	not out	93	178
*MP Vaughan	b Bravo	12	32	c Lara b Gayle	33	98
GP Thorpe	c Lara b Bravo	114	239			
A Flintoff	lbw b Bravo	7	15	(5) not out	57	92
MJ Hoggard	c Sarwan b Collymore	23	79			
+GO Jones	b Bravo	12	37			
AF Giles	c and b Bravo	10	19			
SJ Harmison	lbw b Collins	8	7			
JM Anderson	not out	1	10			
Extras	(10 b, 10 lb, 9 nb, 18 w)	47		(7 b, 3 lb, 14 nb)	24	
Total	(all out, 112.2 overs)	330		(3 wickets, 65.4 overs)	231	

Fall of wickets: 1-0 (Trescothick, 0.2 ov), 2-13 (Key, 3.6 ov), 3-40 (Vaughan, 16.2 ov), 4-217 (Strauss, 67.6 ov), 5-227 (Flintoff, 73.1 ov), 6-283 (Hoggard, 95.4 ov), 7-310 (Thorpe, 105.4 ov), 8-321 (Jones, 109.1 ov), 9-322 (Giles, 109.5 ov), 10-330 (Harmison, 112.2 ov)
Fall of wickets: 1-15 (Trescothick, 5.1 ov), 2-27 (Strauss, 8.6 ov), 3-111 (Vaughan, 39.1 ov)

WEST INDIES	O	M	R	W	Wd	Nb		O	M	R	W	Wd	Nb
Edwards	18	2	68	1	3	5	Edwards	11	0	51	0	-	6
Collymore	26	6	66	2	1	2	Collymore	16	7	33	1	-	3
Bravo	26	6	55	6	1	1	Collins	8	2	24	1	-	5
Joseph	2	0	8	0	1	1	Bravo	12	3	41	0	-	-
Gayle	4	1	7	0	-	-	Mohammed	6	0	25	0	-	-
Mohammed	26	2	77	0	-	-	Gayle	8.4	0	32	1	-	-
Collins	10.2	1	29	1	-	-	Sarwan	4	0	15	0	-	-

ENGLAND v WEST INDIES, FOURTH TEST

Venue: The Oval, Kennington
Toss: England won the toss and decided to bat
Umpires: DB Hair, RE Koertzen
Referee: RS Madugalle

Date: 19th, 20th, 21st August 2004
Result: England won by 10 wickets
TV Umpire: MR Benson
Scorers: JE Booth, KR Booth

ENGLAND	1ST INNINGS	R	B	2ND INNINGS	R	B
ME Trescothick	c Sarwan b Edwards	30	78	not out	4	3
AJ Strauss	c Edwards b Lawson	14	44	not out	0	0
RWT Key	c Baugh b Bravo	10	41			
*MP Vaughan	c Lara b Bravo	66	118			
IR Bell	c Baugh b Lawson	70	130			
A Flintoff	c Lawson b Edwards	72	99			
+GO Jones	c Sarwan b Collymore	22	57			
AF Giles	c Lara b Bravo	52	78			
MJ Hoggard	c Joseph b Lawson	38	52			
SJ Harmison	not out	36	27			
JM Anderson	b Gayle	12	33			
Extras	(5 b, 21 lb, 17 nb, 5 w)	48			0	
Total	(all out, 123.2 overs)	470		(no wicket, 0.3 overs)	4	

Fall of wickets: 1-51 (Strauss, 15.5 ov), 2-64 (Trescothick, 25.6 ov), 3-64 (Key, 26.4 ov), 4-210 (Bell, 63.1 ov), 5-236 (Vaughan, 68.3 ov), 6-313 (Jones, 90.5 ov), 7-321 (Flintoff, 93.1 ov), 8-408 (Giles, 112.6 ov), 9-410 (Hoggard, 113.3 ov), 10-470 (Anderson, 123.2 ov)

WEST INDIES	O	M	R	W	Wd	Nb		O	M	R	W	Wd	Nb
Edwards	19	4	64	2	2	6	Edwards	0.3	0	4	0	-	-
Collymore	23	8	58	1	-	4							
Lawson	24	4	115	3	1	4							
Bravo	29	4	117	3	1	3							
Smith	14	4	50	0	1	-							
Gayle	7.2	2	18	1	-	-							
Sarwan	7	0	22	0	-	-							

WEST INDIES	1ST INNINGS	R	B	2ND INNINGS (F/O)	R	B
CH Gayle	c Jones b Harmison	12	20	c Flintoff b Anderson	105	87
SC Joseph	c Giles b Harmison	9	23	c Jones b Harmison	16	26
RR Sarwan	c Strauss b Flintoff	2	8	c Bell b Harmison	7	11
*BC Lara	c Bell b Harmison	79	93	c Trescothick b Anderson	15	34
S Chanderpaul	c Key b Hoggard	14	27	(6) c Jones b Giles	32	111
DJ Bravo	c Jones b Harmison	16	18	(5) lbw b Hoggard	54	118
+CS Baugh	c Strauss b Harmison	6	19	(8) c Jones b Harmison	34	35
CD Collymore	c Trescothick b Harmison	4	7	(9) c Jones b Anderson	7	20
FH Edwards	run out (Hoggard)	0	2	(10) b Anderson	2	7
JJC Lawson	not out	3	4	(11) not out	4	5
DR Smith	absent hurt			(7) c Anderson b Flintoff	28	54
Extras	(7 lb)	7		(1 b, 12 lb, 1 nb)	14	
Total	(all out, 36.5 overs)	152		(all out, 84.2 overs)	318	

Fall of wickets: 1-19 (Gayle, 5.6 ov), 2-22 (Joseph, 7.3 ov), 3-26 (Sarwan, 10.3 ov), 4-54 (Chanderpaul, 18.5 ov), 5-101 (Bravo, 25.3 ov), 6-118 (Baugh, 31.1 ov), 7-136 (Collymore, 33.6 ov), 8-149 (Lara, 35.6 ov), 9-152 (Edwards, 36.5 ov)
Fall of wickets: 1-73 (Joseph, 11.1 ov), 2-81 (Sarwan, 13.2 ov), 3-126 (Lara, 22.6 ov), 4-155 (Gayle, 30.6 ov), 5-237 (Bravo, 59.1 ov), 6-265 (Chanderpaul, 70.4 ov), 7-285 (Smith, 75.5 ov), 8-312 (Collymore, 82.1 ov), 9-314 (Baugh, 83.1 ov), 10-318 (Edwards, 84.2 ov)

ENGLAND	O	M	R	W	Wd	Nb		O	M	R	W	Wd	Nb
Hoggard	9	2	31	1	-	-	Hoggard	12	5	50	1	-	-
Harmison	13	1	46	6	-	-	Harmison	18	1	75	3	-	-
Flintoff	8	1	32	1	-	-	Giles	22	5	64	1	-	-
Anderson	6.5	0	36	0	-	-	Flintoff	17	3	64	1	-	1
							Anderson	15.2	2	52	4	-	-

Newsday
The People's Newspaper

BUSH FIRES

HERO'S WELCOME FOR LARA

STORIES ON PAGES 3 & 5

LARA 400

Batting for Lara

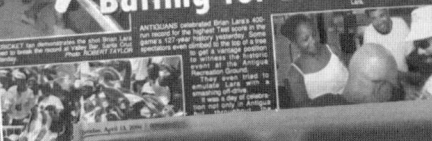

NEWS

Lara's love

STEELBAND WELCOME:

Lar
live
lar

Sporting Academy, Heroes' Park coming –

Laramania grabs the city

The Prince back on top

Lara becomes first Test batsman to score 400

'Coming back six or seven months later to do it all over again I feel great, but to say I knew I would have done it again, no'

ALL IN HIS HONOUR

at Piarco

The Trinidad **Guardian**

MONDAY, APRIL 12, 2004

Back in top form

West Indies captain BRIAN LARA celebrates after getting to his 300th run in the Fourth Test against England at the Antigua Recreation Ground yesterday.

PHOTO COURTESY THE ANTIGUA SUN

LARA conquers England

wee
ges
54,
56

Call him His Excellency

HAIL KING LARA!

BY RICHARD STAPLETON

Govt to name academy, stadium and heroes park after megastar

BY RICHARD LONG

Special gifts

Brian celebrates

Guardian **Sports**

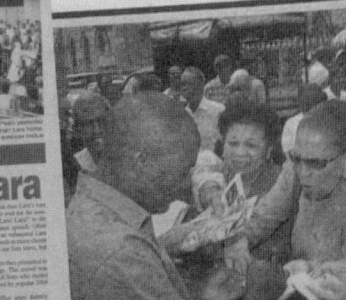

Daily **Express**

5.8%

ra breaks batting record again

ONCE IS NOT ENOUGH

First to score Test 400

NEWS

Rain fails to stop play –

Hundreds wait in town for Lara

Thousands brave rains to celebrate L...

Lara's Day

YOUR EXCELLENCY

- Ambassador of sport for T&T
- $10m Lara Foundation
- Brian Lara Stadium
- $400,000 in travel courtesy B...
- Cantaro cricket ground upgra...

PRINCELY PARTY!

HIS EXCELLENCY!

The Trinidad Guardian
GUARDIAN OF DEMOCRACY
$1
www.guardian.co.tt
TUESDAY, APRIL 13, 200...

The Trinidad Guardian
GUARDIAN OF DEMOCRACY
www.guardian.co.tt
Monday, April 19, 2004

Cabinet powwow on Lara honours

A hero's welcome

England edges Windies in ODI

For love of the game

Record a catalyst for change — Brian

Tobago triumph

LARA rises agai...

Lara spends day with Sydney

King of Port-of-Spain gets keys to Antigua

Lara's party

Daily Express
5.8%
The National Newspaper of Trinidad & Tobago
WEDNESDAY, APRIL 14, 2004

Governor suspends police force

Roytrin

Missing woman found murdered

Babb buried in Lalla's grave

LARA rises again

PM promises 'unprecedented and extraordinary gift'

THE RETURN OF THE KING

Meeting today to plan welcome celebration

THE 400 MAN

Sign changed

SAN JUAN / LAVENTILLE REGIONAL CORPORATION
Welcomes You To The
BRIAN LARA RECREATION GROUND
WORLD RECORD HOLDER
400 Runs - Test Cricket
501 Runs - County Cricket
WELCOME BRIAN LARA

Brian inks it

TEST CRICKET world record holder Brian Lara signs an autograph yesterday for one of his many fans outside City Hall, Port of Spain, following a reception hosted in his honour.

Photo: ROBERTO CODALLO

Sydney cries tears of joy for daddy

Photographs courtesy of Brian Lara, Nasser Khan, Alamy, Getty Images, Graham Morris, Roger Wootton and Warwickshire CCC

Work hard, play hard

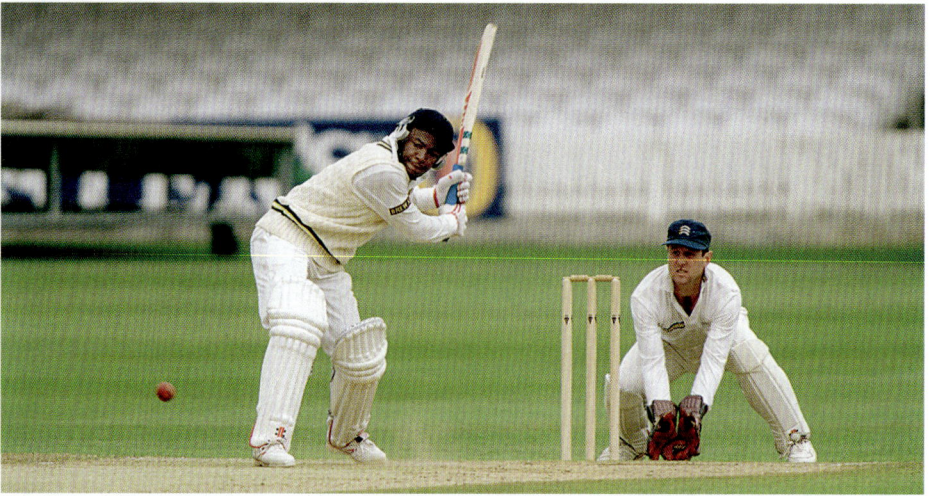

Up and away: almost clearing the pavilion at Lord's off John
Emburey – I've never hit a more effortless six

One of my favourite batting photos; it's impossible to tell which shot I'm about to play

When I wasn't batting, I was a close watcher of the game; I loved
to study how good players went about their business

B&H Cup: our first silverware of a magical summer

The Sunday League completed the treble; the boys always had that one covered

The big one: the 1994 County Championship.
A moment that made all the toil worthwhile

Curtly: Why would you go looking for a battle against the best bowler in the world?

All-timers, and beautiful souls: Malcolm Marshall and Sir Clive Lloyd

The 1998 series win against England kicked off my captaincy on a positive note

The 2000 tour was a tough one; mentally I was unable to give our skipper Jimmy Adams the best version of myself

'Swaggy' Adams: A magnificent teammate and my all-time favourite batting partner

Sir Vivian: The greatest batter I ever saw

In 2004 I became Andrew Flintoff's bunny – he had this incredibly flexible wrist which made it hard to pick up the ball; not ideal at 90mph!

The moment

Like reuniting with an old flame...

At The Oval in 2004, a young kid called Jimmy Anderson
bowled me the best ball I ever faced in my life

Shoaib Akhtar poleaxes me in our Champions Trophy semi-final;
like being whacked around the head with a lamppost

My man Courtney Browne was a constant source of wisdom and good cheer
throughout that amazing tournament; it was fitting that he'd steer us home

Champions

Me and Shiv: the great survivors

My final walk back in a West Indies shirt; the reception from the Barbados crowd
– both from the locals and the English fans – will stay in my heart forever

CHAPTER 11

2004

CHAMPIONS

'Every game we played in that tournament, it worked. It was not luck. When I talk to people about leadership, I always talk about how he pulled that broken, disunited team together to win that trophy'

COURTNEY BROWNE

ONE-DAY CRICKET never quite hit the same, you know? I enjoyed it, but Test cricket was on another level. I made no bones about that. It was the same for everyone. In my time the white ball knew its place.

It was important, limited-overs cricket, don't get me wrong, it offered value and marketability and produced some great moments. We'll always have 1975 at Lord's, Clive Lloyd lifting the World Cup in his thick black specs after licking the Aussies. And it gave us Viv four years later, flicking the final ball of his innings into the stands as we ran out winners for a second time.

Those wins were massive for us growing up. They helped shape the story of West Indies cricket when we were kids. It was proof that we were the best team in the world. Personally though, especially as I got older, comparing limited overs to first-class cricket... well the clue is in the name. *First-class*. That was always my first love, my first priority. First-class cricket was how I measured myself.

The big tournaments were different. It hurts that we never did ourselves justice in the World Cups I played in. Losing to Australia in the semi-finals in 1996, I don't think I'll ever live that down. The World Cups, they stayed with you, lodged in the memory bank, in a way that those best-of-three one-dayers tacked on as an afterthought to a Test series could never do.

So, here's the truth of it: the prospect of the 2004 Champions Trophy in England, a 12-team tournament at the chilly end of their summer – staged on the back of a 10-week tour where we'd been battered everywhere we went – wasn't exactly top of my bucket list. And look, let's be real here, I don't think I was alone in feeling that. Which made what happened next all the more incredible.

* * *

There were minimal changes in personnel. With the core of our Test team still making up most of the one-day squad, we were stuck with each other.

There was one player in particular I pushed really hard for, and that was Courtney Browne, the Barbados keeper-captain. I'd played a bit with him for the West Indies a few years back and we got on well. I knew he was getting on, and he'd need to shape up if he joined us, but I felt he would bring leadership qualities to what was by then a disunited set-up. Barbados was like a rock under Courtney's captaincy. I needed some of that.

As captain, I was lonely. I felt isolated from my own team. Courtney would bring some of that drive and desire that we were lacking. And he'd be someone I could talk to properly about cricket. With Courtney, he *knows* the game.

So, one night I called him up from this hotel in England to sound him out. It would've been quite late in Barbados, I think he was at his cricket club when he answered. I knew he hadn't played since the end of the first-class season some six months back, but he was enthusiastic, if a bit surprised to be asked. I think he'd resigned himself to not playing again for the West Indies. Anyway, Browney wakes up the next morning with some vague recollection of Lara calling him the night before, so he checks his phone and there it is, this +44 number staring back at him. He hits redial. "Brian! I was so pissed when you called, I don't remember a thing about it!" I told him I loved him, that he was an idiot, and that he'd better get up and start training because we had work to do. He was precisely what I needed.

I also asked the selectors for a couple of young players. I wanted some new blood, a bit of freshness. I wanted to let them get a feel for the atmosphere and help to make it less toxic. That's how they settled on Daren Sammy and Sylvester Joseph.

After the Test series, the squad broke up for a few days to lick its wounds before the one-day players, plus our new recruits, met up in Bermuda for a pre-tournament camp. From memory it was OK, quite relaxed. I guess the jagged edges of the Test series had started to soften. It would be pushing it to say there was renewed optimism, but we got our heads around the fact that we were going back to England. As for my own feelings, I knew we were inconsistent, and that the disappointment that lurked in ourselves both collectively and individually ran deep. I could also see, scouting around, that on our day we had a bunch of cricketers who could beat anyone in the world.

* * *

One night pre-tournament, over dinner with Courtney, I proposed the idea of setting up an early morning squad run. He liked the idea, so I went to the management with it. "But I don't want this to be compulsory. I want the guys who want to join up to come out, but those who want to stay in their bed and get some extra sleep are fine by me. Non-compulsory."

I knew that whichever way I went, compulsory or non-compulsory, there would be pushback. The team spirit wasn't strong enough to force everyone out of their beds at 6am. That would not go down well with certain players. If people wanted to go out partying through the night and stay in their bed, then I wanted them to have that option, because it would challenge them to prove that they could still perform. I wanted to allow people to do whatever they wanted to do and then see if it brought out the best in them. They still had to come out and play the game. They could show us in training that they could deliver.

As I suspected, a few guys took to it, and a few didn't. It was fragmented, which was to be expected with our team, because that's exactly what we were. Some guys came along and then dropped out. Other times you'd get a few on one day and then not much the next. I wondered if there was a silent pressure on some players to *not* be a part of it. I remember one morning we ran from our hotel in Kensington up to Lord's and back. It was breakfast time when we returned, and some of the players who hadn't joined us were laughing at those who had.

Me? I did them all except one, the morning after I was smashed up by a nasty delivery from Shoaib Akhtar, but we'll come to that. The only players to appear at every single session along with our trainer Ronald Rogers? One was Ian Bradshaw, our Bajan left-arm opening bowler, and the other was Courtney. Go looking for one of those men at any stage of that tournament, and you'd quickly locate the other. They stuck together right up to the very last ball.

To get one last dance out of this team, I had to accept what we had. At no point did I look at my players in anger. I might have been disappointed with them on a certain day, but I never pointed fingers.

I never accused anyone of creating problems by their behaviour, even when there was a strong case that they were.

The young guys in particular were impressionable, I could see that. They were sponges. And to be honest, I sensed that some former players and administrators were out to poison their minds against me. On a few separate mornings I saw certain ex-players conducting their own private meetings with some of our younger guys on the outfield, and then I'd be feeling that those players would be looking at me in a different way. Look, they could have been saying good things in those huddles, but I had my doubts. In terms of my psyche, if somebody is speaking ill of me, I find it very disturbing. I had to find a way to deal with it.

Usefully, we had a new superstar. By 2004, Chris Gayle was coming through in a big way, and I could see that keeping him onside would be key to our chances. He was always one of the most likeable characters in West Indies cricket. He struck me as someone who had a very extroverted personality on the outside but was actually quite introverted behind it all. He occupied some of the same space that I did; he'd be nervous going out to bat, but he knew what he wanted to achieve. And he didn't just go out and throw the bat, he was smarter than that. He knew he had the skills to motor when he got set and that's why he became successful. I liked him, always did. If I could guarantee 100 percent of his attention, managing Chris Gayle would not be a hard job. The difficulty was securing that 100 percent when there were people circling who wanted to bring me down.

* * *

The tournament schedule meant that every game was basically a knockout. We were put in a group of three with Bangladesh and South Africa and the top team from each of the four groups went through to the semi-finals.

Bangladesh were up first and without being disrespectful, I thought we'd have enough to beat them if we put runs on the board. Gayle was our main guy in the first 15 overs, but he knew not to go too hard too quickly. This was England in late summer, so the white ball would swing for a while, and we were playing in Southampton, a newish venue with a pitch which hadn't really bedded in. When Bangladesh won the toss and chose to bowl, we knew not to get ahead of ourselves. Chris and Wavell Hinds got their heads down to see us through the first hour, and then they got into their work. Wavell made 82, Chris made 99 from 132 balls, and I slapped 20 in seven balls at the death. I was quite happy to have our openers play like that. In those days anything above 250 was a good score and our 269 was way beyond what Bangladesh could face.

Our bowlers were disciplined, Bradshaw was excellent, carrying on his good work from the one-day leg of our England tour, and Merv Dillon bowled well to pick up five wickets. It was a good feeling. We'd forgotten what it was like to walk off a cricket field victorious.

* * *

The win kind of galvanised us. South Africa were a good side, but The Oval pitch suited our way of playing and in Ramnaresh Sarwan we had a classy player on his day. It was a weird game spread over two days due to a little rain and a lot of bad light, which was hardly surprising given we were almost in mid-September. On the second day we held our nerve to chase down their 246 with seven balls to spare. Sarwan made 75, I chipped in with 49 and Shiv Chanderpaul played beautifully for his unbeaten 51 to take us home. One of our youngsters also contributed, with Ricardo Powell smacking a couple of big sixes at the death to make the chase a comfortable one.

Suddenly, we were in the semi-finals, and with Pakistan our opponents, I asked our coach Gus Logie to provide some video analysis for myself and Courtney to study. We'd been watching these videos of our opponents for the group games and it had proven useful. We'd sit in my hotel room, have some lunch, and fast forward through these videos to formulate some plans ahead of a team meeting.

So, I've asked Gus to get this video footage of Pakistan, reminded him a couple of times, made clear how important it is for Courtney and me. A day later he gives me this VHS tape in an envelope and we settle down to watch it. Pop it in the machine, press play, and there it is, presented on screen in full technicolour, this vision of a car park. I fast forward a little. Still a car park. Move it on further. Car park. It's a full VHS tape of a single shot of a provincial English car park. I lose it, I'm cussing the place down, screaming down the phone at Gus, and all the while Browney's trying not to burst out laughing. He later said it was the angriest he'd ever seen me.

Truth was, I didn't have much time for Logie as a coach. I didn't like his style and I don't think he was too keen on mine. We had a lot of baggage from when I was made captain of Trinidad & Tobago in 1990 ahead of him, despite him being an established West Indies player. We just didn't see eye to eye, and seeing as this was my last effort, I felt that I had to shut him down, so I did.

The Pakistan game was a chaotic affair that I don't enjoy thinking about. We won and did so quite convincingly. Bradshaw and Corey Collymore were unplayable with the new ball (after Inzamam-ul-Haq had made the amazing decision to bat first under dark Southampton skies), we'd caught well, pulled off a couple of run-outs, bundled them out for 131, and despite the loss of a couple of early wickets, Sarwan had steered us to a seven-wicket victory. The discomfort for me comes from the memory of being struck on the back of my neck by Shoaib Akhtar. It felt like someone had smacked me with a baseball bat or a lamppost. After staggering to my feet, I was taken off the field, and while I might've been fronting up at the time, I can tell you now I was happy to not be facing another delivery. On that pitch I must confess I wasn't 100 percent confident. I know we still needed a few runs to win the game but that was a pretty hard hit.

Concussion or not, we drank hard that night. I remember that Browne and Bradshaw were with me. They still got up for their early morning session but I chose to duck that one. For various reasons, my head was still a little sore.

Somehow, I'd got my team into a frame of mind where we were in a good space to perform, but we were far from coherent or unified. On one end of the spectrum you had Browne and Bradshaw and a few of the other guys doing whatever they could to stay fit and sharp. And then you had the other side, guys who did whatever they fancied, but because of that, they had to prove themselves.

I'd got us pulling together even though we were doing different things. I could see that the methods I was using wouldn't be solid enough to stand up for long, but I needed to do something in this crisis. I knew the ripped fabric of the team wouldn't be repaired by this method, but for that two-week period, it was the best technique I could think of, and it was working.

We were in the final. The belief was coursing through the team. It was a sweet and welcome respite. But for all that I'd landed on a short-term fix, I still couldn't see how I could captain this team much longer.

* * *

So, the English. *Again*. At the Oval, *again*. We could feel what's at stake. We had a chance to make a play for our own piece of history.

Our trump card was Bradshaw. He was a fascinating bowler. On one level, it baffled me how effective he was. He was hardly your typical West Indian fast bowler. He wasn't tall or bulky. He wasn't much quicker than medium pace. But in all conditions, everywhere, batters struggled to get him away. He was accurate and he got movement as a left-armer, but for me it was his discipline and intelligence. He was a thinking man's bowler.

After Braddy's two wickets in his opening spell, including a beauty to clean up Michael Vaughan, we got rid of Andrew Flintoff cheaply – I took a good one-hander at midwicket – and ran out Andrew Strauss, who was having a good tournament. When Strauss went, Courtney ran over, reminding me that when his name had come up in our pre-game meeting, I'd told him that we'd run him out. They eventually got up to 217 thanks to a hundred from Marcus Trescothick. I remember thinking that the only obstacles in our way were called Harmison and Flintoff.

It's London, it's packed out, it's bitingly cold and something has to give. England's big two quicks share the first four wickets. Flintoff finds my edge and at that point we're 72-4. Dwayne Bravo then follows for a duck: 80-5. A brief recovery between Ryan Hinds and Shiv Chanderpaul takes us up to 114 before Hinds nicks off and Ricardo Powell comes and goes to leave us seven down for 135.

When Shiv departs for 47, we're 147-8. Only Bradshaw and Browne are left to protect Corey Collymore, whose batting, it's fair to say, is not his strong suit.

At that point I'm done. Still 71 runs to get and those two guys out there, neither of whom have batted in the tournament so far? Bradshaw, with his single fifty in List A cricket? Browne, who last batted in a professional cricket match six months ago? I'm not overflowing with confidence.

What they achieve that night is a damn sporting miracle.

* * *

This is what happens. They come together, these great Bajan survivors, smile, look at the scenario, and say to each other: "Right, it's just another night. See off Harmison and Flintoff and we *win this game*. Let's go."

I gather that Harmison bowls pretty fast. The speed gun says he's up at 96 mph, but it's so dark, it's hard to be sure. Our boys have been dealing with bad light every Saturday night back home for most of their lives. Cricket in the Caribbean, bad light is just a state of mind.

Then something wild: England's quicks blow themselves out. They throw everything at us and in response we dodge and weave and go to the ropes. It's like Foreman throwing those booming haymakers in Zaire all those years ago, and Ali just biding his time, waiting to pounce. What's so crazy, almost magical, about those final moments is how, once we get to within about 20 runs needed, it becomes completely inevitable, unstoppable, weirdly nerveless, as if no earthly power can prevent fate from delivering this victory that no one ever imagined could belong to us. It's as if destiny has muscled in again and is calling the shots.

Cricketers are a superstitious bunch and we don't move from our positions as the boys chip away at that target. There's some murmur about taking the light and walking off – that would be madness, and I'll be running on if they even consider it. You don't accept the light when the fates are in play! At one point I'm standing next to Ronald, our trainer. We're arm in arm, shoulder to shoulder, "like Siamese twins" he later says, and I turn to him with a few runs still needed and I say to him, "We're there, Ronald, we're *there*." When Braddy strokes the fifth ball of the penultimate over for four, that's me done, gone.

The immediate aftermath is just chaos really. I lose myself. It's hard to remember. It's just pure release. I'd like to apologise to the English guys for not shaking all their hands straight off. I hope they can understand.

This fractious group of men, given literally no chance, have pulled off a miracle. For one night, and for probably the first time in 10 years, I feel as if everybody is pulling in one direction.

It's beautiful. Fleeting and brief, and we all have to wake up in the morning. But for that one night, beautiful.

* * *

We don't spend much time celebrating. During the tournament, one of the most devastating hurricanes swept through the Caribbean, Hurricane Ivan. It had struck Grenada on September 7 as a Category 3 storm and by the time it reached the Cayman Islands on September 12, it had grown to a Category 5.

It ravaged Grenada, the Cayman Islands and parts of Kingston, Jamaica leaving 58 people dead and resulting in billions of dollars in damage. We couldn't celebrate while so many of our people had suffered such loss. Representing the West Indies team, Courtney Browne and I left England shortly after lifting the trophy to tour these three islands.

We had to give our support to the people who had lost so much.

BANGLADESH v WEST INDIES

Venue: The Rose Bowl, Southampton
Toss: Bangladesh won the toss and decided to field
Points: Bangladesh 0; West Indies 2
TV Umpire: BF Bowden

Date: 15th September 2004
Result: West Indies won by 138 runs
Umpires: Aleem Dar, JW Lloyds
Referee: BC Broad

WEST INDIES		R	B	BANGLADESH		R	B
CH Gayle	c Mashud b Tapash Baisya	99	132	Javed Omar	c Sammy b Dillon	2	7
WW Hinds	c Hossain b Tapash Baisya	82	119	Mohammad Ashraful	c Dillon b Bradshaw	10	8
RR Sarwan	not out	30	26	Nafees Iqbal	b Dillon	2	12
*BC Lara	run out (Tapash Baisya)	20	7	*Rajin Saleh	b Dillon	7	9
S Chanderpaul	not out	18	18	Aftab Ahmed	b Bravo	21	44
SC Joseph				+Khaled Mashud	c Sammy b Dillon	0	9
DJ Bravo				Mushfiqur Rahman	c Joseph b Sammy	21	41
+CO Browne				Mohammad Rafique	c Sammy b Dillon	12	19
M Dillon				Khaled Mahmud	not out	34	51
IDR Bradshaw				Tapash Baisya	c sub b Gayle	8	16
DJG Sammy				Nazmul Hossain	c Bravo b Gayle	4	21
Extras	(6 lb, 2 nb, 12 w)	20		Extras	(2 lb, 8 w)	10	
Total	(3 wickets, 50 overs)	269		Total	(all out, 39.3 overs)	131	

Fall of wickets: 1-192 (Hinds, 39.6 ov), 2-201 (Gayle, 42.4 ov), 3-232 (Lara, 44.5 ov)
Fall of wickets: 1-13 (Javed Omar, 2.1 ov), 2-15 (Mohammad Ashraful, 3.2 ov), 3-23 (Nafees Iqbal, 4.6 ov), 4-24 (Rajin Saleh, 6.3 ov), 5-26 (Khaled Mashud, 8.6 ov), 6-71 (Aftab Ahmed, 20.6 ov), 7-71 (Mushfiqur Rahman, 21.4 ov), 8-94 (Mohammad Rafique, 26.6 ov), 9-105 (Tapash Baisya, 31.1 ov), 10-131 (Nazmul Hossain, 39.3 ov)

BANGLADESH	O	M	R	W	Wd	Nb	WEST INDIES	O	M	R	W	Wd	Nb
Tapash Baisya	10	0	58	2	2	1	Dillon	10	4	29	5	-	-
Nazmul Hossain	10	1	44	0	3	-	Bradshaw	10	2	25	1	3	-
Mushfiqur Rahman	10	0	40	0	1	-	Sammy	6	0	19	1	2	-
Khaled Mahmud	10	1	57	0	2	1	Bravo	9	0	44	1	3	-
Mohammad Rafique	10	0	64	0	-	-	Gayle	4.3	0	12	2	-	-

SOUTH AFRICA v WEST INDIES

Venue: The Oval, Kennington
Toss: West Indies won the toss and decided to field
Points: South Africa 0; West Indies 2
TV Umpire: DJ Harper
Referee: BC Broad

Date: 18th, 19th September 2004
Result: West Indies won by 5 wickets
Umpires: JW Lloyds, DR Shepherd
Reserve Umpire: JH Evans
Scorers: JE Booth, KR Booth

SOUTH AFRICA		R	B	WEST INDIES		R	B
*GC Smith	b Gayle	45	64	CH Gayle	b Pollock	16	19
HH Gibbs	c Bravo b Gayle	101	135	WW Hinds	lbw b Pollock	15	30
JH Kallis	b Bravo	16	33	RR Sarwan	b Ntini	75	99
JA Rudolph	b Gayle	46	39	*BC Lara	b Boje	49	85
M van Jaarsveld	c Powell b Bradshaw	0	1	S Chanderpaul	not out	51	52
SM Pollock	not out	13	11	RL Powell	b Ntini	16	10
+MV Boucher	c Chanderpaul b Bradshaw	7	7	DJ Bravo	not out	4	3
L Klusener	not out	12	10	+CO Browne			
N Boje				RO Hinds			
CK Langeveldt				IDR Bradshaw			
M Ntini				CD Collymore			
Extras	(4 lb, 2 w)	6		Extras	(10 lb, 5 nb, 8 w)	23	
Total	(6 wickets, 50 overs)	246		Total	(5 wickets, 48.5 overs)	249	

Fall of wickets: 1-102 (Smith, 21.2 ov), 2-148 (Kallis, 35.1 ov), 3-198 (Gibbs, 43.3 ov), 4-212 (van Jaarsveld, 44.5 ov), 5-213 (Rudolph, 45.2 ov), 6-222 (Boucher, 46.6 ov)
Fall of wickets: 1-24 (Gayle, 6.6 ov), 2-33 (WW Hinds, 8.1 ov), 3-131 (Lara, 32.5 ov), 4-214 (Sarwan, 45.1 ov), 5-237 (Powell, 47.4 ov)

WEST INDIES	O	M	R	W	Wd	Nb	SOUTH AFRICA	O	M	R	W	Wd	Nb
Bradshaw	10	2	40	2	-	-	Pollock	10	0	56	2	-	1
Collymore	9	0	53	0	-	-	Langeveldt	7.5	2	41	0	1	1
Bravo	9	0	54	1	-	-	Ntini	5	0	26	2	1	1
RO Hinds	10	0	35	0	1	-	Klusener	10	1	32	0	1	2
Gayle	10	0	50	3	1	-	Kallis	6	1	32	0	2	-
Powell	2	0	10	0	-	-	Boje	10	0	52	1	2	-

PAKISTAN v WEST INDIES, SEMI-FINAL

Venue: The Rose Bowl, Southampton
Toss: Pakistan won the toss and decided to bat
Umpires: DB Hair, SJA Taufel
Referee: RS Madugalle

Date: 22nd September 2004
Result: West Indies won by 7 wickets
TV Umpire: DR Shepherd

PAKISTAN		R	B	WEST INDIES		R	B
Yasir Hameed	run out (Bravo->Browne)	39	56	CH Gayle	lbw b Shoaib Akhtar	1	8
Salman Butt	c Sarwan b Bradshaw	0	2	WW Hinds	c and b Shoaib Akhtar	5	12
Shoaib Malik	c Browne b Bravo	17	58	RR Sarwan	not out	56	85
*Inzamam-ul-Haq	c Browne b WW Hinds	21	44	*BC Lara	retired hurt	31	30
Yousuf Youhana	c Browne b Bravo	12	28	S Chanderpaul	c Salman b Shoaib Malik	11	24
Abdul Razzaq	run out (Bravo->Browne)	6	17	RL Powell	not out	6	11
+Moin Khan	lbw b WW Hinds	0	2	DJ Bravo			
Shahid Afridi	st Browne b Gayle	17	13	RO Hinds			
Naved-ul-Hasan	b Collymore	0	4	+CO Browne			
Mohammad Sami	b Collymore	0	4	IDR Bradshaw			
Shoaib Akhtar	not out	0	2	CD Collymore			
Extras	(4 lb, 15 w)	19		Extras	(2 b, 10 lb, 1 nb, 9 w)	22	
Total	(all out, 38.2 overs)	131		Total	(3 wickets, 28.1 overs)	132	

Fall of wickets: 1-1 (Salman Butt, 0.3 ov), 2-65 (Yasir Hameed, 18.1 ov), 3-71 (Shoaib Malik, 21.3 ov), 4-100 (Yousuf Youhana, 29.2 ov), 5-109 (Abdul Razzaq, 32.6 ov), 6-111 (Inzamam-ul-Haq, 34.1 ov), 7-112 (Moin Khan, 34.4 ov), 8-116 (Naved-ul-Hasan, 35.6 ov), 9-125 (Mohammad Sami, 37.4 ov), 10-131 (Shahid Afridi, 38.2 ov)
Fall of wickets: 1-8 (Gayle, 2.2 ov), 2-20 (WW Hinds, 4.2 ov), 3-102 (Chanderpaul, 23.6 ov)

WEST INDIES	O	M	R	W	Wd	Nb	PAKISTAN	O	M	R	W	Wd	Nb
Bradshaw	8	0	23	1	-	-	Shoaib Akhtar	7	1	18	2	4	-
Collymore	9	2	24	2	4	-	Mohammad Sami	3	0	23	0	-	-
Bravo	9	0	41	2	7	-	Naved-ul-Hasan	7	2	24	0	1	-
WW Hinds	10	0	27	2	2	-	Abdul Razzaq	6	0	39	0	3	-
RO Hinds	1	0	1	0	1	-	Shoaib Malik	5	0	15	1	1	1
Gayle	1.2	0	11	1	-	-	Yousuf Youhana	0.1	0	1	0	-	-

ENGLAND v WEST INDIES, FINAL

Venue: The Oval, Kennington
Toss: West Indies won the toss and decided to field
Umpires: RE Koertzen, SJA Taufel
Referee: RS Madugalle

Date: 25th September 2004
Result: West Indies won by 2 wickets
TV Umpire: DB Hair
Scorers: JE Booth, KR Booth

ENGLAND		R	B	WEST INDIES		R	B
ME Trescothick	run out (Lara->Gayle)	104	124	CH Gayle	c and b Harmison	23	33
VS Solanki	c Browne b Bradshaw	4	13	WW Hinds	c Solanki b Harmison	3	16
*MP Vaughan	b Bradshaw	7	18	RR Sarwan	c Strauss b Flintoff	5	7
AJ Strauss	run out (Bravo)	18	33	*BC Lara	c Jones b Flintoff	14	28
A Flintoff	c Lara b WW Hinds	3	6	S Chanderpaul	c Vaughan b Collingwood	47	66
PD Collingwood	c Chanderpaul b W Hinds	16	40	DJ Bravo	c Jones b Flintoff	0	7
+GO Jones	c Lara b WW Hinds	6	18	RO Hinds	c Jones b Trescothick	8	19
AF Giles	c Lara b Bravo	31	37	RL Powell	c Trescothick b Collingwood	14	16
AG Wharf	not out	3	6	+CO Browne	not out	35	55
D Gough	st Browne b Gayle	0	1	IDR Bradshaw	not out	34	51
SJ Harmison	run out	2	2	CD Collymore			
Extras	(1 b, 7 lb, 15 w)	23		Extras	(11 lb, 5 nb, 19 w)	35	
Total	(all out, 49.4 overs)	217		Total	(8 wickets, 48.5 overs)	218	

Fall of wickets: 1-12 (Solanki, 4.2 ov), 2-43 (Vaughan, 10.3 ov), 3-84 (Strauss, 19.6 ov), 4-93 (Flintoff, 22.1 ov), 5-123 (Collingwood, 32.3 ov), 6-148 (Jones, 38.2 ov), 7-211 (Trescothick, 47.4 ov), 8-212 (Giles, 48.3 ov), 9-214 (Gough, 49.1 ov), 10-217 (Harmison, 49.4 ov)

Fall of wickets: 1-19 (WW Hinds, 3.5 ov), 2-35 (Sarwan, 8.1 ov), 3-49 (Gayle, 9.4 ov), 4-72 (Lara, 16.3 ov), 5-80 (Bravo, 18.3 ov), 6-114 (RO Hinds, 24.5 ov), 7-135 (Powell, 29.2 ov), 8-147 (Chanderpaul, 33.4 ov)

WEST INDIES	O	M	R	W	Wd	Nb	ENGLAND	O	M	R	W	Wd	Nb
Bradshaw	10	1	54	2	3	-	Gough	10	1	58	0	5	-
Collymore	10	1	38	0	3	-	Harmison	10	1	34	2	3	-
Gayle	9.4	0	52	1	-	-	Flintoff	10	0	38	3	2	4
Bravo	10	0	41	1	9	-	Wharf	9.5	0	38	0	-	1
WW Hinds	10	3	24	3	-	-	Trescothick	3	0	17	1	2	-
							Collingwood	6	0	22	2	1	-

No turning back

ne leaves for good, but satisfied

GARTH WATTLEY reports — Pa

RAMNARESH SARWAN, WAVELL HINDS, COURTNEY BROWN, BRIAN LA

SSFL round-up
San Juan beat Arima — Page 77

SPORT

Vol. 13 Thursday, September 30, 2004 — FREE

BROTHERS IN ARMS

Windies heroes Bradshaw, Browne celebrate at The Oval

WEST INDIES batsmen Ian Bradshaw (left) and Courtney Browne run off the pitch after the sensational victory over England at The Oval in London on Saturday. Windies won the ICC Champions Trophy.

LASANA LIBURD reports — Pages 6-7

The captain sp

Lara: A grea achievemen for the tear

Vaughan: You have to take your hat off to the opposition

West Indies are under standably ecstatic after their World Indies Champions Trophy final, while Michael Vaughan gave full credit to Ian Bradshaw and Courtney Browne, whose partnership took them to victory.

BRIAN LARA

Guardian

CHAMPIONS

AGAIN

Channa bombs throw at Sat's house

Rastas seek politica power

West Indies 218/8

Penta

4.5% LOW INTEREST RATE

INSIDE

Volume 131

Express SPORTS

September 30, 2004

Athletes of the Week

The West Indies cricket team who got the better of England in the final of the ICC Champions Trophy at The Oval in London last Saturday.

WINDIES' SWEET REVENGE

ICC CHAMPIONS TROPHY

This is an opportunity for the people in the Caribbean, wherever they live, whatever mood they are in, to rejoice.

Guardian
THE GUARDIAN OF DEMOCRACY
www.guardian.co.tt

ICC CHAMPIONS

ara: Champions win an be foundation or 2007 World Cup

NKING in the glow of his team's mir-
s win over England in the ICC Cham-
ns Trophy final, West Indies captain
an Lara believes the victory could be a
ndation to prepare for the 2007 World
p.

"Hopefully this can be the foundation
y the team and this can be the impetus
settle some matters. We're just looking
ward to playing some more cricket,
ra said. "It's an opportunity for us. We
ven't won the World Cup, but it serves
s something we can work with. We have
me tough cricket to come."

the win...

As a team it is a great achievement. For

che and help them rejoice.

On recovering from 147 for eight...

"It's great to see the guys believing in
themselves. I'm not sure they had a knack
in the nets. (Browne and Bradshaw) are
from Barbados and have played together
in many, many matches."

On his catch to dismiss Andrew
Flintoff...

"It was majorly important and it has to
go up with the best of them. It was a great
team effort. We backed ourselves in the
field and against South Africa and Pakistan we wanted to be the better fielding
team and today again

September 26, 2004 | SUNDAY GUARDIAN

Browne and Bradshaw steal a thriller

How Wisden saw it

By ANDREW MILLER

LONDON—Back in the 1970s, the Kensington Oval was to all intents and purposes an outpost in the Caribbean. The legendary Test of 1976, Michael Holding's 14 in a fruit of a sea of exuberant conch-blowing supporters, who have all but disappeared in the intervening years.

Yesterday, at the climax of an extraordinary Champions Trophy final, the spirit of that era was summoned up once again, as West Indies reclaimed The Oval with a victory that will resonate across the ages.

For a shell-shocked England, still beaten from their efforts against Australia, it was almost too much to take in, as from the depths of 147 for eight, Courtney Browne and Ian Bradshaw set about forging an unbroken stand of 71 that at first reduced England, then shattered them...

LARA TIPS GAYL
TO SKIPPER W

Besieged WI break losing spell

EVERARD GORDON

WHEN Ian Bradshaw struck Wharfe to the boundary for the winning runs in the final of the ICC Champions Trophy, West Indies had won a major international tournament for the first time in a decade.

It was the reply of a group of beleaguered young men to the doubters and to the many who have criticised them mercilessly, and sometimes justly, for their real and supposed shortcomings.

Inspiring victory —Manning

PRIME MINISTER Patrick Manning has congratulated WI Captain Brian Lara and his team on their victory in the World Cup Cricket 2004 at The Oval, in London England, yesterday.

Manning described the win as an inspiration to the youth of the T&T.

West Indies Cricket captain BRIAN LARA, centre, and teammates celebrate victory in the final of the ICC Champions Trophy in London, England, yesterday.

RETURN OF THE KINGS

Lara: I want to leave a legacy

Page 3

ENGLAND VS LARA

ICC Grand Finale

LARA'S masterstroke

LASANA LIBURD comments

Howard:
This shows
WI care

— Page 70

Mucho Tem
wins dero

express

CHAPTER 12

2004
ALL I ASK,
DID I ENTERTAIN?

'In movies the star sometimes dies.
So don't be afraid to let me die at the end, please'

BRIAN LARA

I WAS THRILLED when they said the 2007 World Cup would be staged in the West Indies. It was just what our region needed to kickstart our cricket, to bring some money in, tidy up some of our venues – even to build some new ones – and to put us back on the map. Way before it came around, I could see that it would be my last World Cup and I allowed myself to dream about fitting ends and rousing climaxes and maybe, who knows, even raising the cup.

When it finally came around, the culmination of all those years of planning and building, I was back in the chair yet again. My third time as captain of the West Indies cricket team. My third and definitely final time.

It was a big decision to go back. I'd been captain in 1998, and two years later I was scraping myself up off the floor. I'd taken it on again in 2003, worn a few blows but survived, only to side with my players in a dispute over sponsorship rights and lose it again.

After that second time, Shiv Chanderpaul took it on out of duty but it wasn't the right fit and so when Shiv decided he'd had enough, and with few other realistic choices available, it automatically came back to me.

It wasn't exactly a smooth transition. The board president, a prominent and distinguished figure in Trinidad & Tobago called Ken Gordon, came to my house and said that I needed to lead the team until I was finished. Dinanath Ramnarine, president of the players' association, also stopped by to try to persuade me to take over. I was torn. It was a big call. I knew my limits, and what kind of toll it was bound to take. But who says no when they're asked to prepare a team for a home World Cup? It was April 2006, a year away from the big show. I went in again.

* * *

We had a tour of India just before the World Cup at the beginning of 2007, playing a few one-day games, and all the time I was thinking how we were gonna get this World Cup squad pulling together.

There was a kid back in Trinidad & Tobago scoring first-class hundreds in 80 and 90 balls, hitting two quick centuries in his first three matches. Name of Kieron Pollard. We had an injury to one of our team in India and I called the selectors to send Pollard over. They flat out refused. The reason given – and look, maybe it was money, or maybe just a board decision – was that he would be our 'secret weapon' for the World Cup, so it wouldn't be right to reveal him too early.

I'm sitting there thinking how laughable this is. We've got a 19-year-old, just a kid, barely played any senior cricket at all, coming onto the stage of international cricket for the first time, and we're calling him our secret weapon? That was never going to happen. I needed him in India to see what the guy was all about. This was something new for us, to hear about first-class bowling attacks being taken apart. I needed to know if he could cut it at the top level. And in turn he needed to be introduced into the set-up.

The squad for the tournament was selected. I couldn't tell you if I was happy with it or not, but I was high in spirits, I remember that. The blood was pumping again. The old optimism was back. I was thinking about what we could achieve, how we could claim redemption, and build something that we could look back on in the years to come and say we *finally* achieved it. This was it. The World Cup.

The optimism didn't last long. From the very beginning when I first met with the selectors, Andy Roberts, Gordon Greenidge and Clyde Butts, I felt uncomfortable, uneasy, as if there was some ulterior motive that I didn't know about. I didn't feel that it was positive in my direction, that they wanted me in charge. I was challenged at every point. I felt like they wanted to do their own thing and I was just there to toss the coin for them. It reared its head in the very first game of the World Cup. We were playing Pakistan at Sabina Park and despite running out comfortable winners one of my tactical moves was questioned.

We batted first and got 241-9, and when we went out to bowl, I found that the ball was moving around for the seamers, and they had the Pakistani batters playing and missing. We'd gone into the game with three quicks in Daren Powell, Jerome Taylor and Corey Collymore, with Dwayne Bravo as our allrounder and Chris Gayle as our fifth bowler, bowling his off-breaks. But seeing the ball hooping, I decided that Dwayne Smith, who was an underrated bowler, someone who seamed it around, could be our man. I figured if he put it in the right areas he could be a force in those conditions, so I gave him the ball and he bowled 10 overs for three wickets and not much runs conceded. I felt it was a great move. It worked like a dream.

So, we've won the match and I walk into the meeting feeling good, we've got our first game out of the way, and the first question they ask is why I'd ignored the plans we'd had from the selection meeting.

I said, "What are you talking about?"

And they said, "Well, when you left here, Chris Gayle was our fifth bowler, and we want to know why you didn't bowl him."

"You wanna know *why*? It's pretty obvious. The wicket was seaming! Look, if we'd lost the match because of a decision that I'd made…"

"No but, you know, we wanna know if you're just gonna do your own thing."

I could not believe it. It was a gut punch. From that point, I wasn't sure I wanted to be around for much longer. Some former players, you know, they have this feeling of wanting to see another one fall. I've seen it so many times. It hurts deep when former players, people who should understand the reality of the situation, react like that.

You think that sounds destructive? It brought the end of my career. After that World Cup I was gonna play more Test cricket. We had a tour to England straight after the World Cup that I wanted to be on. But right from the start of that World Cup I felt vulnerable, attacked. We'd just put in the perfect performance in our first game of the World Cup and after that reaction I started to get antsy, nervous, about my entire future.

I woke up a few mornings later. We were still in Jamaica, and I could hear this commotion outside my hotel door. I opened it to a bunch of police officers. I asked them what the problem was and they said, "Please, Mr Lara, just carry on with your day, nothing for you to worry about." Downstairs at breakfast was abuzz with talk and rumours.

Later that morning I came to learn that just across from my room was Bob Woolmer's room. I also learned that a chambermaid had found Bob lying unresponsive on the bathroom floor.

By about midday, it was official. The worst of all news.

* * *

Bob's death overshadowed everything. He was my old Warwickshire coach, and by then in charge of Pakistan. A good man. Hugely popular with his players. The day before his death, Pakistan had suffered one of their worst defeats in a big tournament, losing to Ireland on St Patrick's Day. A defeat like that would not be well received in Pakistan. There would be protests, effigies burned in the streets, all that stuff. In the Caribbean, the whole tournament immediately fell into shadow. The story of how Bob died became the story of the World Cup.

A few days after his death, the Jamaican police announced that the cause of death was "asphyxia as a result of manual strangulation". Suddenly, this was a murder case. And it was then that all the conspiracy theories and big rumours started coming. Who killed Bob Woolmer? The ICC's anti-corruption people were closely involved in the case. An English detective, a big man called Mark Shields, became the face of the investigation. Every day he was in the papers and on TV. There were differing accounts about what the pathology reports had found. The bone in Bob's neck that they first said was broken, and which had led to the claim of manual strangulation, was later found by an X-ray not to have been broken at all. There was even some talk that he may have been poisoned, but there was conflicting evidence on that too.

Theories were flying around, stories appearing in the press, lots of them relating to corruption and pushing the idea that Bob knew too much. None of it stood up. All the evidence now points to Bob having died of natural causes. Not that we knew that at the time. It was a mess. And a mess played out in front of the world. The tragedy of Bob's death got turned into an international scandal and even today, the story remains unjustly clouded in mystery. That's what happens when a case as big as this gets handled so badly.

Personally, I was confused and hurt by the whole situation. Bob's death, coupled with India losing to Bangladesh that same weekend and not making the latter stages, leaving our tourism market on its knees with last-minute cancellations and so on, just set this entire World Cup into a doom spiral.

* * *

As for us, we comfortably came out of our group on top, beating Zimbabwe and Ireland at Sabina to go through to the Super Eights. Our next games, against Australia and New Zealand, would take place at the Sir Vivian Richards Stadium, the new ground in Antigua built especially for the World Cup.

Antigua is a special place for me. I'd had some wonderful experiences there, being part of the world-record chase of 418 against Australia, and those two world records, all played out to a fantastic atmosphere at the Antigua Recreation Ground. A lot of our islands had to improve their facilities to host some games at the World Cup, and Antigua had started on this stadium a few years earlier.

It was the same across much of the Caribbean. Back home, our prime minister, Patrick Manning, decided in 2004 to open a cricket ground in my name and was gonna get it ready in time for the 2007 World Cup. Barbados made some renovations to the Kensington Oval. In Guyana, they built the national stadium in Providence.

All of these were welcome. But by building these grounds away from the physical heartbeat of an island, you ran the risk of sacrificing some of the flavour and atmosphere of watching cricket in our part of the world.

I was in shock when we got to Antigua. We were there to play the defending champions. I was expecting it to be sold out. We all were. This would be the first time I'd be seeing the Sir Vivian Richards Stadium, and we walked in there and it was nowhere near sold out. Coming from the Rec, a magical place set right in the heart of the city, it just didn't transfer to this place which was remote and out of the way. There was a good turnout of Australians, but the place just felt flat.

We were playing the world champs, so the lack of buzz was no kind of excuse for us losing the game. But the atmosphere seemed to sum up the overall mood of the tournament. Something was missing. On the pitch we never really got close to them. I made 77 in our run chase but it was nowhere near enough. A few days later we played New Zealand at the same ground and there were even fewer people there, it was honestly no more than half full. We were beaten heavily then too.

We had to play six matches in the Super Eights, and so after Antigua we went to Grenada, where we lost heavily twice, first against Sri Lanka, and then South Africa. Four games in the Super Eights, and four defeats. We were out of our own World Cup with two games still to play.

Did we have a good enough team to challenge? Definitely. I wish I could tell you what went wrong. I don't know if I can articulate this properly, but from about the time I came back after Chanderpaul, I sensed that a lot of times, fingers were being pointed at me for defeats and that the players recognised that and sort of fell into line with it. In defeat I felt I was on my own, and we spiralled downwards.

And look, if the selectors are putting doubts in my mind after we've won a game convincingly, imagine what it's like when we start losing. The doubts that they clearly had about me as a leader definitely affected my confidence. It knocked so much out of me.

It's not an excuse, it's a fact. I doubted my captaincy. I wanted to understand from them how to captain this team. I captained this team partly from selection meetings and discussions, but also on instinct, on what I knew at times to be spontaneous, spur-of-the-moment moves that I'd done all of my life. Their questions put a spoke in my wheels for sure. And again, historically, we do tend to spiral when we're not together. We get into a situation where people fend for themselves and it's not a collaborative effort to stop the flow of things. It makes it all the more impossible to reassess and come back together as a team.

Maybe that's the fault of the captain. Maybe it is. The buck has to stop somewhere. But I couldn't shake the feeling that even though

I was trying to be up for every battle, there was something holding me back. Truth was, my confidence was shot.

* * *

I went into that tournament absolutely wanting to continue my Test career. I still had work to do as a Test player. My first consideration was to stay as a member of the team and get to England for the Test series. Yes, I intended to end my one-day career after the World Cup, to hand the reins over to a younger man, but I still had aspirations to play Test cricket.

The longer that tournament went on, however, the more my mind took me back to the past. And the more I went there, the more I could feel the will to carry on draining out of me.

My mind often ended up back at Sir Viv, who gave up the captaincy in 1991 but still wanted to go to the World Cup in 1992 and yet was left out. There was a definite sense that him giving up the captaincy was used against him as a reason to end his career. Whether that was specifically the case or not, he was dumped against his will as soon as he relinquished the job. I didn't like that for Viv Richards and I wasn't gonna like it for myself.

This was my third go at the job, and it was the heaviest burden of leadership I'd ever known. I'd had sleepless nights and stress before, but never like this. After much consideration, talking and late-night soul searching, I came to a decision to finish the whole thing.

The board president, Ken Gordon, was upset, strongly intimating that he wanted me to reconsider, and I spoke to Sir Hilary Beckles, the historian and vice-chancellor of the University of the West Indies, who was also on the board. He too was upset, and he even said to me, "Look, if they're going to not pick you for England, then let them do that, and let's see the reaction". I also spoke to Lisa Agard who worked for Cable & Wireless which had been a sponsor of West Indies cricket for about 20 years until 2004 and became a significant personal sponsor through my retirement and after. As sponsor, they were quite concerned and wanted my exit from the game to be professionally managed and felt it was better to leave during the upcoming England tour. Ultimately they understood, and supported my decision, telling me that the only voice I had to listen to was my own. I spoke to friends and family, and of course to Joey Carew, who was a man of wise counsel.

I made the decision that week, in the days building up to the meaningless Super Eights game against England. I officially told the media at the end of the pre-match press conference, leaning into the microphone and whispering these words: "I gave extensive consideration to this. I want everybody to know that on Saturday I'll be playing my last international match."

At no point in time, then or now, do I think I made a harsh or rushed decision. Let's stress this point: people talk about my records as if I was obsessed with the numbers. If that was the case, why wouldn't I stick around to make 47 more Test runs to become the first man to make 12,000 Test runs? These things meant nothing to me. It was time.

The day before the England game, Ken Gordon spoke out. "We have to take the whole picture and accept the good with the bad," he said. "But overall, I think he's so much more on the plus side. He's been tremendous for West Indies cricket and I'd really like to see us honour that."

I had no clue by that stage how I'd be received at the Kensington Oval.

* * *

When I was a kid coming up, we played cricket a lot at Guaracara Park, a ground in the middle of the oil fields and the oil refinery in south Trinidad. There was maybe a maximum of a couple-thousand people that could squeeze in there to watch, wedged in along the grass cycle track surrounding a very fast outfield, and man, I loved it there. It was rough and bumpy and beautiful, and every time I walked out to bat there, I imagined I was playing in a stadium with 50,000 people. The anticipation, the eruptions, everything there was just amazing. It was small, but it had a raw energy to it, this little corner of West Indies cricket, throbbing with life. These days it's an overgrown field, abandoned and long forgotten.

At Barbados that day, it was as if all these wondrous places and all these pages of history came to be bottled up into a single moment.

It really *was* my last day. Whatever happened out there on that field, when 5pm came, it would be the end. I tried to gather myself because I knew I had an innings to play, but it was a dizzying feeling. We batted first. The English cricketers formed two lines for me to walk through as I got to the middle. The whole place was on its feet.

Was the match irrelevant? No. I wanted to go out with a win. I wanted to perform one final time, a parting gift, something to remember me by. Then Marlon decided to change his mind, and that was that.

We score 300 but Kevin Pietersen hits a hundred and they chase it down in the final over, nine wickets down. It's a wonderful game of cricket, even though there's nothing riding on it. I'd have loved to have gone out with a win but it's not to be, and that's OK. I didn't play in too many winning teams throughout my career, so why should the last game be any different?

Bajan cricket people are so knowledgeable. And it feels good and right that the crowd should have so many overseas fans in it, and so many English fans. The game is the thing, always, and it belongs to all of us. The crowd's reaction, the walk out, the walk back, that will never leave me.

* * *

I'm standing on the outfield. Michael Atherton is holding a microphone in front of me. I haven't planned anything. The words just come out.

"I've had a tremendous time playing for the West Indies. All I ask is, did I entertain? If I entertained you, I'm happy.

"When I was first playing cricket, the West Indies were at the top in world cricket, and I always wanted us to stay at the top.

"But there was a decline, and we haven't managed to stop that over the last 10 or 12 years, and that's the most disappointing thing. I'm a team player and I want to see this West Indies team get back to the top.

"I came to the realisation some time ago that this was going to be my last game... I felt comfortable and as the day went on, I knew I'd made the right decision.

"I knew it was the right time to call it a day and let the younger players take the West Indies forward. Maybe we can see some change in the future."

Even as I'm speaking, I can feel what it means. I know what I'm really saying. I can hear it in my voice. Some of the crowd won't pick it up, but a good number will. I'm saying that I didn't quite achieve what I set out to do. *At least* did I entertain you? Did I *at least* bring a little pleasure and joy through the way I played the game? *At least* offer some hope to people who lived vicariously through the successes and greatness of West Indies cricket, whose daily moods ebbed and flowed depending on the fortunes of their team? I brought some pride and identity to Caribbean people when I did well, right? At least I did *that*? At least, *at least*.

I remember that interview. I couldn't look Atherton in the eye and say that I left West Indies cricket in good stead. I couldn't say that. So what was left for me to say? I realised I didn't need to say anything. I just had to *ask*.

* * *

In the minds of some, I kept the West Indies afloat. Not as a captain or as part of a great team, but through the consolations of individual achievements. You might call that a blessing and a curse.

What motivated me to make runs, *always*, was the team. Any time I went away from that, turned a bit inward, started thinking about my name on honours boards and things like that, then I'd fall apart.

A man doesn't play cricket by himself. Nor should he play it *for* himself. Cricket isn't golf or tennis. It's not about grand slams and individual titles. Cricket is an expression of collective action, or it's nothing at all.

I was meant to keep the West Indies on top of the world and I couldn't do it. We won a couple of things, I broke a couple of records, but I failed at my main purpose. England didn't win a single match against the West Indies throughout the Eighties. Yet, when I was captain against them, we lost seven Tests out of eight at one stage. You can't hide from those facts. If you sat down with one or two prominent legends in a quiet room and asked them to describe Lara's legacy, they'd say "What legacy? We lost when he was playing!"

Money lurks around the edges of this story too, of course. Wherever there's money, there's envy. So let's be real for a moment, and leave it at that. Back in the day, my salary was one tenth of what I was making overall. What I would have made in one year would have been more than what other guys would have made in their careers. And a generation on again, what a guy might make in a few months is more than Viv might have made in his whole career, and he was the greatest.

I straddle those worlds. I'm the link in that rusty chain. I came up through the great eras of the past, in awe of these players, not being rich in money but rich in purpose, alive to the struggle, fired by the cause. And then there's this other era, the one we're in now, let's call it the age of the individual, where young talented kids – and good luck to them – can make a lot of money very quickly and pick and choose whoever they play for. In spirit, I belong to the former group, though I have a foot in the present. My only purpose was the cause of the West Indies cricket team. If somewhere down the line I happened to put my name to a clothing label or a computer game or whatever, then that was just a side story.

So here's another question: How do we pick a legacy from all of *that*?

* * *

You know what? Perhaps it *is* all entertainment in the end. Perhaps that's enough. Nothing is forever. Great eras come and go. Players move on, teams go through good times and bad. Life is about moments and it's the memories we made that will hang around long after we've gone.

I gave 17 years of my life to West Indies cricket. Actually, hold on. I don't like that idea, that I 'gave'. I'm having none of that. I *received*. West Indies cricket and its people gave something *to* me, this amazing opportunity to live out my dream. I was privileged to represent them.

Would I give up my records to be part of a truly great West Indies team? Of course I would. Would Sachin hand over a few of his hundreds to have won another World Cup? No doubt. The more interesting question is this: Would I swap my career to have played in the halcyon days, with Viv and the boys, when we won everything? And the answer is no. Never. This was my time, my people, our struggle.

* * *

Pearl and Bunty Lara brought me into this world. The tenth of 11 children, our own cricket team. You taught us all how to live, and about the value of dreams. And in return, all you ever asked of me was that I gave my heart and soul to something I cared about. I want to thank you for that.

WEST INDIES v PAKISTAN

Venue: Sabina Park, Kingston
Toss: Pakistan won the toss and decided to field
Points: West Indies 2; Pakistan 0
TV Umpire: BG Jerling (South Africa)
Referee: BC Broad (England)

Date: 13th March 2007
Result: West Indies won by 54 runs
Umpires: BF Bowden (New Zealand), SJA Taufel (Australia)
Reserve Umpire: IJ Gould (England)

WEST INDIES		R	B	PAKISTAN		R	B
CH Gayle	c Kamran Akmal b Umar Gul	2	6	Imran Nazir	c Ramdin b Powell	6	3
S Chanderpaul	c Kamran Akmal b Iftikhar Anjum	19	63	Mohammad Hafeez	c Lara b Powell	11	28
RR Sarwan	c Younis Khan b Iftikhar Anjum	49	65	Younis Khan	c Ramdin b Taylor	9	13
MN Samuels	c Shoaib Malik b Mohammad Hafeez	63	70	Mohammad Yousuf	c Ramdin b Smith	37	72
*BC Lara	c Kamran Akmal b Mohammad Hafeez	37	56	*Inzamam-ul-Haq	lbw b Smith	36	65
DJ Bravo	c Naved-ul-Hasan b Iftikhar Anjum	16	17	Shoaib Malik	c Chanderpaul b Collymore	62	54
+D Ramdin	st Kamran Akmal b Danish Kaneria	1	4	+Kamran Akmal	c Bravo b Smith	0	1
DR Smith	c Inzamam-ul-Haq b Umar Gul	32	15	Naved-ul-Hasan	b Bravo	11	29
JE Taylor	run out (Iftikhar Anjum)	2	4	Iftikhar Anjum	c Lara b Bravo	11	18
DBL Powell	not out	1	1	Umar Gul	c and b Bravo	0	1
CD Collymore	not out	8	2	Danish Kaneria	not out	0	0
Extras	(2 lb, 3 nb, 6 w)	11		Extras	(2 lb, 2 w)	4	
Total	(9 wickets, 50 overs)	241		Total	(all out, 47.2 overs)	187	

Fall of wickets: 1-7 (Gayle, 2.2 ov), 2-64 (Chanderpaul, 19.2 ov), 3-77 (Sarwan, 23.5 ov), 4-168 (Lara, 41.1 ov), 5-181 (Samuels, 43.6 ov), 6-183 (Ramdin, 44.5 ov), 7-223 (Smith, 48.2 ov), 8-228 (Taylor, 49.1 ov), 9-232 (Bravo, 49.3 ov)

Fall of wickets: 1-6 (Imran Nazir, 0.3 ov), 2-17 (Younis Khan, 3.6 ov), 3-39 (Mohammad Hafeez, 10.3 ov), 4-99 (Mohammad Yousuf, 28.6 ov), 5-116 (Inzamam-ul-Haq, 32.4 ov), 6-116 (Kamran Akmal, 32.5 ov), 7-144 (Naved-ul-Hasan, 40.2 ov), 8-187 (Iftikhar Anjum, 46.5 ov), 9-187 (Umar Gul, 46.6 ov), 10-187 (Shoaib Malik, 47.2 ov)

PAKISTAN	O	M	R	W	Wd	Nb	WEST INDIES	O	M	R	W	Wd	Nb
Umar Gul	9	1	38	2	2	1	Powell	10	1	42	2	-	-
Naved-ul-Hasan	9	1	49	0	-	2	Taylor	10	1	38	1	-	-
Iftikhar Anjum	10	3	44	3	-	-	Collymore	8.2	3	27	1	1	-
Danish Kaneria	9	2	45	1	3	-	Smith	10	0	36	3	-	-
Mohammad Hafeez	9	0	39	2	-	-	Bravo	9	0	42	3	1	-
Shoaib Malik	4	0	24	0	-	-							

WEST INDIES v AUSTRALIA

Venue: Sir Vivian Richards Stadium, North Sound
Toss: West Indies won the toss and decided to field
Points: West Indies 0; Australia 2
TV Umpire: BF Bowden (New Zealand)
Referee: BC Broad (England)

Date: 27th, 28th March 2007
Result: Australia won by 103 runs
Umpires: Aleem Dar (Pakistan), Asad Rauf (Pakistan)
Reserve Umpire: RE Koertzen (South Africa)

AUSTRALIA		R	B	WEST INDIES		R	B
+AC Gilchrist	c Ramdin b Powell	7	9	CH Gayle	c Watson b McGrath	2	23
ML Hayden	c Samuels b Bravo	158	143	S Chanderpaul	lbw b Tait	5	12
*RT Ponting	run out (Sarwan)	35	36	RR Sarwan	c Ponting b Hogg	29	58
MJ Clarke	lbw b Bravo	41	47	MN Samuels	c Symonds b McGrath	4	8
A Symonds	c Ramdin b Samuels	13	18	*BC Lara	lbw b Hogg	77	83
MEK Hussey	b Powell	9	18	DJ Bravo	c Ponting b McGrath	9	10
SR Watson	not out	33	26	+D Ramdin	c Gilchrist b Bracken	52	43
GB Hogg	not out	5	6	DR Smith	lbw b Hogg	9	7
NW Bracken				JE Taylor	lbw b Symonds	10	18
SW Tait				DBL Powell	b Tait	5	9
GD McGrath				CD Collymore	not out	1	2
Extras	(1 b, 9 lb, 3 nb, 8 w)	21		Extras	(1 b, 15 w)	16	
Total	(6 wickets, 50 overs)	322		Total	(all out, 45.3 overs)	219	

Fall of wickets: 1-10 (Gilchrist, 4.1 ov), 2-76 (Ponting, 14.4 ov), 3-174 (Clarke, 30.5 ov), 4-208 (Symonds, 35.6 ov), 5-234 (Hussey, 40.5 ov), 6-297 (Hayden, 47.1 ov)
Fall of wickets: 1-11 (Chanderpaul, 3.5 ov), 2-16 (Gayle, 7.2 ov), 3-20 (Samuels, 9.4 ov), 4-91 (Sarwan, 25.2 ov), 5-107 (Bravo, 28.3 ov), 6-156 (Lara, 35.3 ov), 7-172 (Smith, 37.4 ov), 8-199 (Taylor, 42.4 ov), 9-217 (Ramdin, 44.2 ov), 10-219 (Powell, 45.3 ov)

WEST INDIES	O	M	R	W	Wd	Nb	AUSTRALIA	O	M	R	W	Wd	Nb
Powell	10	2	53	2	-	-	Bracken	9	1	25	1	1	-
Taylor	10	0	67	0	3	-	Tait	7.3	0	43	2	7	-
Collymore	10	0	56	0	2	-	McGrath	8	1	31	3	-	-
Gayle	4	0	29	0	-	2	Watson	7	0	31	0	-	-
Bravo	7	0	49	2	2	-	Hogg	10	0	56	3	2	-
Samuels	9	0	58	1	1	1	Symonds	4	0	32	1	1	-

WEST INDIES v NEW ZEALAND

Venue: Sir Vivian Richards Stadium, North Sound
Toss: New Zealand won the toss and decided to field
Points: West Indies 0; New Zealand 2
TV Umpire: Aleem Dar (Pakistan)
Referee: MJ Procter (South Africa)

Date: 29th March 2007
Result: New Zealand won by 7 wickets
Umpires: Asad Rauf (Pakistan), RE Koertzen (South Africa)
Reserve Umpire: BF Bowden (New Zealand)

WEST INDIES		R	B	NEW ZEALAND		R	B
CH Gayle	b Oram	44	56	PG Fulton	b Powell	0	2
S Chanderpaul	c Styris b Bond	4	28	*SP Fleming	run out (Lara)	45	66
RR Sarwan	c McCullum b Oram	19	27	HJH Marshall	c Lara b Powell	15	23
MN Samuels	c McCullum b Oram	9	18	SB Styris	not out	80	90
*BC Lara	c McCullum b Styris	37	49	CD McMillan	not out	33	57
DJ Bravo	c McCullum b Bond	18	30	JDP Oram			
+D Ramdin	c Oram b Vettori	15	22	+BB McCullum			
LMP Simmons	not out	14	26	DL Vettori			
DR Smith	b Vettori	8	6	JEC Franklin			
DBL Powell	lbw b Vettori	0	1	SE Bond			
CD Collymore	b Bond	0	5	MJ Mason			
Extras	(1 b, 5 lb, 3 w)	9		Extras	(1 lb, 2 nb, 3 w)	6	
Total	(all out, 44.4 overs)	177		Total	(3 wickets, 39.2 overs)	179	

Fall of wickets: 1-14 (Chanderpaul, 7.5 ov), 2-66 (Sarwan, 16.2 ov), 3-78 (Samuels, 20.3 ov), 4-81 (Gayle, 22.2 ov), 5-128 (Bravo, 33.1 ov), 6-150 (Lara, 36.3 ov), 7-158 (Ramdin, 41.3 ov), 8-176 (Smith, 43.3 ov), 9-176 (Powell, 43.4 ov), 10-177 (Collymore, 44.4 ov)
Fall of wickets: 1-0 (Fulton, 0.2 ov), 2-36 (Marshall, 8.3 ov), 3-77 (Fleming, 20.6 ov)

NEW ZEALAND	O	M	R	W	Wd	Nb	WEST INDIES	O	M	R	W	Wd	Nb
Mason	6	2	14	0	1	-	Powell	10	2	39	2	1	2
Bond	8.4	0	31	3	2	-	Smith	5	0	24	0	1	-
Franklin	3	0	29	0	-	-	Collymore	9	0	43	0	-	-
Oram	8	2	23	3	-	-	Bravo	8	0	32	0	-	-
Styris	10	1	35	1	-	-	Gayle	6.2	0	35	0	1	-
Vettori	9	1	39	3	-	-	Sarwan	1	0	5	0	-	-

WEST INDIES v SRI LANKA

Venue: Guyana National Stadium, Providence
Toss: West Indies won the toss and decided to field
Points: West Indies 0; Sri Lanka 2
TV Umpire: SJA Taufel (Australia)
Referee: JJ Crowe (New Zealand)

Date: 1st April 2007
Result: Sri Lanka won by 113 runs
Umpires: MR Benson (England), DJ Harper (Australia)
Reserve Umpire: SA Bucknor

SRI LANKA		R	B	WEST INDIES		R	B
WU Tharanga	b Powell	8	24	CH Gayle	c Fernando b Malinga	10	21
ST Jayasuriya	b Powell	115	101	DJ Bravo	b Vaas	21	24
+KC Sangakkara	c Ramdin b Bradshaw	7	10	S Chanderpaul	b Malinga	76	110
*DPMD Jayawardene	b Bravo	82	113	*BC Lara	st Sangakkara b Vaas	2	4
LPC Silva	c Lara b Sarwan	23	31	RR Sarwan	st Sangakkara b Jayasuriya	44	68
TM Dilshan	not out	39	22	MN Samuels	lbw b Muralitharan	3	5
RP Arnold	not out	4	4	DR Smith	run out (Malinga->S'kkara)	0	2
CRD Fernando				+D Ramdin	c Vaas b Jayasuriya	2	5
WPUJC Vaas				IDR Bradshaw	not out	6	17
SL Malinga				JE Taylor	lbw b Muralitharan	13	9
M Muralitharan				DBL Powell	b Jayasuriya	2	4
Extras	(7 lb, 5 nb, 13 w)	25		Extras	(1 lb, 2 nb, 8 w)	11	
Total	(5 wickets, 50 overs)	303		Total	(all out, 44.3 overs)	190	

Fall of wickets: 1-18 (Tharanga, 5.5 ov), 2-35 (Sangakkara, 8.4 ov), 3-218 (Jayasuriya, 38.4 ov), 4-251 (Jayawardene, 44.1 ov), 5-268 (Silva, 46.4 ov)
Fall of wickets: 1-20 (Gayle, 5.2 ov), 2-40 (Bravo, 8.3 ov), 3-42 (Lara, 10.1 ov), 4-134 (Sarwan, 34.2 ov), 5-147 (Samuels, 35.6 ov), 6-148 (Smith, 36.4 ov), 7-158 (Ramdin, 38.1 ov), 8-173 (Chanderpaul, 41.2 ov), 9-187 (Taylor, 43.4 ov), 10-190 (Powell, 44.3 ov)

WEST INDIES	O	M	R	W	Wd	Nb	SRI LANKA	O	M	R	W	Wd	Nb
Taylor	8	1	32	0	4	-	Vaas	8	1	19	2	-	1
Powell	10	1	38	2	2	2	Malinga	5	0	34	2	2	-
Bradshaw	10	0	67	1	1	1	Fernando	7	3	19	0	1	1
Smith	3	0	23	0	-	-	Dilshan	4	0	11	0	-	-
Gayle	9	0	60	0	3	2	Arnold	3	0	9	0	-	-
Bravo	7	0	59	1	2	-	Muralitharan	9	0	59	2	1	-
Sarwan	3	0	17	1	1	-	Jayasuriya	8.3	0	38	3	-	-

WEST INDIES v SOUTH AFRICA

Venue: Queen's Park (New), St George's
Toss: West Indies won the toss and decided to field
Points: West Indies 0; South Africa 2
TV Umpire: Aleem Dar (Pakistan)
Referee: BC Broad (England)

Date: 10th April 2007
Result: South Africa won by 67 runs
Umpires: MR Benson (England), DJ Harper (Australia)
Reserve Umpire: Asad Rauf (Pakistan)

SOUTH AFRICA		R	B	WEST INDIES		R	B
AB de Villiers	c Chanderpaul b Collymore	146	130	CH Gayle	run out (Prince)	32	35
*GC Smith	c Ramdin b Collymore	7	22	S Chanderpaul	c Smith b Pollock	4	7
JH Kallis	b Gayle	81	86	DS Smith	c de Villiers b Nel	33	27
HH Gibbs	not out	61	40	*BC Lara	b Kallis	21	26
+MV Boucher	c and b Bravo	52	23	RR Sarwan	c Pollock b Ntini	92	75
SM Pollock	not out	0	0	DJ Bravo	c Gibbs b Pollock	6	11
AG Prince				KA Pollard	b Kallis	10	17
LE Bosman				+D Ramdin	c sub (RJ Peterson) b Smith	4	9
AJ Hall				IDR Bradshaw	c Hall b Smith	20	45
A Nel				DBL Powell	not out	48	36
M Ntini				CD Collymore	not out	12	12
Extras	(3 lb, 6 w)	9		Extras	(4 lb, 3 w)	7	
Total	(4 wickets, 50 overs)	356		Total	(9 wickets, 50 overs)	289	

Fall of wickets: 1-21 (Smith, 6.6 ov), 2-191 (Kallis, 35.2 ov), 3-261 (de Villiers, 43.1 ov), 4-347 (Boucher, 49.2 ov)
Fall of wickets: 1-5 (Chanderpaul, 2.1 ov), 2-65 (Smith, 10.6 ov), 3-69 (Gayle, 11.3 ov), 4-119 (Lara, 19.4 ov), 5-142 (Bravo, 24.1 ov), 6-169 (Pollard, 29.5 ov), 7-181 (Ramdin, 31.5 ov), 8-213 (Sarwan, 38.1 ov), 9-254 (Bradshaw, 45.3 ov)

WEST INDIES	O	M	R	W	Wd	Nb	SOUTH AFRICA	O	M	R	W	Wd	Nb
Collymore	10	0	41	2	3	-	Pollock	8	0	33	2	-	-
Powell	10	0	78	0	1	-	Ntini	10	1	57	1	-	-
Bradshaw	10	0	73	0	2	-	Nel	10	0	54	1	-	-
Bravo	7	0	69	1	-	-	Hall	9	0	49	0	2	-
Pollard	3	0	20	0	-	-	Kallis	8	0	36	2	-	-
Gayle	6	0	42	1	-	-	Smith	5	0	56	2	1	-
Sarwan	4	0	30	0	-	-							

WEST INDIES v ENGLAND

Venue: Kensington Oval, Bridgetown
Toss: England won the toss and decided to field
Points: West Indies 0; England 2
TV Umpire: BF Bowden (New Zealand)
Referee: RS Madugalle (Sri Lanka)

Date: 21st April 2007
Result: England won by 1 wicket
Umpires: RE Koertzen (South Africa), SJA Taufel (Australia)
Reserve Umpire: SA Bucknor

WEST INDIES		R	B	ENGLAND		R	B
CH Gayle	c Broad b Flintoff	79	58	AJ Strauss	c Smith b Collymore	7	12
DS Smith	c Collingwood b Flintoff	61	106	*MP Vaughan	run out (Bravo)	79	68
*BC Lara	run out (Pietersen)	18	17	RS Bopara	run out (Bravo)	26	43
MN Samuels	c Collingwood b Vaughan	51	39	KP Pietersen	b Taylor	100	91
RR Sarwan	c Nixon b Plunkett	3	8	PD Collingwood	b Bravo	6	11
S Chanderpaul	c Plunkett b Collingwood	34	39	A Flintoff	c Powell b Sarwan	15	20
DJ Bravo	c Dalrymple b Vaughan	13	11	JWM Dalrymple	run out (Smith)	1	6
+D Ramdin	not out	10	11	+PA Nixon	b Bravo	38	39
JE Taylor	c Dalrymple b Vaughan	12	10	LE Plunkett	c Bravo b Taylor	2	3
DBL Powell	run out (Flintoff)	0	1	SCJ Broad	not out	5	5
CD Collymore	run out (Flintoff)	1	2	JM Anderson	not out	0	1
Extras	(1 lb, 3 nb, 14 w)	18		Extras	(6 b, 11 lb, 5 w)	22	
Total	(all out, 49.5 overs)	300		Total	(9 wickets, 49.5 overs)	301	

Fall of wickets: 1-131 (Gayle, 23.5 ov), 2-168 (Smith, 29.3 ov), 3-173 (Lara, 30.5 ov), 4-181 (Sarwan, 33.2 ov), 5-258 (Samuels, 42.5 ov), 6-276 (Chanderpaul, 45.3 ov), 7-277 (Bravo, 46.1 ov), 8-296 (Taylor, 48.5 ov), 9-298 (Powell, 49.2 ov), 10-300 (Collymore, 49.5 ov)

Fall of wickets: 1-11 (Strauss, 2.3 ov), 2-101 (Bopara, 15.3 ov), 3-154 (Vaughan, 26.3 ov), 4-162 (Collingwood, 29.2 ov), 5-185 (Flintoff, 34.2 ov), 6-189 (Dalrymple, 35.5 ov), 7-269 (Pietersen, 46.2 ov), 8-271 (Plunkett, 46.5 ov), 9-298 (Nixon, 49.2 ov)

ENGLAND	O	M	R	W	Wd	Nb	WEST INDIES	O	M	R	W	Wd	Nb
Anderson	6	0	39	0	6	-	Collymore	10	0	61	1	2	-
Plunkett	7	0	71	1	5	2	Powell	10	0	58	0	2	-
Broad	6	1	32	0	1	-	Taylor	10	0	65	2	-	-
Flintoff	9.5	0	59	2	-	1	Gayle	5	0	32	0	-	-
Dalrymple	3	0	19	0	1	-	Bravo	9.5	0	47	2	1	-
Collingwood	8	0	40	1	1	-	Sarwan	5	1	21	1	-	-
Vaughan	10	0	39	3	-	-							

Lara says emotional goodbye to cricket

DID I ENTERTAIN?

—Page 3—

FINAL LAP: West Indies captain Brian Lara waves goodbye to his fans as he makes a lap of honour around the Kensington Oval after the final Super Eight match between West Indies and England in Bridgetown, Barbados yesterday.

Artist Boscoe Holder dies —Page 5   Hinds wants Akon charged —Page 7

LARA A BATSMAN OF RARE GIFTS

Here's LARA'S LAST HURRAH

WEST INDIES captain Brian Lara raises his bat after the match during the Cricket World Cup match in Bridgetown, Barbados yesterday.

WI LOSE THRILLER IN LARA FINALE

PAGE 46A

THE NEXT GENERATION HAS ARRIVED

KIA Rio

West Indies captain **BRIAN LARA**, right, gets a hug from teammate **CHRIS GAYLE** while leaving the pavilion to play his last innings in international cricket during the Super 8s match against England in Bridgetown Barbados, on Saturday. Lara retired from all forms of international cricket, surprising many who had expected his test career to carry on.

AP Photo

Sunday Sport

The National Newspaper of Trinidad &

April 26th 2007

...reer of Lara...

ENGLAND

ENGLAND SPOIL LARA'S FAREWELL

...beat Windies by one wicket

—GARTH WATTLEY reports-Page 86

WORLD CUP SCOREBOARD

End of an era
TONY COZIER comments –Page 83

Fans hail 'the entertainer'

BRIAN LARA signs autographs

LARA ON INDIGO: West Indies captain Brian Lara hits a shot against England while smashing his last innings in international cricket during the Super Eights match of the Cricket World Cup at the Kensington Oval in Bridgetown, Barbados, yesterday. Lara is retiring from all forms of international cricket, surprising many who had expected his Test career to carry on.

Sports sports sports sports sports sports

England dash fairy-tale farewe

BRIDGETOWN. England spoiled Brian Lara's farewell to international cricket with a last gasp victory over the West Indies in the last Super 8s match of the World Cup yesterday.

Kevin Pietersen struck a century as England chased the West Indies total of 300 and wicketkeeper Paul Nixon stepped in and smashed 36 to set England up for a one wicket victory in front of 22,452 spectators at the Kensington Oval with just one ball left.

Bowler Stuart Broad, playing his first match at the World Cup, scored the winning runs as the Barbados gloom.

Lara, with tears in his eyes, bid farewell to the crowd. "Did I entertain you?" he asked before walking off the ground, shaking

crowd at the Kensington Oval who had largely come to say goodbye to a Caribbean cricket legend.

Lara is the world's leading Test run scorer and holds the records for Test innings (400) and First-Class innings (501).

England put West Indies in to bat and against Chris Gayle bludgeoned 79 to 53 for two.

Lara came in at number three, walking past applauding England players and to roars of "Lara, Lara, Lara." He was just beginning to look comfortable, having hit three fours on his way to 18 from 17 balls, when disaster struck the captain.

Runnells called him through for an impossible single and then changed his mind, leaving the captain stranded. Pietersen threw down the stumps from 10 yards away to...

Lara shrugged and walked off.

WEST INDIES fans reach to greet their team captain Brian Lara after he played his last international cricket match in the Super 8s round against England of the Cricket World Cup at the Kensington Oval in Bridgetown, Barbados, yesterday. AP PHOTO

BARBADOS SCOR

WEST INDIES VS EN

ress Sport
per of Trinidad & Tobago
FRIDAY APRIL 20, 2007
Pass It On...
Digicel
$1

LARA LEAVES TOO SOON

Bryan Davis laments West Indies skipper's retirement

WORLD CUP SCOREBOARD — Page 78

Newsday
FREEDOM OF THE PRESS
APRIL 22, 2007   120 PAGES

LARA: DID I ENTERTAIN?

BOSCOE HOLDER IS DEAD

WEST INDIES Captain Brian Lara sets with supporters while he takes a lap of Kensington Oval, in Barbados yesterday, following his final international cricket match against England in the Dhs Brief Super 8s World Cup match.

CROWD YES!

MINISTER: AKON SHOULD BE CHARGED

SEE PAGES 5 & 46A

West Indies captain Brian Lara through a "guard of honour" as takes the field for Saturday's S match against England at Ken Oval, Barbados. Photo: Robert

NEWS

Curtain falls on Lara's career

BY SUNDAY NEWSDAY REPORTER

WEST INDIES Captain Brian Lara brought an end to his illustrious career against the old enemy, England in the last Super 8s match of the Cricket World Cup yesterday.

Lara's glittering career as one of the world's best batsmen has been enveloped with controversy ranging from poor team results, contract disputes and heavy media criticism.

Despite these pressures brought to bear off field, no one can deny the 38-year-old left-hander his place in history as arguably the greatest batsman to ever play the game.

Lara was born in Cantaro, Santa Cruz, the ninth of 11 children to Pearl and Bunty Lara. His father and one of his older sisters Agnes Cyrus enrolled him in the Harvard Coaching Clinic in Port-of-Spain at the tender age of six on weekly coaching sessions.

He would attend San Juan Secondary before moving to Fatima College at the age of 14. This period saw him enter the influence of Michael "Joey" Carew, a former national representative and opening batsman in Woodbrook.

Carew, a long-serving West Indies veteran took Lara under his tutelage and worked with him on his cricketing and mental development.

In 1988 Lara made his First-Class debut for Trinidad and Tobago in the Red Stripe Cup regional tournament against Barbados.

He marked his arrival with a polished innings of 92 against a Bajan bowling attack led by Malcolm Marshall and Joel Garner.

Lara was then selected to the West Indies team but this coincided with the untimely death of his father and he withdrew from the team.

The following year he became the youngest captain of Trinidad and Tobago as they captured the famed sports Golden Grant Trophy.

Lara made his West Indies debut against Pakistan, scoring 44 and six against a bowling attack compromising of Imran Khan, Waqar Younis and Wasim Akram. He would soon signal his arrival on the international stage as a superstar of the game with a magnificent innings of 277 in his Fifth Test match against Australia at the Sydney Cricket Ground.

Lara would then surpass Sir Garfield Sobers' 36-year record for the highest Test score with a magical innings of 375 against England in Antigua in 1994.

He would soon make the highest First-Class score his own in scoring 501 not out for Warwickshire against Durham in an innings where he faced 427 balls smashing ten sixes and 62 fours.

Following the record-breaking season of that year Brian Lara was honoured by Trinidad and Tobago with the Trinity Cross. He was also given the keys to Port-of-Spain at

WEST INDIES captain Brian Lara smiles while watching the fans cheering him after playing his last international cricket match in the Super 8s round against England of the Cricket World Cup in the Kensington Oval in Bridgetown, Barbados, yesterday as represe

ing as he became the first West Indian batsman to pass 10,000 One-Day runs, held the most catches for the West Indies (164) and most Test runs (11,953).

The West Indies team now face a difficult time of England commencing on May 17 a Lord's without their inspirational leader and batting maestro.

Ramnaresh Sarwan is now the clear favourite to take the helm of the West Indies team which has been faltering over the past decade.

The question of who is going to take up the mantle left by Lara is yet to be answered as many of the seasoned players in the team are still unable to produce consistent performances. West Indies cricket looks to be in shambles with the untimely retirement of Lara but there is still talent beckoning to be unleashed.

Hopefully the West Indies selectors can finally get the team selection correct and not undermine the new captain as was done to Lara.

Erlanctedly the retirement of Lara will hurt West Indies cricket as fans would not be persuaded to come and watch a team that is

He reached out to fans from all nations with immortality (0) Ian Dennis Medburys from New Zealand returning a bat and other cricket gear from his slot.

The batting genius has also lost his name to the new Career Research Facility in Trinidad while looking to make a difference in a community which has adored him and gone him most support throughout his career. See Page 46A

WEST INDIES captain Brian Lara
through a "guard of honour" as

Weather

Trinidad and Tobago: Intl. sunny and hazy
Mainly 2 metres in open waters and less than
1 m in sheltered areas
Yesterday's temperature: 34 degrees Celsius
Today's maximum: 32 degrees Celsius
Forecast minimum temperature: 23 degrees Celsius

ge 24 NEWSDAY SECTION C Saturday April 18, 2007

A tribute to Brian Lara

WEST INDIES

FANS show where their loyalties lie during the Cricket World Cup in the Caribbean

BRIAN LARA
takes some time to sign
autographs after playing his final match in the
West Indies on April 21 in Barbados

sports sports sports sports sports sports

final match West Indies

un-out wrecks Lara's farewell

BRIDGETOWN: Marlon Samuels' runout blunder wrecked Brian Lara's hopes of marking his retirement with a big score at the World Cup yesterday. Then he partly made up for it with a big-hitting half century.

Samuels misjudged a call for a sharp single ended in Lara being run out for 18 against England before a packed Kensington Oval crowd.

Samuels called Lara for a sharp single after playing the ball

World Cup reckoning, but per eager to win this match in a precursor to the opening Test and limited-overs series between them starting May 17.

Samuels may have be remorseful as the batsman who ran out, captain Lara in his final innings, a tag he surely would not relish.

His half-century was one of the highlights of the West Indies innings after captain Chris Gayle (79) and Devon Smith (61) had put on 131 runs for the opening partner.

EPILOGUE

I'M BATTING IN THE NETS preparing for a Test match when I see Sobers walk over from the pavilion to stand behind me. He sees me play a few deliveries and picks his moment. "You're not looking at the ball."

I would never address Sir Garfield Sobers without stopping to face him, so I turn, ready to give him and his ideas full attention and respect. He is the greatest cricketer ever to have played the game. It was true when he played and it's true today.

He also loves me, and I love him for that. From an early age he believed in me and expressed it openly. Such outward support from a legend as vast as Sobers might injure as much as inspire a teenager, but his words always gave me strength.

He rejoiced in my successes and now he's volunteering his advice at a time when I wouldn't trust anyone but him. Doesn't mean I'm not gonna shoot back…

"What do you mean?! Of course I'm looking at the ball!"

He smiles back, doesn't say another word. It's his way of saying I have permission to face the next ball.

I knock my bat on the ground and with fierce intensity move back and across then onto my front foot to slap the next ball through the covers. It's a rebuke to his statement and I'm nodding my head in appreciation of the shot. "Now *that's* looking at the ball," he says.

Is the great man here to confuse me, to play with my mind?

I respectfully ask the obvious question. "What did I do differently?" There's a hint of sarcasm in my tone.

"You looked at the ball *before* it was delivered."

I didn't know I had to do that. With all the negative thoughts I had in my head, I just didn't know. I'm dumbstruck. He's right. "You see the bowler at the top of his mark in the distance? Find the ball in his hand and watch it all the way. Don't take your eyes off it till it touches your bat."

The next ball is dug into the surface. I spring back and across my stumps, get up on my toes and smack it right out of the middle, no chance for the imaginary fielder on the square leg boundary. My eyes open wide. I haven't played a shot with this kind of ease and timing in weeks.

He slips away.

The rest of my net session is a joy. I don't see him for the rest of the summer. After a poor start, I end up with the most runs in the series.

* * *

I have taken my eyes off many things in my life and struggled to get back to focusing on the important stuff. This book is my attempt to refocus on the ball right from the start of the action.

For now, I've concentrated on just the one part. My battles against our oldest rival, the team we defined ourselves against, before my era and during it. I wanted to try and capture through my eyes what this rivalry means. What it taught me, how it excited me, the great overflowing moments of joy it brought me, and the times it beat me down.

All of it combined to man me up.

Playing for the West Indies for 17 years was a true privilege. Within that period, there was this one country that brought out the best and the worst in me. England did something to me. All those great highs and sinking lows, those oceans of emotion, and my fight to keep things in check.

And now my focus is moving elsewhere. *The England Chronicles* is just a fraction of my story. The rest is gonna come at you with pace.

Brian Lara
Port of Spain, Trinidad
June 2024

LARA IN
NUMBERS

CAREER BATTING AND FIELDING STATS

	Mat	Inns	NO	Runs	HS	Ave	BF	SR	100s	50s	4s	6s	Ct	St
Tests	131	232	6	11953	400*	52.88	19753	60.51	34	48	1559	88	164	0
ODIs	299	289	32	10405	169	40.48	13086	79.51	19	63	1042	133	120	0
FC	261	440	13	22156	501*	51.88	-	-	65	88	-	-	320	0
List A	429	411	43	14602	169	39.67	-	-	27	86	-	-	177	0
T20s	3	3	0	99	65	33.00	86	115.11	0	1	11	1	0	0

TEST BATTING AND FIELDING STATS AGAINST EACH OPPONENT

Opponent	Matches	Inns	Not Out	Runs	HS	Ave	100	50	Ct	St
Australia	31	58	2	2856	277	51.00	9	11	34	
Bangladesh	2	2	0	173	120	86.50	1	1	2	
England	**30**	**51**	**3**	**2983**	**400***	**62.14**	**7**	**11**	**45**	
India	17	29	0	1002	120	34.55	2	6	22	
New Zealand	11	17	0	704	147	41.41	1	5	13	
Pakistan	12	22	0	1173	216	53.31	4	3	11	
South Africa	18	35	0	1715	202	49.00	4	9	20	
Sri Lanka	8	14	1	1125	221	86.53	5	2	14	
Zimbabwe	2	4	0	222	191	55.50	1	0	3	

ODI BATTING AND FIELDING STATS AGAINST EACH OPPONENT

Opponent	Matches	Inns	Not Out	Runs	HS	Ave	100	50	Ct	St
Asian CC XI	1	1	0	52	52	52.00	0	1	0	
Australia	51	50	3	1858	139	39.53	3	15	19	
Bangladesh	7	6	0	243	117	40.50	1	0	3	
Canada	1	1	0	73	73	73.00	0	1	0	
England	**29**	**27**	**1**	**795**	**110**	**30.57**	**1**	**6**	**11**	
India	42	40	5	1142	89	32.62	0	6	18	
Ireland	1	0							0	
Kenya	3	3	0	129	111	43.00	1	0	3	
New Zealand	28	26	5	1068	146*	50.85	2	7	8	
Pakistan	48	48	7	1771	156	43.19	5	6	29	
Scotland	1	1	1	25	25*		0	0	0	
South Africa	37	37	3	1219	116	35.85	3	6	14	
Sri Lanka	25	25	2	1122	169	48.78	2	9	10	
Zimbabwe	25	24	5	908	113	47.78	1	6	5	

TEST CENTURIES

No	Score	Opponent	Result	Test match start date	Location
1	277	Australia	Draw	January 2 1993	Sydney Cricket Ground, Sydney
2	167	England	Win	March 17 1994	Bourda, Georgetown
3	375	England	Draw	April 16 1994	Antigua Recreation Ground, St John's
4	147	New Zealand	Win	February 10 1995	Basin Reserve, Wellington
5	145	England	Loss	July 27 1995	Old Trafford, Manchester
6	152	England	Draw	August 10 1995	Trent Bridge, Nottingham
7	179	England	Draw	August 25 1995	The Oval, London
8	132	Australia	Win	February 1 1997	WACA Ground, Perth
9	103	India	Draw	April 4 1997	Antigua Recreation Ground, St John's
10	115	Sri Lanka	Draw	June 20 1997	Arnos Vale Stadium, Kingstown
11	213	Australia	Win	March 13 1999	Sabina Park, Kingston
12	153*	Australia	Win	March 26 1999	Kensington Oval, Bridgetown
13	100	Australia	Loss	April 3 1999	Antigua Recreation Ground, St John's
14	112	England	Draw	August 3 2000	Old Trafford, Manchester
15	182	Australia	Loss	December 15 2000	Adelaide Oval, Adelaide
16	178	Sri Lanka	Loss	November 13 2001	Galle International Stadium, Galle
17	221	Sri Lanka	Loss	November 29 2001	Sinhalese Sports Club Ground, Colombo
18	130	Sri Lanka	Loss	November 29 2001	Sinhalese Sports Club Ground, Colombo
19	110	Australia	Loss	April 10 2003	Bourda, Georgetown
20	122	Australia	Loss	April 19 2003	Queen's Park Oval, Port of Spain
21	209	Sri Lanka	Draw	June 20 2003	Beausejour Stadium, Gros Islet
22	191	Zimbabwe	Win	November 12 2003	Queens Sports Club, Bulawayo
23	202	South Africa	Loss	December 12 2003	Wanderers Stadium, Johannesburg
24	115	South Africa	Draw	January 2 2004	Newlands Cricket Gound, Cape Town
25	400*	England	Draw	April 10 2004	Antigua Recreation Ground, St John's
26	120	Bangladesh	Win	June 4 2004	Sabina Park, Kingston
27	196	South Africa	Loss	April 8 2005	Queen's Park Oval, Port of Spain
28	176	South Africa	Loss	April 21 2005	Kensington Oval, Bridgetown
29	130	Pakistan	Win	May 26 2005	Kensington Oval, Bridgetown
30	153	Pakistan	Loss	June 3 2005	Sabina Park, Kingston
31	226	Australia	Loss	November 25 2005	Adelaide Oval, Adelaide
32	120	India	Draw	June 10 2006	Beausejour Stadium, Gros Islet
33	122	Pakistan	Loss	November 11 2006	Gaddafi Stadium, Lahore
34	216	Pakistan	Draw	November 19 2006	Multan Cricket Stadium, Multan

ODI CENTURIES

No	Score	Opponent	Result	Date	Location
1	128	Pakistan	Win	February 19 1993	Sahara Stadium Kingsmead, Durban
2	111*	South Africa	Win	February 23 1993	Springbok Park, Bloemfontein
3	114	Pakistan	Win	March 23 1993	Sabina Park, Kingston
4	153	Pakistan	Win	November 5 1993	Sharjah Cricket Association Stadium, Sharjah
5	139	Australia	Win	March 12 1995	Queen's Park Oval, Port of Spain
6	169	Sri Lanka	Win	October 15 1995	Sharjah Cricket Association Stadium, Sharjah
7	111	South Africa	Win	March 11 1996	National Stadium, Karachi
8	146*	New Zealand	Win	March 30 1996	Queen's Park Oval, Port of Spain
9	104	New Zealand	Win	April 6 1996	Arnos Vale Stadium, Kingstown
10	102	Australia	Win	January 5 1997	The Gabba, Brisbane
11	103*	Pakistan	Win	January 10 1997	WACA Ground, Perth
12	110	England	Loss	March 29 1998	Kensington Oval, Bridgetown
13	117	Bangladesh	Win	October 9 1999	Bangabandhu National Stadium, Dhaka
14	116*	Australia	Loss (D/L)	January 17 2001	Sydney Cricket Ground, Sydney
15	111	Kenya	Win	September 17 2002	Sinhalese Sports Club Ground, Colombo
16	116	South Africa	Win	February 9 2003	Newlands Cricket Gound, Cape Town
17	116	Sri Lanka	Loss	June 8 2003	Kensington Oval, Bridgetown
18	113	Zimbabwe	Win	November 22 2003	Queens Sports Club, Bulawayo
19	156	Pakistan	Win	January 28 2005	Adelaide Oval, Adelaide

TEST RECORD AGAINST ENGLAND, INCLUDING IN ENGLAND AND IN THE WEST INDIES

	Tests	Inns	NO	HS	Runs	Balls	Average	Strike rate	Bpd	100s /50s
Overall	30	51	3	400*	2983	4634	62.14	64.37	97	7/11
in West Indies	15	24	2	400*	1715	2761	77.95	62.11	126	3/5
in England	15	27	1	179	1268	1873	48.76	67.69	72	4/6

TEAM RECORD AS CAPTAIN

Wins	Draws	Loses
10	11	26

TEAM RECORD AGAINST ENGLAND AS CAPTAIN

Wins	Draws	Loses
3	3	8

(not including Sabina Park match abandoned)

OVERALL BATTING AND FIELDING RECORD AS TEST CAPTAIN (v ENGLAND AND NOT)

	Matches	Innings	NO	Runs	HS	Ave	50	100	Ct
As captain	47	85	4	4685	400*	57.83	19	14	72
As captain v England	14	24	2	1181	400*	53.68	5	1	22
Not as captain	84	147	2	7268	375	50.12	29	20	92
Not as captain v England	16	27	1	1802	375	69.31	6	6	23

PROGRESSION TO 11,953 RUNS

Runs	Tests	Average	100s	50s
1000	13	52.76	2	7
2000	22	56.91	4	11
3000	31	60.96	7	16
4000	45	54.10	10	20
5000	61	50.87	11	27
6000	73	49.21	15	40
7000	83	50.49	18	34
8000	94	50.34	20	40
9000	101	52.69	24	43
10000	111	52.91	26	45
11000	121	54.04	31	46
11953	131	52.88	34	48

FIRST-CLASS BATTING FOR WARWICKSHIRE IN 1994

	Matches	Innings	NO	Runs	HS	Ave	50	100
First-Class	15	25	2	2066	501*	89.82	3	9

HEAD-TO-HEAD RECORD v
SELECTED ENGLAND BOWLERS

MOST RUNS

		Runs	Balls	Dismissals	Average	Strike rate	Balls per dismissal
Angus Fraser	1994-1998	375	608	7	53.57	61.67	87
Andrew Caddick	1994-2000	268	430	6	44.66	62.32	72
Chris Lewis	1994	191	248	3	63.66	77.01	83
Phil Tufnell	1994-1998	174	321	1	174.00	54.20	321
Dominic Cork	1995-2000	168	289	3	56.00	58.13	96
Steve Harmison	2004	146	304	4	36.50	48.02	76
Matthew Hoggard	2004	137	161	1	137.00	85.09	161
Gareth Batty	2004	130	161	0	N/A	80.74	N/A
Andrew Flintoff	2000-2004	118	272	4	29.50	43.38	68
Mike Watkinson	1995	108	144	0	N/A	75.00	N/A

MOST DISMISSALS

		Runs	Balls	Dismissals	Average	Strike rate	Balls per dismissal
Angus Fraser	1994-1998	375	608	7	53.57	61.67	87
Andrew Caddick	1994-2000	268	430	6	44.66	62.32	72
Darren Gough	1995-2000	102	192	6	17.00	53.12	32
Andrew Flintoff	2000-2004	118	272	4	29.50	43.38	68
Steve Harmison	2004	146	304	4	36.50	48.02	76
Chris Lewis	1994	191	248	3	63.66	77.01	83
Dominic Cork	1995-2000	168	289	3	56.00	58.13	96
Ashley Giles	2004	45	97	3	15.00	46.39	32
Craig White	1995-2000	76	90	2	38.00	84.44	45

RECORD v DIFFERENT ENGLISH BOWLING

	Runs	Balls	Dismissals	Average	Strike rate	Bpd	4s/6s
Seam	2117	3285	40	52.93	64.44	82	313/6
Spin	866	1349	7	123.71	64.20	193	102/7
RM/RFM/RF	2117	3285	40	52.93	64.44	82	313/6
OB	527	753	2	263.50	69.99	377	63/7
LBG	69	82	0	N/A	84.14	N/A	11/0
SLA	270	514	5	54.00	52.53	103	28/0

SERIES BY SERIES

	Tests	Inns	NO	Runs	Balls	Average	Strike rate	Balls per dismissal	100s/50s
1993-94	5	8	0	798	1168	99.75	68.32	146	2/2
1995	6	10	1	765	982	85.00	77.90	109	3/3
1997-98	5	9	1	417	770	52.12	54.15	96	0/3
2000	5	9	1	239	483	26.55	49.48	54	1/1
2003-04	4	7	1	500	823	83.33	60.75	137	1/0
2004	4	8	0	264	408	33.00	64.70	51	0/2

RECORD-BREAKER

• Brian Lara is the only batsman to have scored a century, a double century, a triple century, a quadruple century and a quintuple century in first-class games

• Brian Lara is the fastest batsman in the history of the game to 10,000 Test runs, in terms of number of matches, joint in terms of innings

• World record highest Test innings score (400*)

• World record highest first-class score (501*)

• Record number of Test runs for the West Indies – 11,953

• Record number of Test centuries for the West Indies – 34

• The only batsman to score two 350 plus scores in Test cricket – 375, 400*

• He is one of the four batsmen to score two triple hundreds in Test cricket. Donald Bradman, Virender Sehwag and Chris Gayle are the other three

• He scored the third-most double hundreds by any batsman in Test cricket with 9. Only Bradman (12) and Kumar Sangakarra (11) have more than him

• Lara scored 53 hundreds in international cricket, making him one of only eight batsmen to score 50 plus hundreds in international cricket

• Lara scored 22,358 runs in international cricket, the eighth-most of any batsman

• His maiden Test century of 277 against Australia in Sydney is the fifth-highest maiden Test century by any batsman, and the highest individual score in all Tests between the two teams

- He is the first man to score seven centuries in eight first-class innings, the first being the record 375 against England and the last being the record 501* against Durham

- He is one of only two players to score two career quadruple-centuries in first-class cricket, the other being Bill Ponsford

- He is one of only eight batsmen to score a century and a double-century in the same Test match

- World record number of runs for a losing team in a Test match (351)

- He is one of only two West Indian cricketers to win BBC Overseas Sports Personality of the Year (1994), the other being Sir Garfield Sobers

- In 2007, he received an Honorary Doctorate from the University of Sheffield

MAN OF THE MATCH/SERIES AWARDS v ENGLAND

MAN OF THE MATCH

- 17th – 22nd March 1994, Bourda, Georgetown. 2nd Test, England in the West Indies

- 16th – 21st April 1994, Antigua Recreation Ground, St John's. 5th Test, England in the West Indies

- 24th – 28th August 1995, The Oval, Kennington. 6th Test, West Indies in England

- 5th April 1998, Arnos Vale Playing Field, Kingstown. 4th ODI, England in the West Indies

- 10th – 14th April 2004, Antigua Recreation Ground, St John's. 4th Test, England in the West Indies

MAN OF THE SERIES

- West Indies in England, 1995 Test Series *(shared with Michael Atherton)*

ACKNOWLEDGEMENTS

ACKNOWLEDGEMENTS AND THANK YOUS? I don't think we have enough pages for me to complete such a task.

Within days of realising my dream of selection on the West Indies team I lost my dad and I never had a chance to say thank you to the man who sacrificed so much to have me here today. Thank you, Dad.

And to Joey Carew, I lost you as well, but what an amazing mentor you were to me. I enjoyed every moment with you and Marion, may you both rest in peace.

I want to say thanks to Cecil Camacho and Steve Singh for the great support and legal guidance you have given me over the years. To Jonathan Crystal and Adrian King, you are both very special people in my life who have given me so much more than legal advice. I've always cherished our conversations about life and family. Thank you for bringing such freedom and openness to our friendship.

Agnes Eustache Cyrus, you are the best sister anyone can ask for. You and all my siblings have been nothing short of amazing, thank you.

St Joseph Boys, San Juan Secondary, Fatima College, I achieved a decent level of education only because of my teachers' consistent encouragement. "Cricket will only get you so far, that's a very short career, you need your education." Wise words. Thank you.

To the Harvard Cricket Club and the Queen's Park Cricket Club, and the Trinidad & Tobago Cricket Board and Cricket West Indies, you laid the foundation for me to bat my way to the top. Thank you. And Warwickshire CCC we didn't make bad choices, did we? I am grateful for my two wonderful years at the club. To say that I have played county cricket and won a treble is just golden.

I can't thank everyone in this one book – I have to save some names for what's around the corner – but it would be remiss of me not to mention the likes of Tim Munton, my former Warwickshire teammate, who when I told him I wanted to do this book, immediately put me on to the managing director of Fairfield Books, Matt Thacker, and my co-writer Phil Walker. Thank you Matt for your instant confidence in the project. Phil, it must have been a hectic few months with me, eh? Come on, tell the truth! It was worth it for many reasons but most importantly I believe we are now stuck together, so good luck to you! Also, big thanks to our editors, Osman Samiuddin and Rob Smyth, and our researcher – and world-class transcriber – Ollie Wright. And a special thanks to Nasser Khan from Trinidad, who helped immensely.

And of course to Jimmy Adams and Dwight Yorke. Two great forewords, first from the man I loved batting with the most, a truly great teammate, I am honoured to have shared a dressing room with you, Swaggy. And Dwight Yorke, what a man, and what a friend. Someone who made it against all the odds, a true inspiration for our Caribbean youth. Thank you, brothers.

To all THANK YOU. And the beauty of doing multiple books is that whoever doesn't see their name here, I'll have something special to say about you soon.

INDEX

Praise for *Brian Lara, The England Chronicles*

"Watching Brian Lara was to understand how batting could be."
MICHAEL ATHERTON

"Couldn't have enjoyed it more. Highly recommended."
GEORGE DOBELL

"No-one batted like Brian Lara, and few cricketers have talked so openly of their lives and their drives – a book worth waiting for."
GIDEON HAIGH

"I thought I had heard it all. I was wrong. Brian Lara's book proves it. Written in the first person it's an intimate account of the emotional complexities of one of the greatest players in history. Once you begin to read this book it will be very difficult to put it down. It confirms something I have always suspected. The minds of great sportsmen are not like ours. They are far greater."
SIR TREVOR MCDONALD

"A hugely captivating book… it's riveting"
AMOL RAJAN

"The epic scale of Lara's batting, his career and life, his highs and lows, reconstructed in evocative detail."
OSMAN SAMIUDDIN

"A vivid and at times shocking insight into the exhilaration and pain of being a true genius."
ROB SMYTH